England's Landscape

The West

NORTH EAST

NORTH WEST

EAST MIDLANDS

WEST MIDLANDS

EAST ANGLIA

WEST MIDLANDS

WEST

SOUTH EAST

SOUTH WEST

Collins

England's Landscape
The West

Edited by Barry Cunliffe

Michael J Allen
James Bond
Barry Cunliffe
Jo Draper
Peter Ellis
Julie Gardiner
Jeremy Harte
Sam Hunt
Trevor Rowley

Series Editor Neil Cossons

ENGLISH HERITAGE

First published in 2006 by Collins, an imprint of
HarperCollins*Publishers*
77–85 Fulham Palace Road, London W6 8JB

www.collins.co.uk

10 9 8 7 6 5 4 3 2
10 09 08 07

ISBN 10 – 0 00 715573 5
ISBN 13 – 9 78 0 00 715573 6

British Library Cataloguing in Publication Data
A CIP catalogue record for this book is available from the
British Library.

Publisher & Commissioning Editor Myles Archibald
Production Director Graham Cook
Edited by Rowan Whimster
Designed by D & N Publishing, Hungerford, Berkshire
Indexed by Sheila Seacroft

Map on previous page:
The regions: the red lines bound the general area covered by
each volume.

ACKNOWLEDGEMENTS

SERIES EDITOR
Sir Neil Cossons OBE
Chairman, English Heritage
President, Royal Geographical Society
The series editor would like to acknowledge the contribution of
the following people:

EDITORIAL BOARD:
Professor David Cannadine
Queen Elizabeth the Queen Mother Professor of British History,
University of London

Professor Barry Cunliffe
Professor of European Archaeology, University of Oxford

Professor Richard Lawton
Professor Emeritus, Department of Geography, University of
Liverpool

Professor Brian K Roberts
Professor Emeritus, Department of Geography, University of Durham

ENGLISH HERITAGE EXECUTIVE EDITORS:
Dr Paul Barnwell, *Head of Medieval and Later Rural Research*
Dr Martin Cherry, *Former Chief Buildings Historian*
Humphrey Welfare, *Northern Territory Director*
Graham Fairclough, *Head of Characterisation*

ENGLISH HERITAGE PROJECT MANAGERS:
Val Horsler, *former Head of Publishing*
Adele Campbell, *Commercial Publishing Manager*

All new ground and air photography was taken specifically for
this series. Thanks to: Damian Grady, Senior Investigator of
English Heritage Aerial Survey and Investigation Team, and to
the photographic and dark-room teams in Swindon; Steve Cole,
Head of Photography, and the staff of the English Heritage
Photography team. Archive material from the National
Monuments Record was researched by the Enquiry and
Research Services teams led by Alyson Rogers (Buildings) and
Lindsay Jones (Archaeology/Air Photos). Graphics lists were
managed by John Vallender and Bernard Thomason. Graphics
were produced under the management of Rob Read of 3's
Company (Consultancy) Ltd by John Hodgson and Martyn
Norris. All other images were researched by Jo Walton and
Julia Harris-Voss.

Printed in Italy by LEGO SpA, Vicenza

Contents

Foreword

The landscape of England evokes intense passion and profound emotion. This most loved of places, the inspiration for generations of writers, poets and artists, it is at once both the source of the nation's infatuation and the setting for grievous misunderstanding. For people who visit, the view of England offers some of their most lasting images. For exiles abroad the memory of the English landscape sustains their beliefs and desire for a homecoming.

But for those who live in England the obsession is double edged. On the one hand we cherish the unchanging atmosphere of a familiar place, and on the other make impossible demands of it, believing that it will always accommodate, always forgive. Only in the last half century or so have we started to recognise the extreme fragility of all that we value in the English landscape, to appreciate that it is not only the metaphor for who we are as a people but that it represents one of our most vivid contributions to a wider culture. At last we are beginning to realise that a deeper understanding of its subtle appeal and elusive character is the key to a thoughtful approach to its future.

The unique character of England's landscape derives from many things. But nowhere is the impact of human intervention absent. If geology and topography set the scene, it is the implacable persistence of generations who since the end of the Ice Age have sought to live in and off this place that has created the singular qualities of the landscape we have today. Not, of course, that the landscape before people was in any sense a static thing; on the contrary, the environment untouched by mankind was and is a dynamic and constantly changing synthesis. Every layer of that complex progression can still be found somewhere, making its own peculiar contribution to the distinctiveness of today's England. It is a compelling narrative. Through this series of regional studies our distinguished contributors – as authors and editors – have distilled something of what has created today's England, in order to decode that narrative.

Unique is an overused term. But it has a special resonance for the landscape of England, both urban and rural. What we hope readers of this series will begin to feel is the nature of the qualities that define the English landscape. Much of that landscape has of course been inherited from cultures overseas as conquest and migration brought here peoples who have progressively occupied and settled Britain. They created what might be called our shared landscapes, defined as much by what links them to the wider world as through any intrinsically native characteristics. The peoples whose common bonds stretched along the Atlantic seaboard have left a legacy in Cornwall more akin to parts of north-west France or Spain than to anywhere else in England. There are Roman roads and cities and medieval field systems that have their closest parallels in the European plains from whence they derived. Great abbeys and monasteries reflected in their art and architecture, their commerce and industry, a culture whose momentum lay outside these islands. And when disaster came it was a pan-European epidemic, the Black Death, that took away between a third and a half of the people. England's are not the only deserted medieval villages.

And yet, paradoxically, much of what today we would recognise as the quintessential England is only some two or three centuries old. Parliamentary enclosure, especially of the English lowlands, was itself a reaction to an even greater economic force – industrialisation, and the urbanisation that went with it. It has given us a rural landscape that epitomises the essence of Englishness in the minds of many. The fields and hedgerows surrounding the nucleated villages of the pre-existing medieval landscape are of course quite new when set against the timescale of human occupation. Indeed, when the first railways came through there remained, here and there, open fields where the rows of new hawthorn hedges were still feeble whips scribing lines across a thousand years of feudal landscape.

As Britain emerged to become the world's first industrial nation its astonishing transformation was at its most visible in the landscape, something new, indigenous and without precedent. It fuelled the debate on the picturesque and the sublime and was a source of wonder to those who visited from overseas. But in its urban and industrial excesses it soon came to be detested, by aesthetes, social commentators and a burgeoning class opposed to the horrors of industrial capitalism. What was perhaps the most decisive contribution of Britain to the human race provoked a powerful counteraction reflected in the writings of Ruskin, Morris, Octavia Hill and the Webbs. It was this anguish that a century ago energised the spirit of conservation in a growing band of people determined to capture what was left of the pre-industrial rural scene.

Today the landscape of England is, as ever, undergoing immense change. But, unlike the centuries just past, that change once again draws its energy and inspiration from forces overseas. A new form of global economy, North American in flavour, concept and style carries all before it. The implications for the long term future of the landscape and the people who live in it are difficult to predict. The out-of-town shopping mall, the great encampments of distribution warehouses crouching like so many armadillos across the rural shires, the growth of exurbia – that mixed-use land between city and country that owes nothing to either – are all manifestations of these new economic forces. Like the changes that have gone before they have become the subject of intense debate and the source of worrying uncertainty. But what is clear is that a deeper understanding of the landscape, in all its manifestations, offers a means of managing change in a conscious and thoughtful manner.

This was the inspiration that led to this new regional landscape series. To understand the language of landscape, to be able to interpret the way in which people make places, offers insights and enjoyment beyond the ordinary. It enables us to experience that most neglected of human emotions, a sense of place. These books set out to reveal the values that underwrite our sense of place, by offering an insight into how the landscape of England came to be the way it is. If understanding is the key to valuing and valuing is the key to caring then these books may help to ensure that we can understand and enjoy the best of what we have and that when we make our own contribution to change it will not only reinforce that essential distinctiveness but improve the quality of life of those who live there.

Neil Cossons

1

What Manner of Place Is This?

BARRY CUNLIFFE

And where is the West? There will probably be as many answers as there are
people who address the question. It is notoriously difficult to divide the British
Isles into regions – a truth all too apparent to the Commissioners who have
attempted from time to time to redefine local government boundaries – and they
have only to deal with the present. For those of us who are interested in a much
deeper time span, the complexities of definition multiply. Our West is a given,
offered by historical geographers having reviewed a variety of the spatial patterns
created by human communities seeking harmony with their environments. It is,
by any standards, a curious, in-between, place where things are not always as
they seem – a zone of merging and of mixing. At various stages in history it was a
place where principal actors like Arthur, Alfred and the Duke of Monmouth
could vanish and reappear: a place of safety where time could be bided. It is
neither the South West – Roman Dumnonia – nor is it the South – Anglo-Saxon
Wessex: and it is certainly very different to the Midlands. By defining what it is
not, the West assumes an identity – it is a liminal zone where all things are
possible.

Take geology for example. The West could not be more in between. To the west
lies the Old Red Sandstone with its granitic intrusions, which give Devon and
Cornwall their highly distinctive character, while to the east are the Cretaceous
chalklands which give the heart to Wiltshire and Hampshire. To the north the
region fades into the dreary river valleys of the Midlands. Our oldest rocks, the
Carboniferous Limestone and the Coal Measures, were laid down and then
thrown into great convolutions by the Armorican earth movements at the end of
the Carboniferous period that brought the Palaeozoic age to a close. The
dominant ridge of the Mendips is a vivid reminder of these distant times. Then
followed the more placid Mesozoic when the Triassic and Liassic rocks were
created, succeeded by the oolitic limestone that provides the spine of our region,
most evident in the grand sweep of the Cotswold Hills. After another period of
faulting and unconformity the Cretaceous sequence – the Gault Clay, Greensand
and chalk – was laid down, the eroded western scarp edge of which provides part
of the rugged eastern border of our region.

Our bedrock, then, gives us variety – perhaps among the English regions a
unique variety. Our region is a kaleidoscope of fragments of shattered rock
formation. Look for the most colourful zone of the geological map and you will
have found the West.

Over this bedrock is not a single blanket of landscape but a rag-quilt of
discarded scraps of landscape giving rise to an amazing variety of ecozones each
with its own highly distinctive character – the Cotswolds, the Mendips, the
Quantocks and the Dorset Downs; the Vales of Evesham, of Berkeley, of
Malmesbury, of Blackmoor and the many others; the broken-up lands of west
Dorset and the open flat lands of the Somerset Levels – the variety is almost

OPPOSITE PAGE:
*View from the open sea looking into Poole
Harbour towards the heartland of the West.*

11

endless. And in that variety, with its rich array of colourful building stone, its proffered mineral wealth – salt, lead, silver and coal, and its almost endless opportunities for agro-pastoral production, offering the world woollen blankets and cider, sail cloth and rope, not to mention Cheddar and blue vinny cheese, lies the endless fascination of the West.

From deep in time our region has been a border zone in its own right or a region crossed by cultural or political boundaries. In prehistory it displays a mélange of cultural influences from both east and west made even more varied by its focal position on major transpeninsular routes leading, via the river valleys, from the Solent ports of Poole and Christchurch to the Severn estuary and thence to Wales and the Midlands. By the early decades of the 1st millennium AD it was divided into the territories of two tribes, the Durotriges in the south and the Dobunni in the north, the boundary roughly coinciding with the marshy zone between the Polden Hills and the Mendips. The Roman invasion imposed a new political geography in which the West became part of a larger territory linked by the famous Fosse Way that ran from the vicinity of Exeter north-eastwards through Ilchester, Bath and Cirencester, and ultimately on to Lincoln. The Romanised culture of the south-east of Britain embraced our region to its western borders.

In the century or two following the breakdown of centralised Roman authority the West once more reverted to its role as a border zone providing, at least temporarily, a barrier to the Saxon penetration from the east. By the end of the millennium it was firmly within England but divided once more, this time between Wessex and Mercia, the boundary now approximating to the Bristol Avon. With the Norman invasion it still played its role as a difficult in-between place, first in the rebellion of 1069–70 against William the Conqueror and later in the anarchy of the civil war between Stephen and Matilda in the middle decades of the 12th century. And so into later history the West continued to play its part – in the Civil War of Cromwell and the rebellion of Monmouth. Dissent and defiance were never far beneath the surface.

The great railway boom of the late 19th century brought people from all over Britain travelling to the region to enjoy the picturesque, to collect their fossils and ferns and to savour the invigorating sea air. In the pre-Second World War years of the 20th century the flood continued, encouraged by gaudy railway posters and democratised by the lure of cheap seaside holidays. With this opening up came a growing nostalgia for times past – a desire for a Merrie England that existed only in the imagination, fuelled by crusty rural melodramas set in Hardy's Wessex or the warm comforting glow of sharing cider with Rosie. In these two centuries of romanticism many stereotypes of our region emerged, which are, in their own right, a fascinating insight into changing perceptions moulded by our changing needs.

Nothing is ever static. The West today is changing fast. Motorways mean that those wishing to enjoy the rural calm of the countryside can with ease commute to weekend homes, while new attractions such as safari parks, country houses with adventure playgrounds, and working farms designed for tourist inspection – complete of course with farm shops – are now significant employers of the rural population. Nostalgia too has moved on, transformed in its New Age guise into a celebration of a reinvented pagan Celtic past, far from any archaeological reality. There are new themes, too. A growing awareness of the importance of biodiversity and a realisation that the ecosystem is fragile have all but halted the indiscriminate quarrying of peat for garden compost and the tearing out of hedges to ease the passage of mega machines. Set-aside schemes and enlightened land management now offer at least a reprieve. But change there will always be and it is these changes, through the *longue durée* of time, that continue to create and re-create the landscape that here forms the focus of our attention.

2

Rhythms of Change;
a Region of Contrasts

MICHAEL J ALLEN AND JULIE GARDINER

DEFINING THE REGION: THE NATURAL LANDSCAPE

Diversity and contrast

The West is a landscape of contrasts rather than unity, containing a great diversity within its relatively small area. It lacks the topographic and geographic conformity, which in many regions provides a unifying framework for both the natural processes and human activity that have subsequently modified them, and it is this apparent lack of physical consistency that has given rise to a complex mosaic of small physically defined areas (Fig. 2.1), each contrasting starkly with its neighbours.

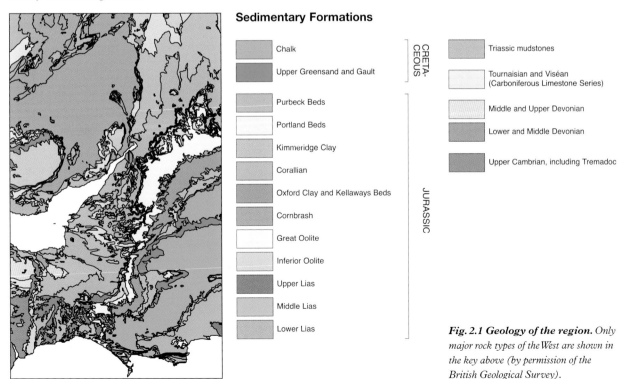

Sedimentary Formations

CRETA-CEOUS

- Chalk
- Upper Greensand and Gault

JURASSIC

- Purbeck Beds
- Portland Beds
- Kimmeridge Clay
- Corallian
- Oxford Clay and Kellaways Beds
- Cornbrash
- Great Oolite
- Inferior Oolite
- Upper Lias
- Middle Lias
- Lower Lias

- Triassic mudstones
- Tournaisian and Viséan (Carboniferous Limestone Series)
- Middle and Upper Devonian
- Lower and Middle Devonian
- Upper Cambrian, including Tremadoc

Fig. 2.1 Geology of the region. Only major rock types of the West are shown in the key above (by permission of the British Geological Survey).

This diversity runs through the kaleidoscope of geology, soils, animals and plants, which have defined the region's natural character and ecology throughout the past 250 million years. More recently, in archaeological and historical time, these differences have provided the stage for the human actors and raw materials within the landscape, as communities have carved their identity into the land, moulding it significantly by both their conscious and unwitting actions. Each area of the region, each landscape, has its own distinct character and history of human land use. None has been consistently rich in terms of natural resources nor wholly self-sufficient, but each has fulfilled a different and varying role, providing food, land and economic, social and non-secular opportunities not available in other areas. The variation between them allowed for complex physical, social and community changes within the region as a whole. The region is composed of a series of internal landscapes, each with its own identity. This internal variation gives a superficial impression of fragmentation, but in reality provides it with a coherent internal strength. The sum of these areas is infinitely greater than its parts, and it is a richer region as a result.

Geological building blocks of the landscape

We should examine first the geological building blocks, the hard skeleton of the region, and then the topography and landscape to which that skeleton gives form.[1] While geology and landscape are inextricably linked, the first does not inevitably produce the other, nor are they mutually exclusive. It is other factors, not least the peopling of the land, that create the landscape we see today.[2] But geology can be a fundamental starting point. The West has a complex story (Fig. 2.1) that can be categorised in eight principal zones (Fig. 2.2).

Fig. 2.2 Landscapes within the region.

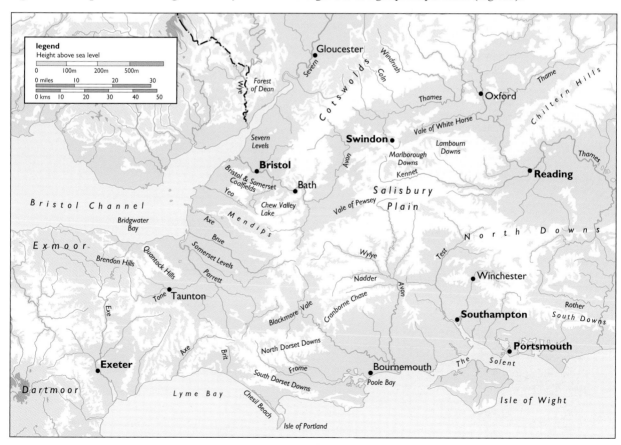

1. The *Cotswold Stone Belt* stretches from north of Bath to Stow-on-the-Wold and is characterised by a steep escarpment facing north-west, and more gently rolling eastern slopes with numerous small valleys. At Bradford-on-Avon and Bath deep gorges create picturesque scenery and expose the yellowing limestone that has for centuries been the ubiquitous local building material here.

2. The *Severn Levels* is the region's youngest building block, in which the soft coastal borders of the Severn, Avon and Gloucestershire Levels are formed of consolidated muds, silts and clays (Fig. 2.3). This low-lying landscape – almost flat and relatively featureless – was created in times so geologically recent that they lie within an archaeological timescale and coincide with the human occupation of the area, after the scouring and tearing of the last ice age.

3. The *Somerset Plain* (*Somerset Levels*) is an area in which the Quantocks (a Lower Old Red Sandstone outlier of the north Devon moors that contains some of the oldest rocks in the area) and younger hills between Minehead and Porlock form the south-western margins of the Somerset Plain and embrace the edge of the Somerset Levels (Fig. 2.4). The Brue valley, and the Somerset Levels through which the Brue flows, provide a second geologically recent landscape, punctured by islands of ancient rock poking up through the clay and peat.

*Fig. 2.3 **The Severn Levels at Crooks Marsh** showing the typical flat landscape with medieval fields (ridge and furrow) intersected by drainage ditches (rhines), and the rise of the new industrial development at Avonmouth.*

*Fig. 2.4 **The iconic Glastonbury Tor** protruding from the mystic vale of Avalon, surrounded by typical field patterns of the Somerset Levels.*

4. The *Mendips* are open, rather bare uplands, characterised by large expanses of nearly level high plateau, such as that between Shepton Mallet and Shipham, in which Carboniferous Limestone has created grey crags and numerous swallow-holes. Their only villages, Priddy and Charterhouse, lie sheltered in broad shallow valleys and the upland plain often ends abruptly at steep-sided incised gorge-like valleys. Caves, caverns, grottos and fissures, such as Aveline's Hole, Gough's Cave, King Arthur's Cave in Cheddar, and Hyena Den and Badger's Hole at Wookey Hole to the south, open out into the gorges – geological orifices that for hundreds of thousands of years sheltered animals and humans alike from the cold and the predators of the ice ages and the harsh early post-glacial period.

5. The *Bristol and Somerset Coalfields* is a complex landscape of steep sharp inclines, short stretches of rolling fields, and irregular limestone uplands, beneath which lie horizontal beds of coal. This convoluted geology was the source of inspiration for William 'Strata' Smith, the father of modern geology (*see* Chapter 12).

6. The *Avon and its tributary river valleys* traverse the region, mainly from east to west. Some, like the Parrett and Brue, are an integral part of the Somerset Levels; others, like the Wylye, Kennet and Avon, form areas in their own right. More important than their local botanical and geological aspects, however, is that they unify the region by providing access into land within and beyond it.

7. The *West Dorset Chalk* – including the Dorset Downs and the edge of Cranborne Chase – is quintessentially 'English' rolling downland, incised by dry valleys and bounded by escarpments. Southwards, however, the South Dorset Ridgeway provides some of the most uncharacteristic chalkland in southern England. Here, acute slopes within the escarpment sweep down to the sea over an undulating coastal plain, with a dip slope that drops to the South Winterborne river and towards Dorchester. In this area, clay-with-flints lying on the chalk creates heavier soils and wooded landscapes, while chalk heathland covers many of the windy hilltops.

8. The *Clay Vales* separate areas of hard rock in the region, including the Vale of Evesham, with its rolling countryside, and the heavier clay soils and lowland of the Blackmore Vale.

A landscape of contrasts

Although each of these zones could be viewed as separate entities, they are far from being self-contained and it is the interaction between them that provides the character of the region. Their contrasting topographies provide a prologue to the peopling of the landscape and they underlie the sense of place, religion and fantasy with which people have imbued the land. While there are rigid divisions between the uplands and lowlands, more fluid boundaries between the Levels and the permanent drylands provide subtle yet significant connections between their resources and histories of land use.

ICE AGES: COMING OUT OF THE COLD

Time, the backbone of archaeological study, has to be viewed at a variety of different scales because without this the human mind cannot cope with its vastness. The further back in time we go, the cruder and longer our subdivisions become, and the hazier and broader our knowledge. The ice age equates to the earliest Stone Ages – otherwise known as the Palaeolithic era. It spans some 2 million years; an almost incomprehensible duration for archaeologists used to dealing in much shorter lengths of time. The post-glacial period (termed the Holocene) covered only the last 10,000 years (into which archaeologists squeeze the Mesolithic (middle Stone Age) to Modern eras) and represents a mere 0.5 per cent of the Palaeolithic epoch. Yet to geologists, the entire Palaeolithic or Pleistocene is 'recent' in terms of the geological history of the West region and it might be thought to warrant only a few lines of description. We, however, need to examine our region in terms of both geological and archaeological timescales in order to set the scene for earliest human interaction with nature.

SOME TERMS (*see* Fig. 2.5, Tables 2.1 and 2.2):

Devensian — the most recent ice age
Glacial — a cold period of advancing ice sheet (glaciers)
Interglacial — a warming period of retreating ice sheet (glaciers)
Stadial — a cold period within a glacial stage
Interstadial — a warm period within a cold glacial stage

Ice and mud

The ice ages are a succession of climatic stages, each comprising a separate series of glacial advances and retreats, that provided a recurrent pattern of change for 2 million years (Table 2.1). These individual ice ages changed rhythmically between intense cold, *glacial* stages (themselves oscillating between colder *stadials* and warmer *interstadials*), and prolonged warmer *interglacials* (Fig. 2.5). We currently live in a period known as the Flandrian that we also call the Post-Glacial – an optimistic label since another ice age will inevitably occur at some stage in the distant future.

Ice ages, the intensely cold phases of major southward advances of the glaciers, were essentially devoid of human activity in the West. They were periods of lower sea level (Fig. 2.6 and Table 2.1) when the land mass extended beyond the Severn into the Irish and Atlantic seas. Rivers engorged by annual summer floods of glacial meltwater carved and sculpted hard rock formations, dumped banks of boulders and gravels and deposited metres of silt, sand and clay. Here, then, is some of the 'soft' geology that was deposited within our archaeological timescale.

Prolonged periods of intense cold (stadials) were not, however, thousands of years of unchanging monotony. Within them there were minor warmer phases that lasted perhaps 2,000 to 8,000 years. These so-called 'short' warmer spells mark interstadials within the glacial epochs (Fig. 2.5).[3] During longer and warmer interglacial episodes retreating and melting

Table 2.1 Simplified table showing the correlation between Oxygen Isotope Stages (OIS), conventional British glacial stages and archaeological periods.

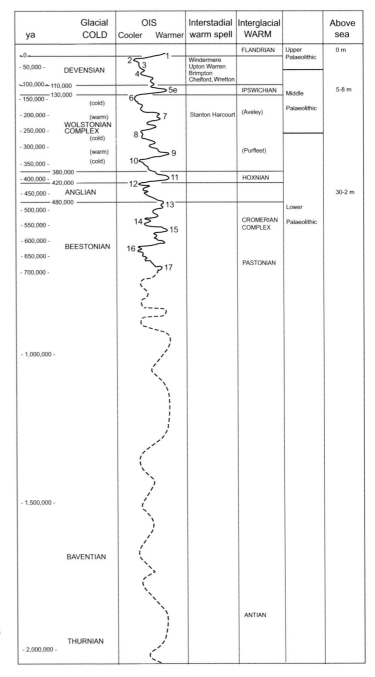

ya	Glacial COLD	OIS Cooler	OIS Warmer	Interstadial warm spell	Interglacial WARM		Above sea
~0		2	1		FLANDRIAN	Upper Palaeolithic	0 m
−50,000	DEVENSIAN	3		Windermere / Upton Warren / Brimpton / Chelford, Wretton			
		4					5-8 m
~100,000 −110,000			5e		IPSWICHIAN	Middle Palaeolithic	
−150,000 −130,000	(cold)	6					
−200,000	(warm)		7	Stanton Harcourt	(Aveley)		
−250,000	WOLSTONIAN COMPLEX (cold)	8					
−300,000	(warm)		9		(Purfleet)		
−350,000	(cold)	10					
−380,000 −400,000 −420,000		12	11		HOXNIAN		30-2 m
−450,000	ANGLIAN						
−480,000 −500,000			13			Lower Palaeolithic	
−550,000		14	15		CROMERIAN COMPLEX		
−600,000	BEESTONIAN						
−650,000		16					
−700,000			17		PASTONIAN		
−1,000,000							
−1,500,000							
	BAVENTIAN						
					ANTIAN		
	THURNIAN						
−2,000,000							

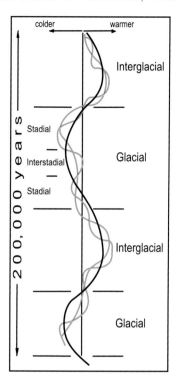

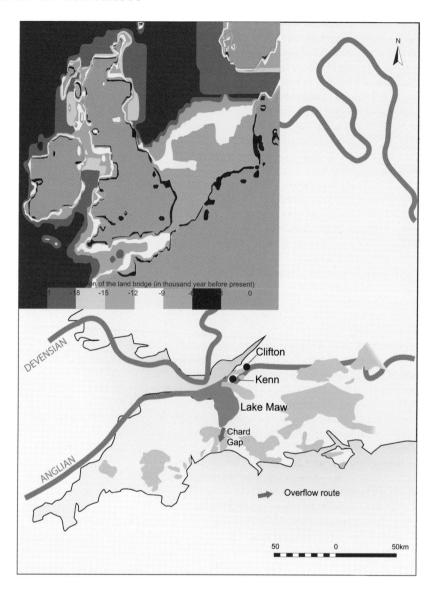

ABOVE: **Fig. 2.5 Schematic representation of general mean temperatures variations** *(solid line), more specific temperature variations showing glacial, stadial, interstadial and interglacial epochs.*

RIGHT: **Fig. 2.6 Glacial maxima of Anglian, Wolstonian and Devensian ice sheets**, *showing the pro-glacial Lake Maw, distribution of loess and location of periglacial features.*

glaciers led to rises in sea levels that drowned the coastal fringes and deluged formerly dry land with water-borne sediment. These ameliorating climatic conditions also allowed plants to grow and animals to migrate northwards – including humans, although their archaeological traces survive only in areas not erased by the next glacial event.

Glacial landscapes

As the ice sheets extended their glacial fingers southwards, they sculpted and moulded the hard rock over which they flowed into the smoothed form it takes today. In periods of the glacial maxima, archaeological and hominid remains are rare. Instead we find traces of our human predecessors mainly in warmer interglacial interludes, when Neanderthal and later Modern humans found the climate and resources sufficiently tolerable to sustain life.

What effect did these glacial episodes have on the first Palaeolithic settlers to the region and what can we see of their impact on our landscape today?

Compared with northern regions of Britain, the action of glaciers and the ice ages in the West was minor. The earliest glacial deposits in the region were laid down in the Anglian cold stage (480,000 to 420,000 years ago; Table 2.1). The courses of rivers fed by meltwater and the edges or frontiers of retreating glaciers can be seen marked out in the fluvial sands with shells that they deposited at Kenn[4] and the glacial till that was left behind at, for instance, Clifton Gorge near Bristol. These deposits provide glimpses of the region when it was cold, bleak, bare of soil and sparse in vegetation. Snow-fields blanketed cold and cracking ground. Few animals ventured into the freezing atmosphere; most herds were further south, grazing on the tundra and steppe of what is now modern-day France.

The subsequent Hoxnian warm interlude lasted for about 40,000 years and afforded a welcome respite from the bitter cold, although little of its placid landscape has been left for us to see. Bones of any animals that ventured this far north have not been preserved because no river or marine deposits accumulated to trap and preserve their remains.

The next glacial maximum, known as the Wolstonian, did not penetrate as far south as its Anglian predecessor[5] (Fig. 2.6), although much of the Bristol Channel was again occupied by ice. A large pro-glacial lake, known as 'Lake Maw', formed adjacent to the snout of the glacier as it bore down from the Bristol Channel (Fig. 2.6). This expanse of water occupied the whole of the area we now recognise as the Somerset Levels, with an outlet to the English Channel at Seaton via the Chard Gap that broadly follows, in fact moulds, the line of the present-day Axe valley. Marine sand and gravels lined the base of the Maw Lake,[6] forming in part the deposits now known as the Burtle Beds. Fluvioglacial bedded gravels and terrace gravel are a testament to the huge discharge with torrents of water that swept through the Axe valley.[7] Taken with the meltwaters and dumped among the hand-sized flint gravel were flint axes, suggesting that humans had ventured to the edges of the Maw Lake in search of food, flint or shelter. The remains of wolverine (*Gulo gulo*), brown bear (*Ursus arctos*), wolf (*Canis lupis*), fox, cave lion, and possibly spotted hyaena (*Crocuta crocuta*) have all been found in Devon,[8] and these species probably occurred in other parts of the region as well.

Warmer temperatures once again ensued and slightly milder climes emerged as glaciers retreated towards the Arctic. In these Ipswichian conditions large mammals including lion, rhinoceros, hippo and elephant roamed elsewhere in Britain (in Trafalgar Square for instance), suggesting climates similar to or even warmer than those of today. It is quite probable that they also foraged and hunted here in the West, although no firm evidence of their presence has yet been found.

The last ice age

The last glaciation, the Devensian, lasted for a mere 60,000 years, from 70,000 to 10,000 BC, and it is from this latest epoch that most evidence survives in the form of sediments, glacial landforms, fauna, flora and, most significantly, intermittent traces of human activity (Table 2.2).

The glaciers of the Devensian ice age did not quite reach the West region, but did cover the Vale of Glamorgan (Fig. 2.6). Meltwaters, deep permafosts, cold icy winds bearing dust and sand, and bitterly cold temperatures led, nevertheless, to uncovered ground freezing to depths of 3 or 4m each winter, before thawing in the following summer. This repeated cycle of winter freeze and partial summer thaw led to the formation of typical periglacial landscape features such as ice-wedge casts. Examples have been found at Kenn near Clevedon, and are seen exposed in the intertidal reaches of the Avon and Gloucestershire Levels. Huge porridge-like semi-frozen masses of muddy

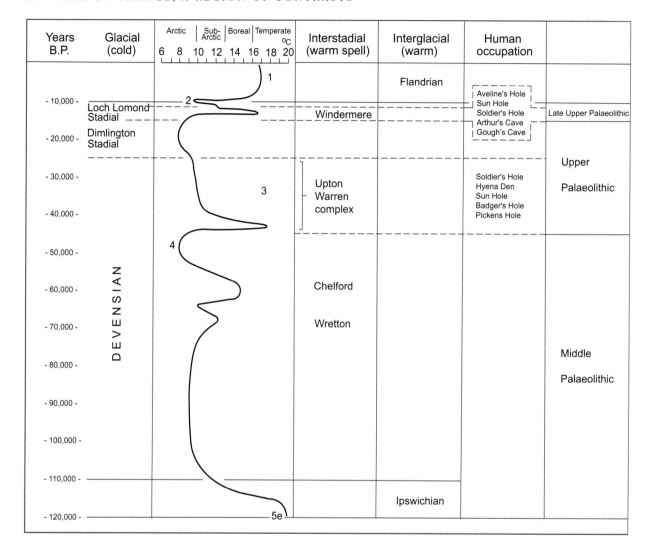

Years B.P.	Glacial (cold)	Arctic | Sub-Arctic | Boreal | Temperate °C 6 8 10 12 14 16 18 20		Interstadial (warm spell)	Interglacial (warm)	Human occupation	
					Flandrian		
- 10,000 -			1			Aveline's Hole	
	Loch Lomond Stadial		2	Windermere		Sun Hole Soldier's Hole	Late Upper Palaeolithic
- 20,000 -	Dimlington Stadial					Arthur's Cave Gough's Cave	
- 30,000 -				Upton			Upper
			3	Warren		Soldier's Hole Hyena Den	
- 40,000 -				complex		Sun Hole Badger's Hole Pickens Hole	Palaeolithic
- 50,000 -			4				
- 60,000 -	D E V E N S I A N			Chelford			
- 70,000 -				Wretton			
- 80,000 -							Middle
- 90,000 -							Palaeolithic
- 100,000 -							
- 110,000 -							
- 120,000 -			5e		Ipswichian		

Table 2.2 Correlation of major stages during the last glaciation, with major sites in the West.

sludge crept down the gentlest of inclines before coming to rest at the base of slopes, and in valley bottoms as 'head' deposits. These can be seen all over the Mendip Hills, in swallets (swallow-holes) and at the base of the limestone cliffs at Brean Down.

In these dry cold conditions, dust and sand blown from the glacial plain that was to become the North Sea, was deposited in drifts across southern England. These cover-sands, or loess, are most famously found in Kent where they are at their thickest nearer their source in the North Sea, but loess has also been mapped extensively across the Bristol area and the Mendips.[9] In contrast, deposits of coarse beach sand were blown from the opposite southerly and westerly direction to accumulate as huge 30m-deep drifts against the limestone cliffs at Brean Down, and as sand bars and dunes along the Somerset coastline from Brean to Hinkley Point. These, and other deposits, mantle the harder geological landscape, hiding its angularity and giving rise to more gentle slopes and profiles. In the colder phases, vegetation was sparse – comprising tundra grassland, stunted trees and bushes.

In the Devensian glaciation's warmer interludes vegetation grew more strongly, soils developed, rivers ran and animals returned. That is not to say that the region was a warm paradise, far from it. The fauna included spotted hyaena, wolf, red fox

Fig. 2.7 The harsh fissured Carboniferous Limestone landscape of Giants Cave, near Bristol.

(*Vulpes vulpes*) and arctic fox (*Alopex lagopus*), brown bear, woolly rhinoceros (*Coelodonta antiquitatis*), red deer (*Cervus elaphus*), giant deer (*Megaloceros giganteus*), reindeer (*Rangifer tarandus*), extinct bison (*Bison priscus*) and wild horse (*Equus przewalskii (ferus)*). The remains of all of these have been recovered from where they sheltered in, or were brought into, Sun Hole Cave in the Mendips.

Caves and swallets sheltered both animals and people (Fig. 2.7); each brought their prey where it could be consumed out of the elements and away from other predators. Caves not only provided refuge for the visitors, but have since protected their remains and rubbish from the ravages of the climate. Numerous caves in the Mendips, including Hyena Den, Badger's Hole, Soldier's Hole and Uphill Cave, contain important clues about the former landscape and its people. Others such as Sun Hole, Aveline's Hole and King Arthur's Cave were regularly revisited and re-occupied, but in general the use of most fell into either a warmer period about 43,000 years ago (the Upton Warren interstadial), or another around 13,000 years ago (the Windermere or Allerød interstadial (*see* Table 2.2)).[10]

TIME AND TIDE

The advance and retreat of ice sheets over the last 2 million years (Tables 2.1 and 2.2) repeatedly locked up and released millions of litres of water. During cold glacial periods the ice stole water from the sea with the result that sea levels were dramatically lowered. Both the western (Bristol Channel) and southern (English Channel) coastlines stretched beyond their present line by many kilometres. At the last glacial maximum, about 20,000 years ago (Fig. 2.6, inset), it was possible to walk from the West of England westwards to Ireland and southwards to France, or even eastwards across the southern counties and the North Sea plain to Denmark and Scandinavia. Over the millennia, repeated transgression and regression (Table 2.1) created many different shorelines, few of which we know much about today (Fig. 2.6). In recent post-glacial times rising and falling sea levels have locally had profound effects in exposing, drowning, or creating land, especially in the lowlands of the Somerset Levels and along the estuarine fringes of the Severn and Avon, and we need to imagine similar events being witnessed by humans on numerous other occasions over the past tens of thousands of years.

Sea-level change: nature versus man

As the glaciers finally retreated, the major valleys of the region were left while their rivers settled into the courses we see today, but many of the coastal margins were entirely different. They have subsequently passed through cyclical existences as sea, wetland, marshland and lowland. Sea level has risen over 55m in the last 12,000 years, much the greater part of this occurring before 5000 BC

This was a complex process, however, and successive sea levels cannot always be easily plotted. The weight of millions and millions of tonnes of ice itself bore heavily on Scotland and England and began to push their land surfaces into the earth's crust. As the ice receded, not only did meltwater feed the seas and raise sea levels, but the land slowly rose again as it was released from the weight of the ice, in what is termed isostatic recovery. To complicate matters further, metres of soft muds and silts that had been deposited over large areas of the Avon and Severn Levels gradually dried out and contracted, so that the land surface in these localised areas began once more to 'sink'. Where these silts conceal upstanding former hard rocks, shrinkage was not as great, causing the development of silt-veiled landscapes in which subtle surface undulations reflect the geology beneath them.

LOOKING WEST

Severn Levels

Marine or estuarine glacial sands covered by fluvial silts and clays occur deep beneath the Severn Levels. Some, dating from before 10,000 BC, are exposed along the present coastline where they are known as the Lower Wentlooge Formation (Fig. 2.8). During the Ipswichian (the last interglacial) the area from Minehead to Gloucester was inundated by the sea, but in the Devensian (the most recent glaciation) became land again, before becoming drowned once more in early post-glacial times (8500 to 6000 BC) by rapidly rising sea levels. Thereafter, the land started to rise again, and as a result of the deposition of clay and sand it became wetland that supported carr and reed swamp and contained small 'islands' of higher dry ground. Between 5500 and 250 BC further deposits of clay and peat were laid down (the Middle Wentlooge Formation). Some of these were several metres thick, within which are the remains of isolated settlements of Bronze and Iron Age date. As a result, the area was used for summer occupation and seasonal grazing, but not for permanent settlement.[11]

Fig. 2.8 Schematic drawing of the **Wentlooge Formation** *and the relative position of the Iron Age farmstead at Hallen.*

This was a diverse landscape; at the foot of the high ground were back-fens of alder and fen carr, dotted with pools of fresh and browning peaty water, and fringed by tussocky grassland that bulged over deeply formed peats (Fig. 2.9). Seawards, herbaceous saltmarsh was punctuated by occasional shrubs. It was also a changing landscape. By

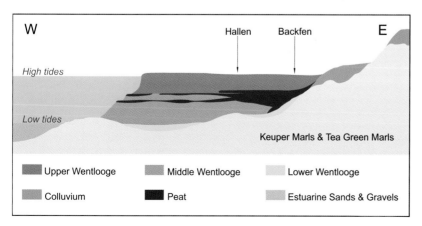

W — Hallen — Backfen — E
High tides
Low tides
Keuper Marls & Tea Green Marls

Upper Wentlooge   Middle Wentlooge   Lower Wentlooge
Colluvium   Peat   Estuarine Sands & Gravels

the early Roman period it was dry enough for communities to set out fields for pasture and to attempt cultivation, but by the later Roman period rising seas were once again regularly flooding the land, covering it in up to a metre of brownish silts of the Upper Wentlooge Formation. Today, this seemingly unchanging and tranquil plain buries a succession of very different landscapes, archaeologies, ecologies and economies.

*Fig. 2.9 **Low tides in the Severn Estuary** reveal the peat and extensive mudflats of the Wentlooge sequence close to the new Severn bridge.*

FEN

This is an ecological term used to describe a rather ill-defined group of wetland habitats. In practice it refers to the kind of marshy vegetation found on lowland lakeshores, or which gradually develops on silt and peat in lake basins. Fen is the first stage in the natural succession from open water to woodland. Waterlogged areas of land dominated by reeds, rushes and sedges form a complicated system of plant and animal communities. It includes vegetation that is fed by groundwater, and permanently, seasonally or periodically waterlogged peaty or mineral soils where grasses do not predominate, and emergent or frequently inundated vegetation.

CARR

Carr is bushy woodland and woody plants that grow on soils with permanently high water levels; it is usually dominated by alder or willow. When fen is left unmanaged small shrubs and trees grow, leading to the natural creation of carr woodland.

TABLE 2.3

1253	Edingworth (Somerset)
1259	Pawlett (Somerset)
late 13th century	Huntspill (Somerset)
before 1312	Avonmouth
1316	Pawlett (Somerset)
1326	Pawlett (Somerset)
1359	Chilton Trinity (Somerset)
1381/2	Crowpill, Bridgwater (Somerset)
1425	Cannington Priory lands (Somerset)
1480s	Cannington (Somerset)
1485	Bleadon (Somerset)
1485	Brent (Somerset)
1485	Highbridge (Somerset)
late 15th century	Avonmouth
1563	Avonmouth
1607	Whole estuary
1687	Avonmouth
1703	Avonmouth and north Somerset

Table 2.3 Documented floods around the Severn Estuary (data from Rippon 1997, Table 10.1).

Fig. 2.10 Somerset Levels; the extent of marine ingression in the Mesolithic.

From Roman times onwards, efforts were made to hold back the waves and to reclaim land from the sea[12] and in the medieval period dryer conditions allowed for isolated settlement and farming. Drainage and furrowing were imperative, but flooding was still inevitable from time to time. Eventually large economies and dispersed populations became well established. Occasional single-event floods brought local disaster, and although they were relatively common across the broad sweep of history, within the lifespan of an individual generation they were rare enough to be stories of their forefathers (Table 2.3).

The lowland landscape is vulnerable to heavy winter river discharges, storms and high winter tides, and a number of historical floods (for example that recorded in 1703, Table 2.3) are attributed to such phenomena. But the cause of flooding is not always so parochial. A major flood on 20 January 1607 drowned land fringing the Severn Estuary and Bristol Channel. It affected the countryside from Barnstaple in Devon to the South Wales coast, and inland as far as Gloucester. Historical records recall a catastrophe; crops, animals and many thousands of householders were lost. As well as flooding land to the foot of Glastonbury Tor, the inundation occurred more or less simultaneously across the entire seaboard, and it has recently been suggested that it was caused by a tidal wave or tsunami.

The Somerset Levels

The same general history of tidal ebb and flow can be seen in the Somerset Levels. These resulted in the formation of the thick and extensive beds of peat for which the levels are, or were, famous. The development of the Somerset Levels is not necessarily more complex than elsewhere, but because of the detailed work carried out over the past 60 years by Sir Harry Godwin, the Somerset Levels Project[13] and other more recent research, we have an unusually clear picture of how it occurred across both space and time.

In the Mesolithic, from 8300 BC to around 5000 BC, the Somerset Levels took the form of a large, swampy estuarine inlet that extended as far inland as Glastonbury, encompassing the Brue and Parrett valleys and engulfing the present shoreline from Brean Down to Bridgwater (Fig. 2.10). During the early Holocene period the brackish estuary and its hinterland started to silt up with blue to grey silts and clays. Inland, where saltmarsh gave way to fresh water, thick deposits of peat formed over the estuarine clay.

By 4500 BC the rate of sea-level rise had slowed down and the estuarine influence was reduced, allowing saltmarsh to give way to freshwater reed swamp. Consequently organic sediments started to form. Reed vegetation prospered, but was soon surpassed by *Cladium* sedge growing in base-rich fen conditions as the waters became shallower (0.4m deep). By about 3500 BC, birch, alder and willow fenwood had become established as peat growth and rising land gained the upper hand. Further marine incursion is recorded in the Axe valley around 2850 to 2500 BC but, further inland, fenwood was superseded by sphagnum raised bog with heather and hare's-tail cotton grass. Peat formed in these bog

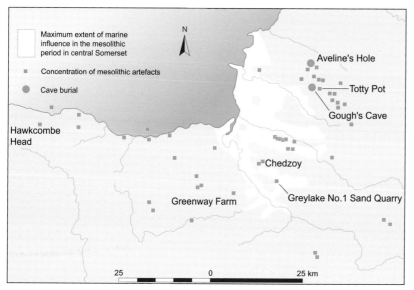

conditions and the raised bog west of the Burtle Beds, started forming by around 2600 to 2500 BC and had reached eastwards to Shapwick by about 2000 BC, its spread being hindered by the islands of Westhay and Meare. Around Glastonbury open lakes and sedge mires formed rather than raised bogs (Figs 2.11 and 2.12). These wet conditions were the impetus for the first phase in the trackway construction between higher drier islands of land (eg the Abbot's Way).

Continued rising sea levels led to the formation of groundwater fen peat rather than raised bog, and to the onset of further floods. Flooding became more common and in some areas land was under shallow water for nearly 400 years from about 700 BC. A later series of flooding events occurred around 100 BC, and these may in part have been the stimulus for renewed trackway building. Peat growth finally ceased in about AD 400.

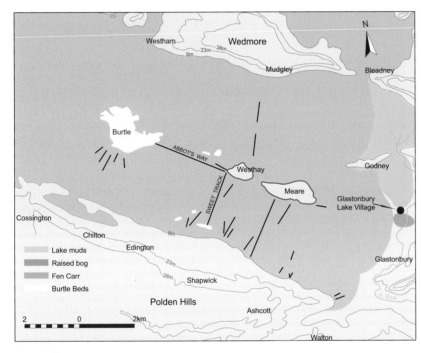

ABOVE: *Fig. 2.11 Schematic section through the deposits of the Somerset Levels.*

LEFT: *Fig. 2.12 Somerset Levels showing the islands, extent of raised bog, principal sites and some of the trackways.*

Brean Down

The very fact that a 25m-high cliff of dune sand lies exposed and eroding on the beach against the southern rock cliff of Brean Down is testimony both to today's rising sea levels and to the lower sea levels that prevailed at the time it was deposited during the last Devensian glaciation some 20,000 years ago. More significant still are the Bronze Age houses that are falling out of this eroding cliff face, some 2 to 4m above the present storm beach. Between 1800 and 1000 BC Brean was not a seaside resort, but a small Bronze Age farming settlement lying perhaps a couple of kilometres inland from the sea.

Islands in the sea?

Relatively small changes in sea level can have dramatic effects on the nature and extent of habitable land. These have sometimes been forgotten or remain unconsidered. Flat Holm and Steep Holm in the Bristol Channel, for instance, may have been accessible by land until possibly as late as 4000 to 5000 BC. It is superficially tempting to consider the early Mesolithic artefacts (dating to around 5500 BC) found on Lundy as the debris of island-dwellers who were exploiting the unique coastal and marine resources of the island. In reality, Lundy was probably part of the mainland, and because there were no marine and coastal resources for Mesolithic communities to exploit, it is necessary to find another story to explain their presence.

LOOKING SOUTH

The southern seaboard of our region is composed of hard rock geology rather than being the creation of sedimentation or drainage. Rising sea levels still drowned former land lying up to several kilometres from the current shoreline – the Isle of Wight was once part of the mainland, separated from it only by the former Solent river (now the Solent). Land has also been lost to the sea as cliffs retreated – the full extent of prehistoric settlement on Hengistbury Head, and offshore from Swanage and Weymouth, has been lost forever through coastal erosion. Further seaward, former dry landscapes have been submerged, as at Boulder on the north coast of the Isle of Wight.

THE HUMAN INFLUENCE ON THE COUNTRYSIDE

Forests and forest clearance: a tangled pattern of woodlands

After the last glaciation, temperatures rose, vegetation started to colonise the warming land, and soils began to form over bare rock and in soft sediment as plants took root. Over the next 4,000 years there was a general development from herbaceous plants to shrubs of birch and juniper, and thereafter from open woods of pine, birch and hazel, eventually to deciduous mixed forest of oak, elm and lime. This process can be seen happening all over Britain[14] (Table 2.4), but in reality this history is too generalised to explain the exact course of events in any specific area.

The West as a whole is not one of the best-studied regions in terms of its palaeo-ecology, yet we are fortunate in knowing a great deal about some of its component elements such as the Somerset Levels. One common assumption, embedded in archaeological thought for more than a generation, is that the whole of our region, indeed the whole of southern Britain, was forested more or less simultaneously and in a consistent developmental sequence (*see* Table 2.4). In reality, however, the landscape of today is a mosaic of different vegetation, plant communities and land uses, and it always has been. Even the most seemingly 'natural' and widespread of ecological communities is in practice a diverse montage.

Uplands

We *assume* that the uplands were covered in deciduous woodland by earlier Neolithic times (4000 to 3500 BC), but often find little convincing proof. This either illustrates the destructive effects of subsequent human land use or requires us to question our original assumption. We are told that much of the mid-west of England, the Cotswolds in particular, were 'clothed' in dense natural wildwood from 4000 BC. However, pollen evidence from soils buried beneath the Cotswold-Severn long barrows of Nympsfield, Ascott-under-Wychwood and Hazleton tend to suggest a much more open and airy woodland of hazel scrub interspersed with oak, lime, alder and birch, and with some open hazel and pine woodland on the higher hilltops of the Cotswolds.[15]

We know from recent work on the downs in both Cranborne Chase[16] and around Dorchester[17] that some areas of dry chalkland may not have become forested at all until very late in the Neolithic, perhaps 2,000 years after the

Table 2.4 Generalised vegetation succession for southern England (after Allen 2000).

TABLE 2.4

Climatic Zone	Godwin/West Pollen Zone	Archaeological Period	Climate and Vegetation	Approx. date calibrated BC/ (BP)
FLANDRIAN			*Deterioration*	
Sub-atlantic	VIII	Roman period / Iron Age / Late Bronze Age	Cold and wet, general deterioration. High rainfall. Decline of lime. Increase of ash, birch and beech	
	Fl. III			1250 BC (*c.* 2900 BP)
		Middle Bronze Age / Early Bronze Age / Final Neolithic	*Stable* Warm and dry, low rainfall, wind-blown deposits. Woodland regeneration in southern England	
Sub-boreal	VIIb			5200 BC (4500 BP)
		Late Neolithic / Middle Neolithic / Early Neolithic	Declining warmth. Landnam and first agriculture. Elm decline: 3800 BC/5050 BP	
				4000 BC (5200 BP)
Atlantic	Fl. II / VIIa	Later Mesolithic	*Optimum* Climatic optimum, warm and wet. Increase of 2°C, poly-climax forest. Increase of alder, some clearances	
				6300 BC (7500 BP)
Boreal	VI	Mesolithic	*Ameliorating* Continental climate, warm and dry. Asynchronous expansions of mixed oak forest with hazel and successional from pine	
	V			
	Fl. I			8900 BC (9500 BP)
Pre-boreal	IV	Early Mesolithic	*Rapid Amelioration* Sharp increase in warmth at 10,000 BP. Birch, juniper + pine woodland	
				10,000 BC (10,250 BP)
LATE GLACIAL Loch Lomond/ Younger Dryas Stadial	III	Later Upper Palaeolithic	Sub-arctic climate; Loch Lomond re-advance tundra	
				11,500 BC (11,500 BP)
Windermere (Allerød) Interstadial	II	Later Upper Palaeolithic	Interstadial, rapid amelioration. Birch, pine and tundra	
				13,500 BC (13,000 BP)
Late Devensian	I	Later Upper Palaeolithic	Sub-arctic climate	
				c. 17,000 BC (16,000 BP)
Main Devensian		Upper Palaeolithic	Sub-arctic climate, full glacial advance Man absent from British Isles	
				(*c.* 24,000 BP)
MID GLACIAL sub-arctic – Upton Warren Interstadial sub-arctic –		Earlier Upper Palaeolithic ? Mousterian	Sub-arctic climate Interstadial Sub-arctic climate	
				(*c.* 60–70,000 BP)

surrounding hills and valleys. Here, then, there was no woodland for the first farmers to cut down. Unwooded areas in and around the Allen valley (Cranborne Chase) and South Winterborne (Dorchester) were fringed by heavier woodland cover. It is perhaps no coincidence that these two areas are centres of widespread Mesolithic activity, later replaced by Neolithic monumental landscapes. Further afield the South Dorset Ridgeway, with its heavier soils on clay-capped hills and harder chalk outcrops, seems to have supported darker and more dense deciduous forest, mainly of oak, ash, hazel and perhaps elm.

The lowlands

Detailed examination of the environmental record for the Somerset and Severn Levels shows the presence of woodland, but this was far from ubiquitous and uniform. Many areas supported open fen and pools or lakes of water; these could not become forested until the landscape had dried. When this began to happen, alder and willow carr woodland developed, often as tangled masses of spindly branches with tussocky reeds and herbaceous marsh plants beneath. This was light woodland, one that was difficult to pass through comfortably, but easy to cut and manage. On the drier fringes where the hills rise from the levels, more typical deciduous woodland became established. Again, a different pattern can be seen in the river valleys. The Severn valley towards Tewkesbury contained woodland dominated by lime, but also with oak and elm and an under-storey of hazel, the latter indicating an open woodland canopy. The floodplain itself and river margins were overrun with alder carr growing in the damper riverside environment. The Kennet valley, from earliest times, contained expanses of *Phragmites* reed beds interspersed with alder and willow carr, while the drier sides supported open pine and hazel woodland in the Mesolithic, later superseded by lime, oak and hazel in the Neolithic. In contrast, recent limited analysis suggests that some of the chalkland valley sides of the Wylye valley may have remained unwooded; the valley floor has still to be studied.

Clearing ground

Laying down the basis of natural woodland succession is an essential prelude to the identification of subsequent clearance and modification by local communities. In very general terms, the woodland was first modified on any scale in the Neolithic, when ground was cleared for a variety of activities, including the construction of burial and other monuments. Woodland was progressively felled through the Bronze and Iron Ages, resulting in the formation by the end of the Roman period of landscapes that would be almost recognisable to us today.

Despite some areas of the chalkland becoming afforested only late in the Neolithic period, other parts of the same wooded landscape may have been cleared, or at least modified, in much earlier times. We have tentative evidence of limited clearings in the Mesolithic in Cranborne Chase,[18] and similar suggestions have been made for the Dorchester chalklands.[19] Clearance, we may suggest, was for the creation or maintenance of open glades that allowed shrubs and bushes to thrive and fruit, and that would provide ideal browsing for deer and cattle. Here then, are both ideal bait for quarry, and soft fruit and berries for the hunter. At the same time, the act of clearing and maintenance provided wooden poles for spears and branches for bows, as well as fuel for the fire.

Other forested areas were also attacked and cleared during the Neolithic. Initially the edges were nibbled away, but later much larger tracts were clear-felled. The growing of grasses was such a success that it provided one of the main impetuses for large-scale forest clearance, the creation of fields and later the division and ownership of land. In the Dorchester and Cranborne[20] areas much of the chalkland had been opened up and divided amongst separate owners by the later Bronze Age, but south of Dorchester large tracts of woodland remained with only a few small settlements.

Within the river valleys clearance was selective. In the Severn valley near Tewkesbury small clearances may have been made in the woodland as early as 3500 BC, but major clearances did not occur until after 1700 BC, centuries later than on the chalklands. Clearance of the lowlands and claylands was local and piecemeal. But compared with the dry uplands, human effort was not always the primary force in removing woodland. Rising tides and dampening soils could clear woodland as extensively and nearly as quickly.

Rising water: man or nature?

As we have seen, the landscape was constantly changed and influenced by fluctuations in the level of the land relative to the sea, but these changes were not entirely the result of nature. As communities cleared and farmed the uplands, one of the consequences was an increase in the amount of rainwater that washed off the land. This eroded soils and caused the build up of sediment in valleys and vales. The natural processes of soil erosion, sedimentation and alluviation have been unwittingly accentuated and accelerated by human activities. Increased levels of flooding and sedimentation accompanied Iron Age settlements such as those at Glastonbury and Meare in the Somerset Levels,[21] while in the Avon Levels similar events may have been associated with Bronze Age settlements at Cabot Park and Iron Age occupation at Hallen.[22] In these lowlands, however, it is difficult to disentangle the effects of man from those of nature – and perhaps that is the point: people here were working in nature, as part of nature.

Woodland as a resource

Woodlands offer not just timber for building and fires, but provide a range of staple foods such as berries, fruits and fungi. They also support habitats for animals, both large and small, which graze and browse within them. As woodland developed, it changed as a habitat, and in turn so did the resources that it provided. From early post-glacial times, human manipulation of the woodland attracted herbivores to browse and graze, and right through to medieval times it provided important pannage for herds of pigs. There is also evidence that trees were being coppiced and pollarded from Neolithic times in the woodland surrounding the Levels to provide timber for the construction of trackways through the peat mires, for hurdle fencing around Iron Age houses and enclosures and as an important medieval trading commodity. Pollarding is well attested in the Forest of Dean from the medieval period, where it allowed light into the woodland and encouraged new growth. In addition it provided lofty boughs for construction and the fabrication of a vast array of implements from cultivation spades to furniture.

Farmscapes: the creation of the modern countryside

The biggest single impact on the landscape in both prehistoric and historic times has been that of agriculture and the creation of farmscapes. From the early Neolithic, trees were felled to create grazing land for cattle on the chalk downlands, the Cotswold limestone and the fringes of the Levels. But it was tillage, the breaking of the sod, that had the greatest direct impact in changing semi-natural countryside into the farmscape we see today. Furrows for the seedbed were initially dug by hand with an ard, but it was when animal-drawn mould-board ploughs were used to turn the soil in Roman times that the farmscape we see today was born. In human terms cultivation enabled larger

Fig. 2.13 Rolling chalk downs of the Dorset Ridgeway *with the Long Bredy bank barrow in the foreground, and relict Bronze Age field systems superimposed by later medieval fields.*

populations to be sustained, and gave rise to the creation of new skills and increased specialisation in crafts and industries right across the West.

The first fields were on the chalk, and those around Dorchester and Cranborne Chase in the Neolithic at about 3000 BC were little more than garden plots where cereals were tended, probably along with blackberries and other fruiting shrubs. These plots were replaced in time by larger portions of land more formally designated for cereal growing. From the beginning of the Bronze Age, fields were established on the chalklands and by the Middle Bronze Age (about 1000 BC) sets of regular rectangular plots of land had been laid out with their borders fringed with longer grasses and shrubs (Fig. 2.13). By the later Iron Age whole hillsides were covered with extensive regular field systems; each year some would have been under crop while others lay fallow to be grazed and manured by animals. The remnants of these systems survive as the low grassy

banks and lynchets that were once hedges or fencelines and that are still a
characteristic feature of today's chalk downlands. As farming became more
widely established, the countryside was divided and allocated by bounded and
apportioned field systems, rather than by individual fields. Around Dorchester
large ranch boundaries defined land owned or utilised by specific communities,
families or tribes.

The chalklands south of Dorchester (the South Dorset Ridgeway) and the
limestone of the Cotswolds were not so extensively farmed, nor probably as
highly populated during earlier prehistory. The limestone provided rock to build
walls, divide fields and contain animals – a material absent from the chalklands.
Although the cultivation of cereals played a part in Neolithic and Bronze Age life
on the Cotswolds, the establishment of fields, or more significantly of large field
systems, occurred much later than on the chalk. The first small field systems in
this area were developed in the Middle to Late Bronze Age. Their patterns were
also less regular, often involving flowing field shapes that followed the natural
contours and topography. On larger hillslopes, field boundaries and shapes were
defined by ownership and long-lost landmarks. It was not until the later Iron Age
that the valleys and hillsides of the Cotswolds were covered by field systems
divided by drystone walls, perhaps a millennium after those of the chalklands.
Although these field systems, which are a characteristic feature of the Cotswold
landscape, are visually very different from those of the chalk downs, their
function and economy was not.

Farming did not always require the formal demarcation of land. From earliest
times grazing of cattle and sheep was undertaken on common, unenclosed land
and herds were driven along droveways to drink at nearby rivers. Droveways are
present throughout the downlands and Cotswolds, and many have their origins
in prehistory. Although the Wylye valley provides an important corridor into the
heart of Salisbury Plain, major droveways run from the high chalk at Corton and
Grovelly in the south, across the Wylye floodplain and the river and on to
Salisbury Plain at Upton Lovell and Codford to the north. Most of these ancient
routes are flanked by prehistoric barrows, including some of the most richly
furnished, if not most visually prominent, in the region. Were these droveways
merely aligned on these ancient monuments, or were they an essential part of the
prehistoric agricultural landscape?

Fields were not a defined feature on the fringes of the Somerset Levels. Iron
Age settlements at Glastonbury and Meare were located on small drier islands
and on the edges of the levels. Lower land provided summer pasture and the
higher drier land was used for winter stocking.[23] Cereals could only be grown on
the drier land (Fig. 2.14), so extensive field systems were never established; the

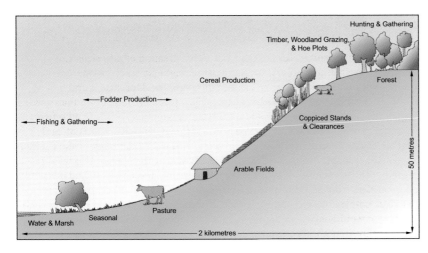

Fig. 2.14 Land-use on the zones of the Somerset Levels (after Coles and Coles 1989).

economy here was based on a much more mixed and dispersed farming regime than the chalklands, in which trade in textiles and metalwork played a more important part than the cultivation of cereals.

This pattern was mirrored in the Avon Levels, where small localised farmsteads were established from the Bronze Age and Iron Age. Unlike Glastonbury and Meare, these were largely for seasonal summer occupation associated with the grazing of cattle, the manufacture of textiles and the cutting of reeds and willow for mats and baskets. The arable fields of these communities lay elsewhere, in a different landscape on the uplands to the east.

One significant consequence of tillage, particularly on the dryland of the chalk and limestone, was erosion of the soil. Slowly, year by year, autumn and winter rains washed soil to the edges of fields, where it formed banks and lynchets against hedges, fences and walls. Elsewhere soil ran unhindered to accumulate at the bottom of dry valleys, or into rivers to be washed seawards before filling river channels and being spread across floodplains. No single event was remarkable or catastrophic, but decade by decade, century by century, upland soils became thinner, the valleys became shallower as they were filled with new deposits, rivers were slowed by thick muddy bottoms, while soils on the alluviated floodplains became deeper and siltier.

Major changes in farming methods occurred in the medieval period. Drying land allowed greater exploitation of the lowland, especially in the Severn Levels, and the creation of large tracts of ridge-and-furrow ploughing. These extended deep into the river valleys of the Kennet and Wylye, and into the now-colluviated (soil-filled) dry valleys of Dorset, Salisbury Plain and the Cotswolds. Previously unviable land was opened up through new methods of cultivation and more effective land drainage and tidal flood management. Prehistoric field systems were amalgamated and incorporated into medieval open fields on the higher and drier land, but the extensive cultivation of these areas was later replaced by the pasturing of sheep, accompanied by cattle-herding. This medieval farmscape, inherited from prehistory and modified by economic necessity, is essentially the landscape we see today.

Creation, management and reclamation

From the Roman period onwards, concerted efforts were made to deliberately manage and modify rather than just utilise the countryside. The lowlands fringing the Severn, including the Levels surrounding Brent Knoll, and encompassing the Brue and Parrett valleys, were marginal landscapes for settlement. They had provided important components of prehistoric economies, but their later exploitation was relatively sparse.

The unpredictable nature of tidal and river flooding limited further exploitation of these extensive tracts of land. Their potential could only be realised by controlling or managing nature. The first evidence of embankment, embayment and land reclamation and protection on the coastal shorelines occurs in the Roman period, especially in the Severn estuary between Gloucester and Bristol. Extensive outworks along the Severn estuary on both the Welsh and English sides were constructed to keep the sea at bay. Watercourses known locally as rhynes were dug through peats and clays to ensure drainage, and to modify dendritic and wandering river channels into regular, maintained courses. As a result, new blocks of open land were created and made available for livestock and cultivation.

By the medieval period extensive tracts of land, particularly on the river shore around South Gloucester, Slimbridge and Oldbury, had been progressively embanked and reclaimed, increasing farmland and the extent of medieval manors. Hand in hand with coastal reclamation came inland land improvement. Attempts to drain land and enclose moors are recorded from the

13th century onwards, again in an effort to increase the amount of workable land available for farming.[24]

Shorelines were more clearly defined and dryland was separated from wetland by banks or wharfs, punctuated with grouts (tidal outlets) from pills (creeks) and rhynes. The river frontage from Gloucester to beyond Bristol supported a burgeoning fishing industry. The Severn's high tidal range and low extensive mudflats made this an ideal environment for setting fish traps, and fishing industries grew throughout the medieval period and early post-medieval period, only being lost to the region within the last two centuries.

Access and transport

The major river valleys of the region, particularly the Kennet and Wylye, provided access into the chalk heartland of the Marlborough Downs and Salisbury Plain. As early as the late-Neolithic period (around 2000 BC), bluestones for Stonehenge were transported from South Wales along the Bristol Avon, Wylye and Wiltshire Avon rivers. These valleys had been routeways and corridors for even longer, and in Mesolithic times (6500 BC) would have provided easy access into central southern England. Neolithic long barrows along the Wylye valley were deliberately located where they were conspicuous and could be seen from the riverside and valley floor, not from the high downs. The importance of this routeway was further emphasised by the almost unique construction of long barrows on the valley floor itself.

The broad river valleys of the Wylye, Kennet and Nadder not only provide access to areas further to the east, but are distinct, if narrow, landscapes in their own right. In Mesolithic times *Phragmites* reed beds offered cover for birds and hunting opportunities for the nomadic human communities. Reeds and rushes also provided materials for matting from earliest prehistoric times, and for thatching from at least the Bronze Age until today. The open floodplains were in addition natural routeways for migrating herds of herbivores, their diverse ecology offering food and shelter while their rivers provided water for drinking and bathing. Not surprisingly these valleys are also the locations of some of the earliest known human habitation sites, such as those around Thatcham near Newbury.

In the medieval period the valley floors and floodplains were farmed with the aid of ridge-and-furrow ploughing, supported by extensive systems of managed water meadows. At a later date they were also important for the cultivation of watercress. Although only small ribbons of land, they are surprisingly important components of the region in terms of economy, transport and ecology.

And what of the clay vales? We have said little of the character of these areas so far, and for good reason. In terms of landscape history we know almost nothing about what was happening there; there is no preserved record of their character in glaciated times or of the effects of sea-level change, and they offer very little evidence of their post-glacial vegetation history and human habitation. These landscapes cannot at present contribute much to our story.

Attrition and abuse: mining, cutting and extraction

Extraction and exploitation of the region's mineral wealth on an industrial scale can be traced back to the Roman period. Peat as a resource for burning had been known since prehistory; fires in Bronze Age houses at Brean Down were fuelled by peat from the adjacent lowlands.

Extensive surface peat, in places many metres thick, occurs throughout the Somerset Levels from Brent Knoll to Glastonbury. It is dark, humified and cohesive, which has made it a rich source of fuel, fertiliser and even building blocks since the Roman period. By the medieval period it had become so valuable that legislation was needed to control rights over its ownership and exploitation. Peat cutting was a major medieval industry, especially within the central Somerset Levels. Areas were defined, drained and cut, initially by hand and more recently by machine.

Industrial peat cutting had a deleterious effect on the hydrology and ecology of the Levels as well as on their appearance. But there was at least one positive result of this development: it was the commercial cutting of this peat that first alerted archaeologists to the presence of buried prehistoric remains in the form of trackways on Westhay Level in 1835 (the Abbot's Way). This discovery spurred interest in other possible hidden sites, and the identification of the Iron Age settlements at Glastonbury (1890s) and Meare[25] (1895) can each be indirectly attributed to the peat-cutting industry. Destructive though this extraction was, without it the initial finds might never have been made and our archaeological knowledge never expanded to the rich level it has reached today – the wetlands, like the clay vales, would instead have played only a small part in our story.

Landscapes as human creations

Each component landscape of the relatively unpopulated countryside of the West, beautiful though it may be, is far from natural. Much of what we see as features of the landscape, and all that we see in terms of ecology, is a human construct. From the wettest wildernesses of the Avon Levels to the windy barren hilltops of the Mendips and Cotswolds, the region's landscape is a direct product of centuries, indeed millennia, of human activity. No search, however thorough, will find a natural, untouched enclave in the region. Despite its generally open and sometimes wild countryside character it is all, ultimately, a human creation.

NOTES

1   Trueman 1977.
2   Fortey 1994.
3   Lowe & Walker 1984.
4   Jones & Keen 1993.
5   Wymer 1999.
6   Jones & Keen 1993.
7   Wymer 1999.
8   Evans 1975.
9   Lowe & Walker 1984.
10 Jacobi 2004.
11 Gardiner et al. 2002.
12 Rippon 1997.
13 Coles & Coles 1989.
14 Evans 1975; Allen 2000, 2002.
15 Darvill 1987.
16 Allen 2000; French et al. 2003.
17 Allen 1997.
18 French et al. 2003.
19 Allen 1997.
20 Green 2000.
21 Coles & Coles 1989; Coles & Minnitt 1995.
22 Gardiner et al. 2002.
23 Housley 1995.
24 Rippon 1997.
25 Coles & Minnitt 1995.

3

Peopling the Landscape

JULIE GARDINER AND MICHAEL J ALLEN

EMERGING FROM THE ICE

The story of how our region was peopled really begins about 40,000 years ago, when the first anatomically modern humans like ourselves (*Homo sapiens*) are found in the archaeological record. But flint and chert hand-axes indicate that as far back as 400,000 years ago parts of the West had been inhabited by earlier types of hominids, but only sporadically in warm phases between periods of glaciation (Fig. 3.1). Although no human bones have been found from the period 250,000 to 40,000 BC, it can be assumed from artefacts and the use of caves that Britain, like much of north-west Europe, was then inhabited by Neanderthals (*Homo neanderthalensis*).[1] Bones of *Homo sapiens* from Kent's Cavern, Torquay show that there were modern humans in our region by some 38,000 years ago, giving a period of around 10,000 years during which *sapiens* and *neanderthalensis* might have co-existed, though we still do not know why the Neanderthal population then vanished.

There is very little evidence from the West for early *sapiens* occupation in what is known as the Upper Palaeolithic,

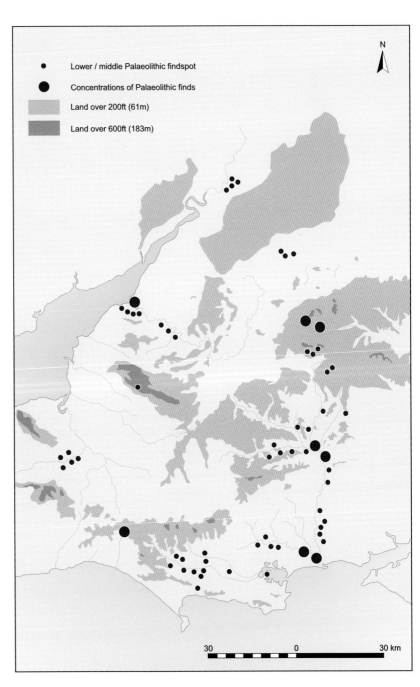

Fig. 3.1 Map showing Lower and Middle Palaeolithic findspots.

Lower / middle Palaeolithic findspot

Concentrations of Palaeolithic finds

Land over 200ft (61m)

Land over 600ft (183m)

N

30   0   30 km

Fig. 3.2 Map showing the cave sites of the Mendips.

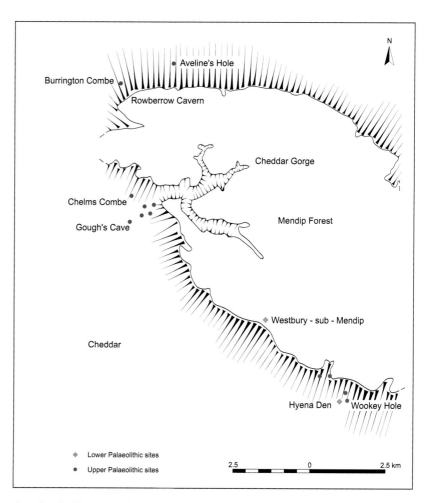

virtually all of it coming from cave and rock shelter sites in the Mendips (Fig. 3.2). Four caves – Hyena Den, Badger's Hole, Soldier's Hole and Uphill Cave – have produced characteristic flint tools associated with large assemblages of bones of animals including hyena, cave lion, otter, ox (aurochs), horse, reindeer, giant deer and brown bear (some of these being hunters rather than hunted!). We can say almost nothing about the lifestyle of these people or make any sensible estimate of their numbers, nor guess at how they perceived their landscapes.[2]

The last (Devensian) glaciation to have affected Britain reached its maximum southern extent somewhere around 20,000 years ago. The thaw began to set in before 14,000 BC, by which time some of the earliest new arrivals in Britain had crossed a shrinking land bridge from the continent into our region. These were hunters, or perhaps more accurately scavengers, groups who followed herds of animals, especially reindeer, and periodically visited caves in the Cheddar Gorge (Fig. 3.3). Here, late Upper Palaeolithic flintwork associated with the butchered remains of horse and deer have been found in Gough's Cave, Sun Hole, Aveline's Hole and Soldier's Hole. Human remains are rare – only two adults, two adolescents and a young child have been found at Cheddar, but isotope analysis of their bones confirms that they relied on a meat diet.[3] Only occasionally have any unprotected open-air sites, such as Hengistbury Head in Dorset and Barnwood in Gloucestershire, survived the thousands of years of subsequent land use.[4]

As the ice passed from memory, the environment was transformed, and a natural succession of vegetation closely shadowed changing climate and ground conditions. Open grasslands gradually gave way to birch and pine forests; the horses, reindeer and other creatures of open country and cold climate left with them. Rivers began to settle into their courses. Sea levels rose and so, freed of its weight of ice, did the land. The two kept pace for a while until the sea gained the upper hand, drowned the Solent valley and inundated vast lowland areas along the Severn.

The varied geology and topography of our region gave rise to an increasingly varied mosaic of vegetation and drainage, even over small areas. Developing floodplains along major rivers like the Parrett, Brue, Sheppey and Axe were probably heavily wooded, supporting wild boar and beaver while the wetland areas of what are now the Severn Estuary Levels teemed with wildfowl and fish. The Mendips and Quantocks supported more open woodland and scrub, providing grazing for deer. The limestone hills were quickly wooded while the chalklands sported a tapestry of pine and birch woodland and grass. Broad east–west river valleys such as the Wylye, Kennet and the Bristol Avon became both rich areas for occupation and important routeways.

Against this background people

Fig. 3.3 Oblique aerial photograph of the Gorge at Cheddar, incised through the Mendips.

thrived. Far from life being 'nasty, brutish and short' as it was once described, the postglacial (Mesolithic) period was a time of plenty. People lived in harmony with the land, moving with the seasons as a succession of resources became most plentiful. These movements were not random but followed a cyclical rhythm within large territorial ranges whose bounds and pathways must have become established through group experience and memory.

Early Mesolithic base camps, where family groups congregated over the winter months, can be recognised as vast concentrations of stone tools sometimes accompanied by broken animal bones and hearths. On the eastern fringes of our region, flint scatters are spread over several kilometres of the Kennet valley around Newbury and Thatcham. These are associated with the exploitation of red deer, elk, roe deer, aurochs, horse, beaver and wild boar – animals whose preferred habitats ranged from dense forest to open grass. Fish and wildfowl were almost certainly hunted too, though their small and fragile bones do not survive well, and plant foods would have included nuts, roots, berries, fruits and even wild seeds and grains. Away from the base camps, smaller flint scatters producing a specialised range of tools indicate the occurrence of hunting stands and specific kill sites.

Flint scatters belonging to the earlier Mesolithic (about 8300 BC) have been found widely spaced across the Cotswolds with large assemblages around Cherington and Long Newnton to the north of Malmesbury, at Bagendon near Cirencester and Syreford Mill and Hazleton near Cheltenham.[5] Flint does not occur naturally on the Cotswolds, so this raw material must have been imported as part of a seasonal round that included the Marlborough Downs or Salisbury Plain or through exchange. In the smaller of our upland areas earlier Mesolithic sites occur on the fringes of the hills overlooking the river valleys and wider vales, for instance at North Petherton on the edge of the Quantocks and around Shapwick on the north side of the Polden Hills. Cave and open camp sites occur on the Mendips with occasional occurrences of human burials. Many small flint scatters have been found close to the present south coast, for instance at Hengistbury Head, around Christchurch Harbour and on the Isle of Purbeck.[6] There are few areas which did not form part of the territories of Mesolithic hunters.

BREAKING NEW GROUND

It did not take long for people to realise the potential for taking greater control of the environment that they exploited. It could not have escaped the attention of Mesolithic groups that if lightning caused forest fires, the new open areas were quickly colonised by grasses, grazing animals and fruiting shrubs such as blackberry. Pollen records from all across southern Britain show that the forests began to be cleared before 5000 BC.[7] By this means, large stores of fresh 'on the hoof' meat supplies could be made available at a time and place to suit the hunters. The appearance of flint axes during this period is surely linked with this pioneering forest clearance. By picking off the young males and older females, of wild cattle in particular, the composition of the herd could be manipulated to provide maximum yields in the presence of a minimum number of aggressive adults. The process of domestication had begun.

Once begun, there was no turning back. Within little more than 1,000 years – perhaps 50 generations – people had altered our region irreversibly and transformed the economic and social basis of their existence. Before 3500 BC large areas of the forest had been cut down. New herd animals – sheep and goat – were brought to Britain from the continent, as were cultivated cereals such as emmer and einkorn wheat and barley. This period, the New Stone Age or Neolithic, saw the rapid spread of pioneering farming across our region. The first areas to be farmed were the hills, where rich, easily worked and extremely fertile soils had developed under the deciduous forests that had replaced the pines.

The effects of the slow change to a settled lifestyle, in which people produced food where they lived rather than following the seasons, were profound. By breeding animal populations that required management and by planting crops that needed constant tending, people tied themselves to the land. A very different concept of landscape must have formed.

As communities started to settle down they began also to establish a sense of ownership as well as a feeling of belonging to the land that fed them. Within a very few generations they developed a sense of history, of acknowledgement that previous generations – their ancestors – had been associated with the same areas that they cultivated and grazed. Soon they began to build extravagant burial mounds in which to place their dead – the future ancestors of their own descendants, thus emphasising the connection between community, land and the past, and in turn legitimising the future.[8] In some cases, such as at South Street at the head of the Kennet valley, traces of ard marks of early cultivation survive actually beneath the burial mound.

Within two or three hundred years during the 4th millennium BC these large, elongated burial mounds built of chalk and earth and designed for multiple or communal burial – long barrows – were raised across all the main uplands of the West. Their presence across a large part of the region indicates that early farming communities not only adopted similar lifestyles but also shared a common set of beliefs. On the chalklands of Dorset, along the scarp slopes of Salisbury Plain and the Marlborough Downs, and on hillsides flanking the major chalk rivers such as the Wylye and the Kennet, they commanded extensive and sweeping views of the new farming territories, and continue to do so to those who seek them out 5,000 years later.[9] On the Cotswolds and parts of the Marlborough Downs, where large slabs of stone such as sarsen were available, the long barrows are even more elaborate, containing passages and chambers roofed and walled with stone slabs. Examples of these so-called 'Cotswold-Severn' tombs include Hazleton North, Belas Knap (Fig. 3.4), Nympsfield, Notgrove and Hetty Peglar's Tump.[10] The West Kennet long barrow near Avebury is the best known of the Marlborough Downs examples.

Neolithic farming communities were not fully self-sufficient, however, and extensive trading networks in a variety of raw materials and objects were also needed.[11] Among the most obvious, and apparently important, was the trade in flint and stone axes, examples of which travelled hundreds of kilometres from their origins. In our region, some stone axes have been found that originated in Cornwall, Wales and the Lake District. Pottery tempered with rock and clay fragments derived from localised outcrops became dispersed over wide areas and probably many other goods were exchanged of which it is more difficult to find archaeological traces, including food, livestock and people. Most of these transactions are likely to have been hand-to-hand – the simple swapping of one item for another – but they helped to maintain contact and good relationships between communities throughout and beyond our region and to ensure harmony and peaceful coexistence.

Some of these transactions seem to have taken place at new large enclosures that began to appear, usually in prominent positions on the periphery of the main areas of settlement. Examples in our region include: Hambledon Hill and Maiden Castle in Dorset; Knap Hill, Whitesheet Hill, Windmill Hill and Rybury in Wiltshire; Crickley Hill, The Peak, Eastleach (Fig. 3.5), Icomb Hill and Down Ampney in Gloucestershire; and possibly Cadbury and Ham Hill in Somerset. These oval or roughly circular enclosures consisted of one or more deliberately discontinuous concentric rings of banks and ditches – hence the name 'causewayed enclosures' that they have been given by archaeologists (Fig. 3.6). They vary enormously in size and complexity and seem to have served a variety of functions.[12] Some, such as Hambledon

Fig. 3.4 Belas Knap Cotswold-Severn Neolithic long barrow.

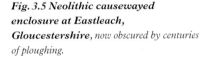

Fig. 3.5 Neolithic causewayed enclosure at Eastleach, Gloucestershire, *now obscured by centuries of ploughing.*

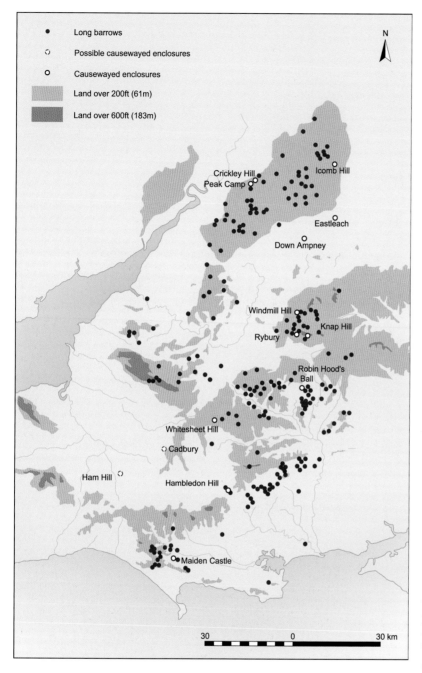

Legend:

- Long barrows
- Possible causewayed enclosures
- Causewayed enclosures
- Land over 200ft (61m)
- Land over 600ft (183m)

Map labels: Crickley Hill, Peak Camp, Icomb Hill, Eastleach, Down Ampney, Windmill Hill, Knap Hill, Rybury, Robin Hood's Ball, Whitesheet Hill, Cadbury, Ham Hill, Hambledon Hill, Maiden Castle

30   0   30 km

Fig. 3.6 Distribution map of causewayed enclosures and long barrows.

Hill in Dorset, contain a great many pits, but the contents of these frequently include carefully selected, often unusual or exotic objects and rarely suggest 'ordinary' domestic settlement. In the ditches deposits of 'rubbish' and human burials are often found during excavation, apparently carefully placed for non-functional reasons. Causewayed enclosures seem therefore to have been largely ceremonial in function; interestingly they appear to have served several communities at the same time: to be places where communities met.

Throughout the earlier part of the Neolithic, then, the people of our region, our pioneering farmers, lived in inter-connected extended family groups and the emphasis of social organisation was on the importance of kin-groups, community and ancestral rights. This egalitarianism was not to last for long.

DEFINING PLACE AND CREATING POWER

Early in the 3rd millennium BC, causewayed enclosures began to fall out of use. A new type of monument, the cursus, had appeared in the landscape – massive elongated earthwork enclosures, sometimes directly linked to the old causewayed enclosures, but sometimes in areas, notably in river valleys, where earlier Neolithic monuments are rare or non-existent. Around the cursuses were built other monuments, including hugely elongated mounds known to us as bank barrows, and new long barrows, often built to emphasise the ends of a cursus. Many other types of monument are also associated with the cursuses: single or concentric circles defined by ditches, pits or timber posts, henge monuments, palisaded enclosures and groups of pits containing deposits of exotic and unusual items.

This new phase of monument-building marked the beginning of a major shift in the social order and was accompanied by the rapid development of complex belief systems that placed great emphasis on symbolism, ritual activity and individual status. A markedly hierarchical exchange system was established, which involved the acquisition and controlled circulation of exotic and elaborate objects and materials. This began with specific types of stone and stone tools and eventually, by perhaps 2700 BC, included gold, copper, amber and jet, as well as decorated pottery vessels known as Beakers (probably complete with their contents). Much of this material originated from beyond our region, and even Britain, some of it coming from as far as central Europe.[13] The importance of the individual is also reflected in a new burial rite – single burials furnished with grave-goods beneath a small but often elaborately built barrow.

Monuments of this period are not randomly spaced but occur in concentrations at focal points of the landscape, sometimes in such profusion and obviously related positions that we can consider calling them ritual landscapes. Even apparently individual structures, such as the scatter of stone settings on the chalk west of Dorchester, can now be seen to be part of a complex of monuments including bank barrows (Long Bredy, Maiden Castle, Broadmayne), henges (Maumbury Rings, Mount Pleasant, Conygar Hill), cursuses (the Dorset Cursus), timber circles (Greyhound Yard), stone circles and coves (Fig. 3.7) (Flagstones, Martin's Down, Mount Pleasant) and round barrows focusing on the Dorset Ridgeway and the valleys of the South Winterborne and Frome rivers.[14] Henge monuments – circular enclosures usually with one or two entrances and, typically, with the bank placed outside the ditch – come in many sizes from small examples defined by a series of

*Fig. 3.7 **The Nine Stones stone circle at Winterbourne Abbas, Dorset.***

Fig. 3.8 Oblique aerial photograph of the Neolithic henge of Mount Pleasant on the chalklands near Dorchester, Dorset, under excavation in 1970–1.

contiguous pits, as at Wyke Down in Cranborne Chase or Conygar Hill near Dorchester, to massive earthworks, as at Maumbury Rings and Mount Pleasant (Fig. 3.8).

Our region is fringed on its eastern side by four of the most famous of these so-called ritual landscapes: around Stonehenge, Avebury, Cranborne Chase and Dorchester-on-Thames, but there are several major concentrations of Late Neolithic–Early Bronze Age ritual monuments elsewhere in the West that display long constructional histories, most culminating in the erection of stone circles. These are around Dorchester and the Dorset Ridgeway (Fig. 3.9), Priddy in the Mendips (Fig. 3.10), Stanton Drew to the south of Bristol, Buscot and Lechlade at the headwaters of the Thames and its tributaries (Fig. 3.11), Condicote and Rollright at the headwaters of the Evenlode, and near Barford in the valley of the

Fig. 3.9 Dorset Ridgeway monuments.

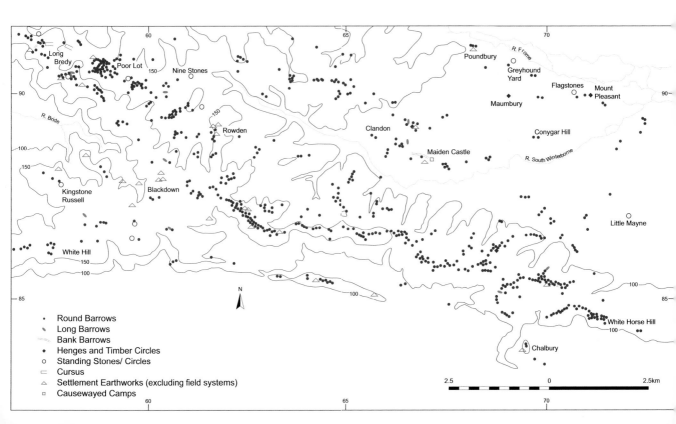

Fig. 3.10 Oblique aerial photograph looking along the line of the Priddy henges.

BELOW: *Fig. 3.11 **Plans of Late Neolithic complexes at Buscot and Lechlade.***

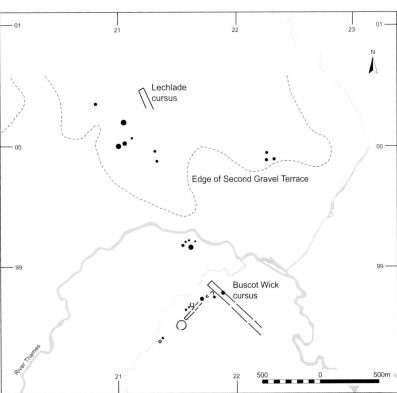

Warwickshire Avon (Fig. 3.12). Apart from the Priddy group, high and dry on the Mendips in an area that shows little coherent evidence of other Neolithic or Early Bronze Age activity, all these are associated with rivers and settlement sites represented by scatters of flint.

While we may understand little of why these monuments were built or what they were used for, they do provide us with important clues about life in our region. They tell us that nearly all parts of the West belonged to the same system of social organisation and were linked through networks of exchange and shared beliefs. They also tell us that our region was wealthy in terms of its agricultural production; a centralised system of governance based on the restriction of luxury objects to an elite and on the use of large labour forces to build elaborate follies could surely not survive without a very secure economic base to provide food, manpower and everyday necessities.

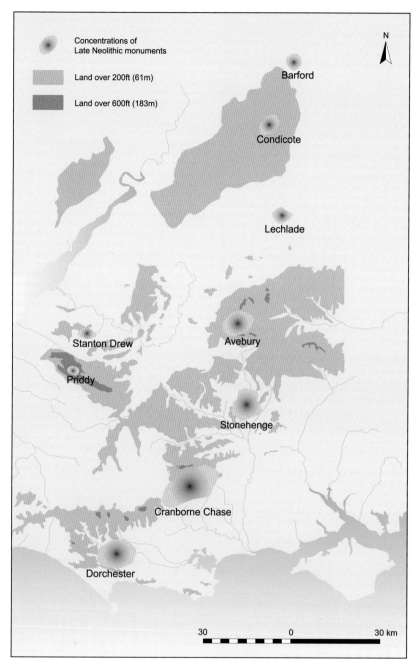

Fig. 3.12 Distribution map showing major Late Neolithic sites.

How that economic base was organised has so far been difficult to determine. All our evidence for settlement in the later Neolithic and Early Bronze Age comes from extensive scatters of flint artefacts, with virtually no surviving structures that could be considered to be domestic. On the chalk downland, however, the extent and distribution of these flint scatters indicates intensive occupation, at intervals of less than 1km in some areas.

In the Cotswolds, flint-scatter sites are also distributed widely across the hills while a number of river valley sites have produced pits that contain what appears to be domestic refuse of flint tools and pottery known as Peterborough Ware. Examples have been found at Cam, near Dursley in the Severn valley, where two pits contained pottery, daub, a perforated macehead made from a local rock and animal remains of pig, sheep and goat as well as red deer and wild boar. Several excavations in and around Gloucester, for instance at Berkeley Street, Barnwood and Longlevens, and at Tewkesbury have also produced domestic pit assemblages and other examples have come to light in the Windrush valley near Bourton-on-the-Water. An elaborately decorated type of pottery known as Grooved Ware is frequently found in what are clearly ritual or symbolic deposits associated with the main monument complexes, but it also occurs in what appear to be domestic contexts, for instance at The Loders and Roughground Farm, Lechlade, and Saintbridge, Gloucester, again associated with pits, flintwork and animal bone.[15]

How can we reconcile this rather diffuse and unimpressive settlement evidence with that of the extremely impressive monuments and the displays of wealth and ritual deposition that characterise the later Neolithic and Early Bronze Age? The answer lies partly in the symbolic function of the monuments which, though we will never know their full meaning, are still evident even 4,500 years after they fell out of use. Many were constructed so that some part of them, or alignments within or between them, were related to predictable, recurrent celestial, solar or lunar, phenomena, most obviously sunrises and sunsets at the solstices. Power and position at this time seem to have been legitimised by an authority that was at least partly based on knowledge of the movement of 'heavenly' bodies in relation to the real world. This primitive form of soothsaying, priesthood or even shamanism would allow otherworldly happenings to be translated into rules for the sowing and reaping of crops, the mating and culling of livestock and, no doubt, other important annual and seasonal events.[16]

The period from perhaps 5000 BC down to the middle of the 2nd millennium BC, from the later Mesolithic to the Early Bronze Age, thus saw many developments in the ways of life (and death) of the communities of the West; this was a period of long, gradual change, but by and large it was change in a uniform direction.

DIVIDING THE LANDSCAPE

The continuum of social and economic development that had characterised the previous 3,500 years came to a fairly abrupt end in the second half of the 2nd millennium BC. The reasons seem to have been primarily economic. Agriculture, on which the growing wealth and size of the population depended, began to take its toll on land that already had been cultivated for more than 2,000 years. Environmental evidence from across southern England shows that the soils were becoming thin and seriously degraded. The tilth that had been so productive for so long began to break down and to be washed away from the farming heartlands of the chalk and limestone hills into the downland valleys, which began to be choked by deep deposits of hill-wash. Other areas, such as parts of the southern coastal zone from Weymouth to the New Forest, had already begun to degenerate into acid heathland.

The effects of this would have been felt only gradually; but eventually pressure on the land would have necessitated a drastic reorganisation of how the land was used, and perhaps a new perception of landscape. There was a major shift too in the economic and social structures of later Bronze Age communities, partly resulting from the widespread availability of new technology and trade in new materials. These factors undermined, and ultimately destroyed, the existing power base and social structure. Their demise is clearly reflected in the abandonment of the rites of richly adorned individual barrow burials in favour of large barrows (Fig. 3.13) that contained multiple cremation burials in urns, followed in turn by a preference for large flat 'urnfield' cremation cemeteries.

Fig. 3.13 A classic example of a Bronze Age linear barrow cemetery, *Priddy Nine Barrows in Somerset, looking across Ashen Hill.*

Fig. 3.14 Excavation plan of Bronze Age settlement and enclosure at Rowden, Dorset.

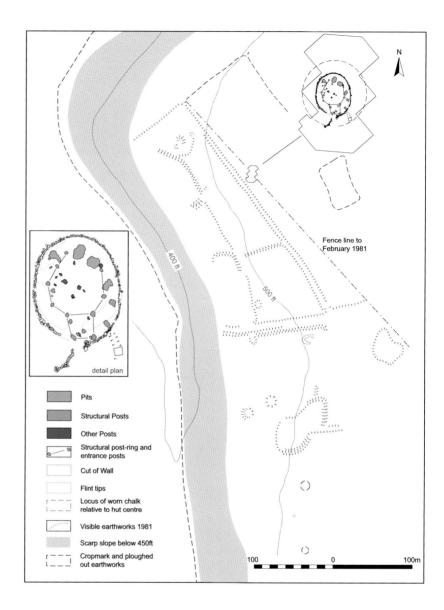

Legend:

- Pits
- Structural Posts
- Other Posts
- Structural post-ring and entrance posts
- Cut of Wall
- Flint tips
- Locus of worn chalk relative to hut centre
- Visible earthworks 1981
- Scarp slope below 450ft
- Cropmark and ploughed out earthworks

detail plan

Fence line to February 1981

400 ft

500 ft

N

100   0   100m

To bring the countryside back to full productivity required major reorganisation of both the land and the farming methods. A new structure was imposed on the chalklands: formal field systems served by trackways, farmed from houses and small settlements set among the fields. These generally consisted of a single circular house, often with a hearth and perhaps a second hut used as a workshop or animal shelter, enclosed wholly or partly by a bank and often approached by well-worn tracks with barrow cemeteries lying close by. Such sites are associated with a distinctive type of pottery known as Deverel-Rimbury Ware. They were permanent settlements and, though each house may have been occupied for a single generation, they were often replaced and the settlement itself inhabited over longer lengths of time.[17]

These single family farmsteads survive well on the chalk and over very extensive areas dozens have been recognised, largely from the air. Examples have been excavated at Shearplace Hill and Rowden in Dorset (Fig. 3.14) and at South Lodge (Fig. 3.15), Angle Ditch and Martin Down in Cranborne Chase where the close integration of fields, living areas and burial grounds can clearly be seen.[18]

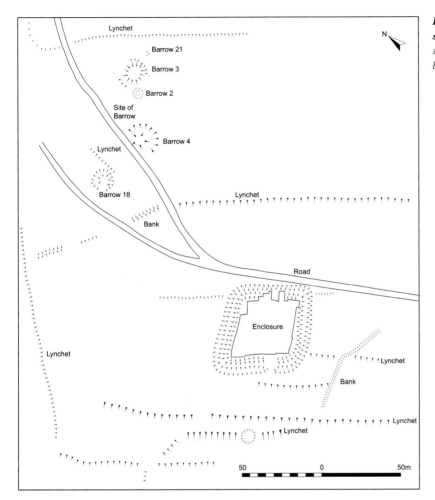

Fig. 3.15 The Middle Bronze Age settlement at South Lodge, Dorset, *set amongst fields and with associated burial mounds.*

Similar sites occur in other upland areas too, such as at Brean Down, a promontory of the Mendips that today extends into the Bristol Channel but which would not have been coastal during the Bronze Age (Fig. 3.16). The demarcation of field systems by banks, fences or hedges not only enabled greater regulation in the specific use of individual fields though crop rotations and manuring by grazing animals, but also helped to slow the loss of soil downslope through erosion. The emphasis was on maximising production.

The Cotswolds may not have seen such reorganisation, because similar enclosures are absent and traces of field systems rare. Deverel-Rimbury pottery is certainly found, however. In the upper Thames valley pits, ditches, post-holes and fences have been identified at a few sites such as Roughground Farm, Lechlade, while large-scale gravel extraction around Shorncote, near Cirencester, allowed excavation of many hectares of field boundaries, scattered settlements and trackways as part of a much wider farmed landscape. Nevertheless, the Cotswolds in this period may generally have experienced a shift towards a more pastoral economy.

This pastoral economy was also revitalised in the later Bronze Age. While meat certainly remained a major product, and cattle in particular probably represented significant capital, many spindle whorls and loomweights from excavated settlement sites show that wool was being used to make textiles. Milk and cheese were further by-products of animal husbandry, and it seems significant that the main types of flint tools in use in the later Bronze Age are scrapers and piercing

Fig. 3.16 Two Middle Bronze Age houses exposed during the excavation at Brean Down, Somerset.

tools most suited to the cleaning and working of animal hides. Bone awls and knives made from animal ribs were also used in leatherworking and have been found in some quantities at sites such as Eldon's Seat, Dorset. Thus, the emphasis shifted towards the secondary products of pastoral farming.

There is circumstantial evidence that whole new areas were opened up to farming at this time. The clay vales region between the chalk and the limestone hills that frame the Somerset Levels would have offered a different mosaic of soils and vegetation to the traditional farmlands. While today these soils are heavy, often waterlogged and intransigent, to Bronze Age farmers they would have presented a fine, workable tilth. We may, perhaps, best envisage the creation of large ranch-like farms based on a mixed arable and pastoral economy.

Parts of the southern coastal plain also became more densely settled in the later Bronze Age. Between Wareham and Christchurch, actual settlement evidence is sparse but there are very large urnfield cemeteries and several environmental sequences that attest to intensive agriculture. The fringes of the wetlands began to be exploited on a more regular basis, as we shall see.

By about 900 BC the junction of the chalk uplands and clay vales may have become an important interface between farming communities. Several large midden-like sites occur on the edge of the Vale of Pewsey, at the foot of the chalk scarp near Devizes in Wiltshire, that seem to have developed as trading centres. Two sites that have been excavated, Potterne and All Cannings Cross, are characterised by the presence of deep organic deposits covering several hectares that contain large quantities of animal bone, pottery, metalwork and equipment for spinning and weaving. Study of the microstructure of the midden deposit at Potterne indicated that large numbers of cattle were repeatedly kept in confined spaces as though at a formal market. These market centres could have served the needs of communities over wide distances and they apparently operated for several hundred years in the later Bronze Age and Early Iron Age.

The economic developments of the later Bronze Age were not entirely based on agriculture, however. The wide availability of bronze and, more significantly, of bronzeworking skills, allowed many communities access to a range of products that would previously have been very restricted in their production and distribution. Utilitarian tools, personal ornaments and a whole arsenal of weapons were made, used and eventually recycled. There were rapid typological changes as new innovations and ideas arrived from the continent and our region became part of an extensive exchange system that involved much of western Europe. Detailed study of bronze typology indicates that the production and distribution of tools, weapons and ornaments involved complex local and more regional groupings. Regional differences can also be seen in the types and distribution of fine ware pottery that suggest the emergence of social territories. In our region, one of these can be seen to be focused in Dorset.[19]

The later Bronze Age in our region was, therefore, a period of rapid change and development, of innovation, large-scale reorganisation of agricultural land and intensification in production. The old system of individual status based on the acquisition of exotic high-status objects was replaced by one in which land was the key, and control over territory and what it could produce – directly or indirectly – became the basis for power. The stage was thus set for the development of tribal society.

But before pursuing that part of the region's human history, it is worth looking in some detail at a different type of environment. Much of this chapter has focused on the chalklands; how does the story of the western wetlands compare?

MANAGING THE WETLANDS

A great swathe of what is now the southern floodplain of the Severn and the Bristol Channel, from Gloucester to Minehead, is low-lying and very flat. All of it was rapidly inundated at the end of the last ice age. For several thousand years thereafter, fluctuations in sea level led to the deposition of layers of marine silts and clays interleaved with peats formed by decaying vegetation under brackish and freshwater conditions (Fig. 3.17). The Somerset Levels became a brackish lake fed by several rivers, which gradually developed into a freshwater reed swamp.

Fig. 3.17 Extent of the Severn Levels.

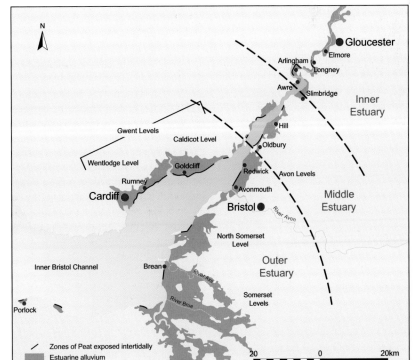

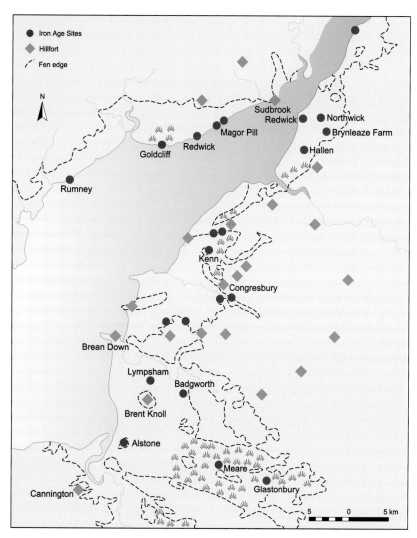

Legend:
- ● Iron Age Sites
- ◆ Hillfort
- ⌒ Fen edge

N

Sudbrook
Redwick • • Northwick
Magor Pill • • Brynleaze Farm
Redwick •
Goldcliff • • Hallen

Rumney •

Kenn

Congresbury

Brean Down

Lympsham •
Badgworth •
Brent Knoll

Alstone •

Meare •
Glastonbury •

Cannington

5   0   5 km

Fig. 3.18 Iron Age sites in the Severn Levels.

At various times in prehistory the peats accumulated to such an extent that they raised the ground surface above water level, even if only periodically, giving rise to slightly drier areas that could support moisture-loving trees such as alder, birch and willow. Their leaf litter helped to extend this light woodland, known as 'carr', and led to very localised and complex patterns of vegetation. From at least the Neolithic we can find evidence that people made good use of the fens whenever the opportunity arose. Around 3500 BC wooden trackways, such as the Sweet Track and Walton Track, were being built out into the Somerset Levels to give access to drier areas that provided good hunting. The pollen record indicates substantial natural changes from reed swamp to alder carr woodland around this time. Further north, in the Avon Levels, forest clearance was taking place along the fen margins and, though direct evidence has not been found, it seems likely that similar forays were made into the levels here.[20] Just a few centuries later, though, all traces of human activity have disappeared from both areas and the pollen evidence points to increasing wetness and the development of raised bogs.

New bog development buried and sealed Neolithic trackways and artefacts and the archaeological record indicates a continuing cycle of activity and inundation throughout the Bronze Age in the Somerset Levels. Extensive hurdle trackways, such as the Meare Heath and Eclipse Tracks, linked the fen islands, either to the dryland or to one another, and many objects – pottery, flint and wooden implements, amber beads and, especially, bronze tools and ornaments such as necklaces and rings – have been found associated with them. Some of the metalwork may have been deposited as votive offerings, an increasingly common practice in the Bronze and Iron Ages, but the tools include sickle blades, which, along with flint examples, indicate the exploitation of the reedbeds for thatch and flooring materials as well as sporadic agriculture (Fig. 3.18).

At least three Bronze Age villages were built on the edges of raised bogs at Glastonbury and Meare. They appear as a series of mounds, resulting from the accumulation of successive clay floors. At Glastonbury these represented houses, workshops, stables and other structures. The village was surrounded by a wooden palisade. The two villages at Meare produced similar pottery and artefacts to Glastonbury but excavations at Meare Village West showed that here there was no palisade and little evidence for permanent structures. The inhabitants at both villages, however, were farmers, keeping sheep, pigs, cattle, horses and dogs and growing wheat, barley and beans on the dryland fen-edge.[21]

In the Avon Levels, unprotected from the sea, such occupation was not possible. In the southern part of this area, several places around Avonmouth, such as at Cabot Park and Rockingham Farm, have been examined and limited evidence has been found for Bronze Age activity, though no convincing structures have been found. This implies repeated but short-lived visits to fen islands.

By the later Iron Age, parts of the seaward side of the Somerset Levels settled into increasingly stable areas of grassland and alder carr and these islands gradually became the focus for small farmstead settlements. Closer to the fen-edge, settlements like those at Glastonbury and Meare thrived and iron and bronzeworking industries developed. Pottery was produced in quantity and traded widely and the large numbers of spinning and weaving tools, awls, pins, needles and polishers indicate the manufacture and trade of cloth and leather goods. These fenland villages were part of a much wider settlement and trading network that extended throughout, and even beyond, the region.

The Avon Levels remained generally wetter, but recent evidence from excavations at Hallen carried out in advance of the building of the second Severn Bridge revealed the temporary but repeated occupation of islands well out into the saltmarshes. Circular huts – shepherds' huts essentially – with ancillary pens were erected and cattle, sheep and horses were brought here during the summer to graze on the lush grasses. Everything else, including grain and pottery, had to be brought to the site. These summer pastures seem to have formed part of a pattern of transhumance that extended the homelands of local farming communities living on the hills to the east.[22]

COUNTRYMEN, FRIENDS AND ROMANS

The 3rd and early 4th centuries AD were a time of peaceful prosperity throughout our region. Its boundaries encompassed a microcosm of the Roman Empire of which it was a small part: planned towns, a spa and religious centre, established ports, excellent communications, wealthy landowners living in (relatively) fine villas and an economy based on intensive agriculture and well-organised industrial production and trade. All this was made possible by the peculiarly Roman model of Imperial rule. The people of our region, mainly 'Romanised' Britons, rapidly accepted the benefits that the empire had to offer. But the economic development of the region remained firmly rooted in tradition – the people were descendants of tribes that had established territories during the Iron Age and whose way of life was already based on agriculture, industry, trade and a clearly defined social structure.

That tradition had its origins way back in the late Bronze Age reorganisation of land, intensification of agriculture and developments in industrial production and trade that we have already outlined. The population of the Early to Middle Iron Age, dating to approximately 600 to 100 BC, inherited an unprecedented economic stability.

Improved strains of wheat and barley allowed a greater variety of soils to be worked to the full and also for the winter sowing of cereals that enabled two crops to be harvested each year. Many small agricultural settlements and single farmsteads, some enclosed by ditches and hedges and some not, are found all across the upland areas of our region. Relatively few have been excavated and most are recognised as cropmarks on aerial photographs, frequently associated with field systems. The general distribution appears random, but, in detail, it can be seen that within the major hill ranges settlement clusters tend to focus on the sheltered river valleys, with field systems extending to the higher ground beyond. In the smaller uplands such as the Mendips and Quantocks, which have few permanent water courses, settlements, by contrast, are based along the springlines in order to utilise both the uplands and the surrounding lowland margins.

The upper Thames valley was intensively farmed. Sites such as Claydon Pike and Roughground Farm, Lechlade, consisted of extensive clusters of round-houses associated with drainage ditches and field boundaries. Elsewhere on the Cotswolds such settlements include large numbers of underground storage pits and elevated granaries represented by rectangular arrangements of four posts, often in considerable numbers. Similar sites occur in great profusion on the chalklands and also include what have been interpreted as two-post drying racks and 'working hollows,' which may have been associated with corn drying prior to storage. Quernstones for grinding corn are common finds.[23]

Such intensive agriculture led to the creation of surpluses that could be traded and exchanged for manufactured goods such as metalwork, pottery and textiles. Many of the traded commodities were the product of what today we would term craft or cottage industries – manufacture based on the by-products of rural life – but metalworking was a more specialist craft that required not only specific skills but also the importation and transportation of raw materials that are rarely found in our region (and whose potential was not fully realised until the Roman period). Many settlements probably had a resident blacksmith whose wares added to the goods that could be bartered. One unusual site, at Gussage All Saints in Cranborne Chase, seems to have specialised in the production of bronze horse-harness fittings including chariot gear.

Chariots were not for ordinary folk but are a reminder that the rapid economic development of the 1st millennium BC was accompanied by the development of an increasingly structured society. The redistribution of agricultural surpluses and trade in both raw materials and finished goods on the scale that was now possible clearly demanded organisation and control. The emergence of a ruling class or elite is reflected in the settlement hierarchy, which included the appearance of fortified hilltop settlements. Many of these housed sizeable resident populations but also became increasingly important as fortified storage facilities, often packed with grain storage pits and raised four-poster granaries. The hillforts became the repositories for the agricultural surplus of the local communities and from where goods could be redistributed.

But it needed more than the straightforward recycling of grain and wool to generate and maintain the trading networks required by a burgeoning society that had risen so far above the subsistence level. The hillforts therefore became centres for trade in more 'expensive' goods which, within our region, included iron, extracted from localised sources near Westbury, Wiltshire, Abbotsbury, Dorset and in the Forest of Dean; salt, produced in the Severn Levels and along the south coast; and shale from Kimmeridge that was worked into jewellery at a number of sites on the Isle of Purbeck, such as Eldon's Seat. These products, in turn, generated the need for increasingly numerous and specialised commodities and for greater control over their production and consumption.

As time went on, large numbers of hillforts were constructed – they occur throughout the hills of our region, often in closely spaced clusters or arranged in lines along prominent ridges, physically and symbolically dominating the landscape. A fine group stretches along the north side of the Wylye Valley to the east of Warminster in Wiltshire, spaced as little as 2km apart (Fig. 3.19). In general, hillforts became more elaborate and ostentatiously defensive as time passed, although only occasionally do they provide evidence for actual conflict. They reflect a period of increasing competition and struggle for power that may well have been exacerbated by a rapidly growing population. Eventually, however, there followed a period of comparative stability with fewer, larger and more complex centres of power more widely spaced across the landscape. Examples of these more 'developed' hillforts include Maiden Castle and Hambledon Hill in Dorset, Battlesbury and Yarnbury in Wiltshire, Ham Hill and South Cadbury in Somerset and Uley Bury and Salmonsbury in Gloucestershire.[24]

OPPOSITE PAGE:

Fig. 3.19 The Wylye Valley, Wiltshire: looking east along a row of Iron Age hillforts (Battlesbury, Middle Hill and Scratchbury) stretching into the distance. The area to the immediate left of Battlesbury (in foreground) is the location of a large Early to Middle Iron Age settlement.

It is now that tribal groupings or confederacies began to emerge. By about 350 BC there appear, based on the distribution of principal pottery types, to have been three main groupings within our region: one centred on the chalklands and coastal plain of Dorset, a second encompassing the Severn Estuary Levels, Mendips and Cotswolds (extending beyond our region into Worcestershire and south Wales) and a third which occupied much of south-east and south-central England, its western boundary roughly following that of the chalk scarp. By the time Vespasian's legion attacked the Dorset hillforts in AD 43–4, out of these confederacies had crystallised tribes whose identity can be recognised through distinctive styles of pottery and coinage, and whose territories roughly coincided with the confederacies. We also know names for these tribes: the Durotriges, the Dobunni and the Atrebates (Fig. 3.20).

For about 100 years before the Roman invasion, our region had been actively engaged in cross-channel trade with the tribes of the Armorican peninsula. The Roman writer Strabo, writing in the early 1st century AD, tells us that British exports included corn, cattle, gold, silver, iron, hides, slaves and hunting dogs. Major ports flourished at Mount Batten, Devon and, especially, at Hengistbury Head, Dorset, which was also a major metalworking centre.[25] Kimmeridge shale armlets and glass beads and bracelets were also made here for trade. Continental goods, most visibly various types of pottery and quantities of coinage but undoubtedly including more perishable commodities, travelled far into Dorset and Somerset while the inhabitants of Hengistbury imported – and apparently drank (since the 'empties' are not often found far inland) – large quantities of Italian wine carried in distinctive ceramic amphorae.

At the time of the Roman invasion, then, while our region was not as 'Romanised' as the south-east of England, its people were no strangers to the idea of a market economy. Vespasian's campaign against the Durotriges and Atrebates may have been rapid and fairly brutal but, within only 30 years, a

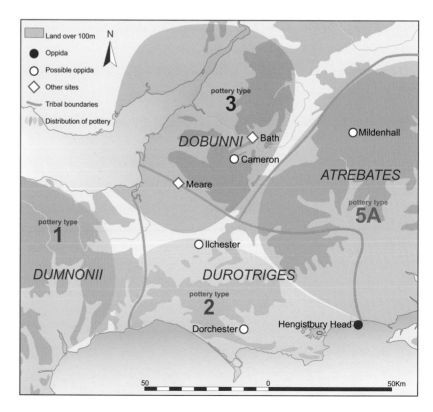

Fig. 3.20 Map of tribal confederacies and Late Iron Age tribes.

'Roman' town was thriving at Dorchester (*Durnovaria*), and the regional administrative centre of *Colonia Nervia Glevensis* (Gloucester) was founded not much later, in AD 96–8. Many forts established along the newly constructed Fosse Way grew into small urban centres in the first half of the 2nd century, and some such as *Lindinis* (Ilchester), *Aqua Sulis* (Bath), *Cunetio* (Mildenhall in Wiltshire) and *Corinium* (Cirencester) emerged as major manufacturing and market towns. *Aqua Sulis*, of course, also developed from an Iron Age antecedent to became a famous shrine and spa town. Smaller, more specialist centres developed, such as Charterhouse in the Mendips from where lead and silver mining was controlled, and ports such as *Abonae* (Sea Mills) near Avonmouth that supplied the military in Wales (Fig. 3.21).

Many smaller markets developed along the roads between the major urban centres: Camerton, Nettleton, Wanborough and Bourton-on-the-Water are examples. Local production in both agricultural and manufactured goods increased dramatically and new industries emerged, such as the quarrying of Bath stone and Purbeck marble for buildings, religious architecture and tombstones. As the process of assimilation of Roman culture progressed, so we see an increasing demand for imported luxuries such as Italian wines, Spanish wine, olives and fish sauce (recognisable from their containers), fine tablewares and glass, and the adoption of Roman fashions in burial, jewellery and personal items.

It was during the Roman period that the wetlands became a major part of the main settlement pattern. From as early as the 1st century AD rural farmsteads were founded on and around the islands of the Somerset Levels, especially Pawlett, Huntspill, Brent Knoll, Banwell and Kenn. These sites are most often now visible to us as areas of pottery, animal bone, charcoal, burnt stone and burnt clay in the ploughsoil, but hearths and occasional crudely built

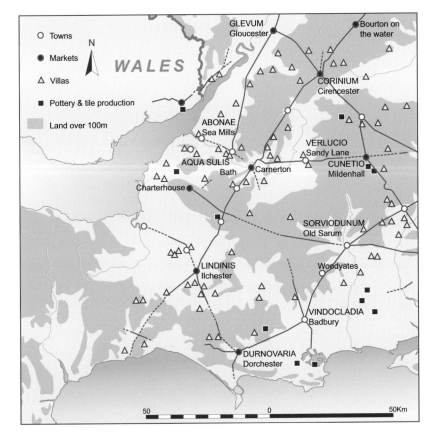

Fig. 3.21 Map of Roman sites.

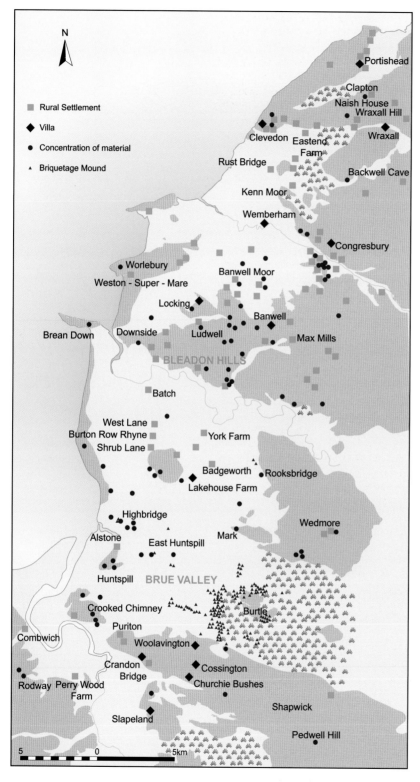

Fig. 3.22 Roman sites in the Somerset Levels.

stone walls attest to the orginal presence of buildings. Salterns and mounds of fragments of the crude pots used for transporting salt ('briquetage') are found in several areas of the Somerset Levels, most notably along the edge of the Brue valley where brackish water could be boiled to extract the salt (Fig. 3.22).

In the Roman period we also see the first serious attempts to control drainage within the levels to make them permanently available for farming. In the area between the River Axe and a former channel to the north of the Brue (called the *Siger* in a Saxon charter) substantial farmsteads were established from the 1st century AD onwards and there is evidence for the construction of seawalls with substantial footings alongside the channels of both rivers. These were permanent settlements and they were clearly successful. At sites such as Lakehouse Farm, east of Brent Knoll, a farm established in the 1st century AD became a small villa by the 4th century with a hypocaust, painted wall plaster, window glass and a tiled roof – and it was not the only one.

Elsewhere the fen-edge became the focus for rural settlements, a number of which developed into villas. The upland areas surrounding the levels supported agricultural farms and those based at the edge of the fen established field systems that extended well into the fens. Few relict landscapes survive from this period but around Banwell, Puxton and Congresbury in the North Somerset Levels large, dense pottery scatters and surviving traces of extensive field systems point to a sizeable population and intensive agriculture. At the same time there was a huge expansion of settlement into the fens and it is possible that much of this took the form of satellite 'outfield' farms belonging to the ring of villas that developed along the fen-edge.

In Gloucestershire, on the Oldbury/Berkeley Levels, the preservation of settlement material close to the modern seawalls suggests the presence of earlier sea defences. Excavations at Oldbury produced evidence of settlement and field boundaries of 2nd to 4th century date with an economy based on growing two kinds of wheat, barley and oats and the keeping of animals, particularly sheep. Industrial activity included iron smelting. Unlike the Somerset Levels, however, fen-edge settlement is sparse and there are no villas. The neighbouring Cotswolds, on the other hand, became heavily settled. This could suggest that fenland settlement here was largely independent of the main settlement hierarchy, or that these were grazing lands held by, but remote from, the developing villa estates.[26]

By the late Roman period, then, large parts of the Severn Estuary Levels had been incorporated into the general farming regime of the region, with a growth in wealthy fen-edge farms almost certainly closely linked to burgeoning villa estates on the hills to the east. Indeed, the greatest settlement density that the fen margins have ever witnessed was probably during this period. But it was not to last. Between these increasingly occupied areas lay the Avon Levels and here we see a premonition of the problems that were to face the fenland farmers in the immediate post-Roman period. The Avon Levels were not tamed by Roman farmers. A few, very scattered farms have been identified. Most seem to have been relatively short-lived and those that survived for a few generations, such as that at Northwick between the two Severn bridges, required considerable maintenance of their field ditches in the face of repeated flooding.[27] By the early 4th century the Avon Levels seem to have been abandoned and, within 100 years, throughout the Severn Estuary, the sea had begun to reclaim its own.

For the most part, the four centuries of Roman rule were a time of peaceful prosperity throughout our region with virtually all of its component sub-regions gradually becoming engaged in intensive production geared to a full market economy. The imposition of state taxes and the ability of individuals to 'make good' financially may have undermined the old tribal hierarchies, but the semi-democratic structure of the new administrative system would have allowed the old nobility, or their descendants at least, to maintain, or regain, a degree of control. The social and political landscapes of the Iron Age were transformed but the economic basis, firmly rooted in agriculture and animal husbandry, was added to rather than replaced. New scars appeared on the land as its valuable natural resources were exploited on a commercial scale; new areas were taken into cultivation and others removed from it by the creation of urban centres; but the rolling hills that characterise the greater part of our region remained essentially as green and pleasant lands.

THE COMING OF KINGS

In AD 350 the barbarian Magnentius – who may have been a Briton – seized the Imperial throne from the Emperor Constans. Although Magnentius was eventually defeated by Constantius II, his reign probably marked the beginning of an end to many aspects of civilisation as the people of our region had come to know it. Within 20 years Hadrian's Wall had been overrun by 'barbarians' who marauded as far south as the River Thames, and seaborne raiders may have attacked the Somerset Levels where signs of destruction have been found in a number of excavations of fen-edge villas, including Kings Weston, Box, Brislingham and North Wraxall.[28]

Many major towns like Dorchester and Cirencester, and even smaller ones like Mildenhall and Ilchester, shrank and fortified themselves with massive ramparts or walls. Some more rural settlements such as Camerton and Catsgore were largely or completely abandoned. After the formal withdrawal of Roman central control in AD 410 large parts of Britain disintegrated into chaos as Saxons and Jutes fought and overcame the native population, and established colonising settlements. By the end of the 6th century south Gloucestershire, along with parts of Wiltshire and Oxfordshire, had fallen to Saxon rule, although it was another 150 years before Dorset and Somerset fell into the control of Saxon kings, during which time a number of the Iron Age hillforts of Somerset were reinhabited and their defences refurbished. By the 8th century, the countryside was probably populated by Britons, Saxons and mixed ethnic groups, and Christianity was the predominant religion.[29]

The 7th and 8th centuries saw the rise of the Kingdom of Wessex under a succession of Saxon kings, not as the result of a peaceful transition but through a history of fierce battles and complex alliances and rivalries until the West Saxon kings finally secured ascendancy. The next 200 years saw a complete remodelling of society and countryside alike, with land and property divided and apportioned according to rank and birth; the landscape was carved into large estates owned by kings (such as the one whose palace has been discovered at Cheddar), noblemen or by the church, and those who worked the land were no longer its masters. Within our region the over-worked soils of the chalklands and Cotswolds could no longer provide a good living, and settlement and farming were increasingly concentrated in the river valleys. Other areas, such as the coastal plain, were virtually unusable for agriculture and there were great swathes of deep forest. Boundary negotiations were endless and complex resulting, in many areas, in such a careful division of the land that it can still be traced in the field and parish boundaries of today.

Out of all this was carved the foundations of the medieval pattern of land use and settlement that still underlies the present-day landscape of the region. Slowly the economy grew again, as did population figures. By the time of the Domesday survey in 1086, our region was thriving: a patchwork of towns and villages, markets and open fields, royal estates and forests, great minsters and abbeys and tiny Saxon churches, green hills, cultivated plains and drained marshes.

NOTES

1   Wymer 1999.
2   Jacobi 2004.
3   Jacobi 2004.
4   Saville 1984, 66–7.
5   Saville 1984, 67–74.
6   Cunliffe 1993, chapter 2.
7   Evans 1975; Zvelebil 1994.
8   Bradley 1993, 1998.
9   Cunliffe 1993, chapter 3.
10 Darvill 1987.
11 Bradley 1990.
12 Oswald et al. 2001.
13 Bradley 1998.
14 Woodward 1991.
15 Saville 1984, 113–27.

16 Bradley 1990, 1998.
17 Cunliffe 1984, chapter 4.
18 Barrett et al. 1991; Green 2000.
19 Cunliffe 1993, chapter 6.
20 Gardiner et al. 2002.
21 Coles & Minnitt 1995.
22 Gardiner et al. 2002.
23 Cunliffe 1993, chapter 7.
24 Cunliffe 1993, chapter 7.
25 Cunliffe 1993, chapter 8.
26 Cunliffe 1993, chapter 8.
27 Gardiner et al. 2002.
28 Cunliffe 1993, chapter 9.
29 Cunliffe 1993, chapter 9.

4

Villages and Markets

JAMES BOND

VILLAGE ORIGINS AND VILLAGE PLANS

Images of picturesque villages abound in the literature of tourism: Cotswold
stone cottages at Lower Slaughter reflected in the rippling waters of the River
Windrush; spring blossom overhanging the black-and-white half-timbered
dwellings of Harvington in the Vale of Evesham; thatched and whitewashed
cottages by the greens at Selworthy or Milton Abbas. In a rootless age of rush
and bustle, such idyllic visions convey a nostalgic glimpse of a seemingly more
tranquil past, a sense of timeless stability. That sense is, however, illusory. Most
villages show evidence of considerable change over the centuries, including
expansion, contraction, moves of site, sometimes even comprehensive replanning
and rebuilding. Indeed, two of the icons mentioned above, Selworthy and Milton
Abbas, are very largely creations of the late 18th and early 19th centuries.

When geographers first began to study patterns of rural settlement in the late
19th century, they made a fundamental distinction between nucleated villages
(usually linked with large communally farmed open fields divided into strips)
and scattered isolated farmsteads with fields in individual cultivation. Initially this
contrast was explained in terms of ethnicity. Most English villages have names of
Anglo-Saxon origin, so they were assumed to have been founded by the first
generations of Anglo-Saxon settlers in the 5th to 7th centuries. Moreover,
because similar villages and strip fields are also found across much of the north
European plain, it was assumed that the invaders had simply introduced forms of
settlement and agriculture familiar from their homeland. Isolated farmsteads and
small hamlets, on the other hand, were believed to represent a more ancient
pattern, surviving particularly in upland areas of western Britain where people of
'Celtic' stock retained their independence longest.

The picture is not as simple as this, however. Even in parts of England dominated
by villages there are also concentrations of scattered farms and hamlets, and these
were assumed to have a different origin. In areas like Marshwood Vale in Dorset,
pockets of dispersed settlement seemed to be linked with distinctive types of place-
name that implied woodland clearance. These were understood to represent a
subsequent stage of colonisation that had begun shortly before the Norman
Conquest, when the subsistence needs of a rising population led to a final assault
upon the remaining wildwood, and had ended with the Black Death.[1] A later stage of
secondary dispersal is well documented in the 18th and 19th centuries, when many
farmers moved out from their old village homesteads to build new farms in the
midst of their newly consolidated fields at the time of Parliamentary enclosure.

Many of the early beliefs about the origins of rural settlement patterns have been
called into question over the past 50 years. The historical and geographical
distribution of nucleation and dispersal is far too complex to be explained simply in
terms of zones of 'Anglo-Saxon' and 'Celtic' settlement. While nucleated villages are
the predominant settlement form in east Gloucestershire, lowland Somerset and

west and central Dorset, they are not particularly characteristic of the areas first settled by the Anglo-Saxons in eastern England; and where early Anglo-Saxon settlements have been excavated, they are not much like villages.[2] Another traditional assumption, that the settlement pattern remained generally stable once colonisation had reached its achievable limits, has been undermined by the demonstration since the 1950s that a substantial minority of villages which existed in the Middle Ages have since disappeared off the map (see Chapter 6). Perhaps the most important realisation of all has been that villages and open fields are really something of an aberration in the landscape, relative late-comers to a countryside that for most of its history has been farmed from scattered homesteads and small hamlets.

When and why did nucleated villages first appear, and how was the landscape organised before they appeared? We can no longer envisage early medieval settlement as taking place within a sparsely populated wilderness. Many of the settlements that subsequently acquired Anglo-Saxon names lay on or near the sites of Romano-British farmsteads and continued to farm the same fields. The earliest documentary evidence suggests a relatively non-intensive form of land use within large 'multiple' estates, in which numbers of dispersed but inter-dependent communities with specialised agrarian functions shared produce both with each other and with the estate centre. The bounds of some of those ancient estates can be reconstructed from early records. In AD 729, if we can believe the evidence of a charter known only from copies made six centuries later, King Aethelheard of Wessex gave to Glastonbury Abbey a large tract of land straddling the Polden Hills. One of the villages that lay within that estate is called Shapwick, which indicates that it was originally the sheep farm. Similar place-names, like Cowley on the Cotswolds, Swindon in the Vale of Gloucester, Wheathill and Whatley in Somerset, and the numerous Woottons preserve distant memories of the cattle farming, pig farming, wheat cultivation and woodland management components of early multiple estates.

The processes by which these estates began to break down into separate parishes and through which villages sometimes started to take shape is not really understood, although some factors can be identified. Pressure upon land resources caused by a growing population may have been relieved by a change in the management of the land itself, particularly if this involved expansion of the hectarage given over to cereals. Some large landholders looking for greater productivity and profit might have found a way of achieving this by dismembering their more unwieldy properties into smaller, more compact, more self-sufficient units. Glastonbury Abbey, reformed by Abbot Dunstan and taking a new interest in its landed property, seems to have broken up its vast Polden estate into 11 separate holdings in the late 10th century. Communally organised strip farming was also a good way of improving arable productivity on those holdings, but it required a bigger labour force. This may be the sort of context in which the larger nucleated village makes its first appearance.

If the creation of new villages and new field systems was a product of deliberate decisions by landholders, then one might expect to find some evidence of organised planning. Several of the villages on the north side of the Polden Hills, which formerly belonged to Glastonbury Abbey, namely Shapwick, Edington, Cossington and Woolavington, have distinctive rectilinear plans based upon a ladder-like pattern of two principal streets linked by short cross-lanes. One of these villages, Shapwick, has recently been subjected to intensive study by historians and archaeologists. Significant alterations to Shapwick's plan have occurred since the 18th century, but beneath these recent changes the underlying regularity of the village plan is more apparent; there are also discontinuities of much greater age, which either imply that the new settlement was laid out in two or three quite distinct stages, or that there was some internal social segregation. On the whole, ten years of research at Shapwick supports the hypothesis that an older, more dispersed pattern of settlement was superseded in the 10th century by a village with a planned layout.[3]

The sheer variety of village forms, large or small, simple or complex, linear or agglomerated, compact or straggling, regular or irregular, with or without village greens, must surely reflect considerable differences in their origins and development. Unfortunately, for most villages we are very lucky if we find any detailed cartographic depiction before the 17th century, and it is difficult to know how much further back we can safely project the earliest known plan. One of the lessons of Shapwick is that, while some components of the village plan may remain stable over long periods, others may be subject to fundamental change. Settlements such as Hawling or Tormarton in the Cotswolds, which display earthworks of abandoned crofts beyond the present built-up area, also provide a warning that some others may have contracted, or perhaps drifted away from an earlier nucleus, before the earliest maps become available.[4] Nevertheless, allowing for such changes, certain repeated patterns can be recognised.

Some villages display strikingly regular shapes, and it is difficult to escape the conclusion that these must derive from organised planning at some stage of their history. Compact linear plans are especially common. Some examples, such as Stockland Bristol near the Parrett estuary, have a single row of dwellings on one side of the street; many more have rows on both sides of the street, as at Wellow, Wanstrow, Leigh-on-Mendip and Weston-in-Gordano, all in Somerset. At Long Load near Ilchester the size and shape of plots is markedly different on opposite sides of the street, perhaps implying some early social differentiation. Sometimes, as at Bradford Abbas in Dorset, a regular linear planned extension has very clearly been added to an earlier nucleus.

By contrast, many other villages appear completely haphazard in their plan – compact jumbled agglomerations like Westbury-sub-Mendip in Somerset or Burton Bradstock in Dorset, or loose-knit straggling settlements such as Frampton Cotterell or Almondsbury in south Gloucestershire. Alongside them are some larger and more complicated polyfocal villages that seem to be on the verge of becoming small towns, like South Petherton or Martock. Within these polyfocal villages different components within the settlement retain their own names, perhaps representing an earlier pattern of dispersed hamlets that have fused into a larger settlement without completely losing their individual identities. Looser-knit villages with more than one central focus, such as West Pennard, Baltonsborough or Compton Dundon near Glastonbury, can perhaps be seen as earlier stages in this process.

Village greens are as varied in size and shape as villages themselves, and must similarly have a wide range of origins. At Halse and at Hinton St George in Somerset the green is no more than a small triangle of open space where three roads come together. At Long Sutton in the same county the green is a regular rectangle, quite clearly part of a planned village, while at Winterbourne St Martin in Dorset it is the verges of the wide street that in effect create a green. At Broughton Gifford near Melksham one part of the village wraps itself around the margins of a large, irregularly shaped common. Some greens were later reduced or extinguished by encroachment or enclosure, as at Stoke Gifford in south Gloucestershire.[5]

Most villages in the West had probably acquired their basic shapes by the 12th century at the latest. Although these would continue to be modified by later expansion or contraction, it was relatively unusual for any fundamental replanning to take place in the later medieval period. One instance is recorded in Somerset, however, the effects of which can still be seen. John Leland, the 16th-century antiquary, ascribes to Abbot Selwood of Glastonbury (1457–93) the replanning of Mells 'to the figure of an Anthony Cross, whereof indeed he made but one streetlet'. St Anthony's cross was T-shaped, so the abbot needed to do no more than create one new street at right-angles to the main road; and, since both sides of the new street incorporate pre-existing buildings, even this action probably involved no more than the straightening and broadening of an older lane to the church. Nevertheless, three of Abbot Selwood's terraced stone-built

Fig. 4.1 Timber building in the Vale of Gloucester; a medieval cruck dwelling in Frampton-on-Severn.

two-storey cottages still survive, each with a projecting polygonal turret containing a spiral stairway to the upper floor alongside the rear door. His monogram was also inserted over the doorways of two of the older cottages.[6]

Although many villages, hamlets and upland farms disappeared in the late medieval period (*see* Chapter 6), many more survived and with the recovery of population after the 16th century expanded once more. With rising prosperity came what we call the 'Great Rebuilding'. Today our impression of any village tends to be coloured first and foremost by the material, style and date-range of its buildings. Medieval dwellings were normally constructed of timber or less substantial materials such as cob or turf, and exposed medieval cruck trusses are still a feature of villages such as Harvington in the Vale of Evesham or Frampton-on-Severn in the Vale of Gloucester (Fig. 4.1). Recent investigations by students

Fig. 4.2 Cotswold stone cottages at Bourton-on-the-Hill, Gloucestershire; the rubble and freestone walling and the fissile limestone 'slates' on the roofs are all from local quarries.

of vernacular architecture have shown that many more medieval houses survive encased within later façades and disguised by inserted ceilings, staircases, fireplaces and new windows than had previously been realised. The main reason that they had escaped notice for so long was the visually dominant legacy of rebuilding in the late 16th and early 17th centuries.

One of the most important aspects of this rebuilding was the increasing use of stone in areas where it was available. The West region is especially fortunate in the rich variety of its local stone, which gives so many villages their strong personality – from the creamy-grey oolitic limestone of the Cotswold belt (Fig. 4.2) to the grey-blue Liassic limestone of the Severn vale, Polden Hills and south-east Somerset (Fig. 4.3), the orange-buff Ham Hill stone and orange-brown marlstone used around Crewkerne, Ilminster, Montacute and Sherborne, the cold grey Carboniferous Limestone of Mendip, the dull brown Pennant sandstones of north Somerset and south Gloucestershire, the red sandstones of Taunton Deane and the Quantocks, and the greensands, chalk and flint of central and east Dorset. Further from the quarries, timber building held its own in parts of the Vale of Evesham and Vale of Gloucester, while cream or pink-washed cob continued in use in parts of south Somerset and Dorset. Roofing materials were equally varied – Cotswold, Pennant and Purbeck slates alternating with thatch where no suitably fissile rock strata could be obtained. This rich range of local materials was not seriously challenged by brick and ceramic pantiles until the 18th century, although brick tends to predominate in villages that achieved their greatest growth and prosperity at later periods.[7]

Fig. 4.3 South Somerset vernacular; *thatch, blue lias walling and Ham stone windows and doorway at Marston Magna.*

While most villages and hamlets in the West have medieval origins, some developed at later periods. Squatter settlements on commons were an especially characteristic feature of areas where there was some alternative to farming, such as coal mining in Kingswood Forest and parts of north Somerset, or stone quarrying in the case of the hamlet of Street End at Blagdon. In the 19th century planned industrial villages were developed by the Clark family at Street and by the Great Western Railway at Swindon. Other settlements were built, or rebuilt, as estate villages by landowners who wished to fulfil some particular aesthetic vision or who had developed a social conscience about the living conditions of their employees (*see* Chapter 5).

A handful of new settlements were founded in pursuit of utopian dreams. Perhaps the best-known were the half-dozen hamlets founded by the Chartist Land Company between 1846 and 1848, where groups of cottages of standard design were set in smallholdings of 0.4 to 0.8ha. These were offered as prizes to the winners of a series of lotteries held among members of the company, the income from each lottery being put towards the purchase of another farm. One example was at Charterville Allotments near Minster Lovell, on the eastern margins of our region. The cottages followed a standard pattern devised by Henry Cullingham, a London builder. They were all single-storey buildings with a pedimented, slightly projecting, central bay containing a doorway flanked by two side windows. The doorway opened directly into the living-room, the two side bays served as bedrooms, and the roof swept down over a rear kitchen, which contained a well and pump. Outbuildings at the back included a privy, a wash-house, a woodshed and a couple of pigsties. Unfortunately most of the settlers had little understanding of agriculture, and the scheme foundered in disorder in 1851. A later venture was the Whiteway Colony near Miserden on the high Cotswolds, where 16ha of land were acquired for a colony of anarchists who believed in Tolstoy's principles of common ownership of land and self-sufficiency in food, shelter and clothing, supported by home-based industry (Fig. 4.4). Having burnt the title deeds to emphasise the communal nature of the colony, the settlers built their own wooden houses, small workshops and village hall. Despite many problems, both practical and bureaucratic, the Whiteway settlement survives.[8]

Leaving aside these special categories, the most decisive factor in village development in the 19th century was the application of the Poor Law of 1846. This placed the duty of relief upon the place of residence of the pauper, the removal of such people becoming illegal after five years of residence. Landowners who paid the poor rate therefore had every incentive to discourage the immigration of paupers from elsewhere. Significant contrasts developed between 'closed' villages dominated by a single powerful proprietor and 'open' villages in multiple ownership, where there was fragmented control over both agricultural and residential land. In closed villages, such as Newton St Loe or Barrow Gurney near Bristol, housing was made available only to agricultural workers on the estate. Because the quality of housing was generally good and the population stable, these villages remained compact, the traditional monopoly of the Church of England held firm, and their social character remained orderly and respectable. Open villages, such as Nailsea or Peasedown St John in the same area of northern Somerset, grew rapidly and possessed much more varied populations that included landless day labourers, artisans, shopkeepers and paupers; housing was cheap, but often of poor quality and lacked gardens. As a result, the village plan developed an

Fig. 4.4 Whiteway Colony; a utopian settlement on the high Cotswolds founded in 1898, based upon ideals of communal ownership and self-sufficiency.

untidy, sprawling character; Nonconformist chapels challenged the established church; and there was often a proliferation of drinking-houses, giving such places a turbulent and rowdy reputation. Some of the Victorian distinctions between open and closed villages are still apparent today, long after the scrapping of the legislation that created them.

ARABLE AND PASTORAL FARMING: THE MAKING OF THE AGRICULTURAL LANDSCAPE

The agricultural landscape of the West, like the settlement pattern, is varied, complex and the product of thousands of years of evolution. Some of its variety stems from the range of possibilities afforded by the natural landscape: pasture was normally the preferred use for the higher uplands, the gravel terraces of the river valleys usually provided good arable land, the flood plains provided meadow for hay or summer grazing, while woodlands were generally limited to the least fertile soils and steepest slopes. In the long term, however, nothing was immutable. Expansion of the cultivated area was prompted by population growth and by improvements in farming technology, but evidence of ancient cultivation in woods or on land now regarded as fit only for pasture underlines the fluctuating nature of the cultivation frontier. The cultivation of crops was a labour-intensive process, so the arable fields normally lay close to the settlement, while other types of land use lay more towards the margins.

Where settlements did not have sufficient variety of land within their own bounds, they often relied upon access to meadow, pasture or woodland further away. Rights to upland pasturage on Exmoor, the Brendons, the Blackdowns and Mendip, and to lowland pastures on the Somerset Levels, were held not just by the surrounding villages, but by others a considerable distance away. Meadowland was an especially valuable resource, and some meadows were shared by neighbouring parishes. Farmers from Congresbury, Puxton and Wick St Lawrence in Somerset formerly assembled on the Saturday before Old Midsummer in Puxton church to draw lots for acre strips in the Congresbury Dolemoors, a custom finally ended by Parliamentary enclosure in 1811–16. Greenwood's Somerset map of 1822 shows at least 10 parishes with interests in West Sedgemoor.

The old belief that vast expanses of primeval woodland survived into the early medieval period, and that the main task of clearing it fell to Anglo-Saxon settlers, has long been untenable. It is now quite certain that permanent enclosed fields covered much of the countryside by the Roman period and that, despite some retreat in the 5th century, early medieval farmers had in general inherited a working landscape. It is still difficult, however, to illuminate the processes by which the rectilinear Romano-British closes became converted over much of our region to the later medieval landscape of open fields laid out in strips.

An intermediate stage may have been the adoption of infield-outfield cultivation, in which an area close to the settlement was divided into strips that were distributed amongst the farmers and cultivated every year through intensive manuring, while the remainder of the land remained subject to common grazing with intermittent relatively short-term intakes for cereal cultivation. Elements of this system seem to have survived at least into the 16th century in west Somerset, where there are occasional records of wheat being sown on the upland commons, and where narrow, irregular cultivation ridges may still be seen over parts of the Quantocks and Brendon Hills and on Exmoor.

Open-field farming in its most developed form was particularly characteristic of the English Midlands, but it extended into many parts of the West. Under this system the arable land was divided into two or three large fields, one of which lay fallow on rotation each year. Each field was then subdivided into furlongs and strips, with all farmers holding a number of strips scattered relatively uniformly throughout the fields. The same farmers also had the right to graze their livestock on those fields in fallow years and after the corn harvest. Meadows were also held in strips and were subject to common grazing after mowing. Finally, all farming operations were regulated by a formal assembly of the farmers through the manor court. Evidence of both two-field and three-field systems occurs in many parts of the region. At Podimore near Ilchester the original two fields were reorganised into a three-field arrangement in 1333, with a 2m-wide ditch being dug as a boundary between two of the new fields. Such fundamental reorganisations were very unusual during the medieval period, but multiple-field systems were widely introduced after the 16th century, when the increased cultivation of leguminous crops permitted the reduction of fallows (*see* Chapter 6).[9]

Surviving working open fields are rare. Strips divided by grass baulks and lynchets still cover about 60ha on the Isle of Portland, though communal management has ceased, while another area of strips at Westcote near Stow-on-the-Wold also escaped enclosure. Far more commonly, relict traces of strips survive in the form of broad ridge and furrow that often displays the reversed-S-shaped curves created by the wide turn of ox-drawn medieval ploughs at either headland. These ridges are still familiar sights in parts of the Severn vale, in the claylands of Wiltshire, and in south-east Somerset, though modern ploughing has levelled huge hectarages. The process of enclosure by agreement (*see* Chapter 6) also often had the effect of fossilising the curvature of the medieval plough strip in long, narrow hedged closes. Where strip fields were pushed into upland areas lynchets (terraces) developed, and some very dramatic staircases of lynchets may be seen on the Cotswold scarp near Wotton-under-Edge, on the south face of Mendip at Westbury-sub-Mendip, in east Somerset at Wyke Champflower (*see* Figs 6.2a and b), and, most conspicuously of all, on Glastonbury Tor.[10]

In some parts of our region open-field farming was more limited in extent and more irregular in form, or, indeed, absent altogether. A very different landscape developed in the Severnside marshes towards the southern end of the Vale of Berkeley and in the coastal belt of the Somerset Levels, where fields behind the sea defences tend to be small and irregular and associated with a more dispersed pattern of settlement. This seems to represent a late-Saxon recolonisation of Romano-British farmland that had been abandoned because of marine encroachment. Small fields of irregular shape are also widely found in Taunton Deane and around the margins of Selwood Forest, where they are a product of woodland clearance between the late-Saxon period and about 1300.[11]

THE ROAD NETWORK AND ITS ORIGINS

People have journeyed around the countryside as long as they have lived in it, because the resources they needed for food, water, fuel, shelter or livestock were rarely available in the same place. Patterns of human movement inevitably became repetitive along particular corridors, and the general courses of many modern roads are of great antiquity. Putting a precise date on an individual road is, however, very difficult. Appearance is no guide: deep, grassy hollow ways which have the air of immense antiquity may be no more than little-used enclosure lanes a couple of hundred years old, while wide dual-carriageways thunderous with lorries and stinking of exhaust may follow thousand-year-old routeways.

The lack of hard evidence for the origins of much of the road system has led to a great deal of speculation. One persistent idea has been that the 'ridgeways' along the crests of so many escarpments across southern England are of prehistoric origin. This hypothesis seemed to be supported by the fact that upstanding prehistoric earthworks, such as round barrows and hillforts, were most densely concentrated along the ridges, where it was supposed that the primeval woodland was thinner and more easily cleared. We now recognise, however, that these concentrations were largely illusory, as the intensified application of aerial photography and other archaeological survey techniques since the 1960s has resulted in the discovery of equally large numbers of prehistoric sites in lowland areas. Notions of ridgeways as routes in an otherwise trackless waste (or as long-distance prehistoric thoroughfares determined by natural topography) have become invalidated by the realisation that much of the primeval forest had already been cleared by the late Bronze Age and that the need for access through the countryside must already have been served by a multiplicity of upland and lowland routes, many of which may well remain in use today.

The Roman army added some distinctive new components to the road network during the 1st century AD. Roman military roads were surfaced with gravel and stone, and were laid out in straight lengths so far as local conditions permitted. The main road network of Roman Britain was at first dictated by considerations of military strategy rather than commerce or local needs, but with the growth of towns and villa estates it was adjusted and extended. Some of the principal roads of the Roman province remained in use throughout the medieval period and continue to serve as main roads today. The modern A37 from Ilchester to Dorchester closely follows its Roman predecessor, as does the A38 from Gloucester to the Roman port of Sea Mills on the Bristol Avon. Until recent upgrading, most of the A417 and A419 from the Marlborough Downs through Cirencester to Gloucester followed the Roman Ermin Way. The Fosse Way linking Exeter and Lincoln survives at least as a minor road for most of its length, though within our region only the section north-east of Cirencester and intermittent lengths between Bath and Ilchester are still designated as A-class roads. Other Roman roads, such as that from Dorchester eastwards towards Badbury Rings, fell into disuse in later centuries.[12]

The density and complexity of the road network by late-Saxon times is well illustrated by the numerous references to paved roads, ridgeways, hollow ways, green ways and paths of various kinds in estate boundary perambulations attached to charters. Long-distance routes which served special purposes can sometimes be identified, such as the saltways running into Gloucestershire from Droitwich, or the 'herepath', or military way, running westwards from the River Parrett at Combwich over the Quantocks towards Exmoor, presumably conceived for the rapid deployment of troops along the vulnerable Somerset coast. The common name 'Port Way' often puzzles visitors when it occurs in inland areas like the Cotswolds, but in Anglo-Saxon records 'port' is a term for a market. The success of markets depended to a large extent upon their accessibility: from some market towns, such as Frome or Sherborne, ten or a dozen roads radiated outwards, linking them with neighbouring towns and with villages in their own hinterland.

Streams and rivers were usually crossed by fords, commonly recorded in place-names such as Bradford ('broad ford'), of which there are examples in Dorset, Somerset and Wiltshire. The Anglo-Saxon word for a ferry, *gelad*, occurs at Cricklade and Lechlade on the upper Thames, and at Framilode on the Severn. Place-names such as Axbridge, Stalbridge ('bridge built on piles') and, less obviously, Bristol, and mentions in charter boundary clauses, indicate that bridges were also numerous before the Norman Conquest, though they may be anything from a plank over a stream to a substantial stone bridge. Early references to hythes and staithes on the Axe and the Parrett show that the rivers were also used for transport.

If we take the 14th-century Gough Map in the Bodleian Library in Oxford as a guide to the principal roads of medieval England, about 40 per cent of those linking the major towns were of Roman origin. The relative ease of long-distance travel throughout the medieval period is indicated by the numerous records of journeys made by kings, barons and ecclesiastical magnates, often accompanied by large retinues; also by the frequent carriage of heavy or perishable goods over considerable distances. In 1231, for example, a consignment of live bream was carried from Feckenham in east Worcestershire to stock a fishpond at Mangotsfield near Bristol, a distance of about 112km.

Medieval roads were regarded as customary rights of way rather than fixed lines with defined boundaries. Those Roman roads which remained in use all developed slight waverings in their course as travellers evaded boggy areas, fallen trees or other obstacles. Deviations occurred particularly where carters and waggoners sought gentler gradients to avoid steep climbs such as Birdlip Hill, where the Ermin Way traversed the scarp of the Cotswolds.[13] Another cause of local diversions was the replacement of fords by bridges. Since the ford was still needed while the bridge was under construction, they are never quite on the same spot: at Burford, for example, the approach to the old ford survives directly alongside the 14th-century stone bridge. However, since fords normally occurred where rivers were at their broadest and shallowest, whereas bridge-builders generally looked for a shorter crossing, more extensive rerouting sometimes resulted. The construction of a new bridge over the Warwickshire Avon between Evesham and Bengeworth in the 12th century had the effect of diverting all the roads on the left bank from the older crossing at Twyford, 1.6km upstream. Other substantial diversions occurred from the medieval period onwards in connection with emparkment: two sharp corners on the Shaftesbury to Blandford Forum road result from its rerouting around the outer perimeter of Iwerne Stepleton park below Cranborne Chase. In the Somerset Levels Glastonbury Abbey built several causeways across Sedgemoor and the Parrett valley moors during the 13th century, which served both as roads and as floodbanks.[14]

Stone bridges were built in increasing numbers through the medieval period, Burford, Chew Magna and Bradford-on-Tone being among the surviving examples. Hermits or chantry priests were often deputed to collect tolls for bridge maintenance from a chapel on the bridge itself. The remains of one example, on the bridge at Bradford-on-Avon, recorded in 1397, were rebuilt in the 17th century as a lock-up. Another stood over the gate on the medieval bridge in Bristol until its destruction in 1646.

In 1555 responsibility for road maintenance was devolved upon the parish and a system of statute labour instituted. For understandable reasons, however, the parish surveyors concentrated their efforts on maintaining the roads most used by local people, with the result that through-routes used more by outsiders were often neglected. By the 17th century the deterioration of road surfaces through increasing volumes of horse-drawn wheeled traffic was becoming all too apparent. Improvements would clearly be necessary if economic growth was not to become, quite literally, bogged down (*see* Chapter 6).

TOWN ORIGINS: ROMAN AND SAXON TOWNS

Gloucester, Cirencester, Bath, Ilchester and Dorchester were all thriving towns during the Roman period, and there is no evidence that any of them came to a violent end after the withdrawal of Roman rule. People continued to live within the protection of their walls well into the 5th century or later. At Cirencester the forum and streets were still being maintained at least into the 430s. At Gloucester the forum court seems to have been extended in the early 5th century and timber buildings were erected over the levelled site of the baths. Extra-mural cemeteries outside Gloucester and Ilchester remained in use. Town life seems to have reached its nadir, not immediately after the withdrawal of Roman government, but around the middle of the 6th century.[15]

It is difficult to find evidence for the resumption of any form of urban life based upon trade or industry before the 7th century, when a new series of international trading emporia began to develop around the North Sea and English Channel coasts. The nature of these settlements is often signalled by place-names that incorporate the Old English element *wic* in its specialised sense of 'trading-place'. One of the best-known examples is *Hamwic*, in the St Mary's district of Southampton, the port for the inland royal estate of Winchester. Imports of exotic luxury commodities under royal control played an important part in this trade. The most important mid-Saxon trading emporia all lay to the east of our region, but minor examples may have existed at Christchurch, at Swanage (*Swanawic* in 877) and possibly even Combwich on the Parrett estuary.

New churches provided another spur to the revival of town life. Two of the earliest local Anglo-Saxon minsters, established in the 670s by Osric, sub-king of the Hwicce, were located within the former Roman towns of Gloucester and Bath. It is unlikely that any vestige of urban life survived in either place by that time, yet their selection is hardly likely to be a matter of chance. Perhaps the

Fig. 4.5 A minster town: Ilminster, Somerset. The loop of streets to south and west of the church may preserve elements of the minster precinct, with an external triangular market-place to the east.

church builders were attracted there simply by the availability of supplies of reusable building stone, which would itself have made a powerful statement at a time when most building was still in timber. Equally it may be seen as a deliberate affirmation of links with the empire's successor, the church in Rome.[16]

Dozens more minsters were established through the 8th century. In the first instance many were founded on royal estates in open countryside. Once settled, however, they provided an economic stimulus, since feeding the minster clergy and maintaining their buildings created demands that could only be satisfied by a nearby settlement of traders and craftsmen. At Wells, Taunton, Ilminster, Crewkerne, Milborne Port and Wimborne Minster, such adjuncts evolved into permanent market towns (Fig. 4.5). The momentum was increased by the Benedictine reform of the 10th century, for the stricter enclosure of monks made them even more dependent upon the services of laymen, while at the same time their extensive estates produced marketable surpluses. Market places developed outside the main precinct gates at Evesham and Glastonbury, reflecting the encouragement of traders by the monastic authorities.[17]

The Anglo-Saxon recovery after the Danish invasions of the 8th and 9th centuries produced a further stimulus to urban growth. Of the 33 new defensive strongholds or *burhs* established by King Alfred across southern England, 23 subsequently developed as towns.[18] There was, however, some inherent difficulty in adapting defensive strongholds to commercial purposes. Places suitable for defence were, by definition, difficult to get at; they tended to be on top of steep hills, or surrounded by water or marsh, where points of entry were limited. By contrast, markets were most likely to succeed where access was easy from any direction. In several local instances urban functions became dispersed within the same area, with defence and commerce assigned to different sites. At the head of the Vale of Pewsey the *burh* of Chisbury was a reoccupied Iron Age hillfort, but markets developed at two nearby settlements on lower ground, Great Bedwyn and Ramsbury. At Watchet the *burh* was on the cliff at Daws Castle, a kilometre west of the present town, which itself had developed as a *port* or market centre by the 10th century. Watchet had no parish church of its own and was served instead by the ancient minster of St Decuman, a little further inland. Even where these functions did develop on the same site, a constricted circuit of defences often left insufficient open space within, so market places developed just outside a gate. This is probably the case at Axbridge, though the precise alignment of the defences there remains uncertain.[19]

Domesday Book gives us a useful if imperfect snapshot of towns 20 years after the Norman Conquest. At least 20 are recorded across the region. Some towns had clearly suffered serious damage since 1066, perhaps during the suppression of the western revolt of 1068–9: of 292 houses in Wareham, 150 were reported as vacant or destroyed, 100 out of 277 houses in Shaftesbury had met the same fate, Dorchester had lost 100 of its 189 houses, while in Bridport, 20 out of 121 houses were reported as destroyed. At Gloucester 16 houses had been removed to make way for the castle. Markets are mentioned only at Thornbury, Bradford-on-Avon, Frome, Milborne Port, Ilchester, Ilminster and Crewkerne, while the markets at Tewkesbury, Cirencester and Berkeley were said to be newly established.

Once political stability had been achieved by the consolidation of Norman power, commercial growth resumed, and the 12th and 13th centuries saw considerable urban growth, with existing towns expanding, new towns being founded and many villages being promoted by the acquisition of market and borough charters.

MARKETS AND MARKET PLACES

During the 12th and 13th centuries the establishment of markets was increasingly seen as a royal prerogative, as a result of which many ancient prescriptive markets became legitimised by charters. Moreover, against a background of landlords' power, which impelled peasant farmers to sell more of their produce to cope with rising rents and taxes, seigneurial applications for new charters led to a huge increase in the number of places where markets were held. Within the three counties of Gloucestershire, Somerset and Dorset, markets are recorded in more than 190 different places between 1066 and 1348. By then the impulse was largely spent, and only a further 15 or so new markets are recorded between 1349 and 1600 (Fig. 4.6).

Despite attempts to limit trade to chartered markets, the notion that any assembly of traders where no toll was taken did not qualify as a market allowed a few unlicensed gatherings to continue. On the Cotswolds, 1.5km west of Chedworth, five ancient roads converge near an upland farm called Newport and a field called Portway. Informal trading had taken place on this spot long before 1348, when Thomas Berkeley acquired a charter to hold two annual fairs there. At Standish in the Vale of Gloucester dairymaids traditionally brought their produce for sale beneath a tree known as the Butter Beech.[20]

Trade operated at several different levels. Small goods and foodstuffs such as vegetables, fruit and eggs, which neither kept nor travelled well, were bought and sold in numerous local markets held in villages and small towns. Cattle, hides, corn and fish were traded mainly through larger towns, fewer in number and more widely spaced. International trade, which in the early medieval period particularly involved the export of wool and the import of wines, spices and salt, was conducted mainly through the ports of Bristol, Bridgwater and Gloucester, and through the medium of fairs.

The spacing of markets was a compromise between several conflicting needs. Customers expected to walk to market and to return home the same day. Traders wished to be able to travel from one market to another on successive days. However, manorial lords and burgesses wanted a trading monopoly over as wide a hinterland as possible, and did their best to quash competing markets nearby. Nineteen years after Henry de Montfort's acquisition of a charter for a Wednesday market on his manor of Nunney in 1260, Nicholas Braunch made an unsuccessful attempt to have it stopped on the grounds that it was injuring his Saturday market at Frome. The burgesses of Bridport complained in 1274–5 that their trade was eroded by the markets at Abbotsbury and Charminster, and in 1278 they objected to the market at Lyme Regis. Between 1260 and 1280 the burgesses of Ilchester raised a succession of complaints about rival markets at

Fig. 4.6 Market centres: markets were established throughout the region, but many small village markets subsequently failed. Only a minority of medieval market centres still functioned as market towns in the 19th century.

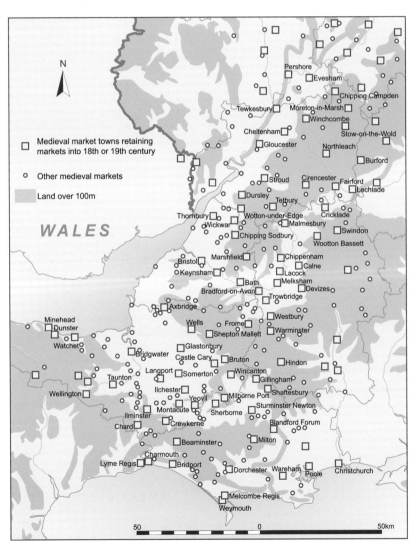

Montacute, Marston Magna, Shepton Beauchamp, Yeovil, Martock, Somerton and Queen Camel. Even the burgesses of such a populous and well-established town as Bristol felt obliged to oppose Maurice de Gaunt's new market at Redwick in 1222 and the abbot of Keynsham's new market at Marshfield in 1234.

Towns like Gloucester or Dorchester which had inherited a partly Roman street pattern within Roman walls, and planned Anglo-Saxon *burhs* such as Cricklade and Wareham, often lacked any dedicated market place, simply accommodating stalls along the streets as best they could. In most towns, however, market places are a familiar feature, and their size, shape and location often provide important clues to their history. Local markets dealing only in 'small wares' needed relatively little space, but livestock sales needed more room than provisions markets. The largest market places, such as the square at Stow-on-the-Wold, tend to occur in areas where pastoral farming was of greatest importance.

We have seen how markets developed outside the gates of monastic and ecclesiastical precincts during the 10th and 11th centuries. The same process continued on a smaller scale after the Norman Conquest, for example at Keynsham, where a new triangular market place was laid out following the abbot's acquisition of market and fair rights in 1303. Market places are also sometimes found outside the gates of castles. Bristol's Old Market, a long cigar-shaped open space with back lanes, had developed outside the castle's east gate by the 12th century.[21] At Devizes the first markets were held in a widened section of the town's main street, which curved outside the walls of the outer bailey. As the castle's military importance receded during the 12th century, the outer bailey itself became available for further commercial settlement, and a second, D-shaped market place developed within its defences.

Several towns acquired more than one market place. At the northern end of our region Stratford-upon-Avon has its Sheep Street and Rother Market, and there were further markets for corn and hay, probably also for poultry and dairy produce. The earliest markets at Evesham were almost certainly held on Merstow Green outside the abbey's west gate, but in the late 12th century trading shifted to a planned market square outside the north gate in the 'New Borough'. Tetbury's market place is at the meeting of three roads in the town centre, but a larger open space called The Cheaping lies just to the north. At Malmesbury the market cross stands in a relatively limited space at the top end of High Street just outside the abbey cemetery. There are traces of a much larger market place, probably mainly for livestock (part of it is still called Horse Fair), in the extra-mural suburb of Westover. Finally, there is a large rectangular open space within the walls at Cross Hayes, which has clearly been created by curtailing the burgage plots on the east side of High Street. The origins of this space may lie in an order of 1223 which required that the Saturday market, previously held partly within and partly outside the cemetery, should be moved to the 'Newmarket'.

Even before the end of the medieval period many market places had been reduced in size by both public and domestic encroachments. A couple of bays of heavily restored medieval timber stalls from the butchers' shambles can be seen in the market place at Shepton Mallet, all that remains of a much more extensive group which survived into the 19th century. Ornate stone market crosses survive at Malmesbury and Cheddar, and are known to have existed elsewhere, for example at Bridgwater. Grander and more substantial shelters were provided by local benefactors during the 16th and 17th centuries: the picturesque octagonal Yarn Market at Dunster was built in 1589 by George Luttrell, while a larger, rectangular gabled structure was built by Sir Baptist Hicks at Chipping Campden in 1627. Another octagonal market shelter in Somerton was rebuilt in 1683. Arcaded market shelters often also carried a council chamber above. Tetbury's splendid rectangular market house, built in 1655, had first-floor meeting rooms supported on an open arcade of stone pillars. Later examples include Wootton Bassett (1700) and Dursley (1738).

Accretions over streets and market places continued up to the 18th century, by which time congestion was becoming a serious problem. During the following century urban improvement schemes began reversing the process. Two parallel rows which had greatly narrowed Bridge Street in Stratford-upon-Avon were removed in 1826, restoring the road to its original width of 27m.

FAIRS

Markets took place one day each week, serving mainly for the sale and purchase of locally produced goods. Fairs, by contrast, attracted traders and purchasers from far and wide, taking place only once a year, but continuing over several consecutive days, a week, or even more. The heyday of the international fairs was during the 12th and 13th centuries, although even Bristol's fairs could not rival the great fairs of eastern England. Nevertheless, there were numerous lesser fairs, which were less affected by the 14th-century decline in international trade, some developing special functions, such as the horse fair at Stow-on-the-Wold or the cheese fair at Frome. Many survive today, though as recreational rather than commercial events.

A few ancient prescriptive fairs were held on open hilltops rather than in towns or villages. Examples include the Whitsuntide fair on White Down east of Chard, which was still held into the 19th century, and the Michaelmas fair on Glastonbury Tor. Montacute Priory claimed a right to hold fairs at St Michael's Chapel on the hill above the town and within the Iron Age ramparts on Ham Hill.

MEDIEVAL NEW TOWNS AND TOWN PLANNING

Visitors to Stratford-upon-Avon are often puzzled by the distance of Holy Trinity church from the town centre. The clue lies in the name of the street leading to it: Old Town. Stratford is a classic example of the most ambitious type of medieval new town development, and the church was the nucleus of the pre-existing agricultural village. In 1196 John of Coutances, Bishop of Worcester, took some 28ha of agricultural land north of the old village out of cultivation, and laid out there two sets of three parallel streets in the form of a skewed grid (the angle at which the streets intersect was influenced by the grain of the underlying open-field furlongs). Along the new streets he laid out burgage plots each of 3.5 perches by 12 perches (about 17m by 60m) and offered them at an annual rent of 1s. The bishop may have been inspired by a similar venture that had taken place some years earlier, lower down the Warwickshire Avon at Evesham, where a new market place and new borough also consisting of three streets in each direction had been laid out on the northern side of the monastic precinct by one of the abbots to supplement or supersede the older market area of Merstow Green.[22]

Only the wealthiest and most powerful landowners were able to plan on this scale. On the Dorset coast the old port of Melcombe Regis had been acquired by King Edward I, and in 1280 he reconstituted it as a borough, at the same time replanning it with a grid of streets. Rectilinear layouts of less ambitious form were employed at several other small boroughs, such as Lacock. Chipping Sodbury provides an interesting example of an ambitiously conceived plan that the promoter failed to complete. In 1218 William le Gras acquired a market charter here, and by 1232 it was regarded as a borough. The site lay astride one of the two main roads between Chippenham and Bristol, which was diverted to accommodate a chequerboard pattern of new streets. Although there were nearly 200 burgesses by 1295, the available plots were never fully occupied, and the town gravitated to a single broad main street, leaving empty vestiges of the grid plan to the south.[23]

Simpler and far more common was the type of plan based upon a single burgage-lined street, wide enough to accommodate a market. Chard, probably founded in 1234–5 by Bishop Jocelyn of Bath, was laid out in regular form along the main road from Crewkerne to Honiton, with 52 regular burgage plots each of 1 acre (0.4ha) offered for an annual rent of 1s. Moreton-in-Marsh was founded by Richard Barking, Abbot of Westminster (1222–46), utilising the Fosse Way as the main street (Fig. 4.7). In both Moreton-in-Marsh and Chard there are earlier agricultural nuclei bearing the name 'Old Town' to distinguish them from the new borough. Similar linear plans occur in many other medieval towns, including Pershore, Cheltenham, Wotton-under-Edge, Wellington, Bruton and Charmouth. Even some of the smallest planned towns, which are now no more than villages, still display a main

Fig. 4.7 Moreton-in-Marsh, Gloucestershire: a planned new town for which a market was first acquired in 1226 by Richard Barking, abbot of Westminster. The Roman Fosse Way was widened to accommodate the market. The church (right) lies within the earlier village.

street of uniform width with regular plots on either side, such as Hindon, laid out by the Bishop of Winchester in about 1220, or Wickwar, laid out by Roger de la Warre after 1285 (*see* Figs 4.10 and 4.11). Variations on the linear plan occur at Chipping Campden, where the main street broadens out into a cigar shape in the middle of the town (Fig. 4.8), and Marshfield, where it broadens into a small triangular market place at one end.[24]

Even relatively small towns can reveal a complex layout with several stages of planning. Single-street extensions to older boroughs were common. At Langport, 12th-century expansion outside the hilltop *burh* was concentrated along the old causeway of Bow Street, with the rear of the burgage plots on reclaimed marshland (*see* Fig. 5.3). At Bridport, where the *burh* occupied a low spur between two streams, the planned axis of East Street and West Street lay outside the defences, at right-angles to South Street, the axial street of the *burh*. At Sherborne in 1227–9 Richard Poore, Bishop of Salisbury, laid out a street called Newland with burgage plots of three different sizes available for annual rents of 1s 6d, 1s and 8d. South Street at Castle Cary is a similar development. The original nucleus of Montacute was the street called Bishopston, which was already a borough with a market before 1102 when it was given to the Cluniac priory founded there by William, Count of Mortain. To expand the monastic precinct the southern end of the old borough was removed and replaced by a parallel burgage-lined street, which included a planned market square, to the east. The adjustments to the plan are clearly seen in the zigzag course of the main road passing through the small town today (Fig. 4.9).

The intrusion of medieval new towns into an older landscape is betrayed by a wide range of topographical, administrative and ecclesiastical anomalies. At Marshfield and Chipping Sodbury streets with dog-leg angles provide evidence for diversions of older routes into new market places. Some boroughs have constricted boundaries containing no agricultural land: Stow-on-the-Wold, for example, originally comprised just 13ha cut out of the rural parish of Maugersbury. The church of Northleach, though close to the town's main street, stood within the rural parish of Eastington. New towns which had no agricultural predecessor often found their nearest church to be some distance away. Melcombe Regis was planted within the parish of Radipole, the church and manor of which lay 2km to the north, while the neighbouring borough of Weymouth was developed within the parish of Wyke Regis, the church of which lay almost as far to the west. If a new town did finally acquire its own church, as was the case in both Weymouth and Melcombe Regis, this was likely to remain a subordinate chapel for some time, often without its own churchyard, as the parochial rector usually resisted any loss of income from burial fees. The church of Moreton-in-Marsh, which long remained a chapelry of Bourton-on-the-Hill, acquired burial rights only in 1512 (*see* Fig. 4.7).

Rarely does an entire block of medieval houses survive in the context of a planned layout, but there are two supreme examples in Wells. The Vicars' Close, laid out by Bishop Ralph Shrewsbury in 1348 for subordinate members of the cathedral

Fig. 4.8 Chipping Campden on the Cotswolds: a 13th-century new borough with a market place along the broad main street, grafted onto an earlier settlement near the church.

chapter, consists of two rows of terraced houses along a street that subtly decreases in width towards the chapel at the end, creating the illusion that it is of greater length. Then between 1451 and 1458 Bishop Thomas Beckington built the 'New Works', a terrace of 12 shops along the north side of the market place; a parallel row to the south, intended to form a square before the gateway to the palace grounds, was never completed. A more opportunistic speculation can be seen at Tewkesbury, where a mid-15th-century terrace of 23 timber-framed dwellings with ground-floor shops along the street front has been beautifully restored.

FAILED BOROUGHS AND DECAYED MARKETS

The acquisition of a market or borough charter was no guarantee of long-term commercial success (Figs 4.10–4.13). Many places which are now only villages reveal traces of past urban aspirations in their plan. The wedge-shaped green at Broadway in Worcestershire was the market place of an unsuccessful new town planned by the abbot of Pershore in 1251, on a promising site where the main road begins to climb the Cotswold scarp from the Vale of Evesham.

ABOVE: *Fig. 4.9 Montacute, Somerset: the older borough of Bishopston in the distance was curtailed by the foundation of a Cluniac priory which stood south of the parish church; in the centre of the view is the new borough with its rectangular market place.*

Fig. 4.10 Wickwar, south Gloucestershire: the bend in the road marks the entry to the main street of Roger de la Warre's planned 13th-century borough.

The old village church was left isolated a kilometre to the south. Despite a subsequent attempt to promote Broadway as a borough, it failed to develop, and by the later medieval period its economy was based entirely on farming. Frampton-on-Severn acquired a market and fair charter in 1254, and in 1308–9 Robert FitzPayn attempted to set up a borough there, but there is no record of either market or fair becoming of any great importance. Nevertheless, a planned new settlement was clearly begun, traces of burgage plots partly surrounding a long green three-quarters of a kilometre north of the older nucleus around the church. Stogursey was a borough in 1255, and evidence of ambition can still be seen in its rectilinear layout and broad main street (Fig. 4.14). Stoford near Yeovil had 74 burgages in 1273, and the present village consists of a large rectangular green, the former market place, with two parallel streets issuing from it. Cerne Abbas never even aspired to become a borough, but the village layout still betrays some evidence of an urban promotion, which probably followed the acquisition of a market charter in 1175. The main street, Long Street, was broadened out into a characteristically cigar-shaped open space that was subsequently reduced by a central block of infill. There are also vestiges of planned tenements terminating in a back lane on the southern side, and another planned street running from the market place up to the abbey gate (*see* Fig. 4.12). Finally, some

Fig. 4.11 Wickwar, south Gloucestershire: the broad main street represents a failed borough promoted by Roger de la Warre in the 13th century. The older village may have been near the now-isolated church to the north (top). The settlement has expanded through suburban growth in recent years.

ABOVE: *Fig. 4.13 Puddletown, Dorset:* the broad street north-west of the church once accommodated a market, granted by charter to the prior and canons of Christchurch in 1301.

OPPOSITE PAGE:

Fig. 4.12 Cerne Abbas, Dorset: in 1175 the abbot of Cerne was granted the right to hold a market, which was held in the wide street to the south (right) of the parish church.

Fig. 4.14 Stogursey, Somerset: the broad street through the centre of the present village west of the priory church is the market place of a failed borough probably promoted by the de Courcy family. In the foreground is the moated castle.

market grants were probably abortive from the outset: there is no evidence that markets were ever held at Kempsford (1243), Creech St Michael (1269), Sampford Brett (1306), Brimpsfield (1354), Bradenstoke (1361) or Enmore (1401), despite the acquisition of charters in the years stated.

STABILITY AND CHANGE IN VILLAGE AND COUNTRY TOWN

Outside the industrial conurbations the pattern of towns and villages that we see today is largely a product of a limited period, the couple of centuries before and after the Norman Conquest. Despite that essential stability, however, settlements have always been dynamic organisms, responding to social and economic changes. The formation of villages as centres of communal agricultural production, whether through seigneurial planning or through more gradual organic processes, represented a significant departure from a much older tradition of dispersed hamlets and farms. Yet the growth of villages did not entirely eliminate the older pattern, nor were villages themselves always successful in the longer term. In later centuries, while some rural settlements dwindled or disappeared from the landscape, others were brought into existence by squatters settling on commons, or through the action of estate owners or utopian idealists. Few rural communities can ever have been entirely self-sufficient, and access to a road network and the development of trade were critical factors in the rise of towns in the early medieval period. While a few towns had Roman or Anglo-Saxon forebears with administrative and defensive functions, the network of smaller market centres was predominantly a development of the 12th and 13th centuries. However, urban status was also subject to change, and many villages were promoted through the acquisition of market or borough charters only to lapse again as they failed to compete with more aggressive or more advantageously sited neighbours.

NOTES

1   Taylor 1970, 26, 68, 99–100.
2   Taylor 1983, 109–50.
3   Aston (ed.) 1988, 73–5; Aston & Lewis (eds) 1994, 230; Bond 2004, 241–3.
4   Saville (ed.) 1984, 279 and 282.
5   Aston (ed.) 1988, 73–80.
6   Bond 2004, 245–6.
7   Clifton-Taylor 1972; Hall 1983.
8   Hadfield 1970, 152–78; Darley 1978, 170–5.
9   Aston (ed.) 1988, 83–7.
10 Finberg 1955, 41–3; Taylor 1970, 88–9 and 99; Aston (ed.) 1988, 85–7.
11 Aston (ed.) 1988, 89; Aston & Lewis (eds) 1994, 241 and 243; Rippon 1997, 149.
12 Margary 1967, 107–16, 123–7, 132–53 and 158–62.
13 Margary 1967, 134.
14 Williams 1970, 53–4; Rippon 1997, 212.
15 Branigan & Fowler (eds) 1976, 81–98; Haslam (ed.) 1984, 345–58 and 361–2; Cunliffe 1986, 44–9.
16 Haslam (ed.) 1984, 347–9 and 365–6; Cunliffe 1986, 49.
17 Haslam (ed.) 1984, 167–201 and 208–29; Bond 2004, 279.
18 Hill & Rumble (eds) 1996.
19 Haslam (ed.) 1984, 94–102, 172–4, 192–3, 232–3 and 234–6; Hill & Rumble (eds) 1996, 189–91 and 197–8.
20 Finberg (ed.) 1957, 61–2.
21 Lobel (ed.) 1975.
22 Beresford 1967, 500–1; Bond 2004, 282.
23 Beresford 1967, 441.
24 Beresford 1967, 429–30, 438–40, 483–4 and 505–6.

5

The Architecture of Power

JAMES BOND

THE NATURE OF POWER

Human beings are not born equal. Social reformers have at various times
dreamed of creating an egalitarian society, but no one has ever succeeded for
long in preventing individuals or groups acquiring power over others, whether by
eloquence and persuasion, threat and intimidation or physical strength and force
of arms; or through religious beliefs and fears, or by social processes of
inheritance, wealth, election or preferential appointment. In all cases, however,
power and status, whether religious, military, economic or administrative,
whether forcibly imposed, tolerated or welcomed, operates in a wider social
system. Together, these social forces have bequeathed to us some of our most
impressive monuments, buildings and landscapes. This chapter looks at some of
the expressions of power and displays of prestige that have coloured the West and
its landscape from the remote past into recent times.

POWER IN PREHISTORY

Priesthoods, mediating between man and the supernatural, may be the earliest
form of power structure outside the family group. In an uncertain world, belief in
a deity seems to meet fundamental human needs. Monuments such as the henge
of Maumbury Rings near Dorchester and the stone circle of Stanton Drew in
north Somerset represent thousands of man-hours of labour, but appear to
contribute nothing to the practical needs of survival: their construction suggests
that priestly power was already strong by the early Bronze Age.

We can see more overtly secular authority manifested in the landscape during
the Iron Age, when Cotswold, Mendip, and Dorset hilltops were crowned with
the earthen ramparts of hillforts. These served many different purposes, and vary
greatly in character. Some provided refuge in times of emergency, but others
were intensively occupied for prolonged periods, serving also as trading and
manufacturing centres. Their construction implies large, stable populations that
regarded particular swathes of territory as their own, to be defended against
outsiders. At the same time, it confirms the emergence of an elite powerful
enough to be able to withdraw labour from the basic chores of food production.[1]

ROMAN ADMINISTRATION

hillforts reflected the centralisation of power within tribal communities, but the
system they represented was replaced by a different form of more standardised
central administration, first military, then civilian, after the Roman invasion of

Fig. 5.1 Hod Hill, Dorset, *showing the Roman fort superimposed over the north-west corner (top right) of the Iron Age hillfort.*

AD 43. In the West, that replacement took a very literal form: as the Roman historian Suetonius tells us, the future emperor Vespasian captured over twenty 'strongholds' as he led the Second Legion westwards to subdue two local tribes. Excavations at Maiden Castle, Ham Hill and South Cadbury have revealed burials bearing evidence of violent death, and most hillforts had been abandoned before the end of the 1st century AD.

Military control over the newly conquered territories was marked in the landscape by new roads and forts. Of the many Roman highways that still feature on today's maps, the Fosse Way is especially notable in shaping our landscape as it passes on its way from Exeter through Ilchester, Bath and Cirencester and on through the Midlands to Lincoln. These roads were built for military purposes but soon became the skeleton of the new landscape of civilian towns and villas. The strategically located forts were, in contrast to hillforts, of more or less standard design. At Hod Hill, as if to underline the change in power structures, the Roman fort actually stands within one corner of the Iron Age hillfort (Fig. 5.1), while South Cadbury and Ham Hill have also produced evidence of early Roman military occupation. At Charterhouse-on-Mendip another fort enabled the authorities to control the exploitation of local lead and silver deposits. Further north, a major base for a legion was built to support the expansion of the Roman province of Britannia into Wales: first standing at Kingsholm just north of Gloucester and then later on the site of the modern city, this base evolved into a *colonia,* a model urban settlement designed to accommodate retired army veterans. From then on Gloucester has remained a centre of power, both as a cathedral city and as a county town.

Cirencester and Dorchester also became important centres of Roman administration in the region, responsible for administrative areas called *civitates* that were broadly based on pre-Roman tribal areas. Cirencester thus became the capital of the Dobunni in the Cotswolds and the Severn valley, while Dorchester, within sight of the abandoned frowning ramparts of Maiden Castle, became the capital of the Durotriges of Dorset. Later, by the 3rd century, Ilchester gained promotion as the centre for the northern part of Durotrigian territory. These new administrative hubs acquired grid-like street plans, substantial public and domestic buildings, water supplies and, later, defensive walls.

The Roman administration of Britain endured for nearly four centuries, and some of its elements survived the sundering of contact with the imperial government in Rome. Even in ruin, the Roman towns seem to have retained a nostalgic glow of prestige, for the Anglo-Saxon Chronicle entry for the year 577 records a tradition that Cirencester, Gloucester and Bath survived as British 'cities' with their own 'kings'. At the same time, however, we see the revival of more ancient centres of power: a significant number of hillforts, including South Cadbury and Cadbury Congresbury, were refurbished in the 5th century.[2]

ANGLO-SAXON KINGS

The imposition of rule by Anglo-Saxon kings is charted in the Anglo-Saxon Chronicle. This records a number of key events including a battle at Dyrham in 577 that brought the West Saxons to the Severn and the subsequent West Saxon defeat at Cirencester in 628 that resulted in the lower Severn and Cotswold region passing into the hands of the kings of Mercia to the north. King Cenwealh of Wessex later fought battles at Bradford-on-Avon (652) and Penselwood (658), on the latter occasion putting the Britons to flight as far as the River Parrett. The Chronicle is not a contemporary witness, being compiled only in the late 9th century, and its reliability is thus sometimes questionable. Nevertheless, it seems probable that most of the region had fallen under West Saxon or Mercian political control by the late 7th century.

Once the Anglo-Saxon kings had embraced Christianity, they wielded a powerful mixture of religious and secular power. They became law-givers: King Ine of Wessex (688–726) drew up the earliest known West Saxon law code, and established a system of local government. The counties of Dorset, Somerset and Wiltshire may all have originated as administrative areas in Ine's time, each under the charge of an appointed *ealdorman*, whose responsibilities included presiding over the shire court twice a year and collecting royal taxes; thus power once again shaped our landscape.

Maintaining royal prestige in the 7th, 8th and 9th centuries required flamboyant display as well as military might, achieved by rewarding followers with costly gifts. One result of this was a boost to international trade and the development of new coastal trading centres (*see* Chapter 4). The minting of coins became another expression of royal power, and mints in turn gave a fresh boost to the re-emergence of urban life in places like Gloucester (under Alfred, 871–99), Bath (Edward the Elder, 899–924) and Langport, Shaftesbury, Wareham, Dorchester and Bridport (Athelstan, 924–39). During the late-Saxon period the West acquired the highest concentration of mints in England, and coins continued to be minted in Bristol up to the early 18th century.

Royal households were itinerant, moving around between scattered royal estates, partly for subsistence reasons, but also because it was politic for the king to make himself visible to his subjects throughout his realm. The very institution of the monarchy thus had a presence in the structure of the landscape. Many of the royal estates contained 'palaces', complexes of large buildings, which could accommodate several hundred people for several weeks, where the king's council could meet, where charters could be witnessed, justice dispensed, taxes collected and entertainment offered. During the 10th century, for example, the king's council met at Chippenham, Frome, Dorchester, Cheddar, Winchcombe,

Fig. 5.2 The climb to a hilltop burh:
Gold Hill, Shaftesbury, Dorset.

Somerton, Edington, Puddletown, Calne, Cirencester and Bath. Many of these places were then rural estates, but it is clear that the former Roman towns also exerted some magnetism. By the 10th century a large timber hall and chapel had been built just outside Gloucester over the late-Roman cemetery at Kingsholm, which may still have retained some aura of ancient sanctity. A royal palace at Cheddar was built over part of the precinct of a minster which itself lay close to the site of a Roman villa. Excavations here in the early 1960s revealed a sequence of timber halls and ancillary structures built after the late 9th century, with a detached stone chapel.

In 789 the first Viking raiders landed unexpectedly near Portland and killed a local official from Dorchester who asked their business. Larger Danish raiding parties defeated local forces raised against them at Carhampton in West Somerset in 836 and at Portland in 840. Soon their purpose changed from plunder to occupation. In 870 a large Danish army invaded Wessex, and by 878 King Alfred was a fugitive in the watery wastes of Somerset, from where he led a brilliant campaign that drove the Danes out of his kingdom. Alfred emerged from the crisis with his own power and prestige greatly enhanced. In order to provide a more effective resistance against future invasion, as well as restructuring the army and 'founding' the Navy, he reorganised the region's landscape by establishing a network of *burhs* – strongpoints and refuges maintained by dues from the surrounding countryside (Figs 5.2 and 5.3).

The West Saxon system of shires was extended to Mercia when it was liberated from the Danes. New counties such as Gloucestershire and the short-lived Winchcombeshire bore no relationship to the old Mercian tribal areas, and were probably designed to highlight the imposition of West Saxon power. By this time the shires were subdivided into hundreds, another important power-related building block of the landscape: they administered local justice and supported courts that met every four weeks. Hundreds were notionally made up of 100 hides (a hide was an area of land deemed sufficient to support a single family) but in practice were much more varied in size, often being based on the existing estates of major landholders. The names of some hundreds, including Badbury, Hundredsbarrow and Culliford Tree in Dorset, Bempstone in Somerset and Brightwells Barrow in Gloucestershire, show that their original meeting places were in the open air, deliberately avoiding centres of power in favour of neutral ground on estate boundaries.[3]

MIGHTY ARISTOCRATS: CASTLES OF THE NORMAN CONQUEST

The dramatic events of 1066 that brought William the Conqueror to the English throne had limited impact in the region until William led his army to Exeter in 1068, following attacks on the Somerset coast and Bristol by three of King Harold's sons who had fled to Ireland. As a response, the new Norman aristocracy built defensible strongholds in the newly conquered western territories. William reallocated land, protecting key strategic points with earthen castles under his own governance or held by his most trusted followers. A new royal castle soon controlled the Severn crossing at Gloucester, the Vale of Berkeley was dominated by the castle of William FitzOsbern at Berkeley, Bishop Geoffrey of Coutances commanded the lower Avon from Bristol castle, while the vulnerable coast was protected by the castles of Walter of Douai at Worle and William de Mohun at Dunster.

William's half-brother, Robert of Mortain, constructed an especially symbolic castle on top of the steep conical hill at Bishopston in Somerset, which the Normans called Montacute. According to a 12th-century chronicle, this spot had a particular significance for the English because a fragment of the True Cross had been found there, and had been adopted by Harold as a symbol of divine support during his campaigns in 1066. For the defeated English, Count Robert's construction over the very spot where the relic had been discovered added insult to injury, and the new castle was besieged by local insurgents in 1069. Severe retribution followed, the effects of which were still apparent 20 years later when the Domesday Book shows many local manors with reduced values.

Castles were the key to Norman supremacy. They protected a lord and his followers in a hostile country, gave a base from which a small force of mounted soldiers could control the country around it, and overawed the local population. The simplest form of Norman castle was the earthen ringwork with a timber gatehouse: William of Falaise's castle at Stogursey (*see* Fig. 4.14) and the castle of Englishcombe (Fig. 5.4) near Bath were of this type. In potentially hostile towns such as Gloucester, Bristol and Dorchester, a more elaborate type – the motte and bailey – was employed, consisting of a tall timber tower built on or partly encased within a large earthen mound, with other domestic quarters and stabling protected within a larger palisaded and ditched courtyard. Motte and bailey castles were also constructed in the countryside, for instance at Upper Slaughter in the Cotswolds, at Downend on the westernmost tip of the Polden Hills, at Fenny Castle near Wookey, and at Powerstock in west Dorset.

Although the Domesday survey shows King William himself holding extensive estates, none of the royal properties in the West ever rivalled Westminster, Windsor, Woodstock or Clarendon as regular royal residences. Nevertheless, the

Fig. 5.3 Langport, Somerset: *the Anglo-Saxon* burh *crowned the hill on which the church stands, in the distance; the straight line of Bow Street in the foreground was an early causeway over the marshes of the Parrett, which became built up with burgage tenements as the town grew in the 12th century.*

Norman and Angevin kings made use of their power to designate about a dozen extensive areas within the region as royal forests, within which their hunting rights were safeguarded. Some areas were also enclosed as royal deer parks, including Gillingham (Fig. 5.5) and North Petherton. The old palace at Cheddar, extensively rebuilt, was linked to hunting in Mendip Forest.

Many castles were subsequently rebuilt in stone. By the early 12th century rectangular stone keeps were the main strong-point of many castles, of which the best example in the region is Henry I's tall keep in the inner bailey at Corfe. Henry had also built a keep at Gloucester before 1108, and another at Wareham, while his illegitimate son Robert, Earl of Gloucester probably built the keep at Bristol in the 1120s. Magnates of the church also built keeps: Roger of Caen, Bishop of Old Sarum, at Sherborne (Fig. 5.6), and Henry of Blois, Bishop of Winchester, at Taunton.

Fig. 5.4 The earthen ringwork at Englishcombe was constructed by the de Gournays, lords of the manor, in the late 11th or 12th century. *Earthworks within the main enclosure include the footings of a round tower, but this may be the remains of a later dovecote which gave the site its name, Culverhay. A slighter rectangular outwork is visible immediately west (right) of the main enclosure.*

Castles designed to keep enemies out were equally useful for containing prisoners, such as Robert, Duke of Normandy, captured after his defeat at Tinchebrai in 1106 by his younger brother Henry I. Robert spent most of the rest of his life incarcerated in a succession of West-Country castles before ending his days in Cardiff. Curiously, this secondary function sometimes continued on the same site long after the demolition of the castles themselves: county prisons were later built over the castle sites at Dorchester and Gloucester, in 1794 and 1821 respectively.

CONCEITS AND CRENELLATIONS: FEUDAL STRONGHOLDS DURING THE HIGH MIDDLE AGES

Fig. 5.5 The site of the royal hunting lodge in Gillingham Park, Dorset: *the buildings erected by King John between 1199 and 1211 were extended by Henry III, but demolished in 1369. The embanked dry moat which survives was constructed in 1211.*

The castles of Wessex (Figs 5.5, 5.6, 5.8 and 5.9) saw little serious military use, except during the dynastic civil war of the 1130s and 1140s – 'The Anarchy' – between Stephen, William the Conqueror's grandson, and Henry I's daughter Matilda, when many of them played key roles. Castles in the region continued to be built and improved in line with military fashion, but as elsewhere their symbolic value became increasingly dominant. Never again did the West become quite such a cockpit as it had been during the Anarchy. Although many of its castles were upgraded during the 13th and 14th centuries, their subsequent development generally had more to do with prestige and fashion: creating an impressive appearance and demonstrating a more luxurious way of living. Thus castles paved the way for later country houses; like them they often sat within carefully constructed landscapes that further

Fig. 5.6 Sherborne Old Castle, *a fortified palace, built by Roger, bishop of Old Sarum, some time after 1107. It was seized by King Stephen in 1139. The residential quarters were arranged around a courtyard and stood in the centre of a large square enclosure with canted corners surrounded by a curtain wall and outer ditch.*

BELOW: **Fig. 5.7 Centres of secular and military power:** *medieval castles and fortified houses and later coastal forts.*

reinforced the aristocratic status of their owners (Fig. 5.7).

While not losing all of their military role (for example, Corfe, Taunton and Dunster were strengthened in John's reign when French invasion threatened, and a new castle was built at Bridgwater after 1200 as part of the establishment of a new market borough), the vision of the castle as a status symbol was more vital. There was also no shortage of 'lesser' men rising up the social scale who wished to embellish their homes with military symbolism to underline their status. A royal licence could be bought to 'crenellate', that is to build a new castle or fortify an existing manor house. Initially intended as a way of limiting private fortifications after the Anarchy, this procedure also served to emphasise royal control over the social structure as well as providing a useful source of royal revenue. Sites fortified under crenellation licences vary considerably, but rectangular arrangements of residential blocks around a courtyard with corner towers were especially popular. Castles built by soldiers returning from the French wars are a particularly interesting group, such as that built in a French style in 1373 by Sir John de la Mare at Nunney, a tall rectangular block of four storeys with round towers at each corner and a continuous machicolated parapet (Fig. 5.8).

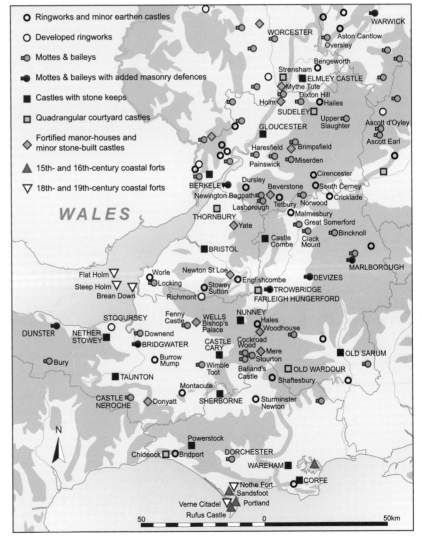

ABOVE: *Fig. 5.8 Nunney Castle, Somerset*, built under a crenellation licence of 1373 by Sir John de la Mare after his return from the French wars, and imitating the form of some contemporary French tower-houses. The projections of a continuous machicolated parapet remain.

RIGHT: *Fig. 5.9 Thornbury Castle, Gloucestershire*, was begun by Edward Stafford, 3rd Duke of Buckingham, in 1511, but left uncompleted when he fell from power 10 years later. Only one corner tower of the inner ward was completed to its intended height.

Two Gloucestershire castles, Sudeley and Thornbury, illustrate the final transition from defence to conspicuous display. Ralph Boteler, Henry VI's Lord Admiral, is said to have built Sudeley Castle using the ransom from a captured French admiral. It had two square courtyards, the inner for the principal domestic buildings, the outer court to house lodgings for retainers. When Boteler fell from royal favour in 1461, Edward IV gave Sudeley to his brother, Richard, Duke of Gloucester, who put in large traceried windows, showing beyond question that defence was no longer a priority. Even more markedly, when Edward Stafford, 3rd Duke of Buckingham, became a leading figure at Henry VIII's court he began in 1511 to build what amounted to a fortified palace at Thornbury in southern Gloucestershire. Like Sudeley it was arranged around two courtyards, and its south range had large bay windows overlooking a walled knot garden, even though other parts still presented towers, arrow embrasures and gun ports to the world (Fig. 5.9).[4]

DEFENCE BY THE STATE

Guns began to exert a significant influence on defence, particularly coastal defence, by the middle of the 15th century. The first fort designed specifically for their use was Rufus Castle, commanding one of the few landing-places on the Isle of Portland. Threats of invasion grew much greater after Henry VIII's break with the Roman church, and after 1540, using the proceeds from the sale of dissolved monasteries, he began to build a chain of fortresses around the coast, including Portland and Sandsfoot guarding Portland Harbour. These were squat in profile, segmental or circular in plan, thick-walled with angled parapets to deflect shot, equipped with cannon, containing rooms for the governor and barracks for the soldiers; these were types of fortifications whose modernity and novelty marks the further emergence of modern systems of government, and a new role for the State. These were public not private fortifications. During a further French invasion scare four centuries later in the mid-19th century, Lord Palmerston urged the construction of new coastal fortifications. This new generation of fortresses included massive sprawling complexes such as the Verne Citadel on the Isle of Portland and Nothe Fort at Weymouth, designed in 1857 to defend the Portland anchorage. Smaller forts were begun in the Bristol Channel in the 1860s on Brean Down, Steep Holm and Flat Holm.[5]

HOLY GROUND: THE POWER OF THE CHURCH

The earliest centre of Anglo-Saxon episcopal power in the region was Sherborne. In 705 King Ine of Wessex appointed his kinsman Aldhelm to be bishop of all territories west of Selwood that had come under West Saxon control during the previous 40 years. The selection of Sherborne, formerly the site of a Celtic monastery, probably reflects the zeal of Ine and Aldhelm to replace Celtic Christianity with Roman customs, since they had already reformed the monasteries of Malmesbury and Glastonbury. Sherborne, like the older West Saxon diocese of Winchester, was subdivided in 909, Sherborne's own diocese being reduced to the county of Dorset, while two older minsters, Wells and Ramsbury, were promoted to serve Somerset and Wiltshire respectively. The northern part of our region lay within the medieval diocese of Worcester, Gloucester not becoming a see until after the Reformation (Fig. 5.10).

During the course of the 8th century dozens of minster churches were established on royal and episcopal estates, serving as bases for teams of priests undertaking pastoral work in the surrounding countryside. King Ine was a major patron of the church in Wessex, supporting Bishop Aldhelm in his foundation of minsters at Bradford-on-Avon, Wareham and Frome. His contemporary in Mercia, King Aethelred (674–704) was equally influential, supporting the first churches at Pershore and Evesham. At Wells and Ilchester the choice of sites for new minsters may well have been influenced by traditions attached to local Romano-British cemeteries.

During the 9th century the church sank to a low ebb. A faltering recovery began with King Alfred's foundation of the monastery of Athelney and the nunnery of Shaftesbury, but the revival gained much stronger momentum under the direction of Dunstan, Abbot of Glastonbury (later Archbishop of Canterbury), and his patron King Edgar (959–75). Through Dunstan's influence

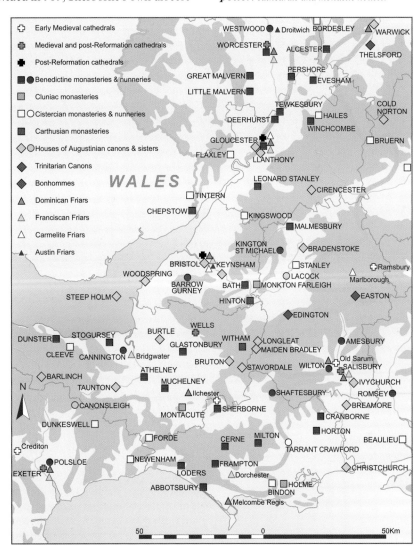

Fig. 5.10 Centres of ecclesiastical power: cathedrals and monastic houses.

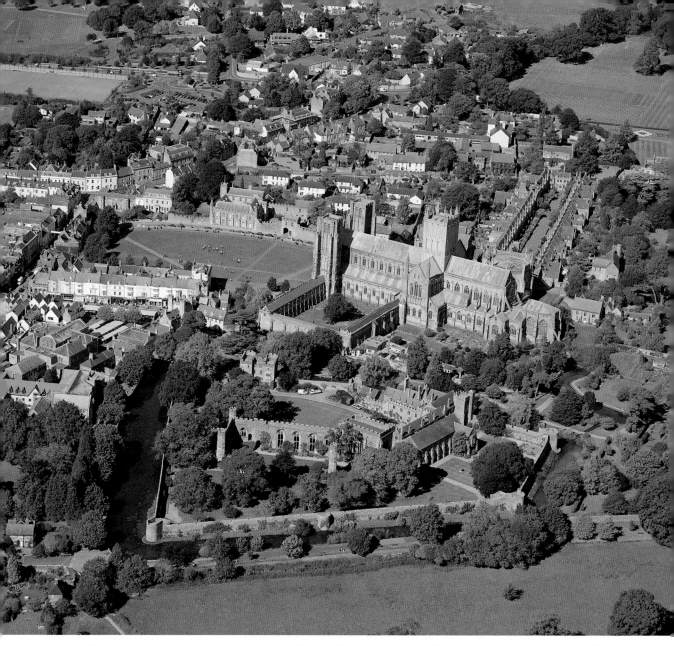

Fig. 5.11 The Bishop's Palace at Wells
lies immediately south of the cathedral. An unfortified palace was begun here by Bishop Jocelyn in about 1230, and extended in the 1280s by Bishop Burnell, who added a large new hall, now ruined. The surrounding curtain wall and moat were constructed under a crenellation licence obtained by Bishop Ralph Shrewsbury in 1341.

new Benedictine abbeys practising a stricter, more contemplative form of monastic life were founded at Malmesbury, Bath, Milton, Muchelney, Cerne and Sherborne. Dunstan's friend and colleague Oswald, Bishop of Worcester, undertook a similar programme in Mercia, reforming the minsters of Winchcombe, Evesham and Pershore and founding a new monastery at Westbury-on-Trym.

The appointment of Lanfranc as Archbishop of Canterbury after the Norman Conquest had two important consequences for the church in the West. One was the relocation of sees from small towns to more important centres, so the bishop of Sherborne moved to Old Sarum and the bishop of Wells to Bath. The second was a comprehensive rebuilding of monastic churches in the continental Romanesque style, exemplified by Gloucester, Tewkesbury and Malmesbury. Of the major Benedictine abbeys in our region only Sherborne retains significant vestiges of upstanding pre-Conquest masonry. A little more survives in the churches of unreformed minsters at Wimborne and Milborne Port and in the scanty ruins of St Oswald's Priory in Gloucester. The only local monastery to retain its Anglo-Saxon church substantially intact was the once-important 7th-century minster of

Deerhurst, reduced to a poor dependency of the abbey of St Denis outside Paris. The Anglo-Saxon cathedral at Wells also initially escaped demolition because of the transfer of its bishop to Bath. However, Wells began to recover its dignity as co-cathedral of the diocese under the third Norman bishop, Robert of Lewes, and in 1180 Bishop Reginald de Bohun began building a splendid new cathedral in Early English Gothic style immediately to the north of the Saxon building, which was then pulled down.

The wealth and power of medieval bishops were reflected in their domestic quarters. Bishop Jocelin (1206–42) began the existing palace at Wells (Fig. 5.11). A much larger hall and chapel were added by Bishop Robert Burnell (1275–92), and then in 1340 friction with the townspeople prompted Bishop Ralph Shrewsbury to acquire a crenellation licence which empowered him to enclose the entire palace within a battlemented curtain wall with bastions and a moat. With further additions by later bishops the whole ensemble survives to perfection, apart from Bishop Burnell's hall, roofless since the 1550s, and further knocked about by Bishop Law to create a romantic ruin in the early 19th century. Of Bishop Jocelin's other palaces, fragments survive at Wookey, which was also once surrounded by a moat, while part of his chapel survives on the site of the palace at Cheddar, which he had acquired from King John. Later medieval bishops built further palaces at Blackford, Evercreech and Banwell.

Benedictine estates dominated the monastic landscape of the West. According to the Domesday Book Glastonbury was the richest abbey in England, with a gross annual income of well over £800. It owned vast swathes of land in and around the Somerset Levels, with further manors scattered over Wiltshire and Blackmoor Vale. Even in ruin the scale of its church gives some hint of its former magnificence. The ancient monasteries of Malmesbury, Cerne and Evesham and the nunnery of Shaftesbury all enjoyed a gross annual income of over £100 in 1086, having acquired extensive estates through their foundation endowments and subsequent acquisitions. During the 12th and 13th centuries many abbeys found it profitable to farm their own demesnes directly, and their investment in farm buildings, dovecotes, vineyards, fisheries, mills, woodland clearance and marshland reclamation had a huge impact upon the medieval landscape.

Nowhere is the economic power of the Benedictine abbeys better expressed than in the huge barns of Abbotsbury (Fig. 5.12), Sydling St Nicholas, Tisbury, Frocester, Bradford-on-Avon, Hartpury and Middle Littleton. After the 14th century more and more land was leased out for cash rents, but individual

Fig. 5.12 The great barn of Abbotsbury Abbey, Dorset, though half in ruin, is the longest surviving monastic barn in England at 83m.

properties such as Glastonbury's houses at Meare, Sharpham and Norwood were developed as sumptuous abbatial palaces. By 1535 Glastonbury's income was said to be over £3,600 a year, while Gloucester and Tewkesbury (Figs 5.13 and 5.14) had overtaken the more southerly houses in the league table of prosperity.[10]

No other religious orders established a toehold in the region before the late 11th century, when the Cluniac priory of Montacute was founded. In 1117 Henry I began building a new house for Augustinian canons in Cirencester, which became the richest abbey of its order in England. The Victorine abbeys of Bristol and Keynsham and the Augustinian priory of Llanthony on the outskirts of Gloucester were also relatively wealthy, but no other houses

Fig. 5.13 Tewkesbury Abbey, Gloucestershire. Founded in 1092, the Norman abbey church survives, with alterations made in the 14th century. The domestic buildings and cloister of the abbey, destroyed after the Dissolution, formerly stood to the south.

Fig. 5.14 St Peter's Abbey, Gloucester, had pre-Conquest origins as a Benedictine monastery, and its church became a cathedral at the Reformation. The monastic cloisters and the arcade of the ruined infirmary are visible on the north side of the church.

Fig. 5.15 Cleeve Abbey, a Cistercian monastery founded in a remote part of west Somerset in the late 12th century. *The outline of the church is visible, but only part of the south wall of its nave remains standing. The refectory on the south side of the cloister was rebuilt on an east–west alignment in the early 16th century, but the footings and pavement of its predecessor can still be seen.*

of canons achieved more than local importance. Cistercian monks were first settled in characteristically underdeveloped country in Kingswood in 1139, but none of the five Cistercian abbeys in the region were of top rank (Figs 5.15 and 5.16). The first Carthusian house in England was founded at Witham in Selwood Forest in 1178, while a second Carthusian community, initally established on the Cotswolds at Hatherop, found the site and endowment inadequate, and moved to Hinton in 1227–32. The Black Death virtually ended the sequence of religious foundations.[6]

THE RISE OF THE NOUVEAU RICHE: TUDOR AND EARLY STUART COUNTRY HOUSES

Fig. 5.16 Hailes Abbey, Gloucestershire, founded in 1246, was one of the last Cistercian abbeys to be established in England. It owed much of its later prosperity to its possession of a relic of the Holy Blood, which attracted many pilgrims. The outline of the cloister and refectory is visible, but the only upstanding fragment of the monastic church is part of its south wall. Earthworks of the monastic fishponds are visible in the foreground.

Land had been the basis of wealth and power throughout the medieval centuries. The 1540s witnessed the biggest upheaval in landholding since the Norman Conquest, as ambitious royal servants scrambled for the lands and buildings of the recently dissolved monasteries: men like Sir John Thynne, once a clerk to the royal kitchen, who bought Longleat Priory; Sir William Sharington, vice-treasurer of the Bristol mint, who acquired Lacock Abbey; and Dr John Tregonwell, one of the inspectors of monasteries in 1535–6, who bought Milton Abbey.[7]

The symbolism of power associated with the medieval castle was never entirely forgotten. Sir Nicholas Poyntz, another ambitious man with court connections, had inherited the moated house of Acton Court and rebuilt it on a grand scale between 1535 and 1555. Although the surviving wing incorporates large windows with mullions and transoms, a Tudor gatehouse built out over the moat has been excavated, and the walled forecourt was battlemented. Imitation castles continued to be built as dwellings, or as parkland follies. Lulworth Castle was begun in 1605 by Thomas, 3rd Lord Howard of Bindon, who at the same time acquired a licence to enclose 1,000 acres (400ha) of the surrounding land as a deer park. Later examples include Enmore (1751–5), Midford (c. 1775) and Compton

Fig. 5.17 Two great houses have disappeared at Low Ham, Somerset: a late Elizabethan mansion pulled down in about 1690, and its uncompleted successor, in ruins by 1823 and entirely gone by 1838. Terraces and other earthworks from the abandoned gardens of the second house are visible on the hill above the 17th-century chapel.

Pauncefoot (1821), all in Somerset. At Banwell a mock castle was built in the 1840s for a London solicitor. Dunster Castle had suffered ruin in the Civil War, and has been patched up since, but it owes most of its present fairy-tale appearance to the reconstruction carried out in the 1860s by Anthony Salvin.

Other men preferred to display and enjoy their wealth in houses with no pretence of defensibility, where the architectural innovations of the Renaissance could be absorbed and the surroundings beautified with formal gardens. In 1517 William Knight, Henry VIII's chaplain, acquired Horton Court in the south Cotswolds. Knight had visited Rome in the king's service, and introduced at Horton some of the earliest Italian Renaissance architectural details ever seen in England: his garden contained an Italian-style loggia decorated with stone medallions bearing somewhat rustic portraits of Roman emperors.

Montacute House, the finest Elizabethan mansion in the region, was built in the 1590s for Sir Edward Phelips, a wealthy lawyer. It typifies the Elizabethan style, tall, symmetrical, E-shaped in plan, with huge windows and Renaissance detail, all in Ham Hill stone. Numerous smaller Elizabethan and Jacobean gentry houses survive, including Little Sodbury, Cold Ashton and Bibury Court in Gloucestershire, St Catherine's Court, Lytes Cary and Cothelstone Manor in Somerset, and Anderson Manor and Wynford Eagle in Dorset. Others have gone, leaving walls and terraces of their abandoned gardens at Kelston and Claverton near Bath and at Chipping Campden. Terraced earthworks in a field at Low Ham (Fig. 5.17) derive from a more extensive series of lost gardens, begun in the 1580s, remodelled around 1690 to accompany a new mansion, then abandoned unfinished on the death of its owner.[8]

THE POWER OF LINEAGE: COUNTRY HOUSES AND PARKS FROM RESTORATION TO REGENCY

Conspicuous display, inadvisable during the Commonwealth, was resumed immediately after the Restoration in great houses such as Kingston Lacy and Badminton. By the early 1700s country houses such as Kings Weston, Barnsley Park, Barrington Park and Frampton Court were moving towards the baroque style. Correspondingly, gardens were becoming even more elaborate, with multiple terraces, parterres and canals, while the formal axes of gardens were often extended out across the surrounding parks by avenues. At Longleat between 1683 and 1700 Sir Thomas Thynne spent £30,000 on creating 28ha of new formal gardens. At the same time Henry Somerset, 1st Duke of Beaufort, was planting lengthy intersecting avenues in his park at Badminton. A generation later

Stephen Switzer was transforming the Cirencester Park estate for Lord Bathurst. Most of the great formal gardens of this period have long since been swept away, but bird's-eye prospects made by the Dutch artist Johannes Kip graphically convey the intricacy of their layout.

The reign of William of Orange saw a brief vogue for Dutch-style formal gardens incorporating asymmetrically set canals. Dyrham (Fig. 5.18), positioned at the foot of a steep combe in the Cotswold scarp, was not, perhaps, the natural setting for such a garden. Sir William Blathwayt, who had married the Dyrham heiress, was, however, secretary to the English ambassador to the Netherlands, and later became Secretary of State to King William. He replaced the old-fashioned Tudor house between 1692 and 1704, employing William Talman to design a baroque east front. Kip's illustration shows this face overlooking a grand parterre, with terraces and a formal wilderness on the hill to the north, and a stepped cascade falling to a canal on the south. Little of this layout survives today, except for a figure of King Neptune, forlornly marooned on top of the hill on the site of the head of the cascade. Enough survived of another Dutch water garden laid out at Westbury-on-Severn in 1696–1705 to permit the National Trust to begin restoration in 1967, and the result is a splendid re-creation of a style which would otherwise be seen only in the Kip illustration. Later echoes of elements at Dyrham and Westbury can be seen elsewhere in Gloucestershire, in the cascade below the pyramid at Stanway, and in the short canal terminating in the gothick orangery at Frampton Court.

Fig. 5.18 Dyrham Park, Gloucestershire: *the great formal gardens made for William Blathwayt on either side of the house between 1691 and 1704 have all been swept away, but remnants of Blathwayt's avenues in the park survived until their destruction by Dutch elm disease in the 1970s. Their alignments have been re-established by recent plantings of lime.*

The great formal gardens had represented not just wealth, but also control: the power to make natural elements such as plants and water conform to the predetermined geometry of parterres, topiary, avenues, canals and fountains. In many respects this reflected the authoritarian style of the Stuart regime. A reaction followed, as English gentlemen returned from their grand tours with a new enthusiasm for classical architecture and the works of nature. Our region has some supreme examples of the early style of informal landscape gardening, in which a pure Palladian mansion is linked with a contrived perambulation around a succession of arcadian scenes involving sinuous lakes, serpentine paths, grottoes, statues, classical temples and sham ruins. William Kent, the pioneer of this style, undertook few commissions in the West, other than the magnificent Worcester Lodge on the edge of Badminton Park. Elsewhere, however, his imitators produced masterpieces of their own, Ralph Allen at Prior Park near Bath, Sir Charles Kemeys-Tynte at Halswell, Copleston Warre Bampfylde at Hestercombe (recently splendidly restored) and, above all, Henry Hoare at Stourhead. Gardens with a more frivolous rococo touch were appearing by the 1740s at Goldney and Painswick.

In the late 18th century this somewhat fussy fashion gave way to a blander, more serene, more distinctively English style, in which the dominant designer was Lancelot 'Capability' Brown. Brown accepted commissions for at least a dozen places in the West, including Dodington, Bowood, Longleat, Sherborne Castle and Milton Abbey, though none rivalled his great masterpiece at Blenheim. Brown's fondness for smooth grassy slopes, natural-looking lakes, rounded clumps and perimeter screens of trees was easily imitated, and many more parks were landscaped by local landowners working with their stewards.

One of the most comprehensive displays of the power of a great landowner can be seen at Milton Abbey (Fig. 5.19). In 1752 this was purchased by Joseph Damer, subsequently created Baron Milton and Earl of Dorchester.

Fig. 5.19 Milton Abbey, Dorset: the abbey church was rebuilt on a grand scale after a fire in 1309, but the projected nave was never begun. To the north most of the domestic buildings of the abbey were demolished to make way for the great mansion built for Joseph Damer, Lord Milton, in the 1770s.

Having closed three roads which passed near his house, he then employed Capability Brown to grade the slopes to north and east in preparation for a large lake and to begin tree-planting on the opposite side of the valley. Apart from the lake, this first stage in the landscaping was largely completed by 1770. Next, Lord Milton turned his attention to the house. He decided to pull down most of the remaining monastic buildings, and engaged William Chambers to design a grand new mansion. Unfortunately employer and architect had divergent opinions on style, Chambers disappeared from the payroll, and the house was completed by James Wyatt.

The resumption of landscaping in 1774 required the removal of the old market town to the south of the abbey in order to complete the lake. Some of the inhabitants were reluctant to move, but Lord Milton resolved this problem by releasing the water that had already been dammed up, sweeping the offending houses out of his way. Despite considerable expenditure, however, the lake was never completed to the scale originally intended. Before his departure Chambers had submitted plans for the rehousing of the occupants of the old town, but the design eventually used was probably conceived by Brown. The new village of Milton Abbas (Fig 5.20) was concealed in a wooded combe so as to be invisible from the great house. It consisted of two rows of evenly spaced houses, uniformly built in cheap traditional materials (limewashed cob and thatch), originally interplanted with chestnut trees, and set back from a gently winding road behind broad green verges.

Country estates had not been the exclusive preserve of the old landed aristocracy for a couple of centuries. Lawyers had been among the first of the nouveau riche owners, such as Sir Edward Phelips at Montacute or Sir Edward Prideaux, who bought Forde Abbey in 1649, followed by bankers such as Henry Hoare at Stourhead and men whose fortunes came from the clothing trade, such as Thomas Jolliffe at Ammerdown.

Another interesting group were men who had made their fortunes in the East India trade, such as Warren Hastings at Daylesford and John and Charles Cockerell at Sezincote, whose house was designed in Moghul style, with an onion-shaped dome, peacock-tail arches and miniature minarets. Their ranks were now joined by successful industrialists and importers. The Dents, who reconstructed Sudeley Castle after 1837, were Worcester glovers. Henry Crawshay, who built

OPPOSITE PAGE:

Fig. 5.20 The estate village of Milton Abbas, built in the 1780s to rehouse inhabitants of the old town removed to make way for Lord Milton's landscaped park, and hidden in a wooded combe to make it invisible from the mansion.

Oaklands Park at Awre in the 1850s, was an ironmaster with interests in the Forest of Dean and South Wales. Tyntesfield was developed in the 1860s on the proceeds of guano imports from South America. After the 1860s the number of new country houses built by new money began to outstrip those built through landed inheritance. Unconfined by inhibitions about 'good taste', the new parks and mansions of the 19th century employed an eclectic mix of formal and informal, classical, Renaissance, baroque, Gothic, rustic and exotic styles.

Clouds were gathering over the gracious style of country-house living before the end of the 19th century, and the era came to a brutal end in the butchery of the First World War. Before it did so there was one last great flourishing of garden design, in which architectural frameworks finally merged with plantsmanship, exemplified by the work of Inigo Thomas at Athelhampton and Barrow Gurney Court, Harold Peto at Iford and Wayford, Edwin Lutyens at Ammerdown and Gertrude Jekyll at Hestercombe.[9]

THE RESPONSIBILITY OF POWER: PATERNALISM IN THE LANDSCAPE

The motives of Lord Milton in building the new village of Milton Abbas had more to do with his own aesthetic ideals than any concern for the well-being of his tenants. Others were more genuinely altruistic, finding a way to combine a picturesque appearance with improved housing standards. In 1789 the Blaise Castle estate was purchased by John Scandrett Harford, a Quaker banker. Having improved its agricultural productivity, rebuilt the house and landscaped the grounds, Harford then purchased 2.4ha of land nearby, employing John Nash, working with George Repton, to provide nine cottages for retired estate employees, informally grouped around an irregular green. Despite their variety of orientation, plan, elevation and building material, the composition is a harmonious one; and, despite their small size, they represented some improvement on the standards of most contemporary housing.

The picturesque style was also adopted by Sir Thomas Dyke Acland in about 1828, when he created a similar hamlet for pensioners on the Holnicote estate around Selworthy Green, on the steep slopes overlooking the Vale of Porlock. Acland knew Harford personally and had stayed at Blaise Castle. The half-dozen Selworthy cottages resemble each other more closely than those of Blaise Hamlet, through the common use of vernacular materials and design details – thatched roofs, walls rendered with cream limewash, tall rectangular chimney stacks and windows with diamond-leaded panes. However, they were not all newly built; two were of medieval origin while another dated from the 17th century. Rather than make an entirely fresh start, Acland did what he could to upgrade and adapt existing cottages. Little Bredy in Dorset provides another example of an estate village in the Blaise Hamlet tradition composed around an irregular green.

Estate cottages in self-consciously picturesque style are to be found in many other villages. Thomas Wright designed a small group of cottages at Badminton with Gothic windows and overhanging thatched roofs. Sandy Lane, on the Bowood estate, was remodelled with thatched stone cottages in the early 19th century. At Erlestoke, below the northern face of Salisbury Plain, Joshua Smith built a series of thatched Gothic cottages around 1800 with mock timbering pillaged from older buildings. When Cobbett rode through Erlestoke in 1826, he was struck by the houses, 'at a few yards from each other, on the two sides of the road; every house is white; and the front of every one is covered with some sort or other of *clematis*, or with *rose-trees*, or *jasmines*.'

Investment by landed proprietors in rural housing was rarely devoid of some element of self-interest, but during the first half of the 19th century aesthetic considerations were overtaken by more practical concerns, as landowners began to recognise that men who were decently housed might work more efficiently than those enduring the misery of cold and dripping hovels. Later estate cottages were more solidly built and roomier, with decoration applied almost as an afterthought. Bargeboards, finials and Gothic porches decorate the Cotswold stone cottages in Westonbirt and Beverston, designed by Lewis Vulliamy between 1842 and 1858.

In 1830 Joseph Neeld, who had inherited nearly a million pounds from his silversmith great-uncle, purchased a 5,250ha country estate near Chippenham that included the villages of Alderton, Grittleton and Leigh Delamere and the hamlet of Sevington. Between 1835 and 1856 these settlements were transformed by the reconstruction of older houses and the addition of new gabled semi-detached cottages in Tudor style. Around 1842 Neeld embarked upon the building of a monstrous Jacobean-style mansion at Grittleton, quarrelling with the original architect and engaging James Thompson to complete the job. Thompson also designed the vicarage and almshouses at Leigh Delamere and the school and lodge at Sevington, and rebuilt the churches of Alderton and Leigh Delamere.

The 19th century saw the apogee of the great estates. Along the borders of Wiltshire and Somerset a parliamentary enquiry of 1872 noted that the Marquess of Bath's Longleat estate comprised some 11,300ha, while Sir Henry Hoare at Stourhead and the Duke of Somerset at Maiden Bradley both owned about 4,850ha; but the power of the landowners was soon to be broken by the agricultural depression of the late 19th century.[10]

ELECTORAL POWER: SHIRE HALLS AND ROTTEN BOROUGHS

Today, power comes from the ballot box, being vested in a hierarchy of democratically elected organisations, from national government down to parish council. By the late 18th century the role of the counties or shires at the highest level of local government was beginning to demand purpose-built quarters in county towns. Dorchester's Shire Hall was built in 1795–7 to the design of Thomas Hardwick, with a seven-bay, two-storey façade of Portland ashlar, with a rusticated arcade and a pediment over the central three bays. Of the original building of Gloucester's shire hall, designed by Sir Robert Smirke in 1816, only the giant Ionic portico and the polygonal assize courts survive. Somerset's first purpose-built shire hall in Taunton was an irregular complex of buildings in early Tudor style designed by W B Moffatt and built in 1855–8.

The Local Government Act of 1888 extended and standardised the responsibilities of county councils in the areas of education, public health, law enforcement and highway maintenance. To accommodate the growing bureaucracies required to administer these functions, old county buildings were extended and new ones built. A new council chamber at Gloucester was begun in 1894, Taunton's neo-Georgian county hall was built in 1936, while lack of space near the old shire hall in Dorchester resulted in a new hall being erected in Colliton Park in 1938. In each case subsequent needs for office space have led to further expansion.

Voting rights in the shires had been restricted in 1430 to freeholders whose income from property exceeded 40 shillings a year, a limitation that remained in force until 1832. Representation of the shires, therefore, lay largely in the hands of the great landed families. The franchise in the boroughs was more varied. In some, most households had suffrage; in others voting rights were limited to the holders of certain tenements, to freemen or to members of the corporation. At Wootton Bassett in about 1830 there were just 20 voters in a town of 1,700 people. Particular abuses arose out of the anachronistic retention of parliamentary seats by once-important boroughs whose electorate had dwindled to the point where they could be coerced by the leading landowners to elect their nominees. William Cobbett did not restrain his disgust at 'the vile rotten borough of Calne ... I could not come through that villainous hole without cursing Corruption at every step'; or at Westbury, 'this miserable hole ... a nasty odious *rotten-borough*, a really *rotten* place'. On the eve of the 1832 Reform Act the small Somerset borough of Milborne Port had 80 voters out of a population of 1,440. After a contested election in 1818 the two rival political factions both promoted new housing developments to increase votes from their own supporters: New Town, mockingly known as 'Blue Town', was built by the Earl of Darlington a short distance west of the old borough, while the Paget family built Waterloo Crescent on the extreme northern edge of the parish.

The Reform Act of 1832 extinguished the parliamentary seats of 56 rotten boroughs, including Corfe Castle, Minehead, Milborne Port, Ilchester, Hindon, Great Bedwyn and Wootton Bassett. While it widened the franchise, it did not abolish property qualifications, nor did it redress the huge imbalances in constituency populations. The first stage in the redistribution of parliamentary seats to reflect the population shift from the countryside to the industrial towns did not take place until 1867.

THE CONTINUITY OF SITES OF POWER

As the nature of power changed through time, so too did the manner of its expression and the type of sites through which it was exercised. Yet power could also generate its own momentum and its own traditions. The recurring importance of the Severn crossing at Gloucester, and the sequence at Dorchester from the Neolithic henge of Maumbury Rings through the Iron Age hillforts of Poundbury and Maiden Castle to the Roman *civitas* capital, Norman castle, medieval and modern county town, show how locations chosen in one period might be adapted and reutilised through a long historical time-span.

NOTES

1 Cunliffe 1991.
2 Branigan & Fowler (eds) 1976; McWhirr 1981; Leach 2001.
3 Hill 1984, 82–95, 126–32 and 143–4; Heighway 1987; Costen 1992, 111–13 and 162–5.
4 Platt 1982; Kenyon 1990; McNeill 1992; Dunning 1995.
5 Saunders 1997, 46–50 and 53–5.
6 Aston 2000; Dunning 2001; Bond 2004.
7 Bettey 1989.
8 Kingsley 1989, 45–7 and 109–11;

Dunning 1991, 43–53, 83–9 and 96–104; Bettey 1993, 45–57; Bond 1998, 50–2 and 67–9; Mowl 2002, 24–6.
9 Stroud 1975, 85–6, 90–2, 118–20, 134 and 239; Darley 1975, 35–8; Kingsley 1992, 54–61, 62–7, 68–70, 100–3, 128–33, 144–8 and 167–70; Bond 1998, 81–94, 104–31, 133–43; Kingsley & Hill 2001, 3–17, 198–9, 231–6; Mowl 2002, 48–56, 67–74, 83–8, 105 and 117–22.
10 Darley 1975, 63–70 and 105.

6

Dynamics and Demography

JAMES BOND

POPULATION AND FOOD SUPPLY

It is not easy to guess the size of populations before the start of censuses in the 19th century. Some estimates for earlier periods can be derived from parish records and medieval tax returns, but it is not always clear exactly what they count. Before the late 11th century we are dependent upon archaeologically based estimates, with even more difficult issues of interpretation.

Population size obviously depends on the availability of food, but at the same time the amount of food that can be produced also depends on the number of people available to gather or grow it and the methods available to them. The greater stability and control over food resources that came with the domestication and improvement of livestock and cultivation of crops also required greater inputs from people. Expansion of the area of land under cultivation was labour-intensive but in return may have supported larger populations. Assumptions based on archaeological evidence suggest that the population began to rise significantly in the later Bronze Age (around 1000 BC). A peak of 4 or 5 million people in Britain may have been reached in the Roman period.

The collapse of the Roman administration during the early 5th century AD was accompanied by social disruption, warfare, pestilence and the ruin of commercial farming, all contributing to a corresponding demographic collapse that may have reduced Britain's population to 3 million or less. Settlements and fields were abandoned, especially in our region along the Bristol Channel coast, where renewed flooding followed the decay of the Roman sea walls and many occupation sites became sealed beneath deposits of alluvium.

Recovery began around the 8th century, and more rapid growth was maintained to a new peak of perhaps 6 million by the year 1300. During this period of expansion our first statistical glimpse of contemporary society comes in the Domesday survey of 1086, a tenurial and tax record that counts various categories of landholders and other heads of households within each vill. Of the three counties which occupy most of our region, Somerset had a recorded Domesday population of nearly 13,000, followed by Gloucestershire with over 8,000 and Dorset with nearly 7,400. The heaviest densities of rural population appear across parts of south and east Somerset. We know that these figures did not include everyone in a household, however, and they must accordingly be multiplied by a factor of perhaps five to accommodate this. Accepting a wide margin of error, an overall total for the three counties of at least 140,000 people seems likely. For the whole of England, figures between 1.5 and 2.25 million people have been suggested, still much below the assumed figure for the Roman period and also well below the 6 million estimated for 1300.[1]

SETTLEMENT AND CULTIVATION: FRONTIERS IN THE EARLY MEDIEVAL PERIOD

With this rise in population went an increase in farmed land. The precise chronology of settlement expansion is difficult to document, but place-names offer some pointers. The spread of secondary settlements is indicated by the numerous Nortons, Suttons, Eastons, Westons, and above all, Newtons. Domesday Book names some 611 places in Somerset, 363 in Gloucestershire and 319 in Dorset. When the distribution of recorded names is examined, certain areas appear still to be sparsely populated, particularly the uplands of west Somerset and Mendip, the Somerset Levels, the Forest of Braydon north-west of Swindon and the Dorset heathlands around Poole Harbour. However, the Domesday record is a selective one. Some single farms are noted, such as Maidenbrook Farm in Taunton or Trowle Farm near Bradford-on-Avon, while larger settlements such as Halstock in Dorset, known to have existed from earlier charters, go unmentioned. The fact that settlements such as Ryme Intrinseca, Priddy and Nempnett Thrubwell appear for the first time in documents of the 12th century is more a reflection of developments in record-keeping than of actual settlement expansion. Occasional Domesday records of single farms in inhospitable locations, such as Hethfelton on the sandy heathland west of Wareham or Hurst Farm on the marshland edge of the Vale of Berkeley, show that settlement was not confined to the best farmland.

The effects of population growth during the early medieval period are seen more clearly in the expansion of farmland into woodland, heathland, upland and marshland (Fig. 6.1). The Old English word *leah*, commonly used in place-names first recorded between the 8th and 11th centuries, has several meanings; but concentrations of such names, for example in the Vale of Berkeley and along the Cotswold edge (Stanley, Coaley, Mobley, Nibley, Dursley, Alderley, Hillsley), usually indicate woodland clearances. The name of Road or Rode, a village between Frome and Trowbridge, has nothing to do with transport, but derives

Fig. 6.1 The Forest of Neroche, south Somerset: view northwards from Castle Neroche. Tree-lined hedgerows in the middle distance result from piecemeal clearance at various times between the medieval period and 17th century. The woods in the foreground are a product of later planting and woodland encroachment over former grazing commons.

from another Old English word meaning 'clearing'. For the most part these are not clearances of virgin forest, but of secondary woodland that had colonised abandoned Romano-British fields. The name of Frith Farm in Stalbridge, first recorded in 1244, implies scrub or overgrown land on the edge of a larger wooded area. The same element occurs in the names of Grafton Flyford and Flyford Flavell on the southern edge of Feckenham Forest in the Worcestershire claylands. In Blackmoor Vale the older villages were surrounded by open fields, but cultivation was pushing out into the wastes and woodland beyond, sometimes creating additional furlongs which were added to the communal fields and at other times producing irregular enclosed fields farmed from isolated homesteads. Variations on this pattern appear in the Severn Vale, in Taunton Deane and around Mendip. On the Dorset heathlands a number of scattered farmsteads are surrounded by irregular fields produced by piecemeal clearance. By the 13th century, when detailed records of new clearances of waste and woodland first appear in proceedings of Royal Forest courts, the process had been going on for several hundred years, and had already passed its peak.[2]

By the 13th century open fields had extended over much of the Dorset chalkland. Ridge and furrow was fitted into abandoned Romano-British fields on the high downs near Compton Valence and Alton Pancras, while strip lynchets at Plush near Piddletrenthide and elsewhere underline the pressure to bring even steep slopes into cultivation (Figs 6.2a and b). Open fields also occupied large areas of the Cotswold plateau, and lynchets are similarly to be found on the scarp at Hinton by Dyrham and near Wotton-under-Edge.[3]

Piecemeal reclamation of alluvial marshlands along the Severn Estuary and Bristol Channel shores had been resumed before the 11th century. Henbury Saltmarsh, at the southern end of the Vale of Berkeley, had largely been drained by the end of the 12th century, while the Berkeley family were still reclaiming substantial areas around Slimbridge in the 14th century. The most extensive areas of wetland were in the Somerset Levels, where the success

Figs 6.2a and b Strip lynchets near Wyke Champflower, east Somerset: *the terraces were created as medieval strip cultivation was extended on to the steeper slopes overlooking the upper Brue valley.*

of early reclamation is reflected by the fact that the abbot of Glastonbury's property of Brentmarsh rose in value from £15 to £50 between 1066 and 1086. During the 13th century the abbots of Glastonbury and Athelney and the bishops of Bath and Wells took a more direct hand in reclamation, initiating works on a larger scale, constructing new sea walls and inland embankments and diverting watercourses.[4]

TOWN GROWTH AND URBAN POPULATIONS IN THE EARLY MEDIEVAL PERIOD

As trade revived during the medieval period, the urban population began to expand. Our first glimpse of the potential size of particular towns comes in the early 10th century, with the assessment of forces required to defend King Alfred's strongholds. Wareham would have needed 1,600 armed men, Cricklade 1,500, Malmesbury 1,200, Bath 1,000. Smaller towns in the region would have required between 800 and 400 men. Obviously these figures reflect garrisons in times of emergency rather than normal conditions.[5]

The record of towns in the Domesday Book is, unfortunately, incomplete and unsatisfactory. From other sources we know that Bristol was trading with Ireland by the late 11th century but Domesday Book makes only passing mention of an unspecified number of burgesses on the royal manor of Barton, giving no hint of the town's character. Whereas the Domesday survey noted only 73 burgesses in Gloucester, another near-contemporary record from Evesham Abbey placed 528 burgesses there, perhaps implying a total population approaching 3,000. A similar discrepancy occurs in the recorded figures for Winchcombe: 29 burgesses in Domesday Book, 141 in the Evesham text. Some towns had suffered population loss, probably as a consequence of the uprising of 1068–9: in Wareham, Shaftesbury, Dorchester and Bridport, a total of 370 out of 879 houses lay empty or destroyed.[6]

Throughout the medieval centuries most towns remained relatively small. Their industrial economy generally rested upon cloth-making, with spinners, weavers and fullers present almost everywhere. Tanning and smithing were also important urban trades. Because the basis of medieval taxation was so variable, it is rarely possible for the records to give us any adequate idea of population. They do, however, offer some possibility of ranking towns in order of size or wealth. Bristol does not figure in the borough 'aids' paid to the crown in 1130 or 1156, but Gloucester then held eighth or ninth position among English provincial towns, with all others in the region well down the scale. By 1334 Bristol had rocketed to the top rank of towns, with a population perhaps approaching 10,000, about a fifth the size of London, while Gloucester had slumped to 16th place. Bristol's medieval prosperity was largely built on trade with Gascony, importing wine and salt and exporting wool and corn. The city's rapid expansion was reflected in its street plan, unusually complex defences and in its extensive suburbs beyond the city walls.[7]

FAMINE AND PLAGUE: THE EARLY 14th CENTURY

The early medieval growth of cities like Bristol, and the widespread promotion of new markets and new towns, could not have been achieved without increased productivity from the countryside. Land resources were not infinite, however, and the effort of further expansion into marginal land became unjustified by the returns. Demands for food began to exceed supply. At the same time, there is evidence of climatic deterioration by the late 13th century, leading to colder, wetter summers, harder winters, and early autumn and late spring frosts. Poor harvests and food shortages became increasingly common after 1272. Successive crop failures, such as occurred between 1315 and 1317, led to widespread famine and further disastrous harvests were recorded in 1332, 1345 and 1348.

In the summer of 1348 two ships from Gascony docked at the small Dorset port of Melcombe Regis. They brought a deadly cargo. Sailors on board had contracted a virulent form of bubonic plague spread by rat fleas. The first English victims of the Black Death died at Melcombe on 23 June, and the plague had reached Bristol by 1 August. Its impact upon a population already weakened by the years of famine was devastating. Overall, between a third and a half of the entire population lost their lives. However, the proportion of deaths varied greatly from place to place: at Bibury in the Cotswolds the bishop of Worcester had 29 tenants in 1299 but only 7 in the autumn of 1349, a reduction of 76 per cent, whereas at Henbury near Bristol the reduction over the same period was only 19 per cent.

The disease spread rapidly in the overcrowded quarters of the larger towns. Bristol was the first major English city to be affected. The parishioners of the Temple Church there were forced to acquire an additional half acre (0.2ha) of burial ground in November 1349 because their churchyard had been filled up by plague victims. Ten institutions of new priests are recorded within the year to the 18 city churches. Even the most prosperous inhabitants did not escape: a register of Bristol's town council in 1349 has lines drawn through the names of 15 of the 52 members, indicating their recent death.

In the Somerset village of North Petherton excavation has revealed what appeared to be an emergency plague pit and a substantial 14th-century extension to the cemetery, which remained in use for only a short time. Nearly half the clergy of the diocese of Bath and Wells died during the plague. On a buttress on the west front of Wells Cathedral is a poignant inscription in memory of John Pitney, chantry priest at Crewkerne, who died in December 1348; the inscription was never completed, probably because the carver himself also succumbed.

Manorial incomes plummeted. At Bere Regis and Charminster in Dorset it was said in July 1349 that 'the mortality of men in the present pestilence is so great that the lands thereof are untilled and the profits are lost'. In 1342 rents from one manor in Crowcombe (Somerset) came to nearly £9, but seven years later they were only 5s because 'the tenants were dead of the plague'. There were also concerns about national security. In September 1352 the king learned that the Isle of Portland had become 'so depopulated on account of the late mortality … that the men left there will not be sufficient to defend the same against attacks by his enemies', and he ordered all survivors to stay there to safeguard it, forbidding the removal of men, crops or victuals for any royal service.

Further plague outbreaks are recorded in 1361, 1369 and 1375. Infant mortality was especially severe. At the same time the birth rate itself declined, as more women found employment, married later and had smaller families.[8]

DESERTED VILLAGES

Observant travellers through the English countryside had been noticing evidence for lost villages since the 16th century. John Leland described Deerhurst in Gloucestershire as 'now but a poor village' where 'there remain yet divers names of streets, as Fisher Street and others; but the buildings of them be gone'. The 18th-century antiquarian Collinson identified a dozen depopulated places in Somerset, such as Hartrow in Stogumber, 'in ancient times a considerable village, the ruins of the dwellings being frequently discovered in the gardens and the fields'. Yet the true extent and significance of late-medieval rural depopulation in the West remained largely unappreciated until the 1970s.

One reason why investigations of deserted settlements in the West lagged behind research elsewhere was that hamlets and farms were more widely affected than full-scale villages. Nevertheless, clues to desertions are widespread, and even a conservative estimate would now place the number of deserted villages and hamlets in the region at well over 150. Churches were left isolated in the fields, such as Widford in the Windrush valley, or fell into ruin, like Stanton St Gabriel on the Dorset coast, while others, including Sezincote on the Cotswolds, Rowley near Bradford-on-Avon and Lazerton in the Iwerne valley, disappeared completely. Abandoned clayland villages like Upper, Middle and Lower Ditchford near Moreton-in-Marsh show today as low earthworks intersected by ditches and hollow ways (Fig. 6.3), while Cotswold sites

ABOVE: *Fig. 6.3 The deserted village of Holworth near Chaldon Herring in Dorset: the earthworks represent a row of house enclosures along the main street with long rectangular crofts to the rear.*

Fig. 6.4 Farmington, Gloucestershire: a shrunken village on the Cotswolds. Earthworks of abandoned houses are clearly visible in the fields beyond the occupied buildings.

like Upton or Hullasey, where the last generation of peasant buildings was in stone, reveal clear traces of building foundations. While some settlements disappeared from the map entirely, many others merely contracted: earthworks beyond the built-up areas of Farmington (Fig. 6.4), Hampnett and Tormarton, all on the Cotswolds, show that they were formerly of much greater extent.

Local myth often attributes village depopulation to the Black Death, and in a few cases this may be correct. In 1352 the curate of Earnshill in Somerset petitioned for his church to be combined with that of the neighbouring village of Curry Rivel, since no people remained because of the pestilence. However, few sites owed their desertion solely to this cause. Many villages subsequently recovered, like Blagdon below the Mendip hills, where a survey in 1353 noted 'divers tenements which fell into the lord's hands by the dearth of tenants during the plague'. Other settlements were clearly in decline some decades earlier, since abandoned and uncultivated holdings are often noted in early 14th-century rentals. Equally clearly, many villages and hamlets that are now deserted were still occupied into the 1420s or later. Perhaps the most important effects of the Black Death were to weaken seigneurial controls by pushing up the costs of labour while at the same time making more land available. The consequent withdrawal of monasteries like Gloucester and Glastonbury from demesne farming opened up new economic opportunities for enterprising peasants willing to abandon their holdings in order to seek a better living elsewhere.

The fact that so much land went down to pasture after the Black Death had more to do with the difficulties in maintaining an arable demesne than with any immediate growth in demand for meat, hides, wool or dairy produce. However, by the late 14th century, the revival of the home cloth industry was once more increasing the demand for wool. The mid-15th-century chronicler John Rous claimed that many villages and hamlets had been destroyed within his lifetime by greedy lords, eager to profit from sheep farming, who had evicted their tenants in order to enclose and convert their lands to pasture. Amongst the places he listed were several in the valley of the Warwickshire Avon, Cotswolds and Vale of Evesham. Similar events are recorded in other sources. At Didcot in the Vale of Gloucester 30 people left their homes in 1491 when 122ha of land were converted to pasture, leaving one single tenant farmer. The village of Little Marston in south-east Somerset had disappeared by 1503, when its two former open fields were grazed by sheep. On the whole, however, enclosure and conversion to pasture were consequences, rather than causes, of depopulation.[9]

TOWNS AFTER THE BLACK DEATH

Despite the severity of the plague in Bristol, its economic recovery was rapid. Though the burgesses were reduced in numbers, some of them were able to amass huge fortunes, such as Richard Cheddar, William Canynges and Richard Spicer, all of whom served several times as mayor. Cloth exports through the city increased sevenfold during the two decades after 1350. Many of the city churches were rebuilt during the late 14th century, with substantial contributions from wealthy merchants and shipowners. The Poll Tax of 1377, the only medieval tax directly based upon population, records 6,345 adults in Bristol; only York and London contained more people.

Elsewhere economic and demographic recovery was patchy, and some towns show evidence for prolonged stagnation. Borough rents in Wells continued to decline into the 16th century, and a new street laid out just before the Black Death contained only two occupied houses 130 years later. Leland says of Ilchester that it was in 'wonderful decay' and that there had been four parish churches standing 'within living memory'. Even the surviving church of St Mary Major was reduced in size when its side aisles were taken down in the 15th century.

POPULATION RECOVERY AND THE CLOTHING TRADE, 1480–1800

England's population did not regain the totals reached before the Black Death until about 1600, but economic recovery was under way by the last quarter of the 14th century. A key factor in this revival was the resurgence of the home cloth industry, based upon Cotswold, Mendip and downland wool. Gloucestershire, north Somerset and north-west Wiltshire developed a specialisation in broadcloth production which made them the most important industrial region of England in the late 15th and 16th centuries. Their new prosperity made possible a lavish rebuilding of parish churches. In Cotswold towns huge bequests by wool merchants such as William Bradbury at Chipping Campden, John Tame at Fairford and the Forteys of Northleach produced buildings of almost cathedral-like majesty. By contrast, the matchless proliferation of glorious perpendicular towers in Somerset's village churches was funded not by supremely wealthy individual benefactors, but by numerous prosperous parishioners. Housing growth is evident in villages like Castle Combe, where 50 new dwellings were built by clothiers between 1409 and 1454.[10]

Fig. 6.5 Lightpill Mill, Rodborough, in the Nailsworth valley near Stroud. A clothing mill has been documented on this site since 1651, but the existing buildings date from successive reconstructions and extensions in 1818, 1850–4, the 1870s and 1910. After the cessation of cloth-making here in 1907, the mill was for 50 years employed in the plastics industry.

In the Cotswolds during the 16th century the cloth industry gravitated towards the south, where streams cutting through the scarp and draining towards the Severn had sufficient gradient to power large numbers of fulling mills. Leland noted a thriving industry in Wickwar, Wotton-under-Edge and Dursley near the Cotswold scarp, whereas cloth-making was in decline in the vale towns of Berkeley and Thornbury. The greatest expansion of all took place in the valleys around Stroud. Stroud itself was a mere hamlet of Bisley through the medieval period, but it acquired markets and fairs in the 16th century, while Painswick, Chalford, Minchinhampton, Nailsworth and Avening shared its rapid growth (Fig. 6.5). Defoe described this area as 'famous not for the finest cloths only, but for dyeing those cloths of the finest scarlets … The clothiers lie all along the banks of this river for near 20 miles, and in the town of Stroud …'. A painting in Stroud Museum shows the valley side covered with scarlet and white cloths stretched out on racks to dry.[11]

In Wiltshire and north Somerset cloth manufacture developed more in the established towns, but its impact was no less significant. William Stumpe created one of the earliest factories at Malmesbury by installing weaving looms in vacated buildings of the abbey. Individual clothiers rose to great prosperity during the 17th and early 18th centuries, building grand houses in towns such as Bradford-on-Avon. Defoe was especially impressed by the prosperity of Frome, where a complete new artisan suburb with its own church had been laid out between 1665 and 1725 by a local clothing dynasty. Serge-making developed as a new speciality in Taunton and south

Somerset in the 17th century. Clothing continued to be an important component of the economy of the West into the 19th century.[12]

THE IMPROVEMENT OF AGRICULTURE 1500–1890

By the end of the medieval period the rural landscape of the West was a patchwork of rough upland grazing, woodland, marshland, meadowland, open-field strips, old enclosures and new pastures occupying the fields of abandoned settlements. Between the 16th and 19th centuries farmers increased their productivity to meet the demands of a rising population by adopting a wider range of crops, introducing improved strains of livestock, undertaking irrigation and further enclosure and improving farm buildings.

New crops were introduced for human consumption, for fodder to enable farms to carry greater numbers of stock and for industrial use. Sainfoin was one of several new fodder crops introduced from the Low Countries. A leguminous plant that returned nitrogen to the soil and permitted the reduction of fallows, sainfoin was first grown in about 1650 by John Hastings at Daylesford in the Evenlode valley and by Nicholas Hill at North Wraxall near Chippenham. It became widely grown over the Cotswolds. Sir Anthony Ashley began growing cabbages for fodder in the 1620s at Wimborne St Giles, and many other Dorset farmers followed his example over the next 50 years. Turnips became a common field crop in the Vale of Taunton Deane, in the sandy country around Crewkerne and Yeovil and in the Vale of Pewsey in the 18th century.

Tobacco, introduced from North America in the 1580s, was grown with considerable success for nearly a century around Winchcombe, Tewkesbury and Cheltenham, until protests by Virginia planters and shippers led to government action to eradicate it. Carrots were introduced as a field crop at Beckington near Frome in 1668. Potatoes were extensively grown after the 1790s, particularly in the lower valley of the Warwickshire Avon, on Mendip, on the sandier soils of Wiltshire and in west Dorset, until the onset of potato blight in 1845.

Industrial crops included woad, grown after the mid-16th century in coastal Dorset, around the margins of Cranborne Chase, around Keynsham and Cheddar, and in parts of the Warwickshire Avon valley. Teasels, used in cloth manufacturing for raising the nap, were grown in the Vale of Wrington and Chew valley on the north side of Mendip, and large quantities were shipped out from Bristol during the 18th century for the clothing mills of the north. Hemp and flax, widely grown in west Dorset and south Somerset, supplied the rope, net and sailcloth industries of Bridport, Crewkerne and Beaminster.

Another way of remedying the lack of fodder in April, when winter stores of hay had come to an end, was to advance the new growth of spring grass by means of irrigation. On Exmoor and on the Brendon and Quantock hills streams were diverted into contour leats, often several to one slope, to create 'catch meadows'. More sophisticated forms of floated water meadows were developed in the chalklands, making their first appearance in the Piddle valley in Dorset in the early 17th century. At intervals through the winter, sluices were opened to admit river water into parallel feeder leats along the tops of broad, low ridges. The water then spilled over the brim of each feeder, running in a thin film down the ridge sides into drains, which returned it to the river. Water from chalk springs was usually several degrees warmer than early spring air temperatures, and the chalk content of the water also acted as a fertiliser. Irrigation would be maintained until all danger of spring frosts had passed, and by the middle of March the grass would be up to 150mm high. The water was then drained off, the grass allowed to dry out, and sheep admitted for grazing through to April or May. The meadow would then be irrigated again to produce two or three hay crops. Floated water meadows made it possible to carry far more breeding stock and to bring forward lambing by a month or more. Meadows of this type were appearing elsewhere in Dorset and Wiltshire by the 1640s. Daniel Defoe estimated that 600,000 sheep were grazed within a 10km radius of Dorchester in the 1720s, the water meadows enabling the farmers to produce fat lambs early for the London market. Away from the chalk downs, floated water meadows are uncommon and usually later in date: some 60ha were laid out on the Sherborne estate on the Cotswolds during the Napoleonic War.

Many improved breeds of livestock adapted to local conditions were developed. The long-woolled Cotswold sheep, descended from the medieval flocks, was greatly improved in the 18th century by the use of Leicester rams to produce fat mutton. The hardy Old Wiltshire sheep foraged on the scanty herbage of the chalk downs by day, and were then driven down to be folded on the bare fallows, where a penned flock of 1,000 could manure 0.4ha of land in a night. The Gloucester Old Spot pig was developed in the Vale of Berkeley, sty-fed on whey from cheese-making for part of the year, then turned out into the orchards to feed on windfall apples. The Wessex Saddleback pig, suitable for both pork and bacon, evolved in the late 19th century, and was widely kept throughout the southern counties. Dairying was of increasing importance. Cheddar was noted for its cheeses by the 17th century, and Defoe describes the village herd grazing on the common, and the making of the cheese as a communal operation. Among the many local breeds of cattle to emerge at this time were the maroon-coloured Old Gloucesters, once widely kept across the Wiltshire claylands, the Vale of Gloucester and lowland Somerset, producing rich milk for Single and Double Gloucester cheeses. Eventually continuing imports and improvements reduced the commercial viability of the local breeds; many now survive only in small numbers, and some, such as the Sheeted Somerset cattle and Black Dorset pig, have become extinct.

Open-field farming was portrayed by most of the agricultural writers of the 18th and 19th centuries as backward and wasteful. Pitt, who travelled through the Vale of Evesham in 1805, saw in the unenclosed fields of Comberton 'fallows and corn stubbles foul with weeds … the common thistle shedding its seed, which flies all over the country ... land lost in mears or turf land marks, which are often incumbered with rubbish and bushes'. Thomas Rudge complained that much of the open tillage in the Vale of Gloucester was infested with weeds, while the crops were devoured by vast flocks of pigeons.

Yet, if open-field farming had really been so inefficient, it is difficult to see how so many parishes could have tolerated it for so long. In fact, considerable advances were made without the final step of enclosure. Restructuring the medieval two- and three-field arrangements into multiple-field systems accommodated more flexible rotations, including more leguminous crops. The old North and South Fields of Charlton Mackrell and Charlton Adam near Somerton, for example, were each subdivided into two during the 16th century, thereby reducing the annual fallow to one quarter of the arable land. Some parts of the Vale of Gloucester were cropped continuously for a century or more, while poorer land was rested each alternate year. Even Pitt admired the enterprise of open-field farmers at Eckington and Bredon in the valley of the Warwickshire Avon, where he noted the experimental breaking down of some of the old broad, high ridges for the cultivation of turnips and potatoes as well as beans, wheat and clover.

During the 16th and 17th centuries enclosure of open fields normally progressed by agreement between lords and tenants. Sometimes, as at Iwerne Courtney below Cranborne Chase in 1548, enclosure was comprehensive. More often only part of the parish area was involved. About half the land of Frocester had been enclosed by 1547, the remainder lying in two large and six small open fields. At Charminster near Dorchester a redistribution of land was organised in 1577 so that tenants who were unwilling to submit to enclosure were able to continue open-field farming into the early 19th century. At West Pennard near Glastonbury each farm was half-enclosed by 1604, but also retained strips in seven open fields. A map of Shepton Beauchamp in south-east Somerset in 1755 shows half the land still in unenclosed strips. Since the new closes were normally created out of bundles of consolidated strips, they tend to be long and narrow, with the longer side retaining the reversed-S curvature of the medieval furlongs. This distinctive field pattern is particularly widespread in Somerset. Some areas of sheepwalks on the Cotswolds and Dorset downs were also enclosed by agreement.[13]

Enclosure of open fields or commons by agreement depended upon the consent of all tenants. An alternative method was established in 1602, when the enclosure of the open fields of Radipole near Weymouth was ordered by an Act of Parliament. Under this procedure the lord of the manor applied for a private Act which authorised a committee of prominent local men to employ surveyors to reallocate the land. Inevitably this tended to benefit the larger farmers. These measures were not widely employed before 1750, but over the following century most of the remaining open fields and commons succumbed, and the characteristic chequerboard pattern of square and rectangular closes was superimposed over the countryside (Fig. 6.6). The areas enclosed by Parliamentary Act varied from parish to parish, depending upon the extent of earlier enclosure. At Piddletrenthide in Dorset a complete three-field system was enclosed in 1817, whereas in neighbouring Cheselbourne and Dewlish only 10 to 15 per cent of the land underwent Parliamentary enclosure. A few places in the Vale of Gloucester remained stubbornly resistant to change. At Upton St

Fig. 6.6 Parliamentary enclosure on the Mendip Hills, Somerset: the rectilinear fields around Hill Farm, between East Harptree and Priddy, were enclosed under an Act of 1794.

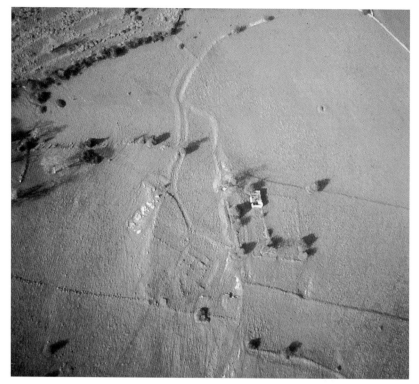

Leonards 1,120 strips covering 210ha still remained unenclosed in 1897. In Elmstone Hardwicke intermixed holdings in small parcels covered about 400ha until 1918, when an enclosure award was finally made.[14]

These improvements had resulted in food production almost keeping pace with the needs of the rising population up to about 1750, by which time Britain probably had a little below 8 million people. Three-quarters of the population continued to live and work in the countryside, but mining and manufacturing industries were beginning to offer enticing prospects of better-paid jobs for far larger numbers of working men, and during the following century this led to a fundamental change in the balance of employment. At the very time when the urban and industrial population was rising most sharply, the safety net of supplementing home production by food imports was threatened by the loss of the American colonies and the struggle against Revolutionary France. In 1793 the government set up a Board of Agriculture to investigate means of improving farm production. The county reports issued by the board provide a valuable record of contemporary farming methods.

The golden age of British farming lasted from 1840 to the 1870s. Among its most conspicuous monuments are a number of model farms designed on scientific principles, with steam engines, tramways, covered yards and a wide range of specialised buildings (Fig. 6.8). One of the earliest was the Whitfield Example Farm at Falfield, built on the Earl of Ducie's estate in 1839. Five model

Fig. 6.7 Rams Pits, an abandoned farm site on the Mendip plateau above Westbury-sub-Mendip, Somerset. A ruined building set within a square earthwork enclosure survives from a complex of new farm buildings erected about 50 years after Parliamentary enclosure in 1788. Immediately below and to the left are the earthworks of a deserted medieval farmstead, inhabited in the early 14th century but probably abandoned not long afterwards.

Fig. 6.8 Flaxdrayton Farm, South Petherton, Somerset: a mechanised estate farm of the 1860s. The chimney served the engine-house and boiler of a farm involved in grain, oil and flax production, fatstock rearing and cider production.

farms were built on the Westonbirt estate in the 1840s. Eastwood Manor Farm was the centrepiece of a holding of 360ha on the north side of Mendip. Built in 1858–60, this vast complex covered more than 0.4ha and included a great barn with both water- and steam-powered machinery, livestock housing, storage for produce and fodder and slurry-collection systems, with two large rectangular yards roofed over by iron and glass.[15]

Highly mechanised farming, notably Victorian steam cultivation, could have a devastating effect upon the landscape, foreshadowing the hedgerow destruction of recent times. At Pitchill north of Evesham, one of several local properties farmed by Benjamin Bomford, it was reported in 1869 that 'the fields ranged originally from six to twenty acres [2.4 to 8ha] in extent, … but now … nearly the whole of the internal fences have been taken up to admit of steam-tackle being more readily and conveniently employed. Eventually the few fences that remain will be taken out, and the farm will then be intersected by steam-roads a quarter of a mile apart, that being the length of the rope'. By this time only the farm's boundary hedge would remain.

TRANSPORT IMPROVEMENTS

The road network was already extensive by the 17th century, but maintenance was failing to keep pace with increasing traffic. Ridgeways, once thought to have been the backbone of the prehistoric road system, in fact may not have become particularly important as corridors of long-distance movement until drovers began taking large numbers of cattle and sheep from Wales and the west of England to the London market. This trade reached its peak between the 17th and 19th centuries. The journey would take several months, so overnight rests with grazing were needed every 16km or so. Other types of long-distance travel were becoming increasingly difficult. One innovation to aid travellers in the 17th century was the erection of guideposts by public-spirited benefactors. Surviving examples include Nathaniel Izod's tall finger post erected on Broadway Hill on the Cotswolds in 1669, designed to be read from horseback or carriage, or Edmund Attwood's inscribed stone pillar at Teddington in the Vale of Gloucester, set up in 1676.

By the late 17th century the inadequacies of the Elizabethan system of road repair by statute labour were becoming all too apparent. One alternative was to require travellers to finance road maintenance by paying tolls at turnpike gates. The first turnpike trust in Gloucestershire was established in 1698 to repair a short length of the Roman road running eastwards from Gloucester, with alternative climbs up the Cotswold scarp at Birdlip or Crickley Hill. Daniel Defoe reported with some satisfaction in the 1720s that 'the road from Birdlip Hill to Gloucester, formerly a terrible place for poor carriers and travellers … [is] now repaired very well'. By then permanent trusts, empowered to collect tolls by private Act of Parliament, were taking over several other roads in the Severn Vale, including the important route between Gloucester and Bristol, turnpiked in 1726–7. The imposition of tolls where there had previously been free passage was greatly resented, however, and on several occasions through the 1730s and 1740s rioters destroyed turnpike gates around Bristol, the miners of Kingswood being particularly implacable in their opposition. The first turnpike trust in Somerset was established in Bath in 1707–8. This trust was characteristic of many in the West, in that it acquired responsibility for a whole series of routes radiating out from one centre, rather than confining itself to one single road.

For the most part, the turnpike trusts contented themselves with improving old roads, though even that task sometimes involved substantial new works, such as at Tetbury, where the engineer Thomas Webb spanned the deep valley south of the town with a new stone viaduct in 1775, high above the older bridge.

Diversions were sometimes made to ease gradients, for example south-east of Frocester, where the turnpike road of 1783 diverges from the old packhorse road to climb more obliquely up the Cotswold scarp.

Some of the routes authorised by later Turnpike Acts included not just local improvements but long stretches of entirely new road. In 1780 a route was opened through the Nailsworth valley to provide travellers between Gloucester and Bath with an alternative to the notorious climb up Frocester Hill. By about 1825 access to Stroud had been transformed by new turnpike roads along each converging valley. Cheltenham's growing importance as a spa similarly resulted in it becoming a hub of new turnpike roads between 1792 and 1825. Three new bridges were built over the Severn by turnpike trusts in the 1820s. That at the Haw has since been replaced, but Thomas Telford's cast-iron span at the Mythe near Tewkesbury and his stone arch at Over Causeway by Gloucester remain. By the late 18th century the territories of particular turnpike trusts could be recognised by the distinctive designs of their milestones, and their toll cottages, which all incorporated some form of projecting front to give a clear view of traffic.

Slowly the new turnpikes cut journey times. In the early 18th century London passenger coaches took three days to reach Bristol. Mail coaches inaugurated in 1784 at first took 16 hours between Bristol and London, but by 1836 three hours had been lopped off the journey. The heyday of the turnpike roads was brief, however, brought to an abrupt end by the railway.[16]

Changes in the network of minor roads were mostly a product of Parliamentary enclosure. Long straight lengths of new road were employed particularly where commons were enclosed, for example over Clevedon Moor and Kenn Moor in north Somerset. Parliamentary awards specified their widths, which were usually sufficiently generous to permit some latitude of movement. When minor roads acquired a metalled surface for the first time, this characteristically left broad green verges on either side.

The River Severn had been a major artery of trade since the early medieval period, but other rivers were improved for navigation during the 17th and 18th centuries. Locks were installed on the Warwickshire Avon in the 1630s, and 90 years later Daniel Defoe could describe a great traffic in sugar, oil, wine, tobacco, iron and lead moving upriver from Bristol towards Warwick, returning with cargoes of corn and cheese. In 1638 John Malet was authorised to make the River Tone navigable from Bridgwater to Ham Mills, and by 1717 this navigation had reached Taunton.

The canals of the South West never rivalled those of the Midlands or North West in economic importance, but several ambitious undertakings were completed. The idea of breaking through the Cotswold watershed to link the Severn and Thames had been mooted as early as 1610, but lay dormant for many years. The first step on the road to success was the Stroudwater Canal, opened from Framilode on the Severn up to Stroud in the 1770s. The line was then extended eastwards by the Thames and Severn Canal, opened in 1789, which pierced the Cotswolds by a 3,490m-long tunnel at Sapperton and continued to a junction with the Thames at Inglesham near Lechlade.

As the canal engineers gained experience and confidence, two further schemes to connect the Thames and Severn by water were brought to fruition. The Kennet and Avon Canal, begun in 1794 and completed in 1810, ran from the Bristol Avon at Bath to the River Kennet at Newbury, and included some major engineering works, particularly the Dundas Aqueduct over the Avon and the flight of 29 wide locks at Caen Hill near Devizes. The Somerset Coal Canal was planned in 1794 to provide the collieries around Radstock and Paulton with an outlet to the Kennet and Avon Canal, though technical difficulties prevented the completion of either of its branches. A third connection, joining the Kennet and Avon at Semington to the Thames at Abingdon, was made by the Wilts & Berks

Canal, opened in 1810. Branch canals were built to Chippenham and Calne, while the North Wilts Canal was opened in 1819 to link the Wilts & Berks with the Thames and Severn Canal at Latton.

The biggest artificial waterway in the region was the Gloucester & Berkeley Canal. First authorised in 1793 to enable ships bound for Gloucester to bypass the dangerous currents and sandbanks of the lower Severn, the project collapsed in 1801, but the government revived it in 1817, advised by Thomas Telford, who recommended a shorter route. When opened in 1827, this was the largest canal in

Fig. 6.9 Gloucester Docks:
(left) the Mariners' Chapel was opened in 1849 for the use of boatmen who claimed that they could not attend church in the city because they lacked sufficiently smart clothes. The warehouse behind, built in 1840, was used by a succession of corn merchants and millers. (below) The docks were developed at the inland terminus of the Gloucester & Berkeley Canal, in its time the largest canal in the world. Excavations of the basins began in 1794, and the great warehouses were built between 1826 and 1899.

the world, and the extensive docks and warehouses at Gloucester still reveal something of its ambitions (Fig. 6.9). The greatest dream of West canal promoters, however, was to avoid the dangerous sea passage around Cornwall by building a ship canal to link the Bristol Channel with the English Channel, for coal to be brought directly from south Wales and the Midlands to the south coast, but this was never realised.[17]

Railways, like canals, were slow in penetrating the West. The first was the Birmingham and Gloucester Railway, opened in 1840. Like most early main lines, this minimised construction costs by taking a direct route from terminus to terminus, ignoring intervening towns like Tewkesbury. Brunel's Great Western Railway opened between London and Bristol in 1841, and his Bristol and Exeter Railway reached Bridgwater in 1841 and Taunton in 1842. Slowly the main network was completed (for example the Oxford, Worcester and Wolverhampton Railway

opened in 1852, and the Somerset and Dorset Joint Railway linked the Bristol Channel to the English Channel in 1862) and rural areas were then opened up by a maze of secondary routes and branches. Most of the rail network had been completed by the 1880s, though a few links were still being added up to the time of the First World War.[18]

EXPANSION AFTER 1780

From about 1780 the graph of population increase began to steepen sharply. There was little additional employment in farming, but a growing demand for industrial workers, so most of the increase was absorbed into the towns. Some factory owners contributed to the expansion of towns in a very direct way by providing housing for their workers, as did Wilkins's Broadcloth Manufactory in Bath and the Tonedale woollen mills at Wellington. The government's decision to organise the first census in 1801 was taken against a background of concern about how food production could keep pace with the rising number of mouths to be fed. At the time of the first census in 1801 the population of Britain as a whole had risen to 10 million. The combined populations of Gloucestershire, Somerset and Dorset (including Bristol) amounted to nearly 640,000. Growth was maintained at a generally steady rate throughout the 19th century, except in Somerset, where population declined a little through the last two decades of the century following a peak of nearly 470,000 in 1881. By 1901 the population of the three counties stood at nearly 1.35 million, of whom 330,000 lived in Bristol.

NOTES

1   Darby 1977, 57–94 and 336; Bolton 1980, 48–65; Fowler 1993, 32–6.

2   Finberg 1955, 64–6; Taylor 1970, 61–4, 67–70 and 90–98; Havinden 1981, 106–9; Aston (ed.) 1988, 89; Gelling & Cole, 2000.

3   Finberg 1955, 39–43; Taylor 1970, 88–9.

4   Williams 1970, 25–81; Rippon 1997, 186–219.

5   Hill & Rumble (eds) 1996.

6   Darby 1977, 289–320 and 364–70.

7   Lobel (ed.) 1975; Keen (ed.) 1997.

8   Ziegler 1970, 30–34, 120–40 and 138–9; Taylor 1970, 117–8; Bettey 1974, 46–7.

9   Saville (ed.) 1984, 276–93; Bettey 1986, 110–15; Aston (ed.) 1988, 80–1; Aston et al. (eds) 1989, 105–28.

10 Finberg 1955, 73–5; 1977, 92–105; Aston (ed.) 1988, 59–62.

11 Tann 1967, 28–42.

12 Ponting 1971, 21–41 and 122–32; Finberg 1977 106–20; Bettey 1986, 115–20, 137–42 and 189–97.

13 Finberg 1955, 98; Taylor 1970, 130–2; Bettey 1974, 49–52 and 54; 1986, 107–10, 121–36 and 197–205; Aston (ed.) 1988, 89–94.

14 Finberg 1955, 98; Taylor 1970, 150–3; Bettey 1986, 253–9.

15 Brigden 1986, 29–32, 55–7, 59 and 61–2.

16 Finberg 1955, 101; Buchanan & Cossons 1969, 177–80; Taylor 1970, 171–2; Hadfield & Hadfield (eds) 1973, 145 and 148–51; Bettey 1974, 84–5; Smith & Ralph 1982, 93–4.

17 Hadfield 1967, 16–65 and 76–115; Buchanan & Cossons 1969, 184–6; Hadfield & Hadfield (eds) 1973, 163–7.

18 Buchanan & Cossons 1969, 209–17; Hadfield & Hadfield (eds) 1973, 167–77; Bettey 1974, 86–9; Booker 1977, 16–40; Christiansen 1981, 15–102.

7

A Kaleidoscope of Regions

JAMES BOND

DEFINING THE REGION

The area covered by this book is a zone of transition and a region of contrasts (Fig. 7.1). It straddles the geological divide between the scarplands of south-east England and the more complex outcrops of older strata to the west. Travellers passing through it will be more aware of the scenic contrasts between its alternating uplands and vales, than of any broad similarities. For many people it is defined mainly by being far enough west to escape the shadow of London, but without the sense of separateness found in Wales or Cornwall. It has never formed a political entity. Sometimes it has been bisected by frontiers, as in the Iron Age when it fell into three tribal territories, and between the 6th and 8th centuries AD when its eastern portion formed part of the West Saxon kingdom and its western part remained under British control. Even when the domination of the Anglo-Saxons was complete, it was divided between Wessex to the south and Mercia to the north.

Human territories do not always match physiographic boundaries, and some may be relatively transient. In the early medieval period, and surely in prehistory as well, separate sub-regions with contrasting landscapes were often exploited by the same community within complex tenurial frameworks. This was because communities cultivating fields on the lowlands also needed access to grazing, fishing, wildfowling, timber and fuel resources provided by neighbouring woodlands, uplands, marshlands or coast. For an entirely different reason, after the Norman Conquest, the legal device of Forest Law set aside tracts of land of variable

Fig. 7.1 Sub-regions of the West.

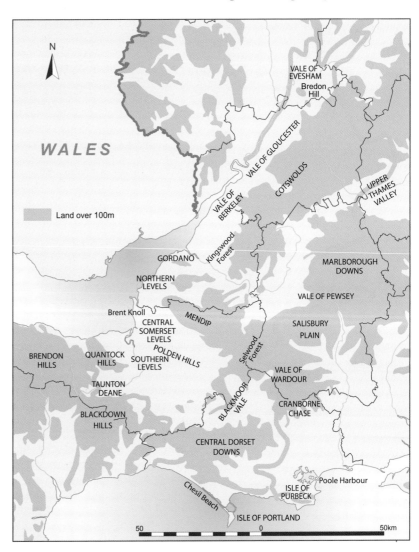

Fig. 7.2 The chalk downs of central Dorset, looking south towards Sydling St Nicholas.

size as royal game preserves within clearly defined bounds, and often spanning different types of countryside. Some medieval forests, like Selwood, retain a lingering identity, while others, such as North Petherton Forest west of the Parrett, are now almost forgotten.

The attraction of the region thus lies in its rich diversity rather than its uniformity. It is in some ways a federation of sub-regions. Many of these sub-regions are sufficiently embedded in local consciousness to bear traditional names, such as Blackmoor Vale, Taunton Deane, Mendip and the Cotswolds. Each contains, within more or less sharply defined boundaries, some combination of nature and culture, geography and history to make it recognisably different from neighbouring sub-regions. In reality, every part of our region has its own character: here a few sub-regions are selected because they seem to stand out as particularly distinctive.

THE CHALK DOWNS OF CENTRAL DORSET

The Dorset Downs form the south-westernmost extremity of a long series of chalk escarpments that extend across England from Yorkshire to the Isle of Purbeck (Fig. 7.2). West of Cranborne Chase the Stour cuts through the escarpment, reaching the sea in Christchurch Harbour. To the west, the downs rise over 240m in places, with a steep scarp face overlooking the Blackmoor Vale to the north. Most of the smaller rivers, like the Piddle, the Cerne and the Frome, rise on the dip slope of the chalk, and there are many dry valleys and seasonal streams. The chalk then curves around the Poole Harbour heathlands in a great arc, narrows to the coast, and terminates dramatically in the Old Harry stacks beyond Handfast Point.

Where they have not been disturbed by modern ploughing, the downs are covered with the earthworks of prehistoric barrows, enclosures, field systems and hillforts. Lack of water on the high downs drew settlement in the medieval period down into the valleys, where, particularly in the Iwerne, Winterbourne and Piddle valleys, nucleated villages with churches are interspersed with hamlets and farms. The modern block-shaped parishes encase a more ancient pattern of smaller, strip-like townships, separated one from another by continuous hedge lines that extend up the valley sides to the local watershed on either side. Arable strip fields flanked the valleys. During the 14th and 15th centuries some of the valley-bottom settlements contracted to a single farmstead or disappeared entirely, and the cultivated area was reduced. At the same time, there was also a considerable increase in sheep flocks. Milton Abbey, for example, had over 7,000 sheep grazing on its downland manors in 1535.

Between the 16th and 18th centuries even more open-field arable and downland were enclosed by agreement between lords and tenants to form large rectangular sheep pastures. This happened at Iwerne Courtney in 1548, at Long Bredy in 1597, at Toller Porcorum in the 1620s and at Bradford Peverell in 1741.

Even as late as 1793, one writer was still able to describe 'the open and unenclosed parts, covered by numerous flocks of sheep, scattered over the Downs', but much of that remaining downland would succumb to enclosure within a couple of decades. A complementary development was the construction of floated water meadows along the valley bottoms, begun in the early 17th century, and greatly extended in the 18th century. Thomas Hardy, in *The Return of the Native*, mentioned 'meadows watered on a plan so rectangular that on a fine day they looked like silver grid-irons'.

During the 'high farming' period of the mid-19th century there was a considerable extension of plough land at the expense of pasture. More than 800ha of downland were ploughed up around Cerne Abbas in the late 1840s and early 1850s. In the agricultural depression that followed, much of that land was returned to grass, and water meadows were abandoned. Farms stood untenanted, farm buildings were neglected and many villages lost a third or more of their occupants. The numbers of sheep fell from about 500,000 in 1850 to 47,000 in 1947. Sheep farming has never recovered, and modern flocks are negligible compared with those of the past. Since 1950, the plough has once more regained its supremacy, and great swathes of waving barley now cover the surface of the downs.[1]

BLACKMOOR VALE

Blackmoor Vale is a clay lowland drained by the headwaters of the Dorset Stour (Fig. 7.3). To the north-west a broken escarpment of oolitic limestone extends from Lillington Hill to Windmill Hill near Charlton Horethorne, where it rises to

Fig. 7.3 Blackmoor Vale: view south towards the chalk downs. Parkland in the centre of the view belongs to the 18th-century house of Stock Gaylard.

just over 180m above sea level. Its northern end has a string of villages along its dip slope at the junction with the chalk, including North and South Cheriton, Horsington and Temple Combe.

To the south-east a second scarp, of corallian limestone, rises to about 90m, beyond which the Vale of Wardour extends a deep bite into the chalk downs. This scarp has an even stronger line of villages along its scarp face, including Cucklington, Buckhorn Weston, Kington Magna, Fifehead Magdalen, Marnhull, Hinton St Mary, Sturminster Newton and Hazelbury Bryan. Its southern limit is the chalk scarp, from which viewpoint Thomas Hardy vividly described the vale in *Tess of the d'Urbervilles*:

> *this fertile and sheltered tract of country, in which the fields are never brown and the springs never dry … the fields are mere paddocks, so reduced that from this height their hedgerows appear a network of dark green threads overspreading the paler green of the grass … Arable lands are few and limited; with but slight exceptions the prospect is a broad rich mass of grass and trees, mantling minor hills and dales within the major … till comparatively recent times, the country was densely wooded. Even now, traces of its earlier condition are to be found in the old oak copses and irregular belts of timber that yet survive upon its slopes, and the hollow-trunked trees that shade so many of its pastures.*

Within the clay vale itself there are a few large nucleated villages such as Henstridge, Stalbridge and Stourton Caundle, but these are widely spaced among the dominant pattern of hamlets and isolated farms connected by winding lanes. Islands of open fields once surrounded villages like Stalbridge in the heart of the vale, with the isolated farmsteads beyond produced through clearance of woodland, which continued into the 14th century. More extensive open fields accompanied the villages on the limestone hills, but at Purse Caundle, Marnhull and Hazelbury Bryan these had been replaced by large enclosed fields of permanent pasture by the 1430s. By the 18th century, relatively little unenclosed land survived, though about a third of Holdwell was enclosed by Parliamentary Act in 1797, and in 1847 two new farms were built over a hundred or so hectares of privately enclosed common east of Glanvilles Wootton.

Hemp and flax were grown on the clay soils from the 17th century, supplying the rope-walks of Bridport and the sailcloth industry of Beaminster. Gloving also provided employment in the villages in the 19th century. The construction of the Salisbury and Yeovil Railway (later the London and South West Railway) in 1860 provided access to more distant markets, and dairying and beef production have been important since the late 19th century. Yet much of Thomas Hardy's landscape of whitewashed thatched cottages and small hedged fields remains today.[2]

THE QUANTOCK HILLS

The Quantocks are a prominent ridge of red sandstone and gritstone, about 5km wide by 20km long, rising at Will's Neck to a height of 390m above sea level (Fig. 7.4). The south-western flank of the hills rises steeply from a vale of red marl drained by the Donniford Stream, which separates them from the Brendon Hills and Exmoor further west. The eastern slopes fall equally steeply towards the Parrett estuary, but are more deeply dissected by numerous narrow, steep-sided combes.

A 16th-century transcript of a lost, but probably genuine, late 7th-century charter, refers to 'the famous wood which is called *Cantucuudu*'. Patches of ancient sessile oak and holly woods and beech plantations still cling to some of the steeper slopes, but the eastern and southern spurs and combes are blanketed

Fig. 7.4 The south-west face of the Quantock Hills: view over West Bagborough towards the coast.

by commercial plantations of larch, pine, spruce and fir established by the Forestry Commission since the 1920s. More extensive planting of conifers was prevented by a vigorous protest campaign in 1949 and the top of the ridge remains open common, with whortleberries, heather, furze and bracken and a few wind-blasted birches and rowans. The hills fall away more gradually into farmland towards the south-east.

Small villages such as Bicknoller and West Bagborough on the south-west and Kilve and Spaxton on the north-east cling to the foot of the hills on both sides. Between them are numerous hamlets and farmsteads. This was never open-field country, most of the land having been enclosed piecemeal long before the 18th century. There were a few plans to enclose upland commons by Act of Parliament, for example on Bagborough Hill in 1810, but it is doubtful whether many of the allotments were ever actually fenced and within about 50 years much of the common had become a large plantation attached to Bagborough House.

Liassic limestone from outcrops towards the coast has been used for building in local villages, and numerous limekilns testify to the burning of lime during the 19th century to make fertiliser. Red sandstone is also much in evidence in local buildings. Copper was mined in the late 18th and early 19th centuries near Dodington on the east side of the hills, but apart from the ruins of a couple of engine houses, has left few scars.[3]

TAUNTON DEANE

Between the Blackdown and Quantock hills is a broad, fertile red-marl lowland that rises gently westwards into more broken country and is drained by the River Tone and its tributaries (Fig. 7.5). In contrast to the lowlands of south-east Somerset, there is little evidence of open-field farming here. Most of the villages

are small, and there are numerous hamlets and scattered farmsteads. Limited infields of arable land near the villages had been enclosed at an early date, leaving extensive common pastures where intakes were occasionally made for cereal cultivation, and which then underwent piecemeal enclosure over many centuries. Remnant patches of commons survive at Langford Heathfield and Ash Priors. Thomas Gerard, writing in 1633, commented on the rich meadows, cider orchards and cherry orchards of Taunton Deane, while Billingsley in 1797 also commended the rich loam soil of the vale, a country of elm hedges, wheat, turnips and dairying with cider orchards on the heavier clays. Kingston St Mary, on the rising ground towards the Quantocks, was the birthplace of the Kingston Black, a famous local cider apple.[4]

Fig. 7.5 Gortnell Common on the north face of the Blackdown Hills. The rectilinear fields of Parliamentary enclosure on Buckland Hill (right foreground) contrast with the irregular patterns of ancient enclosure in the Vale of Taunton Deane (middle distance).

THE SOMERSET LEVELS AND MOORS

The landscape of the Somerset Levels, England's second largest expanse of wetland after the Fens, is relieved from scenic monotony by the views of the surrounding uplands. Variety is also created by the intervening ranges of hills, which separate the flat moors into four distinct basins (Fig. 7.6):

- the southern levels (including Sedgemoor and the Sowy 'island') between the Blackdown and Polden hills, drained by the River Parrett and its tributaries (Fig. 7.7)

- the central levels (including the Wedmore 'island' and Brent Knoll, a more prominent hill towards the coast) between the Polden and Mendip hills, drained by the River Brue and River Axe

- the less extensive northern levels beyond Mendip (including the Nailsea 'island'), drained by the Congresbury Yeo, the Kenn and the Clevedon Yeo

- the Gordano moors, the smallest of the four basins, almost fully enclosed by the Failand ridge and the coastal ridge between Clevedon and Portishead.

Each of these basins is subtly different in character, because of their varied topography and reclamation histories. They all originated, however, as broad estuaries that were inundated by rising sea levels after the last Ice Age. The deposition of alluvial silt, and the growth and decay of sedges and reeds to produce peat, slowly converted these estuaries into swamps, but complete drying-out was inhibited by several factors. More than 1,000mm of rain falls annually on the Mendip and Blackdown hills, causing regular riverine flooding on the inland levels. Moreover, the outlet to the sea was often hindered by the high tidal range in the Bristol Channel, where coastal incursions resulted in the peat becoming sealed by a thick layer of marine clay. The localised development of coastal sand dunes, which provided some protection against the sea, also further impeded inland drainage.[5]

The marshes were exploited by prehistoric man, and the waterlogged peat has preserved a series of wooden trackways, the oldest of which has been dated by dendrochronology to 3806 BC. By about 300 BC farming communities had settled on the edge of the inland marshes at Glastonbury and Meare and the slightly higher clay belt along the coast was extensively occupied during the Roman period. After the 5th century, renewed inundation buried many farmsteads beneath further deposits of flood-silt.[6]

The recovery of the coastal claylands began during the late-Saxon period through the construction of sea walls and river embankments to restrain flooding, and by the digging of drains to remove freshwater run-off. The earlier areas of reclamation on the higher parts of the coastal strip are characterised by irregular enclosed fields, sinuous drainage rhynes, long winding droveways and scattered farmsteads. Pioneer

Fig. 7.6 The low ridge of the Polden Hills, *separating King's Sedgemoor from the central Somerset Levels, can be traced by the thin discontinuous line of woodland extending from the large wood rightwards into the distance. In the foreground some of the fields around Ashcott village have the characteristic long, narrow shape produced by enclosure of open fields by agreement.*

Fig. 7.7 King's Sedgemoor in the Somerset Levels: *view west over Greylake Bridge. The King's Sedgemoor Drain in the middle of the view was cut following the Act of 1791 for the draining and reallocation of the moor, providing the River Cary with a new outlet to the Parrett estuary. Peat-cutting is visible in the middle distance.*

settlements in these areas often bore the name 'huish', meaning a holding comprising sufficient land to support one family, or 'worth', meaning an enclosure, and these are sometimes associated with oval 'infields' which probably represent the first arable fields on slightly higher ground. The D-shaped bend in the road east of Puxton church in the northern levels, for example, curves round one such infield.

Piecemeal reclamation and improvement continued after the Norman Conquest, pushing out from the margins and from the islands. By the 13th century episcopal and monastic landowners were becoming more directly involved in ambitious works further inland. The River Brue was diverted away from its old confluence with the Axe at Bleadney and directed towards a new outfall below Highbridge, while other rivers were straightened and embanked. Causeways such as the Burrow Wall and Beer Wall were built to link the islands with the margins, which also had the effect of containing floodwaters within particular sectors of the moors. However, by about 1320 momentum had slowed, and little more was done before the 17th century.[7]

The inland peat moors remained a valuable resource even in their unreclaimed state. Farmers from the uplands and islands pastured livestock on them in summer. Fish and wildfowl were available from the rivers and from natural lakes such as Meare Pool. Osier beds were coppiced annually to provide wands for basketwork and fish traps. Alder beds and turbaries (peat diggings) provided fuel. New ways of exploiting the resources of the peat moors were slowly introduced. Duck decoys (artificial ponds used for trapping duck) were introduced in the 17th century. Some 45 examples have been identified in Somerset, concentrated mainly within the inland levels, but most had gone out of use by about 1900. Peats were traditionally cut by hand using long-handled square-bladed turf spades and the turves dried in conical or domed stacks with air spaces, but after the 1930s machines were increasingly used to excavate the peat, and this method of extraction still continues today.[8]

Drainage attempts on a large scale were renewed in the central levels after 1770, when the improvement of the Axe and Brue outfalls facilitated reclamation between the Poldens and the Wedmore island and between Wedmore and Mendip. In the southern levels in 1791 the River Cary was diverted away from its old confluence with the Parrett at Burrowbridge, into the King's Sedgemoor Drain, a wide straight cut 19km long taking the water more directly into the Parrett estuary (see Fig. 7.7). Extensive work took place in the northern levels and Gordano valley in the early 19th century. Apart from the Parrett, the mouths of all the main rivers were sealed by 'clyses', tidal sluices that could be closed against high tides. In the southern levels the first of eight coal-fired steam-powered pumping stations was built at Westonzoyland in 1830, and by 1870 these had done much to improve the drainage of the Parrett valley. Local Parliamentary Enclosure and Drainage Acts, which had to take account of the common rights of numerous small proprietors, resulted in the division of the open moors into innumerable rectangular closes defined by new rhynes and ditches. Crack willows were planted along the drainage rhynes, to reduce erosion, and along the roads and droveways, to define them in flood-time. They were pollarded to provide hurdles and thatching spars. In contrast to the anciently settled coastal claybelt, the inland moors remained largely empty of settlement, except for occasional straggling lines of low, often whitewashed cottages along the causeways and embankments.

The latest stage in the saga of improvement began during the Second World War, when the King's Sedgemoor Drain was widened and the Huntspill River, a straight broad cut 8km long, was dug to improve the drainage of the Brue valley. In the northern levels most of the waters of the River Kenn were similarly diverted into a new outfall, the Blind Yeo, in 1949–50. The old pumping stations were replaced with more efficient diesel pumps. Yet even now there are times when nature regains the upper hand and standing water remains on the inland peat moors for weeks at a time. The wetlands still provide a rich wildlife habitat, supporting otters, herons and curlews, while marshland plants survive along the rhynes and in abandoned peat-diggings, and hay meadows support a wide range of flowering species.[9]

MENDIP

The Mendip Hills are an outcrop of Carboniferous Limestone extending for over 40km from Frome to the Bristol Channel (Fig. 7.8). The central section is the most prominent part of the range, a steep-sided plateau about 8km wide, slightly dished at the top, reaching an average height of about 230m above sea level, rising to 325m on Beacon Batch. The coastal promontories of Brean Down and Worlebury, on either side of Weston-super-Mare, are detached outliers. Caves and potholes are numerous, and collapsed cave systems have produced gorges in the face of the hills at Burrington Combe, Ebor Rocks and, most famously, at Cheddar (Fig. 7.9).

Mendip's oldest industry was lead-mining. Lead spindle whorls and net-sinkers were found in the excavations of the Glastonbury lake villages. There were extensive Roman workings at Charterhouse-on-Mendip and documentary references to mining continue through the medieval period. The characteristic 'gruffy ground' around Charterhouse and Priddy is evidence for surface working along the seams. The mines were at their most productive during the first three-quarters of the 17th century, but declined thereafter although the last lead mine, St Cuthbert's Works at Priddy, did not close until 1908. During the middle of the 19th century many of the old spoil tips were reworked, and remains of furnaces survive at East Harptree and Charterhouse. Zinc-producing calamine ore, discovered near Worle in 1566, was also mined around Shipham and Rowberrow up to about 1850, to supply the Bristol brass foundries.[10]

*Fig. 7.8 **The south face of Mendip, looking west over Wavering Down and Crook Peak.** The limestone plateau narrows towards the Bristol Channel, detached portions forming the promontory of Brean Down and the island of Steep Holm, visible in the distance. The scattered settlement of Compton Bishop occupies a fertile combe to the south (left) of the ridge.*

Fig. 7.9 Cheddar Gorge forms a dramatic cleft through the southern edge of the Mendip Hills, *providing access up to the high plateau from the Axe valley to the south.*

Two long lines of villages extend below the northern and southern faces of the Mendip Hills, where springs issue from the limestone. These villages once cultivated open fields on the lower ground, most of which were enclosed by private agreement in the 16th and 17th centuries. The fossilised pattern of consolidated and hedged strips can still be seen, for example around Draycott. The only village on top of the hills is Priddy, a stone-built settlement around a triangular green on which sits a thatched hurdle stack, a reminder of the great annual sheep fair held every August since 1348.

The Mendip upland was traditionally common pasture, carrying large flocks of sheep. In 1791 the Somerset antiquarian John Collinson emphasised its bleakness when he wrote, 'The air, especially in winter, is moist, thick and foggy, and so very cold that frost and snow inhabit these heights longer than they do almost any other parts of the county; and the few remaining trees, their leaves blasted and discoloured by the severe winds from the Channel, never attain to any considerable size.'

There was good grazing for both sheep and cattle around Priddy, but other parts of the upland remained a wilderness of bracken and gorse. John Billingsley, who farmed some 1,600ha at Ashwick, writing a few years later than Collinson, made a distinction between those parts of the plateau with deep, loamy, free-draining soils, and certain recalcitrant areas of ill-drained acid peaty soils underlain by hard iron pans, which occurred particularly on the northern side of the hills on Black Down above Burrington and Blagdon, and on the southern side above Wells, Dinder and Croscombe. Artificial rabbit warrens had been established in many areas, and groups of their distinctive pillow mounds can still be seen, for example within the Iron Age hillfort at Dolebury; but their profitability was always limited by poaching, vermin, and occasional hard winters, and by 1797 working warrens survived only at Charterhouse, Temple Down and Ubley.

The enclosure of the upland commons had commenced in 1770, and over the next five years some 1,000ha were divided up above East and West Cranmore, Ubley, Doulting and Stoke St Michael. Collinson described how 'many of the hills, a few years since unacquainted with the plough, are now, by improvements in husbandry, brought to such a state of cultivation as to produce large crops of grain ... hemp, flax, teasles and woad are cultivated in considerable quantities'. By 1794 Billingsley estimated that some 5,500ha had been enclosed, with 4,650ha of common waste remaining.

By 1813, 9,700ha of Mendip had been enclosed by Parliamentary Act, in addition to some 1,400ha enclosed by agreement. In all, something like 2,650km of new hedges and walls were established. Initially most of the new enclosures were allocated to farms in the villages below the hills, but from the 1820s new farmsteads began to appear on the plateau, their late arrival often indicated by names such as Upper and Lower Canada Farms on Bleadon Hill and Wellington Farm above Cheddar Gorge. In all, some 50 new farmsteads were built, most of them centrally located within their fields, usually taking advantage of any lee slopes or hollows for shelter, and commonly equipped with a large barn and cattle stalls on one side and a wagon-house and granary on the other, with further provision for pigs and poultry.

Billingsley was an enthusiastic supporter of enclosure, being convinced that productive mixed farms could be carved out of rough grazing by establishing shelter-belts, hedges and stone walls. On his own farm he planted nearly 160km of quickset hedges, using one and a half million hawthorn plants. Drystone walls up to 1.5m high and 0.6m wide were used in other areas, for example around Priddy. He recommended planting 'judicious and well-disposed belts and clumps of trees [to] increase the beauty as well as the value of the new inclosures', and also suggested planting fir, larch, beech, ash, sycamore and birch every few metres along the hedges. His recommendation of planting timber trees in hedgerows was not widely carried out, but numerous shelter-belts were successfully established.

The enclosure of Mendip was not, however, an unqualified success. The costs often greatly exceeded the estimates, and many farmers tried to recover their expenditure by taking six or seven successive crops of wheat and oats without manuring, to the detriment of longer-term fertility. Perhaps fortunately, the high demand for grain was beginning to recede during the 1820s. During the 1830s potatoes were alternated with oats on some farms, but this practice was ended by the outbreak of potato blight in 1845. By the middle of the 19th century most of the Mendip upland had been returned to sheep pasture and summer grazing for cattle brought up from the moors.

Small portions of ancient ash, oak and lime woods cling to the steeper slopes on both sides of the hills, augmented in places by ornamental planting. The Forestry Commission has established some 600ha of mixed commercial plantations since 1939, the most extensive being at Rowberrow Warren and Stock Hill near Priddy.[11]

THE VALE OF PEWSEY

A deep wedge-shaped inlet of low-lying Greensand country extends from Devizes almost 32km east towards Savernake Forest, separating the two chalk massifs of Salisbury Plain and the Marlborough Downs. Streams rising along the southern edge of the Marlborough Downs unite to form the Salisbury Avon, which cuts through the scarp of Salisbury Plain at Upavon to drain southwards towards the English Channel. Place-names at the east end of the vale, such as Wootton Rivers and Durley, hint at a more wooded landscape around the fringes of Savernake Forest, but names ending in -ton, indicating settlements in open country, predominate elsewhere. Through the medieval period this was a country of nucleated villages and open fields, though along both edges of the vale the parishes extend in long strips up on to the downs in order to include upland grazing. John Leland in the 1540s described the vale as 'fruitful of grass and corn, especially good wheat and barley'. By the 1630s some streams were watering irrigated meadows, feeding larger numbers of sheep, and water-meadow management continued into the 19th century. Most townships also had small copses in remoter, less fertile corners, or on the edge of the downs. Most of the open fields were enclosed by Parliamentary Acts between 1770 and 1850, though some strip cultivation survived at Stert until 1928. Following enclosure many downland sheepwalks were converted to arable fields by 'burnbaking' (using ash from burnt turf as a fertiliser). Dairying has remained important in the lower-lying parts of the vale, while wheat has returned to the hillslopes.

Many of the villages consist of a single street, sometimes with a green, and appear to have been planned in the early medieval period. The older houses are timber-framed and thatched, but brick and ceramic tiles came into use after about 1700. A few villages, like Milcot and Isterton, disappeared during the late medieval period, but many more show evidence of contraction, with earthworks of house platforms visible beyond their present bounds. Some villages have moved away from their earlier sites, leaving isolated churches at Rushall and Manningford Abbots. Other villages, including Milton Lilbourne, Potterne and Urchfont, expanded considerably between the late 14th and 17th centuries. Farms have tended to remain in the villages here, and there are relatively few isolated post-enclosure farmsteads.[12]

Fig. 7.10 The western fringes of Selwood: view over Alfred's Tower on the Stourhead estate. Piecemeal woodland clearance since disafforestation in 1627 has produced the fields in the middle distance, but the woodland on the near slopes has mostly been planted since the 1790s.

SELWOOD FOREST

Along the borders of Wiltshire and Somerset between Frome and Penselwood the infertile Greensand escarpment forms a belt of heavily wooded upland rising to more than 245m in places (Fig. 7.10). According to Asser, writing in the late 9th century, this area was known to the Britons as *Coit Mawr*, the 'Great Wood', and it may, for a time, have marked the western frontier of Anglo-Saxon territory, since its function as a boundary is mentioned several times in the Anglo-Saxon Chronicle. During the medieval period this formed the core of Selwood Forest, which once extended from Pewsham and Melksham forests in the north to Gillingham and Blackmore forests in the south. The area is still relatively sparsely populated, with a few upland villages like Corsley, Horningsham, Kilmington and Penselwood, all of which have loose-knit polyfocal plans. In 1627 Charles I decided to disafforest Selwood and to sell off the crown estate there. Much of the forest was enclosed during the 17th and 18th centuries and converted to pasture or meadow. In 1791 Collinson described the cutting down of large tracts of woodland around Frome and the establishment of small farms. Several years later Billingsley estimated that something like 7,300ha of forest had been cleared and converted to farmland, leaving about 800ha of oak and ash coppice. More than 200ha of commons and marshes survived at the southern end of the forest between Kilmington and Wincanton and were finally enclosed by Parliamentary Act in 1814. Much of the existing woodland along the ridge and scarp face is a result of extensive replanting for timber undertaken by the Stourhead and Longleat estates since the 1780s.

THE VALE OF BERKELEY

The Vale of Berkeley occupies the east bank of the lower Severn between the Bristol Avon and Stroudwater (Fig. 7.11). Much of the vale rests upon Liassic clays and limestones, and red marls and sandstones, but between Sharpness and Iron Acton erosion has exposed the Carboniferous Limestone and other more ancient rocks.

The clay soils towards the Severn were drained and enclosed during the 12th and 13th centuries. They provided rich pasture for cattle, and Cotswold sheep flocks were traditionally overwintered in the vale. Dairying, particularly cheese-making, dominated agricultural production in the 16th and 17th centuries, with bacon an important secondary product from whey-fed pigs. Cider orchards were also important from the 17th century, and several farms still have cider mills and presses in their outbuildings. As in Somerset, the growth of the cloth industry encouraged the cultivation of the fuller's teasel on the heavy clay soils, and this was still grown in some places into the 19th century.

There are few villages, but many straggling hamlets and numerous isolated 16th- and 17th-century farmhouses. In contrast to the Vale of Gloucester further upstream, timber-building is rare in the Vale of Berkeley, and most of the older dwellings are built of various types of rubble, particularly the blue-grey Liassic limestone. Although brick made an early appearance in the chimneys of Thornbury Castle, brick-built houses were rare before the 18th century, and even then were mainly limited to the coastal parishes below Berkeley. Pennant and Cotswold stone tiles were once widely used for roofing, but during the 19th century they were often replaced with the lighter ceramic Bridgwater pantiles.[14]

The broad ribbon of the Severn forms an important backdrop to the vale, providing transport, power for mills, and fishing. At one time tidal effects were felt as far upstream as Worcester, but after the construction of locks in 1871 Gloucester became the tidal limit. In the estuary below Gloucester basketwork traps were set in fixed wooden frames to catch fish on the outgoing tide. This technique was practised from the early medieval period into the 20th century. Several types of trap were in use, the commonest, known as 'putchers', being designed for salmon. They were cone-shaped, 1.5 to 2m long, 0.6m at the mouth and about 125mm at the tip with a weave open enough to allow other fish to escape. They were put in place in April, set in three or four tiers in ranks up to 50m long and 3m high, and removed in September.[15]

Fig. 7.11 The great bend of the tidal River Severn below Framilode, looking west towards the Forest of Dean. In the foreground the Gloucester & Berkeley Canal passes by the village of Frampton-on-Severn.

129

KINGSWOOD FOREST

A description of the bounds of Kingswood in 1228 shows that the royal forest had once covered all the southern half of the Vale of Berkeley between the Cotswold scarp, the Little Avon, the Bristol Avon and the Severn. Much of the area had probably been cleared well before 1228, but after that date the Berkeleys began acquiring and exchanging common lands to be leased off for enclosure. By this means Michael Wood in Alkington was much reduced between 1230 and 1320. To compensate for the diminution of woodland, Maurice, Lord Berkeley, enclosed Whitcliff Wood in Ham and converted it to a deer park before 1280, not without some opposition from the commoners. Proximity to Bristol encouraged the development of market gardening on the richer soils around Frampton Cotterell and Iron Acton in the 17th century.

The southern parts of Kingswood have now been engulfed by the eastern suburbs of Bristol, but the north retains evidence of an interesting mix of agricultural and industrial activity, ancient farms and villages being interspersed with squatter settlements such as Coalpit Heath. Red sandstone rubble is used for building around Winterbourne and Frampton Cotterell, while there are many walls of grey-brown Pennant sandstone between Iron Acton and Mangotsfield.

Both coal and ironstone have been worked in Kingswood at least since the early 13th century. Before 1800 there were numerous small shallow workings, but larger more productive collieries were developed during the 19th century to supply the industrial districts of Bristol, aided by the construction of coal tramways from Coalpit Heath to St Philips and Bitton in the 1830s. Exhaustion of the best seams and competition from elsewhere resulted in a prolonged decline of the industry during the first four decades of the 20th century.[16]

THE VALE OF GLOUCESTER

The Vale of Gloucester is an expanse of low-lying, fertile countryside in the Severn valley, extending from the Stroudwater upstream to Tewkesbury. The soils are mainly heavy, derived from Liassic clay, but localised bands of limestone, marl and sandstone provide some lighter soils. Above the riverside meadows, the vale is diversified by low, rolling hills rising 60m above the general level of the valley floor, often with small patches of woodland, while further to the east there are several prominent outliers of the Cotswolds (Fig. 7.12).

The medieval agricultural landscape was a mix of open-field and old enclosure. Ridge and furrow is still visible in some areas. According to William of Malmesbury the vale was also noted for its vineyards in the 12th century. Cobbett, travelling westwards from Pitchcombe in the 1820s, saw 'dairy-farms and orchards all the way to Gloucester', and commented on the productivity of the pear orchards. He also praised the rich meadows and pastures around Tewkesbury, where 'the number of cattle and sheep feeding in them is prodigious'.

The villages are closely spaced, and are small, irregular and straggling in form. Houses and farm buildings are generally timber-framed or of brick, their roofs thatched or tiled. The cream, grey and pale-blue Liassic limestones were also used where available. By contrast, many of the churches are built of better stone brought down from the Cotswolds.

Fig. 7.12 Parliamentary enclosure in the Vale of Gloucester south-west of Cheltenham: view east from Churchdown Hill towards Shurdington.

Today this landscape appears more open than at any time since the medieval period. The small cider and perry orchards, once liberally scattered throughout the vale, are much reduced in extent. Moreover, the area was devastated by Dutch Elm disease during the 1970s and the stately trees which once lined so many of its lanes and hedgerows have all gone. Fortunately sufficient hedgerow oaks survive to save it from bareness.

THE COTSWOLDS

Today the Cotswolds are a tourist honeypot, attracting thousands of visitors every year. Yet they have not always been admired. The churchman Sydney Smith (1771–1845), travelling westwards by coach, expressed his preferences in no uncertain terms:

> You travel for twenty or five-and twenty miles over one of the most unfortunate desolate countries under heaven, divided by stone walls, and abandoned to the screaming kites and larcenous crows; after travelling really twenty, and to appearance ninety, miles over this region of stone and sorrow, life begins to be a burden, and you wish to perish. At the very moment when you are taking this melancholy view of human affairs … there bursts upon your view, with all its towers, forests and streams, the deep and shaded Vale of Severn.

William Cobbett, too, thought the Cotswolds 'an ugly country … having less to please the eye than any other I have ever seen'. It took a long time for attitudes to change, and the first popular guidebook to the Cotswolds did not appear until 1905; but for J B Priestley, writing in 1934, the Cotswolds had become 'the most English and the least spoiled of all our countrysides'.

The element which unifies the Cotswolds and gives them their distinctiveness is the rock beneath, the oolitic limestone that moulds the landscape and provides building stone. The hills present a steep scarp face to the west and a long, very gentle dip slope to the east. Variations in relief and drainage further break them up into several scenic sub-regions. On the north-eastern margins of our region, the limestone escarpment is broken by a wide re-entrant clay vale containing the town of Moreton-in-Marsh. Here the Evenlode and Windrush cut deep valleys through the scarp, draining south-eastwards towards the Thames. A second smaller re-entrant at Winchcombe, etched out by the headwaters of the Isbourne, drains northwards towards the Warwickshire Avon.

Beyond Winchcombe the hills rise to their greatest altitude, 330m, above Cheltenham (Fig. 7.13). From here the scarp face continues southwards in an unbroken line as far as Painswick. The top of the Cotswold plateau is generally flat, and in this section the dip slope is drained south-eastwards towards the Thames by smaller rivers, the Leach, Coln and Churn.

South of Painswick, between Haresfield Beacon and Wotton-under-Edge, where the scarp still rises to

Fig. 7.13 The highest point of the Cotswold scarp: Cleeve Common near Cheltenham, looking south. *The Iron Age hillfort on Cleeve Cloud is clearly visible in the upper centre of the view; the dyke in the foreground is a boundary earthwork probably also of Iron Age date.*

between 200 and 250m, it becomes dissected into a confusion of tumbling hills and deep, narrow valleys by the Gloucestershire Frome or Stroudwater and its tributaries draining towards the Severn. The southern Cotswolds, between Wotton-under-Edge and Bath, are less dramatic: the line of the scarp is persistent, but the crest is lower, the rivers that flow down its dip slope smaller and the only deep intersection of the scarp is made by the Avon itself at Bath.

Thin brashy soils predominate on the high Cotswolds, and until the middle of the 18th century much of this land was unfenced sheepwalks. The wealth of the wool trade is reflected in the wonderful late-medieval churches in the Cotswold towns. Between 1770 and 1830 Parliamentary enclosure transformed this open landscape into one of large rectangular fields, with drystone walls criss-crossing the wolds, or hedges on less exposed lower ground. The ancient upland pastures were broken up by the plough, barley and oats being grown along with turnips, vetches, sainfoin and trefoil for sheep feed. Wheat was more commonly grown on the heavier ground. Following Parliamentary enclosure a number of isolated farmsteads built around big, square courtyards, like Dilley's Farm on Baunton Down, appeared on the plateau top, with water pumped up from hydraulic rams.

Beech hangers cling to many of the steeper slopes of the scarp face and valley sides, especially around Stroud, where many were planted in the late 18th century. Intermittent belts of trees also occur on the plateau top, serving as windbreaks. The beeches of the Bathurst estate at Cirencester are particularly noteworthy. Great landed estates with walled parks such as Batsford, Sherborne, Cirencester, Westonbirt and Badminton have long been a special feature of the Cotswolds. The remains of palatial Roman villas at Chedworth, Woodchester and elsewhere show that such estates have been a long tradition.

The villages of the north Cotswolds occur in two characteristic locations. One group hugs the base of the scarp along the spring line, with its open fields formerly occupying the lower land in the vale. The other group nestles in the valleys of the dip slope, with its fields climbing up to the plateau. By contrast, in the central and southern Cotswolds many of the villages and their surrounding open fields gravitated towards the plateau rather than the valleys; valley-bottom settlements like Brimscombe, Thrupp and Nailsworth grew later as a result of the exploitation of water-power for the cloth industry.

The character of the villages and farms is derived from an almost exclusive use of local Cotswold stone, perhaps the most glorious building stone in England. No one has conjured up a better description than J B Priestley, who thought that, even on the most lowering of days, the Cotswold walls remained 'faintly warm and luminous, as if they knew the trick of keeping the lost sunlight of centuries glimmering about them'. The hallmarks of the 'Cotswold style' are long, low-fronted dwellings, steep-pitched stone-slated single-span roofs with gabled dormer windows, flat moulded gable copings sometimes with ornate finials, and small rectangular mullioned windows beneath moulded dripstones. These developed during a period of considerable rebuilding between 1580 and 1690. By the end of that time, coursed rubble walls were giving way to dressed stone, windows were becoming taller, and classical detail was beginning to appear around the doorways. The essential harmony remained, however, and the region's resistance to the intrusion of brick, slate and ceramic tile is now firmly endorsed by local planning policies.[17]

THE VALE OF EVESHAM

The Vale of Evesham is a broad clay lowland drained by the lower valley of the Warwickshire Avon. The flood plain provides rich meadow land and the gravel terraces, where most of the villages stand, provide lighter soils that have been settled and farmed since the Iron Age. Many traditional dwellings of half-timber and thatch survive (Fig. 7.14), Blue Lias stone also being employed, while red brick and tile were increasingly used from the 17th century.

The landscape of the Vale of Evesham derives its present character mainly from the comparatively recent market-gardening industry. This distinctive culture has produced a multi-coloured patchwork of vegetables grown in unhedged strips, interspersed with orchards and glasshouses. It cannot be traced back beyond the 18th century, when horse-drawn carts began to carry fruit and vegetables up to Birmingham and the Black Country, returning loaded with pig and horse manure. Further afield, however, the prosperity of the vale still rested mainly upon cereal production. Many villages continued to be surrounded by open fields, and vestiges of ridge and furrow can still be seen in odd plots of pasture dotted around between the garden plots.

Fig. 7.14 A Vale of Evesham village: thatched and timber-framed cottages at Harvington, Worcestershire.

The expansion of market gardening into the rural parishes began only in the middle of the 19th century. The opening of the Birmingham and Gloucester Railway in 1840 provided a means of transporting large quantities of fresh produce in prime condition to the urban markets. For some years, until the railway network was extended, growers at the west end of the vale in villages such as Eckington enjoyed a considerable advantage over those around Evesham. The second major boost, ironically, was provided by the great agricultural depression of the late 1870s, when land fell out of cultivation on the larger farms and some farm labourers instead took to renting small plots for gardens, working them part-time, and saving up to acquire additional plots until they held sufficient land to cultivate full-time. In Badsey the number of holdings rose from 92 to 244 in the 30 years after 1876, while the amount of land under gardens increased 20-fold. Garden smallholdings came to dominate the landscape east of Evesham, particularly around Offenham, Badsey and Wickhamford. As livestock farming disappeared, hedges became redundant, and the landscape reverted to something like an open-field appearance, though the crops were now asparagus, spring cabbage, lettuce, sprouts, broccoli, broad beans, carrots, radishes and bush fruits rather than cereals. By contrast, market gardens west of Evesham tended to be more than 100ha in extent, employing hired labour and specialising in particular crops.

Market gardening continued to expand and prosper through times when other forms of farming were facing considerable difficulties. Worcestershire County Council had accepted a responsibility to provide smallholdings in the 1890s, and during the slump of the 1920s it acquired many more farms for this purpose. By the late 1930s, when market gardening was at its peak, the Vale of Evesham contained some 2,000 holdings of 6ha or less.

The market gardeners of the vale have always had to be adaptable and innovative to compete in a changing market. James Myatt, son of a Camberwell gardener, took up a lease of 28ha at Laurels Farm in Offenham in 1852, where he introduced the cultivation of rhubarb and strawberries. Following a visit to Vitry in 1905 to inspect French methods, J N Harvey began growing lettuces, radishes, cauliflowers, turnips, cucumbers and melons under glass forcing-frames and bell cloches on his holding at Bengeworth. Unheated glasshouses began to appear after 1910. The first irrigation systems were introduced in 1906, and overhead irrigation using water pumped up from the Avon was appearing during the 1930s. The first marketing co-operatives were set up towards the end of the first decade of the 20th century.

Dutch and Italian farmers who settled in the vale during the Second World War introduced a number of innovations, particularly specialisations in early-season crops and glasshouse production of lettuces and tomatoes. Large numbers of new glasshouses appeared, especially around Offenham. Since the war, circumstances have favoured larger combines covering thousands of hectares at the expense of the small family holding, and the numbers of the latter have dwindled accordingly. Many former smallholdings on the heavier clay soils were absorbed back into larger farms and reverted to cereals and dairying. The cultivation of asparagus, once the standby of the clayland smallholder, was drastically reduced, and sprouts, beans, peas, cauliflowers and root crops have also declined with increasing competition from elsewhere. Soaring fuel costs made the growth of tomatoes in heated greenhouses uneconomic. By about 1980 the overall extent of garden cultivation had contracted to half what it had been before the war. At the same time experiments began with new crops such as Cape gooseberries, Chinese cabbages and peppers and new techniques such as hydroponic cultivation.

Between about 1950 and 1980 the extent of orchards around Pershore was reduced by more than a third; but much of the loss was caused by the grubbing-up of badly sited orchards past their prime, and fruit production was little affected. Many low-lying orchards along the Isbourne and Badsey Brook have gone, but there has been a compensatory expansion, particularly of plum orchards, on the higher ground around Craycombe and the Lenches, and on the southern side of the Avon on either side of Evesham. In newer plantations east- or north-east-facing slopes, where blossoming is delayed until the dangers of late frosts are over, have been preferred to the south-facing slopes generally chosen in the 19th century.

NOTES

1   Taylor 1970, 25–33, 49–59, 111–21, 127–32, 150–3 and 156–7; Bettey 1974, 44–60.

2   Taylor 1970, 120, 155–6, 170–1 and 204–6; Bettey 1974, 50, 60, 86 and 139.

3   Lawrence 1952, 13–212; Waite 1969, 15–21 and 158–82; Havinden 1981, 36, 178–9, 195 and 197.

4   Lawrence 1952, 60–1; Havinden 1981, 34, 106–8 and 231–3.

5   Williams 1970, 6–17; Storer 1985, 14–17 and 23–6; Rippon 1997, 31–46.

6   Storer 1985, 18–22; Coles & Coles 1986; Rippon 1997, 47–50, 56–7, 60–91 and 104–27.

7   Williams 1970, 38–81; Storer 1985, 27–31; Rippon 1997, 142–65 and 168–239.

8   Williams 1970, 25–38; Storer 1985, 124–31; Williams & Williams 1992, 101–4.

9   Williams 1970, 82–122 and 237–60; Storer 1985, 32–7; Williams & Williams 1992, 78–85 and 147–63.

10   Buchanan & Cossons 1969, 101–11, 115–16 and 124; Atthill (ed.) 1976, 146–50.

11   Atthill 1971; Atthill (ed.) 1976, 39–41, 75–125 and 205–7; Havinden 1981, 128, 137 and 200–4.

12   Chandler 1991, 11–36 and 45–88.

13   Havinden 1981, 235–8.

14   Finberg 1955, 14, 16 and 44; Wilshire 1980; Hall 1983.

15   Jenkins 1974; Waters 1987.

16   Braine 1891; Finberg 1955, 65–6; Buchanan & Cossons 1969, 76–100; Hall 1983.

17   Massingham 1937; Priestley 1977, 50–1; Finberg 1955, 77–84 and 96–100; 1977, 23–38; Hadfield & Hadfield (eds) 1973, 21–47 and 110–24; Brill 1987, 5–29 and 98–103.

8

Revenue from Rocks

PETER ELLIS

The relationships between landscape and people in the West become very clear when the focus is on how the rocks beneath the landscape were exploited. This chapter, which looks at quarrying and mining from the Roman period onwards, is about what people have done to the landscape in search of rocks and minerals, and, less obviously, what the search has done to people. So the subject is not just the visible remains of two millennia of work but also the less tangible ways in which lives have been influenced by it. If geology is landscape's destiny then this chapter looks at how it might be seen as people's destiny as well. The way in which this comes about is really no more than a factor of the different timespans occupied by places and people – a building or a mine lasts longer than its originators and remains to exert its influence on their descendants. Thus looking at mining and quarrying makes for a tension between a sense of people's mastery and a sense of place's mastery. In this chapter we shall see the energies driving people on to seek out stone and metals, but we will see also how stone and metals become linked with our sense of identity, an identity that with neat circularity often concerns itself with a quest for the reality beneath the surface of things.

QUARRYING

The clearest place to see an area's geology is in its stone buildings. They are the landscape turned inside out – what was hidden is now exposed and extruded from below ground. Although the relationship is obvious – you can go up close and see the geological layering and contents of an epoch in a single block of building stone – there is a gap between the stone in the building and the stone in the ground. Quite apart from the process of quarrying and transporting stone, an enormous amount of pre-planning and site work, great quantities of materials and many different skills have gone into a building's construction. However, just as the scaffolding is removed leaving no traces when the building is finished, so all the processes of building vanish leaving a final apparently inscrutable product. The building appears rather like the product of a magician's abracadabra or a director's *coup de théâtre*. The historian's and archaeologist's task is to restore this gap and to revivify the processes. By re-linking work practices and their aesthetic products, so often regarded as quite separate, work can be repositioned so that it lies not at the periphery of civilisation but at its centre.

The typical stone house, standing or as unravelled in excavation, tells us that there are different kinds of stone. Rough rubble, whose property is simply solidity, will have been used in the foundations. A second level of more manageable rubble stone appears in the walls except where a third type of stone, cut into exact squared blocks, was used for effect in the façade or in unplastered interiors. Finally there is stone used for decorative work around windows and doors and for other features. In the West only certain quarries supplied the third and fourth types of stone so this material may have been carried from a distance while quarries close by supplied the first two types of stone which, of course, represent the great majority of stone used. The different appearances of buildings in our region, unparalleled in any other, is a reflection of the many different sources of building stone, and this variety can also be seen in the stone used for roofs and paving.

Excavation of urban and rural sites of all periods up to very recent ones reveals how much stone was valued, for stone is seen to have been robbed even down to the bottoms of the foundation trenches. If this was the case for foundation rubble then how much more so for the stone used in façades and decoration? At Sherborne monastic structures were carted away and re-erected. At Wells Bishop Stillington's chapel was blown up in 1552 to get at its stone. This recycling of materials introduces complexity to any attempt to rebuild the link between house and quarry. The quarries that served surviving buildings were not always the bramble-tangled open space on the hillside near by but were very often a previous stone building. This process is an economically logical one since in an abandoned structure there are materials that are ready prepared for the exact purpose intended in the new building, and moreover that have to be carted a shorter distance than from a quarry. The process also involves an attitude to former structures that lies between the destruction and levelling of what went before or the total retention of past structures – the two conflicting approaches with which we view old buildings today. This reuse means that buildings in the landscape often have greater time depth than their appearance suggests.

The great majority of the surviving records to do with quarrying and virtually all of the stone that has an individual significance belong to the third and fourth categories of stone – material that can be sawn into sharply angled, tight-fitting blocks that are mortared to form the façade of a building, or that can be sculpted and carved to decorate the building or to make objects. This is the material for which the West is famous: the Cotswold-edge quarries north to Taynton in Oxfordshire and south to the Bath stone quarries at Bath itself and to its east; the Wiltshire quarries of Tisbury and Chilmark; quarries at Dundry, Doulting and Ham Hill in Somerset; and finally those at Abbotsbury, Portland and Purbeck in Dorset. Cotswold stone is the material forming two architectural set pieces, Bath and Cheltenham. Tisbury, Chilmark and Doulting are the quarries that supplied Salisbury and Wells cathedrals as well as numerous other buildings, Dundry supplied stone to Bristol and by sea to Irish medieval churches. Ham Hill and Abbotsbury stone is widely used for architectural features locally and in buildings outside the region, Purbeck marble appears at Salisbury cathedral and in London and was used nationally for memorial stone, while Portland was the source of Wren's London churches as well as St Paul's.

Of these the Gloucestershire quarries have had, perhaps, the greatest landscape impact, for much of the westward-facing scarp edge has been quarried making this a linear landscape sculpture, unintended but nevertheless impressive as a whole, while others are much less noticeable and have now retreated back into their surroundings. Many of them are very old, such as the great quarries at Temple Guiting, Bath, Dundry, Ham Hill and Purbeck, which were first located and exploited by the Romans.

Bath stone can be taken as a case study to illustrate different uses of stone through time and to focus on how stone delivers identity. The Roman province of Britannia was one of the few areas in the Roman Empire where there was no tradition of building in stone. However, stone for buildings and portable objects was at the heart of the Roman self-image and thus, in a newly won province, of the business of creating identities – representing and marking out 'Romanitas', what being Roman meant and what distinguished Romans from others. Thus stone buildings (temples, palaces, baths, commemorative monuments) and portable stone objects (altars and tombstones) were of vital importance to the whole concept of Romanitas.

The Bath stone industry began early in the Roman period and served Bath and the villas and temples in its hinterland through the period. Masons were brought over from northern Gaul to construct the early buildings for the baths and it would seem likely that quarrymen were also brought over to seek out and exploit the stone sources. The Roman ideology needed quarries so that its ideas could be translated into stone. From the beginning Bath stone was transported great distances, with uses known in Colchester and in London (for tombstones) soon after the conquest, and later at Eccles, St Albans, Caerleon and Silchester.[1]

Without the need to express the essence of the Roman identity, building in stone lost its meaning and quarrying disappeared as an activity with the departure of the Romans. This was very much in contrast to what happened on the continent and meant that for several centuries buildings of importance were constructed of timber, as they had been in the Iron Age. It was only with the spread of Christianity that quarrying began again, and once more stone was used to put beliefs and ideas into physical form. Iconographic meaning was attached not only to church buildings but also to objects associated with the Christian liturgy, such as crosses, fonts and grave covers.

At the end of the 8th century freshly quarried Bath stone was found beyond Salisbury; later in the Anglo-Saxon period it was used in London, as it had been during the Roman occupation. At Winchester Old Minster a sculpted stone, the Sigurd Stone, came from Bath and was the only survival of a frieze depicting events from the Norse *Volsunga Saga*. Large stones, one at Braemore in Hampshire weighing half a tonne, indicate the availability of heavy wheeled transport. Local distributions in the Anglo-Saxon period are as far as Porlock to the west and Deerhurst to the north, stone arriving at both sites by water, while to the south and south-west no Bath stone is known south of Glastonbury.[2]

The Bath stone quarry at Hazelbury, just east of Box, supplied the stone for St Lawrence's church at Bradford-on-Avon in the late 10th or early 11th century. This material had been carefully selected and came from deep beds, evidence of an expertise which contrasts sharply with the story about how the stone for St Lawrence's was found. The account was first written down by John Aubrey, and tells that St Aldhelm, the church's dedicatee, was riding at Hazelbury when he threw down his glove and, telling his companions they would find great treasure there, ordered them to dig. Perhaps this story can be read not as marking the reintroduction of quarrying to the area, but as an origin myth for the building, one that is centred on natural resources and so links Christianity with pagan beliefs about Nature. As with the Romans, once again there is a link between building and identity.

In the medieval period products of the Bath stone quarries are found at many churches, monasteries and great houses in the area. But transporting the stone from the quarries was expensive; the cost of carriage to Marlborough in 1237 was more than seven times that of quarrying. When canal transport became available in the 18th century the industry expanded since its products at once became two to three times cheaper than those of its former competitor quarries at Chilmark and Tisbury. In addition, during the 18th century, the concept of stone as the benchmark of status became universal and increased demand forced producers to introduce new quarrying methods. The post-medieval Bath stone quarries were worked principally as mines rather than open quarries, with mines and tunnels recorded at Corsham in 1770. By the 19th century cavernous spaces were opened with the building stone lying beneath solid capping strata, and by the beginning of the 20th century there were 97km of tunnels and annual outputs of 85,000 cubic metres, with stone being carried to Canada and South Africa. There, the material was used for government buildings or banks, buildings once again expressive of empire and so a repetition of the Romans' ideological use of stone.

Fig. 8.1 Quarrying at Combe Down
shown in a print from 1798. Across the valley
is the eastern part of Bath with Camden
Crescent beneath Beacon Hill.

At Bath itself the Combe Down quarries were reactivated in the 18th century by the entrepreneur Ralph Allen (Fig. 8.1). The impetus for this was the completion of the work to make the Avon navigable in 1727, though Allen's hopes of exporting stone by sea were not realised. He bought an estate on Combe Down and invested in the latest handling machinery introduced from the north of England. In 1731 a 2km-long gravity tramway was in use from the quarries and stone was carried from the foot of the hill to boats at the Avon quays. The quarries were opened up underground from existing hillside quarries and were systematically worked to a preconceived plan using the pillar-and-stall method (quarrying around rock that has been left as a support), a procedure that had already been used in the region's mines. The façade of Allen's own town house, too, is an exuberant exhibition both of the skills of the masons and of the wealth and status of its owner.

The iconic status of modern Bath is based on its stone buildings. The colour of Bath stone makes the buildings homogeneous while the ability of the stone to take decoration allows it to carry architectural features easily and gracefully – for example, it is difficult to picture the 'ancient British' theme of John Wood's Circus, based on the circular Neolithic monuments at Avebury and Stonehenge, in, say, Radstock stone from only 10km away to the south. Bath stone has thus become an integral part of the identity of Bath, or, it seems, the identities of Bath since it can be shown that these have changed through time. In the last 40 years there has been a transformation in the attitudes of planners, from the requirement in the 1960s to rebuild the bomb-damaged city to suit the demands of a post-war community regardless of whether buildings were Georgian or not, to the recent desire to preserve Georgian terraces precisely because they *are* Georgian, the *raison d'être* for the city's designation as a World Heritage site. The image of Bath represented by its stone buildings has been argued to be rooted in a pre-industrial past peopled with a colourful cast of *ancien régime* characters. The modern inhabitants of Georgian buildings thus give themselves meaning through their stone dwellings.

The link between the buildings back through working processes to the quarries is best illustrated by stone working in the medieval period. In the quarry, stone was freed in blocks by cutting down vertically with axes and wedges. The blocks were then levered out with crowbars and shifted using ropes, cranes and winches.[3] Quarry workers were paid at the rate of unskilled labourers, with women, documented at one Devon quarry, paid at two-thirds that rate to cart the stone away. Recent re-excavation of one of the Purbeck quarries found a medieval seam that was less than a metre high, which means that the quarryman had to work on his side to get the stone out.[4] Carrying stone to the building site was expensive – for distances beyond 19km the cost of transporting stone outstripped the cost of quarrying it.[5] Water transport was used as far as possible, with Dundry stone, for example, carried to Wells via the port at Bristol and out into the Bristol Channel and then by river transport up to Coxley, a few kilometres south of Wells.

Masons and quarrymen were linked in that either the same person carried out both tasks or those who worked at quarries later graduated to being masons. Their tool kits were identical, and the mason's use of stone demonstrates knowledge of the material that could only come from quarry experience. Since building work was seasonal – mortar does not set during the winter – it is possible that masons were on site in the summer months and at the quarry in the winter. Some stone was roughly cut and then carried to workshops on site, but often the stone was worked at the quarry. This was the case with the Purbeck marble quarries near Corfe, where large architectural components have been found at the quarry known to have supplied Salisbury cathedral. From the 13th century smaller stone items such as fonts, altars and tombs were prepared in workshops staffed by Corfe stoneworkers in London and elsewhere.[6] At Wells cathedral, the new carvers taken on for the west front figures came from the Dundry stone workshops in Bristol.[7] Essentially schools of carving and stoneworking were quarry-based in the sense that the mason worked on stone from one quarry – the one, presumably, where he learnt his craft. In lists of town craftsmen masons are not common and there is little evidence of craft organisation, perhaps because stonemasonry was not an urban but a rural-based craft (Fig. 8.2).

The industry was hierarchical and progression may have been from rough mason through to stone carver or quarryman. At the west front of Wells cathedral, for example, the quatrefoils over the lowest-tier niches are occupied by demi-angels (quite a few recently replaced) that are not done to a model but are all wildly differing. One possible explanation is that these were test pieces to try out the skills of prospective carvers – an example of equality of opportunity. While some stonework shows this sort of individual approach, much was done to a formula. Ham Hill products were thoroughly standardised, judging from the drip moulds, windows and doors in local houses (Fig. 8.3). Nineteenth-century zinc templates

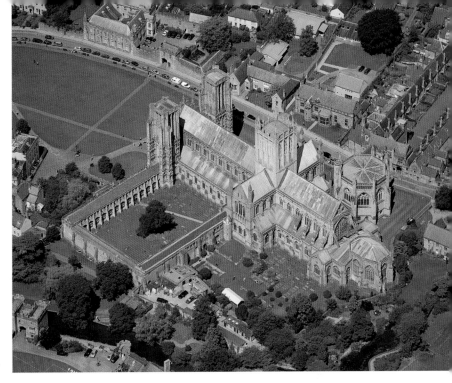

Fig. 8.2 Analysis of the stone sources used at Wells cathedral *has allowed different building campaigns and schools of stone-workers to be differentiated, as well as an unravelling of the sequence of building.*

Fig. 8.3 Quarry workers at Ham Hill quarry. *Its quarry products then were principally standardised mass-produced door and window mouldings in the buff-coloured iron-stained stone; earlier quarrying goes back to the Roman period.*

have been found at the quarry and earlier, less permanent ones must be assumed back into the medieval period. A similar standardisation of products can be seen in the Purbeck marble industry, where not just architectural features but also fonts, tombs and monumental brasses were mass produced. The products on offer were available according to a hierarchy of cost and this is reflected in the monuments and buildings themselves, which very subtly express the wealth of the owner by means of slight elaborations. The Purbeck marble process was dynamic. Changing tastes led to changing production patterns over a period that began in the 12th century, saw a flowering of the use of marble in the 13th and 14th centuries and ended at the turn of the 16th and 17th centuries. Documentary references occur then that show the industry was organised as a company, the 'Marblers and Stone Cutters of Purbeck'. To become a freeman of the company an apprenticeship of seven years was to be served followed by payment of 6s 8d, and presentation of a loaf of bread and two pots of beer. Wives of freemen could join and were able to continue the trade in the event of the death of their husbands.

The rise and decline of the Purbeck marble industry took place within a larger process – the rise and decline of stone building and of the kind of quarrying with which it was associated. Stone from the Portland quarries for instance appears in the 14th century in Exeter cathedral and the royal palace of Westminster, but it came to its greatest prominence in the 17th and early 18th centuries, when Inigo Jones used it for the Whitehall Banqueting House and Wren for St Paul's and the post-fire London churches. As at Purbeck the traditions of quarry use showed a liberal autonomy, with the right to work the quarries restricted to those who were 'free of the island', irrespective of gender. An account in 1635 says there were 'about 200 workmen, some hewing out of the cliffe aloft, some squareing, some carryeing down, others ladeing'. This was for work on old St Paul's. In 1678, when stone was being quarried for new St Paul's, the islanders felt they had been cheated out of their customary right to an ancient levy and in protest vandalised the infrastructure of transport to the ships so that pieces of the carts were found 'above a mile distance one from ye other'. In the end the islanders won. Like other quarries in the West, Portland benefited from the 18th-century fashion-driven popularity of stone (Fig. 8.4). Morton Pitt at Kingston Maurward in Dorset encased his beautiful brick house in Portland stone because George III, having been shown round it, said gloomily 'Brick, Mr Pitt, brick'.[8] In 1812, 800 men and boys, 180 horses and 50 ships were engaged in the stone trade – this was out of a total local population of 2,000 and must have included workers from elsewhere. However, between 1847 and 1862, labour for both the stone quarrying and the construction of the great naval harbour breakwater at Portland was provided by convicts from the prison specially established for the purpose.

Fig. 8.4 Stone quarries on the Isle of Portland with early workings on the cliff side. *Quarrying began on a large scale in the 17th century with export by sea to London for old and new St Paul's, and later to the continent and America. The working methods and ownership of quarrying rights were unique to the island and continued unchanged for centuries.*

Elsewhere, too, quarry methods changed from the careful use of stone for different purposes, to processes such as that at Lyme Regis at the beginning of the 20th century, when rock on the cliff face west of the town was simply dynamited and then dumped in the sea, before being shipped off to be made into cement. Further along the Dorset coast, the Charmouth Cement Mill was beset by labour troubles in the late 19th century and only functioned for 17 years. Here there is a rare mention of women, with two employed to carry stone to the mill and carry the cement away (at 3d per 40lb basket). Changes in demand meant that the industry had to adapt its products. At Box and Tisbury, for example, production in the 20th century changed from the manufacture of decorative church fittings to that of garden ornaments.[9]

In the Anglo-Saxon and medieval periods quarries serviced particular structures and were often owned by the great religious houses or leased out to them over long periods of time. In the late medieval period quarries increasingly began to be run for profit, and this became the normal practice apart from the great public rebuilding projects, such as at London after the fire. A local parish quarry might be opened up simply when stone was required, but increasingly quarries serviced road, canal and sea-port constructions, or supplied limekilns. Gradually the use of stone has become more mundane and less specialised. As well as the change in methods and demand, the quarrying discussed here also differs from its modern counterpart in its scale (Fig. 8.5). The gigantism of modern quarries cannot be fully appreciated on the ground since they are now

Fig. 8.5 Whatley Quarry on Mendip.
Hard limestone from Mendip quarries is used as aggregate by the construction industry. It is cheap because it is easy to quarry and near the markets of the south-east, and also because amenity loss has not been a charge to the quarry companies.

hidden behind giant bunds, and the Mendip roadstone trains and the convoys of Dorset Heath, Quantock Hills, and Gloucestershire Vale lorries soon merge with other forms of transport. From the air the change in scale is obvious. The modern quarry exists in a work environment worlds apart from that of its predecessors.[10] It is impossible to imagine these modern quarries marking their own end with the pillar of stone, known as the Devil's chimney, playfully left by quarrymen at Leckhampton when they shifted to a new quarry in around 1800.

Old quarries are a source of great interest in the modern landscape. Few are registered on databases and hardly any have been examined or excavated, but many can be picked out on Ordnance Survey maps. They can be predicted alongside the newer 19th-century roads as the latter climb out of the valleys, or along major rivers or the sea coast. On scarp edges they can often be missed because they represent absence but the tracks leading away from the faces can still be found, and in places earlier features simply disappear at what seems to be a natural edge. Stone from the quarry faces can be matched with that from local stone structures and so the link reforged between old-fashioned quarrying and building in stone, two processes now more or less dead.

LEAD MINING

The Mendip Hills plateau, the focus of lead mining in the West, has been rendered more orderly by enclosure in the 18th and 19th centuries – later than in other areas – and this disguises what must have been a much wilder place when it was open country. Once the plateau edge with its views has been left behind the rather featureless horizon closes in making it a landscape sharply different to those to north and south. Though pock-marked with swallets (water-eroded swallow holes), the surface of Mendip gives no real inkling of its nether world of caves and underground rivers. The pattern of land use in the western half of the hills – the location of lead mining – was that settlements at the foot of the hills to north and south each exploited a portion of the plateau as well as the hillslopes and the rich land on the lower ground. This is attested in the medieval period by the layout of the parish boundaries, each of which takes a portion of the hilltop and contains a settlement at the foot of the hillslope, but this apportionment of different resources is prehistoric in origin. In the medieval period, the break between hillslope and the plateau would have been sharply marked by a physical boundary between the managed environment below and the open plateau above, where stock grazing was the main use with the presence of lead- (and hence silver-) yielding rocks less important but nevertheless a competitor.

The physical evidence of mining takes the form of long, parallel, half-backfilled trenches and rough pitting. In places, at Charterhouse for instance, what appears to be the natural ground is instead the surface of mining spoil so that what were once valleys have been turned into hills (Fig. 8.6). The surface evidence of mining comes principally from the Roman period and from the

Fig. 8.6 This lead-mining landscape at Charterhouse-on-Mendip is a product of workings since at least the late Iron Age. In the centre of the picture is a two-phase Roman military depot dated AD 50–70 with later Roman settlement in the fields on the far side of the road. Reworking of earlier spoil took place in the 19th century resulting in most of the dumps in the valley. A miners' chapel with an Arts and Crafts interior is to the far left of the photograph.

last few centuries. The existence of a Roman road running directly from Silchester to the Mendip Hills gives the key to the Roman activity here, for the promise of silver was one of the reasons for the occupation of the province and so a road was driven through immediately after the conquest. At Charterhouse on Mendip a fort of the Second Legion, attested here by stamps on lead pigs, can still be seen and is dated by 1st-century pottery from its ditches. Once they had built the road and opened up the mines, the soldiers would have been replaced by civilians exploiting the mines as an imperial concern with slave labour. A small town was established with an amphitheatre near by, and the presence of deep stone drains suggests that there was a bath-house. Lead pigs, lead weights and brooches were found there in the late 19th-century, turned up by fresh workings. To the south of the fort, Roman trenching has been recognised and excavations here suggest that these were preceded by Iron Age mining. Roman buildings, possibly the headquarters of the official procurator, are known at St Cuthbert's, where there was one of the few water supplies on Mendip. Since water was vital to working lead ore this was presumably where smelting took place.[11]

The later evidence, from the late 19th century, is more tangible. Earlier spoil was then re-smelted and the brick structures and furnace chimneys involved survive at Charterhouse, St Cuthbert's and at Harptree. In addition to the buildings there are long, horizontally laid flues at Charterhouse, which ran from the smelting furnaces and were intended to collect the metal from the furnace vapour. At the very end of the life of the mines there was considerable investment in new machinery, including the construction of a plant to extract silver at Charterhouse and new smelting works at St Cuthbert's.[12]

The medieval written evidence records grants to religious houses and to the church of mining rights – the first a grant to Bishop Reginald of Bath by Richard I in 1189. The foundation charter of the Carthusian monastery at Witham in 1181/2 granted land on Mendip to the monks, hence the name Charterhouse on Mendip, but not until 1293 does mining appear as one of the monks' activities. In that year they were granted leave to work the lead mines there, presumably some time after they were already doing so. Much of the plateau top was the property of either the Bishop of Bath and Wells or of Glastonbury Abbey.[13]

Mining courts, unique to the Mendips, dispensed an additional justice to the legal system. The basic document outlining the 'Old ancient custom of the occupation of the mineries' on Mendip dates to 1554 and includes material from diverse sources. Some of the codes embodied miners' rights and customary ways of managing differences by the local communities, others codified the right of the lord to a tenth of each miner's profit, a right that was first recorded for the crown in 1292, and the duty of the miner to work his ore at one of four mineries.

To win the ore miners first located surface veins of galena (lead ore) by trenching, supported by a process of dowsing with a divining rod, which had been introduced from Germany during the Elizabethan period. These veins were then followed either in long trenches or in a series of pits. Fires were lit to break up any rock strata blocking the ore veins. A reference to a framework of timber suggests that winding machinery was used. At depth, water began to fill the workings and this was bailed out by buckets until such time as the mine was abandoned. Once brought to the surface, the ore was broken up with a hammer and then washed in buddles or troughs. Women, from parallels elsewhere, may have undertaken this task. After cleaning, the ore was smelted in furnaces ranging in sophistication from simple hearths relying on the strength of the wind, a method used in prehistory and known ethnographically, to more elaborate structures using bellows to create an artificial blast. An elaboration of the earlier hearths was to turn them to follow changes in the direction of the wind. Methods changed very little over time. From the 17th century, gunpowder rather than firing was used to break open non-ore-bearing rocks, but methods of draining the workings were slow to change, and the shift from hand lifting to the use of engines came about only very gradually. Changes to the furnaces, too, were apparently minimal until the 19th century, when the reworking of earlier spoil necessitated modifications.

After smelting the purified lead was cast into pigs of lead. Apart from sheets used for roofing, lead was used by the medieval building industry for clamping iron fittings into stone and for window cames (the metal strips in leaded lights). Other uses were for coffins – used for special burials by the Romans – church fitments such as fonts, and for personal items such as weights, badges and pen nibs. Lead was also used to produce pottery glazes and paint pigments.[14] Winning silver involved further heating of the ore to a temperature at which the lead oxidised to litharge, which then sank into the hearth material leaving silver behind.

Lead from Mendip was not of as good quality as that from other areas in England. In the 16th century it was said to be inferior to Derbyshire lead and mostly used for export, and for bullets and shot – 'May foreigners enjoy wild lead [the Mendip kind] to kill men' said Fuller in 1662 in his *Worthies*. For the Romans the province supplied a great deal of their lead requirements, from other sources as well as the Mendips, and Pliny records that output had to be controlled to maintain the price. Neither in the Roman nor in the medieval period is there evidence of a successful silver output. Fluctuations in the price of lead were common in recent centuries and changes in world prices finished the industry off in the early 20th century. Essentially lead was used because it was cheap, so trying to make a profit from it was not easy.

The actual mining process itself was not organised but was done by one or two men. Judging by the similarity between the known Iron Age and Roman trenching and the trenches of later periods, winning the material would have involved individual workings, even with the use of slave labour in the Roman period. Fitting the activity into the evidence for other uses of the plateau it must be suspected that mining was a seasonal activity interlocking with low labour demands in the farming year. Through the medieval period this may have changed and that there were full-time miners is suggested by the fact that they were liable to be sent to work in other mines if so demanded by the Crown.

The miner might dig anywhere outside churchyards, gardens and roads, but he had to demonstrate his right to a particular spot by standing in a pit up to waist level and claiming the area within throwing reach of his 'hack' – a pick weighing 3lb 14oz (1.8kg). He also had to have erected a wooden structure to mark his claim. Any miners falling foul of the community were liable to be banished from the hill and all their mining equipment destroyed. This 'burning from the hill' anciently involved the burning of the miscreant himself, who was locked in his hut with his tools. In Derbyshire an equally savage custom is recorded whereby a miner who stole other miner's ore more than three times would have his hand pinned by a knife to his windlass. The mining community also had duties with regard to the miners. They were to be dug out and given burial in the event of rock falls, drowning or stifling by fire. While mining may have been an individual or one partner activity, smelting the ore would have involved larger numbers at the mineries. At Bere Alston in Devon, in 1335, there was an overseer, a boler with assistants, a furnaceman with blowers, two men concerned with providing timber, a smith and a chandler (the latter making candles to be used underground).

The Dissolution of the monasteries introduced new landowners and new land uses on the plateau. The post-medieval mining world seems to have been a much harsher one than in the medieval period, with mining coming increasingly to resemble the 19th- and 20th-century experience in the Americas.[15] Individual pitches were so close that one miner's shaft might break into another, inevitably resulting in disputes. There were cases of gangs carrying off ore by violence and miners being driven off by claimants to the land with drawn swords. Confrontation was exacerbated by drink from the notorious Mendip alehouses. There was added pressure in agricultural downturns when agricultural labourers also sought a living from mining.

Given this background, it is hardly surprising that scientific enquiry into mining, as for instance that by John Locke in 1666, was resisted by the miners, although it is hard to see any changes of methods that might have made the industry more profitable. In the history of lead mining on Mendip there was much talk of wealth. In 1314 a lead reeve wrote to the Bishop of Bath and Wells of a 'splendid mine of lead' with 'a great deal of silver in the lead' about 2m below the ground. Later a Galias de Lune was licensed to dig for gold in Somerset in 1462 and this may have been on Mendip. In the 16th century Bevis Bulmer gained the support of the Crown and the Privy Council but had to abandon his attempts to drain abandoned workings. He was followed by the engineer Thomas Bushell who promised Cromwell 'such store of treasure as to maintain a mint in your city of Wells' and who proposed to bring in galena from as far as Ireland via the port at Uphill to be smelted in a new system bringing 'inestimable riches'. In the end his works were described as 'very costly and expensive' as well as 'ineffectual and unprofitable'. Other optimists included John Billingsley, who in 1794 proposed to cut a tunnel from Compton Martin to Wookey Hole that would drain all the plateau workings, giving a possible yield of £100,000 an acre, and a Horatio Hornblower whose prospectus in 1862 suggested that half a million pounds (23 tonnes) of lead could easily be recovered from spoil on the surface. Another prospectus in 1870 promised profits that were 'not a speculation or theoretic calculation but one of practical results', but this was based on a high in world lead prices that fell soon after.[16]

COAL MINING

Now abandoned and shut off, the Somerset coal mines, the focus of this section, were formerly peopled by men with their own language – of guggs, toppos, dipples, twinways and hudges – to describe their work methods. Over the long period of coal mining in Somerset, continuously from the medieval period until 1973, changes took place in lifting machinery, pumps, and the transportation of coal but very little changed underground. Focusing on change tends to miss the essence of industrial work – that its repetitive nature creates routines. Unchanging work practices become more fixed the more the work is demanding and the erratically lying Somerset coal seams made mining extremely difficult. The seams were rarely level and were invariably shallow – usually about 0.6m high – and the hand-mining methods established early on remained unchanged until almost the end of the life of the mines.

Solinus, writing in the 3rd century AD, described the 'stony balls' left as ashes by the sacred fire at the temple of Minerva in Bath, and this coal may have been located in surface drifts at Stratton on the line of the Fosse Way (Fig. 8.7). The first records, from the late medieval period, come from

*Fig. 8.7 **In the Nettlebridge valley, west of Stratton Common**, coal veins outcrop or are just below the surface. This landscape comprises ploughed-down surface spoil heaps and later bell pits and shafts dating back 600 years or more. The Roman Fosse Way crosses the valley at the top of the picture and coal from here may have been used in the temple at Bath.*

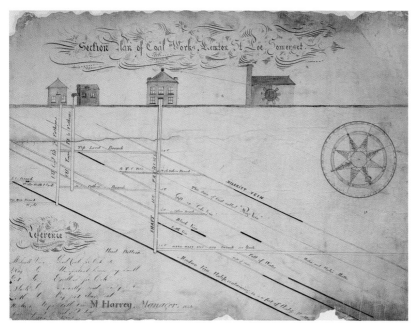

Stratton, and mining seems likely to have begun as opencast quarrying before being extracted from bell pits – open shafts cut down to the seam and then hollowed out till they were too dangerous to work further. From here the next step was to mining proper.[17]

Workings in the 17th and 18th centuries were by a small number of men. At Clutton in 1610 there were two or three men underground with four or five boys for carting, and at the end of the 17th century 88 men and boys at the five Kilmersdon pits. The average early 19th-century pit employed between 100 and 150 employees all told, and for this period a typical way of working underground can be described that differed only in scale from that of previous centuries (Fig. 8.8). To enter the mines each

ABOVE: *Fig. 8.8 A section through the coal veins at an otherwise unknown colliery at Newton St Loe from a coloured drawing of 1844. It is notable that the buildings over the shafts are disguised as neo-Georgian domestic non-industrial structures.*

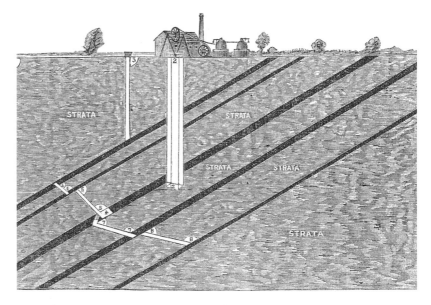

Fig. 8.9 Sketch drawings from a book of 1884 showing the basic, hardly mechanised methods used by the colliery boys to raise and lower coal loads on the subterranean inclines (From Five years of colliery life *by J Presto, 1884).*

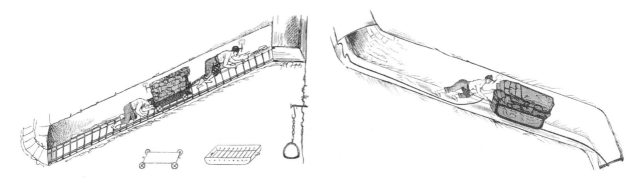

man, at the top of the shaft, sat with a boy on his lap in a rope loop attached to a chain at the end of the main winding rope. The pair were then lowered out of sight and then the next pair attached, until a team of a dozen or so had been lowered to the shaft foot, the men holding the rope with one hand and fending themselves off the wall of the shaft with the other. At the shaft foot was a wider area where further sloping shafts led down and away. These would in turn run into roads, which were more level, and from these further cuts were made on either side on an up or down gradient as the coal seams were followed. Two men would work at a face – hardly ever standing since the seams were so thin – and often having to kick the coal out from under them with their feet. Two boys, barefoot to give themselves a grip and wearing hats as protection from rock falls, then hauled or lowered the coal on wooden sleds up or down to the main road. When hauling the boy in front crawled with a rope round his middle and a hook running between his legs to attach to the sled, the one behind pushing with his head (Fig. 8.9). On the main road the coal was transferred to wagons and drawn by ponies back to the main shaft and then lifted in tubs to the surface. Elaborate tally systems were used, such as each coal-face miner sending one of his personal tallies to the top, or chalking an identification picture on the tub (banjo, cartwheel, gateway, circle and dot, square and dot and cockspur are recorded). The miner's shift was completed once a certain number of tubs, varying according to the width of the coal seam, had been lifted. A typical shift in the early 19th century lasted from 6am to 3.30pm.

Originally, mining would have been an additional occupation to agricultural work for almost all involved and throughout there was a close two-way connection between the two sources of employment. When pits were exhausted or closed because of some mishap, miners had agricultural work to turn to and they were often taken on at harvest time when summer-time coal output was low. Equally, whenever agricultural work was depressed, and as the cloth-making industry declined during the early 19th century, the coal-mining workforce expanded. Yet many must have become miners early and remained so all their lives (Fig. 8.10). The numbers of children employed were considerable – the Child Employment Commission report of 1842 recorded 20 of the 100 employed at Coal Barton near Coleford as under 10 years old, and 50 under the age of 18 – and the mine workings were thus a technical training ground for future faceworkers.

Fig. 8.10 This torn and creased image of a below-ground break at Coleford pit, c. 1933, lacks any explanation of what occasioned the photograph, why the woman was there, or hers and the miners' names.

Fig. 8.11 Camerton New Pit viewed from the top of its 20th-century spoil tip, with the Somerset Coal Canal and the railway to the left. The 19th-centry spoil mounds are beyond the pithead in the middle distance. At 554m, this was one of the deepest shafts in the Somerset coalfields.

There were many complaints about thefts and burglaries set at the door of miners as well as accusations of drunkenness. However, the geological pioneer William Smith, who prospected the Somerset Coal Canal and recorded working conditions as well as the geology of the mines, thought the miners civil and communicative with some exceptionally well informed about the geological strata (Fig. 8.11). There were certainly strikes and violent protests especially in the 18th and early 19th centuries, some ending in bloodshed. Others were settled amicably, as with the group of 4,000 strikers in 1792 who 'dispersed quietly and all returned to work' after a lecture and promises from the High Sheriff of the county. In the 20th century at Dunkerton pit, a strike started by the carting boys led to a confrontation outside the owner's house, during which the owner's son fired on and wounded a number of the protestors.[18] During the General Strike of 1926 Somerset miners stayed out, but confrontation was uncommon. A touching photograph on the cover of a book of one miner's memoirs shows two miners stripped to the waist kneeling in a narrow seam in silence at the funeral of George VI.[19]

Emerging above ground the miner daily returned to a landscape in which nucleated villages clustered around the church and the squire's house. Unlike the Mendips the ground above the mines was privately owned, enclosed land dominated by the estates and large houses of a handful of wealthy landowners, following a pattern perhaps originating in the villa estates known here from the Roman period. In the early centuries of mining some landowners personally opened up mines on their land and were later involved in working partnerships. Others opened mines on common land and then ran their shafts out under private land, provoking angry disagreements with landowners. One landowner married the daughter of an opposing landowner seemingly in order to gain access to his land. Often, the upper levels of the mines were rapidly and irresponsibly exploited, making access to lower levels impossible. Here, for instance, the pillar-and-stall method was used but in such a way as to make any further work too dangerous. Not knowing where previous works lay could have terrible consequences, as when seven miners and four boys died when they broke through to flooded workings in February 1845. Where tunnel roofs were held up on undug sections of the mine, there was always the temptation for the unscrupulous to over-excavate the tunnel sides, eventually eroding the support so that the roof collapsed. Ventilating and draining the pits, and raising men and coal, were all procedures that tended to retain old methods and to resist modern techniques.

Direct involvement by the landowners had declined by the 19th century though the same families still dominated mining. While they provided investment, their managers can be seen reinventing themselves as small squires as James MacMurtrie did at Radstock. The layout of the pithead buildings and the position, often overlooking the works, of the manager's house, suggests that the buildings were intended to underscore power relations at the mines. The positioning of the manager's tennis court on the levelled spoil tip at Upper Writhlington in the 20th century may be a more subtle repetition of this emphasis. The provision of miners' housing by the mine owner can also be interpreted as expressing more than a social concern for the well-being of employees. Among buildings intended to blend in with the countryside were engine-house chimneys that were disguised as towers by folly-like decoration at Upper and Lower Conygyre collieries (Fig. 8.12), and miner's cottages at the entrance to Braysdown colliery that had crenellated towers. Terraces of miners' houses at Radstock provided by the Waldegraves were not intervisible with the historic village and the slightly larger houses at the end of each terrace, which housed colliery officials, marked the work hierarchy in stone (Fig. 8.13).[20]

Coal from the Somerset fields was of different qualities and served different functions. Certain seams were good for house coal and this was supplied to the east of the coalfields to Bath and Frome and their hinterlands. Much of the poorer

Fig. 8.12 The inclined plane at Lower Conygyre colliery photographed c. 1907. The boiler chimney could be seen from Timsbury Manor and so was built as a castellated folly.

Fig. 8.13 Lower Writhlington colliery
Fig. 8.13 Lower Writhlington colliery
was worked from 1829 to 1973 when it was
the last to close. The winding ropes from the
engine houses on the left crossed the highway to
the heapstead or building at the shaft head on
the right.

quality coal was used to fire limekilns. Other uses were for the ironworking industry, first noted in Tudor times, for lead-mining machinery, and for gas lighting in the 1820s in Bath and in neighbouring towns thereafter; coke in particular was used by brewers for drying malt. While the greatest impact on the landscape of mining was the growth of Radstock and of Midsomer Norton (Fig. 8.14), and so the imposition of two small towns into the medieval landscape, a second, rather different impact, came from the methods of transporting coal from the pithead to the consumers. Over the early centuries coal was shifted by wagons or by packhorses, and of this little physical evidence specific to the mines remains. But with the Somerset Coal Canal, originally two canals, and their succeeding rail lines, the impact is marked.[21] The northern canal, running down the valley of the Cam brook, was completed, used and gave great profits. The southern length, running along the Wellow valley, failed and the towpath was converted into a tramway. Both were then reused as the line of railways. The connecting inclines and roads to the canal, and the coal branch-lines to the collieries can all be traced, principally on maps but also on the ground.

This picture of mining in our region has left out iron mining, zinc mining and calamine mining, nor has it included the Bristol coalfields. Adding these to the story would alter the basic picture little. Mining was a local activity, initially undertaken by individual workers who later became more or less organised, depending on the industry. Labour skills were self taught rather than the result of outside contacts. The workers were neither separated from the community nor self-consciously a class apart. The enterprises were undercapitalised and run on conservative lines. The landowners, often continuing families, are of greater importance than the occasional entrepreneurial figures who appeared like Bushell on Mendip or Smith in the coalfields. Those latter who succeeded tended, like McMurtrie, to camouflage their origins and merge into the squirearchy. The various mines remained as small concerns and were never, except for the Somerset Coalfield in the period 1947–73, subjected to overall planning and large-scale organisation.

OPPOSITE PAGE:

Fig. 8.14 The Old Mills and Springfield
collieries' spoil tip at Midsomer
Norton was one of the few coal-mining
features deliberately retained after the
National Coal Board ceased production in the
Somerset coalfields in 1973, just before the
modern interest in heritage would have made
the wholesale clearances scandalous.

The traditional interpretation has been to place the mining industries of our area and the West in general in a backwater away from the mainstream industrial areas. By one of those quirks of historiography the traditional views underpinning interpretations of the Industrial Revolution have been overturned in recent years.[22] This revisiting of the British Industrial Revolution by economic historians might instead see the Somerset mines as the type-site of British industrialisation. For this is now seen as occurring within a continuing *ancien régime* with traditional landowners maintaining and not ceding power to any new bourgeois entrepreneurial class, and with industrialisation itself occurring in a context of under-investment and *ad hoc* solutions to technical problems, where the short-term search for profits dominated enterprises, and where advancement of the working class through education or insurance provisions was viewed in terms of social control. The working class itself remained disunited and kept a strong residual loyalty to authority. In this new picture of Britain the industries of our region can be seen as the exemplars.

The new analysis of the Industrial Revolution has come about in an attempt to explain the sluggishness of the British economy and the continuing and vexing problem of its low productivity. The argument is therefore part of a contemporary debate – one that is posited on the assumption that Britain's failure to develop is a bad thing. Archaeological findings are not so driven and it is not necessary to follow the line of thinking that makes investment and the spread of technical ideas necessarily a good. There are no axes to be ground in emphasising again and again how little rapid change there has been, and how deep in the past the roots of activities lie. The theme of this chapter has been the relationship between geology and people and the conclusion must be that it is the effect of geology on people that is important rather than vice versa.

NOTES

1   For Roman exploitation of quarries in the province *see* Parsons 1990, 33–50.

2   For Anglo-Saxon stone quarries *see* Jope 1964; Blair & Ramsay 1991, 1–27; and Tatton-Brown 1998, 27–32. The latter also describes the Sigurd Stone.

3   For quarries *see* Muir 1986, chapter 9; Salzman 1913, 82–3; 1952, 124–6; Parsons 1990, 1–15.

4   *See* Tatton-Brown 1998, 52.

5   Calculation in Salzman 1952, 119.

6   Blair & Ramsay 1991, 41–56.

7   For Wells cathedral *see* Sampson 1998.

8   George III's views on brick are from Clifton-Taylor 1972, 37.

9   For ornaments from Tisbury *see* Tatton-Brown 1998, 55–8.

10 For modern limestone quarrying on Mendip *see* Stanton 1994.

11 For the Roman town *see* Burnham & Wacher 1990, 208–11.

12 Gough 1967, 186–202 describes the last phases in detail.

13 For Mendip lead mining *see* Gough 1967; Salzman 1913, 38–61

14 *See* Blair & Ramsay 1991, 64–6.

15 For instance *The Treasure of the Sierra Madre* by B Traven.

16 Gough 1967.

17 For early coalmining *see* Salzman 1913, 1, 7. The two articles by Bulley, 1952 and 1953, and Down & Warrington 1972 are the main sources for the Somerset coalfield.

18 Down & Warrington 1972, 121–4.

19 The memoirs are by Fred Flower (1990).

20 This paragraph is taken from Gould 1999.

21 Described by Clew 1970.

22 The revisionist interpretation was first summarised by Cannadine 1984.

9

Looking Outwards

BARRY CUNLIFFE

Our area is unique among the English regions for having two quite different maritime interfaces: one, Severn-side, looking westwards, washed by a sluggish sea depositing sediments to create vast expanses of marsh and fen; the other, Channel-side, looking southwards along the Atlantic face of Europe, where the driven sea erodes the land to create cliffs and constantly shifts and sorts the pebble beaches at their foot. This broad generalisation does not, of course, take account of the many different microenvironments – headlands protecting embayments, fast-flowing rivers scouring out valleys and so on – which have provided opportunities for the people of the coast-lands to establish ports and harbours in their struggle to use the sea to communicate with other worlds and as a rich resource in its own right. So it was that from prehistoric times onwards, the communities clinging to these very special ecological niches articulated the interchange between the varied landscapes of the West of England and the lands beyond the oceans.

In a memorable text the great French historian, Ferdinand Braudel, writing of the Mediterranean, refers to 'those imbalances productive of change,' which, he says, would 'set the rhythm of its entire life'. In these few words he has encapsulated a universal truth – in our desire to redistribute the resources spread unevenly about the face of the earth lies one of the prime causes of the changes reverberating through human society. The sailors of Lyme or Bridport and the ferrymen of Pill were agents for change, and to help them in their task they sculpted the edge of the land creating wharves, jetties and embracing harbour-works, and of course building the ships that made the all-consuming redistribution possible.

Redistribution is a balancing activity. For all the commodities brought into the country equivalents have to be generated for export. These could be raw materials or, better still, manufactured goods with value added. Thus in the 19th century clay for pottery-making left Poole Harbour and ironstone was shipped out from Hengistbury Head. Earlier, high-quality textiles crafted from Cotswold wool were stockpiled in the warehouses of Bristol while the rope-walks of Bridport were busy turning Dorset hemp into much sought-after ships' cables. It was the productivity of our region in the hinterland of its ports that provided the impetus for trade fuelling the ambitions of entrepreneurs, from the ships' masters plying their own small vessels to the august companies of Merchant Venturers who grew rich on commerce, investing their wealth in fine town houses and country estates. The dynamic cycle of productivity–redistribution–profit–reinvestment drove the technology of communications – shipbuilding, harbour construction, roads, canals and railways – and sculpted the landscape, leaving the indelible marks that give our region its infinite variety. The canvas is broad – in this chapter all we can do is to sketch in the outline of that edge between land and sea and add some colour.

BETWEEN LAND AND SEA

The Bristol Channel and the Severn Estuary is a remarkable waterway, unparalleled in Britain – a gradually narrowing arm of the sea thrusting deep into the soft underbelly of England. Of even width at its western extremity it begins to narrow, gradually at first and then, past its confluence with the Usk and Avon, rapidly up to Gloucester where, though still navigable, it becomes little more than a Midlands river. The effect on the incoming tide is to constrict the water into a surge creating massive tidal ranges of 10m to 14m. The rising or ebbing tide could greatly speed a ship homewards or abroad. But there were added advantages. Such was the intensity of the flow that the main channel was constantly scoured creating a safe passage while the tributary rivers benefited in a similar way, at low tide the flow of fresh water carrying sediment far out into the main channel and away. On the rise, as the tide flowed back up the rivers, easily navigable waterways were created allowing vessels to sail far inland to convenient bridging points such as Bristol on the Avon and Bridgwater on the Parrett, where ports could develop to facilitate the transshipment of goods from ocean-going ships to river barges, road transport and, later, the railways.

Fig. 9.1 The Chesil Beach, looking westwards from above Portland, is built by the process of longshore drift driving pebbles steadily eastwards. Between the beach and the indented land lie the placid waters of the Fleet.

River ports such as these were particularly favoured, but otherwise much of upper Severn-side presented the uncongenial face of sandbanks backed by marshland. Indeed, from Gloucester to the Quantocks the sea rarely came into contact with solid rock. Aust cliff, where the first Severn bridge crossed, the Portishead–Clevedon ridge and the isolated rocky promontories, once islands, of Middlehope, Worlebury Hill and Brean Down are lonely outliers of hard ground in a great flatness of treacherous marsh. Little harbours like Clevedon and Weston-super-Mare developed but they were never of commercial importance and even the Victorian fascination with sea-bathing provided them only a brief respite.

Westwards from the muddy estuary of the Parrett more solid geology confronts the sea in a series of cliffs and steep descents fringing the uplands of the Quantock Hills and Exmoor. Here there are no wide rivers to provide convenient niches for ports, and such small harbours as there are – places such as Watchet and Minehead – cling uncomfortably to the edge of the land, confronting the sea with man-made harbour-works.

The southern, Channel-facing, edge of our region is altogether different. Here the predominant force is the unconstrained ocean beating hard against the land, eroding it back, creating steep cliffs, while the waves and the currents, driving inexorably from west to east, carry the detached debris with them, depositing it in high beaches of shingle and cobbles. Between the estuary of the Exe and the western entrance to the Solent the physical evidence of these two processes is vivid. On the western side of the great sweep of Lyme Bay the coast is dominated by cliffs – the red sandstones of Sidmouth, the sombre slumping Liassic beds around Lyme and the golden oolitic limestones of the Bridport coast – all subject to constant pounding as the Channel currents sweep north-eastwards. Beyond the mouth of the Brit the scene changes. The ancient cliff line from Abbotsbury eastwards has mellowed behind the protective barrier of the remarkable Chesil Beach, a massive storm beach of cobbles gently curving 23km out from the mainland before coming to rest on the north-west corner of the Isle of Portland (Fig. 9.1).

Lyme Bay offers little help to the maritime community. At Lyme itself an artificial breakwater, the Cobb, was needed to provide a haven for ships, while further east at the mouth of the Brit, successive communities have laboured desperately to keep the small harbour clear of silt and shingle. Beyond, Chesil Beach effectively sealed off access between land and sea, and the sluggish backwater behind it, the Fleet, had no attraction for mariners.

Once around Portland Bill the processes of erosion and deposition are again visibly at work. Immediately in the lee of Portland the sea has bitten a great semicircle from the land which, when completed with breakwaters built between 1849 and 1903, became Portland Harbour, thereafter home to the British Navy (Fig. 9.2).

Immediately to the north, longshore drift built a storm beach fringing Weymouth, from Nothe Point to Redcliff Point and broken at only one place where the River Wey cuts through to the sea. The benign geomorphology here provides an ideal setting for a harbour with a well-protected backwater linked to the sea by a deeply scoured channel. All the sediment brought down is swept away by the sea. Here the harbour towns of Weymouth and Melcombe Regis confronted each other across the river mouth.

Fig. 9.2 The Isle of Portland joined to the mainland by Chesil Beach, *the two protecting the naval harbour of Portland. The Isle of Portland was, and still is, the source of a fine limestone much used in monumental buildings. The quarries scar the northern part of the island.*

155

East from Weymouth, the sea is once more in an erosive mode sculpting the spectacular cliff scenery of Purbeck to feed the Victorian love of the picturesque with such wonders as Durdle Dore, Worbarrow Bay and Lulworth Cove. Dramatic though the landscape is, it is bereft of good anchorages until the projecting promontory of Purbeck is turned. Rounding the towering chalk crag of Old Harry the calm of Poole Bay, and beyond it Christchurch Bay, is reached, soft sands and clays having been eroded into gentle sweeps with naturally replenished shingle beaches offering reasonable protection to the low cliffs behind.

Along this stretch, apart from the sea, the major formative influence has been the great volume of water flowing off the chalklands of Wessex. The flow from the Frome and Piddle creates the ragged estuary of Poole Harbour, while the Stour and the Avon empty their flood into Christchurch Harbour. At both, the outlet to the sea is conditioned by the fine balance between the outflow of fresh water and longshore drift drawing gravel across the estuary mouth. At Poole the entrance is wide and comparatively easy to navigate, while the protected harbour behind is extensive with ample deep water. It clearly has distinct advantages over Christchurch Harbour where the water is shallower and the entrance much narrower, and there is a fierce race to contend with. It is factors such as these that favoured Poole, so that here the major medieval port developed.

The two maritime faces of our region were moulded in strikingly different ways by the action of the sea, but each provided opportunities for coastal communities in their quest to interact with the open sea. Each harbour had distinct potential and limitations. As time passed, the individual ports forged their own histories, which in the following pages we will explore.

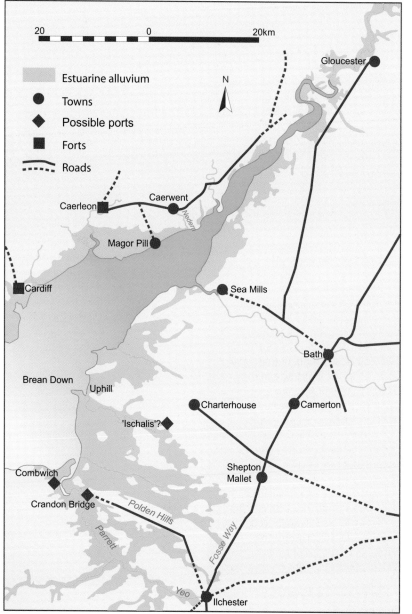

Fig. 9.3 Roman roads, settlements and ports in Somerset and Gloucestershire flanking the Severn Estuary.

BRISTOL AND THE BRISTOL AVON

The medieval town and port of Bristol could by about 1500 be numbered among the three most important cities in Britain next to London and York.[1] Its position, 11km up-river from the shores of the Bristol Channel near the confluence of the Frome and the Avon, gave it a number of advantages. It was also close to the lowest point where the Avon at that time could be bridged, as its name makes clear – it was 'Bricgstow' (the settlement by the bridge). To make the long haul up-river vessels had to pass through the Avon

Gorge, which provided a considerable degree of protection from prevailing south-westerly winds, while the unusually steep tidal range (a massive 7m at the Town Quay) could be used to good effect to flush a vessel up to the port on a rising tide or back out to sea on the ebb. But such a range also created a ferocious current, which required precise timing and a high degree of seamanship if a vessel navigating the sinuous bends in the river was not to turn broadsides and break up.

Long before *Bricgstow* was established, the chosen port on the Avon had been much further down-river, at Sea Mills where the Trim joins the main flow. It was here that the Romans established *Portus Abonae* at the terminal of a road leading direct from London (Fig. 9.3).[2] For transshipment purposes *Abonae* was well sited about 3.5km from the river, mouth and sheltered by a great bend in the river but it depended for its existence on a stable infrastructure. With the breakdown of Roman authority and the onset of raiding it seems to have simply been abandoned. Once the economy was in a state of collapse and the rampaging Irish were in the Bristol Channel, *Abonae* lost its attraction.

Avon's port was re-established in a new world, when the economy was beginning to grow again from the 10th century. The new port was moved to a new position upstream, to a bridging place at Bristol, which allowed control of movement by both land and by sea. Bristol's early years are obscure but coins were minted there in around AD 1000 and pottery found in excavations suggests trade with Dublin was under way in the 11th century.[3] One of the commodities brought from Ireland was slaves, a traffic condemned by Bishop Wulfstan but one which was to feature large in the city's later history, reaching its peak in the mid-18th century.

The late-Saxon settlement occupied the narrowest part of a ridge between the Avon and the River Frome, here barely 150m across. Archaeological evidence suggests a well-established community engaged in the normal activities of a late-Saxon town – spinning, leather-working and ironworking. On three sides the settlement was protected by its river and by extensive areas of encircling marshland, but the eastern approach, along the ridge, was vulnerable and here, soon after the Norman Conquest, a castle was established that remained through successive modifications a prominent feature of the city until the 17th century. The town soon outgrew its protective peninsula, however. New walls were built in the 13th century, and the town extended northwards, south-westwards on to marshland, and across the Avon to incorporate a broad swathe of land (Temple Meads) in the bend of the river within the protection of a new line of defences, the Port wall (Fig. 9.4).

The vitality that led to these medieval expansions came from Bristol's maritime trade, and from the beginning its docking facilities were of prime

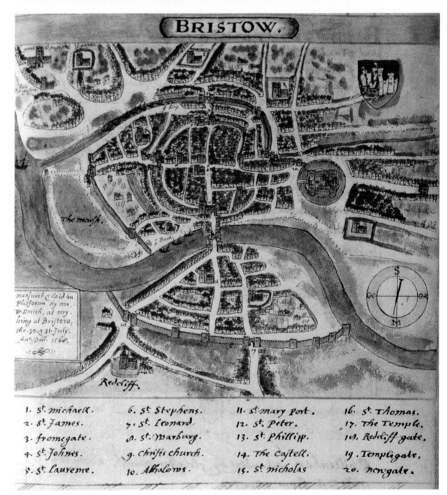

1. st michaell.
2. st James.
3. fromegate.
4. st Johns.
5. st Laurence.
6. st Stephens.
7. st Leonard.
8. st warburg.
9. Chrifts church.
10. Alhalows.
11. st mary port.
12. st Peter.
13. st Phillipp.
14. The Caftell.
15. st nicholas
16. st Thomas.
17. The Temple.
18. Redcliff gate.
19. Templegate,
20. newgate.

Fig. 9.4 Bristol in the 16th century.
The medieval city, originally protected by its two rivers with a castle guarding the landward approach, has by this time begun to spread to the higher land to the north and to the south of the Avon where the suburb of Temple Meads developed defended on the landward side by a city wall of its own.

importance to its livelihood. By the 14th century there were three main areas of quays. At the west side of the town, along the Frome, lay Broad and Narrow quay providing space for ocean-going vessels, while to the east of the old town flanking the Avon was The Back (now Welsh Back), where the local coastal shipping docked. Both were public quays. On the other side of the Avon – the left bank – within the suburbs of Temple Fee, the riverfront was lined with slipways and wharves belonging to private proprietors. It was in this area, in the 1970s and 1980s, that several rescue excavations were carried out bringing to light a wealth of information about harbourside development, manufacturing activities and the range of commodities that passed into and out of the city.

The nature of the waterfront development was conditioned to a large extent by the considerable tidal range of the river. Without special provision, a falling tide could easily have stranded vessels on the steeply sloping mud banks; even with wharves built far out into the river, the times when ships could be loaded and unloaded were strictly limited. Because of this, Bristol was exempt from an Act of 1559 that prohibited vessels from loading and unloading during the hours of darkness.

Impressive and costly efforts were made to provide adequate docking facilities, as archaeological trenches through the Avon waterfront have shown.[4] At Dundas Wharf, about 100m south of the bridge, the sequence of harbourside development began in the mid-12th century with the construction of two revetting walls 4m apart, one relating to the low-water mark the other to high tide. The same pairing of walls was repeated farther out in the river in the 13th century, although a further extension in the 14th century was sufficiently far out for a single wall to suffice.

Further south, at Canynges House, the river bank had a shallower slope, and more extensive reclamation was needed to provide a sufficiently deep anchorage. Here it is estimated that up to 70m was reclaimed over 250 years or so of development. Work began in the 12th century with a simple wattle revetment but in the 13th century the waterfront was totally remodelled, with a stone-built river wall and a slipway leading down to a stone-paved jetty in front, about 3m below the level of the main wharf. Later still, in the 14th century, the riverfront was extended outwards yet again. A succession of docks dug alongside it and later forward from it neatly reflect a change in mooring practice from broadside to stern first.

These two examples give some idea of the structural detail available from high-quality excavation. What they show, above all, were the strenuous efforts made by the men of Bristol to provide a harbour infrastructure appropriate both to the tidal range of the river and to the increasing size of the vessels. That so much energy was invested is a measure of the value of the trade that passed through the port.

By the 15th century Bristol had become one of the busiest and most prosperous of the manufacturing and trading cities of the country. Of the many reasons for this the most significant was its position in relation to the trade routes now in operation. Bristol lay at the hub of a network of regional routes extending out in all directions – routes by road, river and sea – along which a wide range of commodities could flow. From the heart of England came wool from Hereford and Buckingham, cloth from Ludlow and Coventry, sculpted alabaster from Nottingham, iron and timber from the Forest of Dean, and wheat, malt and barley from Worcester and Tewkesbury. Local vessels sailed up the Severn bringing wool, cloth and hides from the ports of southern Wales, and from Cornwall and Devon came fish, tin and yet more cloth. Overland by road, close links were maintained with the merchants of London and Southampton, whence came rarer commodities like the silks carried to Southampton by Venetian galleys.

Of the raw materials that poured into Bristol some came there for redistribution and were shipped onward, others came to supply local craftsmen who, through the application of their craft skills, added value. Leather from south-west Wales, for example, was converted into parchment, horse gear, gloves, shoes and purses – valuable trade goods, most of which went abroad. These craft-workers were simply converting a high-bulk–low-value product – the leather – into high-value–low-bulk consumer durables. There are many other examples – iron was made into guns, copper and its alloys into church bells, and tin and lead into pewter tableware.

But by far the most important activity was the manufacture of cloth and clothing. While raw wool and cloth were brought in from afar, Bristol lay in the heart of one of the most prolific cloth-producing regions in the country. The upland pastures of the Cotswolds and Mendip produced wool of excellent quality while the villages fringing the uplands had copious supplies of water to power the fulling mills. Within these communities the spinners, weavers, dyers and tuckers were busily at work producing cloth to be sent in bulk shipments to the markets of Bristol, there to be traded for money, a variety of consumer goods and the raw materials they needed for their work – the dyestuffs, principally woad and madder, coming from south-west France, Picardy and from Flanders, and alum from the Mediterranean, all imported by the Bristol merchants. The city, too, had its own cloth-works, which seem to have been concentrated in the Temple Fee suburb in the bend of the Avon. In Touker Street, close to the river, the cloth was fulled (by tuckers) and stretched out on tenter racks to prevent it from shrinking as it dried. The dyers occupied the same part of the town while the linen-workers congregated in St Thomas' Street. In Temple Street the Weavers Hall and the nearby Weavers Chapel provided the craft-workers with a sense of community offering support and cohesion.

Of the many activities which thronged the densely built-up waterside – the dyers, fullers, cloth-workers and the tanners, horn-workers and soap-makers – there is vivid trace in the archaeological record. At Dundas Wharf a range of dyestuffs, including madder, dyer's greenweed, weld and possibly woad, have all been identified while wool fibres from a 14th-century dock at Canynges House were found dyed red, blue and black. At another site at the south end of Redcliff Street the bases of three dye-vats were uncovered in a 14th-century context together with freshwater tanks for washing the cloth. The same site also produced post-holes that may have been part of a horizontal loom, suggesting that several of the processes involved in the manufacture of cloth took place in single establishments.

All of these industries produced a range of noxious and unpleasant waste products which, together with organic debris from food production and human waste, were dumped into the river or used as fill behind the ever-advancing river walls. By modern standards it cannot have been a pleasant place to live and yet throughout the medieval period industrial production went on alongside the residences of the wealthy merchants whose lifestyle it supported. It was not until the 17th century that the local elites began to move to more airy and salubrious parts, leaving the suburbs of Redcliff and Temple to decline into an industrial zone where, towards the end of the 17th century, Bristol's famous glass-works were established.

While local production and regional trade were crucial to Bristol's success, its fame and fortune rested on its overseas network reaching to Ireland, the north Atlantic and America and to most parts of Atlantic-facing Europe. From these far-flung sources came an amazing array of products. In the 16th century Iceland and the west coast of Ireland were producing fish, with the Irish ports adding bales of hides to the cargoes. Salt, so essential for preserving fish and meat, was coming from the coastal salterns to the north and south of the Loire estuary. Wine in huge quantities – the main product of Gascony – was being loaded at Bordeaux together with woad from up-river in the vicinity of Toulouse. The Basque country offered iron from the foundries clustering around the port of Bilbao and from south-western Iberia – from the many ports between the estuaries of the Douro and Guadalquivir – came wine, fruits of many kinds and oil. At the height of the season activity in the port of Bristol must have been frenetic with ships from all parts of Atlantic Europe jostling with Bristol-based vessels for wharf space to unload and take on new cargoes.

The 15th century was to see a significant change in the organisation of the business of trade.[5] To begin with the merchants, responsible for the production and distribution of commodities, focused their activities on land, entrusting to shipowners the tasks of fetching and carrying. But later we find merchants buying shares of ships and eventually owning vessels wholly themselves. Some men became very considerable owners. In the late 15th century William Canynges the Younger appears to have owned 10 vessels, amounting to about half of Bristol's ships at the time and a quarter of the ships using the port. He made his fortune not as a dealer in commodities but as a contractor carrying freight for others. In contrast, William Canynges the Elder, who died in 1396, a merchant in the old style, seems to have owned but one ship; one of his sons, John, continued to trade like his father, sending his cloth to Spain and south-western France in return for iron and woad but investing the returns in property: when he died in 1405 his property in Bristol included three halls and five gardens, six tenements, 22 shops and other land.

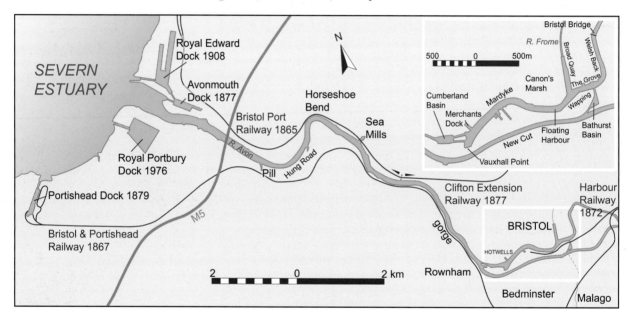

Fig. 9.5 The Port of Bristol: principal features of the River Avon between the city and its later ports that grew up along the Severn Estuary.

The port of Bristol had always been difficult to reach from the sea, not so much because of the distance (11km) but because the sharp bends in the course of the river combined with the ferocity of the tidal flow made navigation hazardous under sail (Fig. 9.5). The larger the vessels became the greater the risk of being wrecked. From the medieval period onwards the normal procedure was for the approaching vessel to heave-to at the anchorage called Hungroad 4km up-river, just beyond the village of Pill, there to wait for a favourable tide (Fig. 9.6). Local rowing boats, manned by 'hobblers', were then attached to the prow to guide the vessel up-river with the tide. The tide, and sometimes the careful use of topsails, provided the power while the hobblers maintained the course in centre channel. Such was the volume of traffic that most of the male inhabitants of Pill were hobblers and the tradition continued after the rowing boat gave way to steam-powered tugs. Pill hobblers are still employed as pilots and as quayside workers under the Port of Bristol Authority.

By the beginning of the 18th century the great tidal range in the port of Bristol and the propensity for silt to accumulate rapidly against the quays were presenting problems to the rapid turnaround now becoming a commercial imperative.[6] One early attempt to bring some relief came with the construction of a large wet dock at Sea Mills, in about 1712, close to the Roman port. Here it was

Fig. 9.6 Eighteenth-century merchants' houses in Princes Street, Bristol. The centre and right-hand houses were built in 1725 for John Hobbs, a deal merchant.

BELOW: *Fig. 9.7 Aerial view of the River Avon looking up-river towards the site of the medieval town of Bristol, showing Cumberland Basin and its locks completed in 1809. The water-course to the right (south) is the New Cut created between 1804–9.*

intended that ocean-going ships would unload, but the disadvantage remained that the cargo still had to be transferred up-river to the main port aboard smaller vessels. The project failed and the company was wound up in 1761. More successful was the substantial wet dock constructed much further upstream at Hotwells a year or two later. A contemporary account suggests that it could take 40 fully laden vessels, but this was only a very partial answer.

It was not until 1809 that the problem was finally solved by an audacious scheme to turn the entire river upstream from Hotwells into one large non-tidal 'floating harbour' that would incorporate all the existing port installations lining the Frome and Avon. This necessitated a system of locks across the Avon at Cumberland Basin to retain a constant level of deep water above. As an ancillary work it was necessary to provide the Avon with a new channel, New Cut, to the south of the river to take the overflow from upstream. The project was completed between 1804 and 1809, providing 32ha of tidal water space, and the next year was linked to London by the Kennet and Avon Canal. The Floating Harbour, or the City Docks as it became known, remained functioning until about 1970, since when major redevelopment schemes have transformed its surrounding buildings, leaving only the expanses of water contained by the surviving dock walls to remind us of its former glories (Fig. 9.7).

But the story does not end there. In spite of the failure of the Sea Mills Dock the attraction of the river mouth remained. In 1877 the new Avonmouth Dock was opened, to be followed two years later by Portishead Dock linked direct to the Severn estuary 3km south of the Avon. The Royal Edward 'Ocean Dock', completed in 1908, further extended the facilities at Avonmouth while in 1976 a new container port – the Royal Portbury – sited midway between the two complexes, came into use to service the rapidly growing needs of the bulk transport industry. The new docks, which extend along 5km of waterfront, with their intricate infrastructure of road and rail links and vast parking lots, can hardly be called an attractive addition to the environment but they are most certainly a part of the historic process, representing as they do man's most recent attempt to maintain the Avon as one of the principal ports of entry into Britain.

THE SMALLER PORTS OF THE SOMERSET COAST

In contrast to the almost epic history of the port of Bristol, the other Severn-side harbours pale into insignificance but they have their own interest.[7]

The River Parrett lacks the grandeur of the Avon. Snaking through its sodden landscape of marsh and fen it has to make its way in a great horseshoe curve, cut deep into a vast expanse of tidal mud, for some 10km before reaching the real sea. From the point of view of a mariner seeking a safe port it is an unpromising entry. That said the Parrett is the only convenient outlet along many kilometres of coast and so, with some ingenuity, convenient port sites were developed along its course.

In the Roman period the place chosen lay at Crandon Bridge on a now-silted deep-water channel close to the west end of the Polden Hills, linked by road to the Fosse Way just north of the Roman town of Ilchester. Aerial photography suggests a large installation covering at least 7ha. From here it would have been possible to sail north up the coast and cross the Severn, past the Holme rocks, to the vicinity of Cardiff or to take a westerly route to access the remoter ports of the north coasts of Somerset and Devon.

By the early medieval period the focus of activity had shifted up-river to Bridgwater, at the time the lowest convenient bridging point on the river and a place where land traffic could meet with sea traffic sailing up the Parrett. It was already a significant regional transshipment point by AD 1200, when King John granted a charter making Bridgwater a town and (among other benefits) allowing the burghers to collect duty on freight vessels calling there. Through the medieval period the town grew, the wealth of its merchants based largely on the production of cloths, most notably a distinctive type of broadcloth known as 'bridgewaters'.

In the early 18th century, a deliberate attempt was made by the Duke of Chandos to develop his land to the north of the town as an industrial estate by building a glass-works. Other industries followed and in 1827 the Bridgwater and Taunton Canal was built, further enhancing the town's importance as a route node. A few years later, in 1841, the Bridgwater Dock was opened to provide improved docking for ships and transshipment facilities for cargoes to be moved efficiently between sea-going vessels and canal barges. The arrival of the railway in the same year was a further boost to trade, linking Bridgwater to Bristol and Exeter.

One of the principal industries to develop during the 19th century was the manufacture of bricks and tiles, which utilised the extensive deposits of alluvial clay found in the immediate vicinity. The products were widely adopted regionally but the more entrepreneurial of the manufacturers made good use of the facility to transport bulk cargoes by sea, and over the period 1850–1914 huge quantities of tiles were shipped to ports along the north coast of Brittany between Morlaix and Saint-Brieuc, at a time when it was the fashion to replace thatch.[8] So successful was the product that roofs of Bridgwater tiles are still a notable feature of this Breton landscape. One of the firms involved in tile production, Colthurst, Symons and Co, developed an inspired marketing ploy. Having been awarded a gold medal in the Paris Exhibition of 1867 they took the medal's emblem, a head of the Emperor Napoleon III identified with the emperor's name and title, and encircled it with their own company name, using it as a stamp with which each tile was prominently impressed. The visual evidence that the product appeared to be endorsed by the French emperor seems to have commended it to the Breton customers.

To the west of Bridgwater the coast is not particularly congenial to a sailor in search of a safe anchorage. For the most part it is a coast of high cliffs giving way, in places, to a fringe of marshland with few significant rivers to provide access to the sea. But so long a coastline needs a port-of-call and one had developed by the late-Saxon period at Watchet at the mouth of the Washford river. The settlement and port were in existence by the time of King Alfred and in the early 10th century it was listed as a fortified place in the Burghal Hidage. It was significant enough to be attacked by Vikings on four occasions during the 10th century – a fate that the more affluent ports of Bridgwater and Bristol escaped by virtue of their remoteness from the sea.

The fortified settlement probably occupied a promontory between the stream and a marsh and faced directly on to the sea. Since there was no natural haven it is likely that from the outset a breakwater or quay had been constructed to provide some protection for vessels. A pier of timber is recorded at the end of the 16th century. Ships sailing to Ireland were using the port in the early 17th century but by this time it was already in decline. The present harbour, built in 1861 to facilitate the transport of ironstone to Wales, was an attempt at revival but it came to little.

In the medieval period Watchet was only one of several small ports clinging to the southern shore of the Bristol Channel, its near neighbours to the west being Dunster, Minehead and Porlock. Together they shared the coastal trade, but in the 17th century Minehead began to grow as the others declined and by 1700 it dominated the local trade with Ireland and was beginning to engage with the Americas, most notably Virginia and the West Indies, and with the Mediterranean. Daniel Defoe, visiting the port in 1724, gave as the reasons for Minehead's success the fact that its harbour was deeper and better built than its rivals and was thus able to accommodate the larger ships that were now increasingly employed for ocean voyages. Another factor was that the anchorage was very well protected from the prevailing westerly weather by the upland massif immediately to the west. Yet for all its benefits the port and its town began to decline in the early 18th century and never truly recovered.

The failure of the little ports of the north Somerset and north Devon coasts to develop is not difficult to understand. They looked outwards across the sea but they lacked populous hinterlands and natural routes of land communication. Whereas Bristol, and even Bridgwater, sat like fat spiders in the centre of a web of communications, the northern coastal ports clung to their cliff edges looking forlornly out to sea as the well-laden ships bound for their rivals passed them by.

POOLE AND CHRISTCHURCH HARBOURS

The harbours of Poole and Christchurch (Fig. 9.8) are near neighbours separated only by the sweep of Poole Bay, now encrusted with Bournemouth and the bungaloid growth that the Victorian creation has attracted around itself (Fig. 9.9). The two harbours have many similarities: both can boast large

Fig. 9.8 Map of the Dorset coast from Poole to Lyme Regis showing coastal defences and beacons in 1539–40.

expanses of sheltered inland water; both control major river routes leading into extensive hinterlands; and both are well signed for approach from the sea – the first sightings, St Alban's Head on Purbeck and St Catherine's Point on the Isle of Wight giving way to the comforting sight of the chalk sentinels of the Foreland and Old Harry to the west and The Needles to the east. Thereafter the passage, to Poole Harbour or Christchurch Harbour, is assured. Both harbours have, over the centuries, shared the maritime traffic coming this way, first one and then the other taking the lion's share, but it is probably best to consider them as partners.

The region is rich in natural resources. Hengistbury Head, overlooking Christchurch Harbour, is laced with large nodules of ironstone known as doggers

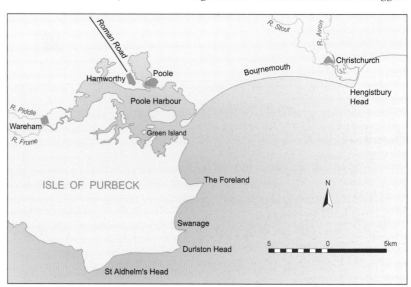

Fig. 9.9 The harbours and ports of the east Dorset coast.

that erode out as the cliffs recede and accumulate on the foreshore (Fig. 9.10).[9] The ironstone was exploited from the Iron Age for its metal. In Saxon and medieval times it was taken up-river by boat to be used as a building stone for churches and the like, while in the 19th century an enterprising local man transshipped large quantities to Wales, bringing back coal for the local markets. In stripping the foreshore of its protecting doggers he allowed the sea more easily to erode the cliffs, creating a serious threat to the survival of the headland.

Poole Harbour is even better endowed. On the nearby Isle of Purbeck the black shiny Kimmeridge shale outcropping in the cliffs was widely used from the Early Bronze Age to the late-Roman period for the manufacture of armlets and finger rings, vessels, trenchers and even furniture. The same region produced salt extracted by evaporation from sea-water which, packed in coarse ceramic briquetage containers, was traded far inland in the Iron Age. The Romans were soon to exploit Purbeck for building material, in particular the attractive blue-grey fossiliferous Purbeck 'marble' and also a white siltstone, both used for decorative purposes from within a few years of the invasion. The fashion for Purbeck marble continued into the medieval period, during which time huge quantities were transported for decorative fittings in churches and cathedrals throughout the country. Nor should we forget the most enduring of Poole

Harbour's extractive industries – clay for potting. Ceramic production was already well under way in the 1st century BC and by the 2nd and 3rd centuries AD had reached colossal proportions, with regular cargoes being taken north to provide for the troops manning the frontiers in northern Britain. The Poole pottery manufactured today is the successor industry.

The south coast of Wessex, then, has much to offer by way of return cargoes for the ships using its ports. But in addition to its own immediate resources it also commands a very rich hinterland – the chalklands of Wessex – productive of corn and wool and other agrarian products in plenty.

Poole and Christchurch must have been visited by ships from the coasts of what is now Normandy and Brittany throughout the prehistoric period. In the second millennium BC the elites of Armorica and Wessex exchanged prestige goods through Christchurch Harbour, the favoured port at this time: amber acquired from the North Sea coasts and decorated gold-work made by Wessex craftsmen were given in return for fine copper alloy daggers, their wooden hilts decorated with hundreds of small gold pins. One of the local elite, no doubt involved in this exchange, was buried with gold and amber ornaments in a prominent barrow on Hengistbury Head.

Fig. 9.10 Christchurch Harbour protected by the mass of Hengistbury Head and the gravel spit built out from it. *Hengistbury was an important prehistoric site and became a port in the 1st century BC when maritime trading links developed with Brittany.*

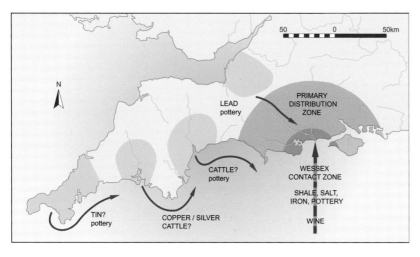

Fig. 9.11 The trading system in operation in the 1st century BC of which Christchurch and Poole harbours were focal points. Hengistbury was the main port-of-trade at this time.

Hengistbury continued to be an important port of entry throughout the first millennium BC culminating, in the 1st century BC, in a frenzy of maritime activity that has left a vivid mark on the archaeological record (Fig. 9.11). On the sheltered north side of the headland excavations have shown that the firm gravel of the shoreline enhanced with hards projecting seawards was used to draw up vessels for loading and unloading. All around were broken Roman wine amphorae from north Italy and large quantities of pottery from the bay of Saint-Brieuc on the north coast of Armorica. Other foreign commodities arriving at this time included purple and yellow glass, bronze vessels and figs, all probably originating in the Mediterranean. Exactly how this complex exchange system worked is a matter of speculation, but the simplest explanation is that the exotic goods were transshipped in a series of short-haul operations to Armorica and that it was the shipowners of the northern Armorican coast – the tribe known as the Coriosolites – who assembled cargoes for the final leg of the journey to Hengistbury, stopping off at Guernsey en route. For their return cargoes they could have taken on board local products, particularly corn, wool and hides, but they also had access to a range of metals including gold, silver, copper and tin, all of which were transshipped to Hengistbury from various parts of the country and refined there, before entering into the exchange network. One of the principal sources of metal would have been the south-west peninsula whence came copper and tin by coastal cabotage. The silver, alloyed with lead, was a product of the Mendip and was probably carried to the port down the River Stour.

While the archaeological finds are sufficient to show something of the products being transshipped, what remains in the archaeological record is only a pale reflection of the variety of goods that must have been carried. Nor is what survives sufficient to explain the social mechanisms involved, but the sheer quantity of Armorican pottery and coins found on Hengistbury Head strongly suggests that Armorican traders may have stayed there for extended periods coming, perhaps, every year for a summer season. Once the pattern was established traders from other ports of southern Britain would have known where and when to take their goods for exchange.

The existence of other ports-of-trade along the south coast is highly likely. In Poole Harbour at this time a major harbour-work of stone and timbers was built out to one of the deep-water channels that separate the mainland from Green Island, where imported pottery from the 1st centuries BC and AD has been found. Concentrations of exotic imported materials are also recorded on the Isle of Portland and the Exe estuary, and there is clearly a lot more to learn about trade in the pre-Roman Iron Age.

By the time of the Roman invasion in AD 43 Hengistbury had lost its pre-eminence as a port but Poole Harbour was still functioning, not least because of the growing importance of the Kimmeridge shale and pottery industries around its southern shore. It was probably as part of the invasion strategy that, in the summer and autumn of AD 43, a military store base was established at Hamworthy, a peninsula on the north side of the harbour, just opposite the medieval and later port of Poole. Linked to the early road system it would have served as an important supply base in the months when the army was subduing

*Fig. 9.12 **The quay at Wareham** facing on to the River Frome, with the parish church of St Mary in the background.*

the West Country and in all probability the port continued to function commercially throughout the Roman period.

We can confidently assume that both harbours remained actively in use in the Saxon period. In Christchurch Harbour settlement began to focus at the end of a narrow promontory of gravel between the Avon and the Stour just above the confluence of the two rivers. This was Twynham ('the place between the waters'), later to be known as Christchurch.[10] Twynham was chosen to be one of the fortified burghs strengthened by King Alfred as protection against Viking attack. In the 11th century the establishment of a castle and a priory provided the town with a degree of status but it never seems to have flourished, and though William Camden describes it, in 1586, as 'a small and populous sea port', in the early 18th century Defoe considers it to be 'a very inconsiderable poor place' and so it remained, eclipsed by the growth of its neighbours, Wareham and Poole.

From the late-Roman period the economic activity of the region focused on Poole Harbour. In the Saxon period the similarities to development in Christchurch Harbour are interesting for here, too, the place chosen as the focus of settlement was the narrow ridge between two rivers, the Frome and Piddle, close to their confluence. Here the town of Wareham developed (Fig. 9.12).[11] Its origins are obscure but a remarkable collection of inscribed memorial stones, dating from the 6th to the 8th centuries, suggests the existence of an important cemetery or shrine and from about 700 it is several times referred to in Saxon sources. By the 9th century it had become one of the fortified places defending the south coast from sea-borne Viking raids – though rather ineffectually it seems, for in 876 it succumbed to a Danish attack.

The town and its port were significant enough to warrant the construction of a castle in the late 11th century and the town quays on either side of the bridge across the Frome attracted a variety of shipping, including coasters carrying goods from port to port, as well as cross-Channel vessels engaged in the wine trade, but like Christchurch the town failed to develop. There were various reasons for this. Its hinterland, largely heathland, was highly unproductive; it was sited inconveniently far from the open sea (from Wareham to Poole Bay was some 18km); but probably more important, the river was beginning to silt up and

was unsuited for the larger vessels which, from the 13th century onwards, were coming into regular use. So it was that as Wareham lost its maritime trade a new port began to emerge on an alluvial promontory – now Poole – just opposite the Hamworthy peninsula, which the Romans had chosen centuries before.

Poole was conveniently sited only a few kilometres from the open sea where the tidal outflow from the large expanse of inland water, Holes Bay, scoured a deep channel (Fig. 9.13).[12] The peninsula was almost an island cut off from the mainland by a creek and a wide muddy inlet. Its growth as a port can be traced from the early 13th century, when it is recorded to be a landing place for the king's wines and the main port used in transshipping stone from Purbeck (Fig. 9.14). By the mid-14th century trade had considerably increased.

Fig. 9.13 The port town of Poole occupies a promontory between Holes Bay (top) and Poole Harbour. *The promontory of Hamworthy opposite Poole (to the left) was the site of a Roman settlement, probably of military origin.*

Fig. 9.14 The topography of Poole.

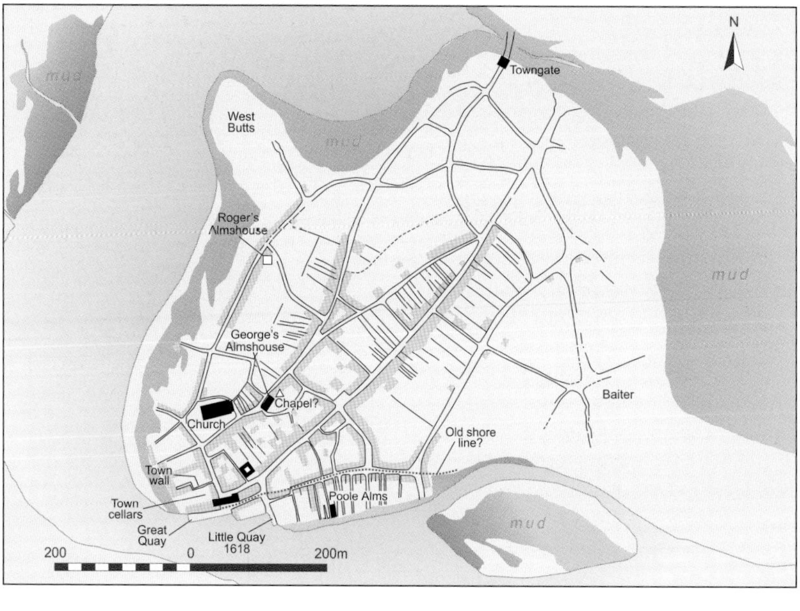

Now Poole was one of the main ports dealing with wine from Gascony. Other imports, listed in 1341, include fish, codfish, salt, hides, skins, wool, resin, pitch, corn and oil, commodities that for the most part could have been gathered along the ports of western France. With the loss of Gascony the maritime links began to refocus on Brittany, Normandy and the Channel Islands.

The main public harbour-works, the Great Quay, lay along the tip of the promontory with a number of private wharves and jetties projecting out into the channel from the old shoreline (Strand Street) immediately to the east. At the end of the 16th century much of this area seems to have been reclaimed partly for warehousing, with a new quay – Little Quay – built alongside the reclaimed zone at right angles to the Great Quay to serve the adjacent fish market.

The building of Little Quay and the fish market in 1618 marks the beginning of Poole's involvement in the lucrative Newfoundland fish trade.[13] The Newfoundland fishing grounds were first brought to public notice in Britain by the Bristol-based explorers John and Sebastian Cabot at the end of the 15th century, just at the time when Britain's traditional fishing grounds off Iceland were being increasingly threatened by the Danes. To begin with a group of entrepreneurs, hoping to gain a monopoly of the new fishing grounds, established the London and Bristol Company for the Plantation of Newfoundland in 1610, but conditions were so tough for the settlers that the monopoly was impossible to maintain. By the middle of the 17th century series of Royal Charters were being issued vesting rights to develop the fishing in a number of West Country towns including Poole, Weymouth, Melcombe Regis and Lyme, but the individual agreements were replaced by the single Newfoundland Act of 1699, which established the working regulations that were to control the trade for the next century and a half – a period during which the entrepreneurs of Poole and other Dorset ports were able to grow rich on the profits of this highly lucrative activity.

The basis of the trade was straightforward. The principal products of the Newfoundland fisheries were salt cod and 'train oil' made from cods' livers, but the cargoes could also be augmented with salmon, sealskins and furs. In return the settlers were provided with the necessities of life, tools, fishing equipment and clothing, as well as the salt used in great quantities to preserve the fish. Thus in April 1709 the *Willing Mind* left Poole with a typical cargo comprising clothing, malt, flour, sail cloths, nails, cordage, rugs, woollen cloth, serges, shoes, blankets, nets and lines – a cargo mostly gathered from the Dorset hinterland. But serious competition soon developed from New England merchants, forcing the Poole traders to include in their Newfoundland run American consumer goods of their competitors, such as large supplies of tobacco, molasses, sugar and rum – goods that were first imported from Virginia by shippers based on other Dorset ports, notably Weymouth.

Once the Poole ships had taken on their cargoes of salt fish and train oil in Newfoundland they made for the ports of Spain, Portugal and Italy – all Catholic countries where fish formed an important food at times when religious observance forbade the eating of meat. In these southern ports they sold their fish for gold and silver and took on cargoes of wine, olive oil, currants, figs, raisins, almonds and citrus fruits, mostly to satisfy the increasingly sophisticated tastes of the affluent British elite, but some carried onwards to relieve the tedious diet of the hard-working Newfoundland settlers. En route from Iberia they also picked up supplies of pitch and salt, so necessary to maintain the momentum of the system, from the ports of Atlantic France.

For nearly 150 years Poole benefited from its pivotal position in this Atlantic-wide network. From their accumulated wealth the merchants invested in country estates and town houses and so Poole took on a new affluence. The 18th century saw the town transformed.[14] Whole streets were rebuilt and in place of timber, daub and stone, elegant brick façades were everywhere to be seen, a number of which still survive in High Street, West Street, New Street and Thames Street (Fig. 9.15). The notable Guildhall in the centre of Market Street was erected in 1761, while other of the community's needs were satisfied by the Congregational Chapel built in 1777 in Skinner Street. Even the owners of the smaller houses and cottages joined in with this desire to upgrade in good brick (Fig. 9.16).

Fig. 9.15 The Custom House at Poole, built in 1813 as a replica of a late-18th-century Custom House destroyed by fire: an elegant building in a less elegant modern setting.

But the boom did not last. Competition from America and from Newfoundland's own increasingly entrepreneurial fishing fleet began to bite while merchants from Bristol, Liverpool and London further undermined these old systems by concentrating on the highly profitable triangle that offloaded cheap British products on West Africa in return for slaves, which they took to America, bringing back to England sugar, tobacco and cash. Added to this were the recurring problems of harbour silting and the increasing tonnage of the ocean-going ships. With profit margins slashed and less to reinvest in infrastructure Poole toppled into a spiral of decline from which it has only comparatively recently begun to emerge. One fortunate result of the downturn is that a surprising amount of the 18th-century city managed to survive the 'improvements' of the Victorian period and of the first 70 years of the 20th century, and today remains quietly resplendent to remind us of the quality and scale of life that could be built on the unstable foundation of salt cod and fish oil.

THE SMALLER PORTS OF THE DORSET COAST

Fig. 9.16 Eighteenth- and 19th-century warehouses: a reminder of Poole's once vital maritime commerce.

Fig. 9.17 Weymouth and its approaches, looking south-west. The entrance to the harbour is protected by Nothe Fort (left of harbour entrance). Radipole Lake to the west of the town provides extensive anchorage for small boats.

For a ship's master sailing west from Poole, the mass of the Isle of Portland would, in adverse weather conditions, have proved a formidable obstacle, making more appealing the attractions of the ports of Weymouth and Melcombe, two small ports facing each other across a narrow race leading from a well-protected harbour beyond.[15] Whatever the origins of the two settlements, by the 12th century they were beginning to grow and by the early 14th century they were populous and flourishing with Melcombe, on the less restricted alluvial peninsula to the north of the channel, becoming the more important of the two. Prosperity was based on fishing together with the exportation of wool to western France and the importation, from Gascony, of corn and wine. Little, however, is known of the intensity of this trade (Fig. 9.17).

The early topography of the two towns can be reasonably easily deduced. Weymouth, on the south side of the channel, was focused around a small cove – Hope Cove – where the quays were sited, and spread to the west in a narrow strip between the water's edge and the cliff behind (Fig. 9.18). Melcombe, on the other hand, occupied a spacious peninsula between the Backwater and the sea. The earliest settlement was sited at the south-western corner, with its quays stretching northwards along the Backwater. In 1280 it was awarded the status of a borough by Edward I and replanned on an extensive grid pattern, still evident in its entirety in the street plan surviving today. At this stage the east side, washed by the tides and now the preserve of sunbathers, was used as the town's rubbish tip. In the later part of the 15th century the Dominican Friars, already established in the town, were given the right to build a fortified jetty extending along the southern side of the wide sandy beach immediately against the edge of the estuary. The present railway

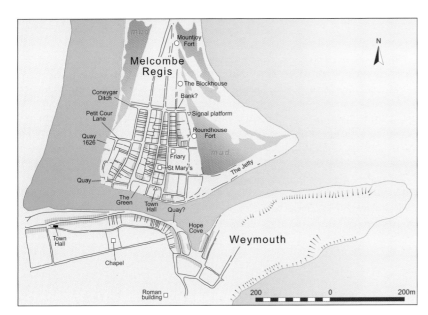

Fig. 9.18 The topography of Weymouth and Melcombe Regis.

BELOW: **Fig. 9.19 The Isle of Portland** showing its dominant effect on coastal land forms and the protection it affords to Weymouth and the naval harbour of Portland.

station serving the vehicle ferry port lies part way along the friars' jetty – a reflection of their sensible investment in harbour installations.

In 1571 the curiosity of the two competing ports was brought to an end when the towns were united by Act of Parliament, the first bridge being built 26 years later. Thereafter the fortunes of Weymouth as a port followed those of Poole, as trade with Newfoundland and Virginia began to develop, but it was always a minor player, eventually losing out as Poole grew to dominate the south coast shipping. Only the rise of popularity in sea-bathing in the 1760s saved it from total decline and set it off on a new trajectory (Fig. 9.19). A further impetus was given by the foundation of the Portland Naval Base in 1845 – a major development that has sustained the maritime energy of the town to the present day. This constant change of identity has given Weymouth a somewhat bewildered appearance – and an all prevailing sense of 'where next?'

West of Portland lies the great sweep of Lyme Bay. Seen from a distance it can be deceptively calm, but its treacherous cliffs and steep shingle beaches lacking in safe havens have justifiably earned it the name of Deadman's Bay. With no natural ports the inhabitants of the region have had to use their ingenuity. Bridport and Lyme Regis are the result.

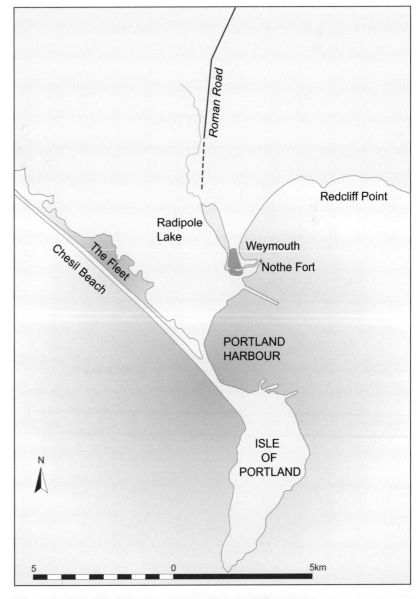

Bridport occupies a promontory between the rivers Brit and Asker, just above their confluence.[16] Three kilometres further south the Brit cuts through the coastal cliffs and the wide shingle beach to the sea. Without human intervention the modest river would have flowed across and through the shingle ridge constantly replenished by longshore drift (Fig. 9.20). But over the centuries strenuous efforts have been made to keep the river mouth open to provide a sheltered anchorage for vessels and a point of transshipment for smaller boats using the river.

The position of Bridport itself, safe between its two rivers, is very similar to the locations chosen for Christchurch and Wareham, which strengthens the view that Bridport is to be identified with *Brydian*, one of the fortified settlements listed in the late-Saxon Burghal Hidage. The port, 3km south at West Bay, would have

Fig. 9.20 The valley of the River Brit with the port of Bridport at its mouth. *The successive harbour-works are designed to protect the harbour from silting by longshore drift.*

been in continuous use from this time but for small vessels the river was navigable as far as the town. This is documented in the late 13th century when, it appears, vessels were docking on the Brit at the southern extremity of the town close to the Chantry. But it was at the river mouth that the real problem lay and it was probably here that in 1385 it was decided to create a harbour 'where there was none' – and so the struggle with the sea began. By the mid-15th century the harbour was in disrepair and in the early 16th century it had become choked with silt and sand. There were major rebuilding schemes in the early 18th century, and again in the 1770s, when moles were built out into the sea in an attempt to keep the channel open and navigable. Finally in 1823–5 a highly experienced engineer, Francis Giles, was employed in a major scheme that has created the harbour we see today – a large harbour basin with the river kept back by sluices that can be opened at low tide to scour out the accumulated sediment. The new works led to a period of prosperity that lasted for 40 years, by which time the railway had largely undermined the significance of sea trade.

That so much effort was lavished on the little port over nearly half a millennium is a reflection of its economic significance in a very special market – the manufacture of sail cloth, cordage and rope from locally grown flax and hemp. In the age of sail these products were in massive demand and Bridport became famous, its many rope-walks proliferating. In the mid-19th century so intensive was the production that hemp and flax had to be brought in from Riga and Archangel. A number of factors combined to bring the production to an end.

Fig. 9.21 Lyme Regis and its artificially constructed port, the Cobb.

The little port could no longer accommodate the larger ships that were coming into use and in 1881 lost its Head Port status to Weymouth. This meant that officers had to be sent out from Weymouth to customs-clear foreign cargoes, causing considerable delays. By itself this was not disastrous, but combined with the demise of the sailing ship, and with it a decline in the demand for cordage and sail cloth, it was a death blow. Today the port at West Bay – a monument to Victorian engineering – is a forlorn curiosity in the heart of a community trying to reinvent itself as a tourist resort.

Lyme Regis is another example of man's ingenuity.[17] The little medieval town that grew up at the mouth of the River Lym was entirely without a natural harbour, so to provide shelter from the prevailing south-west winds and tides for small ships a large breakwater called the Cobb was constructed towards the end of the 13th century. The original structure was built of a casement of vertical timbers infilled with large rocks gathered from the nearby coast: periodic rebuilding from the 14th century onwards has since encased it in increasingly good stonework. As a small sea port the town prospered for much of the 14th century, but in 1378 the town was 'for the most part destroyed and wasted by the sea ... the Cobb ... having been swept away last Martinmass by the sea, stoppping all navigation'.

The Cobb was reconstructed and trade began to revive in spite of attacks from the French (Fig. 9.21). Leland, writing in the early 16th century, talks of it as a 'pretty market-town' which has 'good ships and uses fishing and merchandise'. By the end of the century its merchants were trading with France and West Africa, but its tiny harbour could not compete with Weymouth and Poole and inevitably overseas venturers fell away, leaving the Cobb to shelter fishing boats and local coastal traffic as the little town declined into a gentle picturesqueness beloved of fossil hunters and fiction writers.

CONCLUSION

This brief survey of the outward-looking borders of our region gives some flavour of the constant interplay of land and sea – a dynamic which has involved so many generations in a very particular form of struggle. All this activity has impacted on the land, moulding it with wharves and jetties, with basins and channels and surrounding it with warehouses, canals and rail terminals, the infrastructure of storage and distribution. It has also moulded the character of the region more deeply, creating a landscape than can only be fully understood in terms of the thousands of years over which its inhabitants have been part of a wider, more global world. It is an intricate story of change, each energetic move forward creating structures that eventually become redundant and are replaced or remain fossilised in new developments. The container port of Bristol serving the world and the ferry port of Poole providing quick access to Brittany are but the most recent manifestations of this timeless man–sea interaction.

NOTES

1 The classic description of Bristol trade at this time is to be found in Carus-Wilson 1967, Chapter 1.

2 For excavations at Sea Mills, *see* Bennett 1985.

3 There has been much excavation within the medieval town of Bristol. For an overview of work on the town *see* Ponsford 1987. A useful summary of work on the waterfront is given in Jones 1991. The historic map of the town (Lobel & Carus-Wilson 1975) is an invaluable source.

4 Summarised in Jones 1991.

5 Carus-Wilson 1967, Chapter 1.

6 The later development of the Port of Bristol is helpfully summarised in Elkin 1991.

7 The development and topography of the smaller towns and ports of Somerset is discussed in Aston and Leech 1977.

8 Meirion-Jones & Batt 1985.

9 A brief summary of the archaeological evidence from Hengistbury Head is given in Cunliffe 1978.

10 *See* Penn 1980, 38–44.

11 *See* Penn 1980, 105–13.

12 For the topography and archaeology of Poole *see* Penn 1980, 78–83 and Horsey 1992.

13 Trade with Newfoundland is conveniently discussed in Davies 1979.

14 The eighteenth-century buildings of Poole are fully discussed and illustrated in RCHM(E) 1970.

15 *See* Penn 1980, 114–20.

16 *See* Penn 1980, 23–9 for the topography of the town. The evolution of Bridport Harbour is fully treated by Hannah 1986.

17 For a lively account of the history of Lyme Regis *see* Fowles 1982.

10

Landscape and Legend

JEREMY HARTE

Bristol may be the largest city of the West, but it is only minutes away from one of its wildest and most dramatic landscapes, where the River Avon cuts a deep gorge through folded and broken rocks on its way to the sea. This deep romantic chasm became a favourite spot for lovers of the sublime, both amateur and professional, from the 1820s onwards. Francis Danby and the Bristol School painted the scene, as did many other less famous names. Of course the gentleman amateur would expect to hire a guide – some local character who, once the party had stopped at the edge of Durdham Downs and the tea things were brewing up, might be invited to tell a tradition or two about the place. And this was their story.

Long ago, these bare downs were the home of two giant brothers, Vincent and Goram. Vincent was a fine, hard-working young giant but Goram was a bit of a slob, who liked to let the days slip by as he snoozed in his armchair, a great outcrop of rock near Blaise Castle. All this time Vincent was busy at work on his great task, carving a passage through the hills that kept the Avon from the sea (Fig. 10.1). Goram felt rather shamefaced about this, so he decided to cut a

Fig. 10.1 An opening in the centre of this cliff leads to Goram's Cave, an inaccessible spot overlooking the Avon Gorge, where a hermit was said to have lived.

gorge of his own; but as he spent most of his time knocking off for forty winks, the valley at Combe Dingle is much less impressive. Besides, the two brothers only had one pickaxe between them, which they used to throw from hill to hill as it was needed. Now Vincent was feeling particularly proud of himself – he had just hacked out a fine cave in the crags below Clifton Camp – and he paused for a moment, shouted 'Catch!' in a voice of thunder, and hurled the pickaxe through the air, over towards Henbury way. But by this time Goram had stopped off for another nap in his armchair, so he did not hear the warning cry. Down came the pickaxe, and it struck him just between the eyes, killing the giant instantly. Vincent was devastated. He carried his brother gently out into the Bristol Channel, placing a few rocks over his lifeless form to create what is now an island at Steep Holm. Then it was back to work, but the effort was too much even for a giant's strength and he died of exhaustion, just as the current of the Avon broke through, carrying his body out to sea where it became the island of Flat Holm.[1]

This is one of several versions that you can still hear today. There are multiple variants on the Vincent and Goram story, a sign of their continued vitality in Bristol life: they have inspired Giant Fairs, they appear as the heroes of mumming plays, and they maintain a lively presence on the Web. It is a kind of creation myth, but for all that it is not a very ancient story, not as stories go. The first person to express an interest in the traditions of St Vincent's Rocks was John Aubrey, the father of English folklore, who thought that 'perhaps some sparke of Trueth might be pick't out in this Mist': but this was in the 1690s, when the site at Clifton was still associated with its patron saint. It was not until 1779, by which time the work of the Reformation had filtered through and St Vincent had become plain Vincent the Giant, that the first gorge-cutting legend was told.

But the bare bones of the story were familiar from many other places; for instance, from Badbury and Spetisbury in Dorset. 'They d'zay that when the people were diggin' out an' makin' up Badbury Rings and Castle Rings there were only one pick an' shovel between 'em, zoo they did pass the tools back an' for'ard, when oone were pickin' tother were shovellin'.' Here the action takes place at hillforts, as it does in the Avon gorge.[2] Maiden Castle likewise was the work of giants, and Maesbury 'was built on a lofty hill by the giant Merk. It has been thrown down, but more than a hundred thousand cartloads of stones are heaped there.'

That was what they told William Worcestre when he passed through Somerset in the 15th century.[3] He jotted the information down without surprise, as a historical fact rather than a local legend. Giants, like other larger-than-life characters, could easily slip from one genre to another. How should we respond now if we were told that the hot springs at Bath were enclosed by giants? And yet a thousand years ago, this fitted naturally into the vision of past days in *The Ruin*.

> *Shattered by fate, the fortifications have given way,*
> *The buildings raised by giants are crumbling ...*

This is not in line with current archaeological thinking, but it is not quite folklore either. The author of the Anglo-Saxon elegy was a learned man, not a superstitious rustic, and he knew quite well that the baths had been built by Romans. But in a poetic sense, the Romans *were* giants. They belonged to that distant pagan world that had done such mighty things, but which was also monstrously Godless – the world of Nimrod and Cain's kin, and of those proud emperors who had killed the saints. 'Giant' was a kind of shorthand for power and menace.[4]

Legends are a way of talking about what places can mean – perhaps the oldest way. There have been stories attached to the hills, wells and woods of the West since people first lived among them. These stories have always been changing, and without some very careful readings in the historical record, we will never be able to tell what is old and what is new, nor to say with any confidence what the stories meant to those who told them. Coming from a later tradition, we have to pick our way through this landscape like strangers lost in some foreign city, looking up at every sign and guessing at the meaning of a word or phrase. But not all the words mean what we might think.

Take the Devil, for instance. Here is a figure who carries centuries of theological and spiritual interpretation – the accuser of man, the enemy of souls, the roaring lion seeking whom he may devour. But none of this will quite account for the Devil who features in the story of Cam Peak. Many long years ago, they say, the fiend came across the Gloucestershire plain, struggling behind a colossal wheelbarrow, which he had piled high with stones and dirt. This would all be necessary, as he stopped to explain to a passing cobbler, for his great plan: which was to heave the lot into the

Fig. 10.2 Cam Peak, *an isolated conical hill of sandstone to the south of the Cotswolds, is the scene of an annual procession from the village of Cam at its foot.*

Severn, and so drown all the towns upstream. Pausing to wipe a little sweat off his hairy brow, the Devil asked his new friend if it was much further to the river. 'Oh, much further,' said the quick-witted cobbler, as he swung his sack of old shoes down onto the road. 'Look at these poor shoes,' and he began to count them, one by one – every pair of them had been worn out since he came from Severn side. 'That's the devil of a way,' thought the weary Devil, so he tipped all the dirt out of the barrow at once, and set off for home. Hence the hill of Cam Peak (Fig. 10.2).

The Devil has worn many guises in Christian teaching over the years, but no one has ever suggested that he might be ... stupid. Yet that is the message which comes over, time and again, in these folktales. Huge, slightly menacing, but reassuringly gullible, he is the exact double of the giants who created other landscape features. So the moral, if there is a moral, is that you can always fool the Devil if you keep your wits about you. This is to be expected in the world of the folktale, where it is usually better to be clever than to be good, but it is not what they teach in church. And when we consider the gleefully non-Christian tone of these legends, and the fact that many of them concern ancient stone monuments, we may well wonder if they represent some kind of survival from an earlier, pagan state of things. The search for lingering traditions of this kind kept an earlier generation of folklorists busy for many decades, and although it has now been abandoned as a scholarly pursuit, it continues to motivate much work at the local level.

It is true that old monuments – standing stones, barrows and so on – have always been associated with other-worldly beings. The stories did not appear in records until comparatively recently, but the place-names did, being useful for charters, field surveys and so on. We find that in the earliest records from the West, old places are named after the *eotens*, those pagan giants who had raised the walls of Bath, or after Woden, the most fearful god in the Northern tradition. Other names refer to Grim, who may have begun as a secondary personality of Woden but later came to be identified as a human hero. Not until the 17th century are stones and hillocks named after the Devil. Then we find that the Wansdyke loses its original connection with Woden, and Grims Ditches turn into Devil's Dykes. There is a genial tone about some of these landmarks. Beckington has a Devil's

Fig. 10.3 The triangular folly built by Thomas Farr on Blaise Castle Hill in 1766. Roman coins were discovered while digging out its foundations.

Bed and Bolster, while there is a Devil's Spoon and Trencher in Iwerne Courtenay. Certainly the Devil's Punchbowl in Priddy has a very Georgian feel to it. So the gradual replacement of gods and giants by the Devil took place, not in an age of faith, but in one of the most secular periods of English history. The Nine Stones at Winterbourne Abbas, down the valley from Maiden Castle, are linked with the Devil all right, but this is because they *are* the Devil, petrified along with his wife and children. Making the fiend into a family man is not some obscure Dorset heresy, it's a joke. Place-names like this were never taken seriously by anyone, except perhaps a folklorist of the old school.

But as often as not, the places that feature in these cheerful stories of giants and the Devil had possessed earlier, more spiritual meanings. Vincent the Giant took over from St Vincent, and what was once a rock-cut hermitage becomes a monster's cavern; Goram blots out the memory of St Blaise, just as the ruins of the saint's chapel disappear under the folly of Blaise Castle (Fig. 10.3). In both cases places of worship had been built within the boundaries of hillforts, so that before secularisation there had been Christianity, and before that the prehistoric tradition. Old earthworks had been given new life as protective rings around the sacred place. This is a common pattern in the region, and we find the same at Woodbury, near Bere Regis, where a chapel dedicated to the Nativity of the Virgin was built within a hillfort, some time before 1205. The tradition must have been earlier than Christianity, since pagan temples had been constructed inside the rings at Maiden Castle and South Cadbury. Sometimes, as at Cadbury/Congresbury, a Romano-British shrine was eventually converted to Christian use. So clearly there are some popular practices that go back into the deep past, but it would be a false emphasis to think that everything traditional is unbelievably old, or to pick out only those aspects of folk belief that strike us as archaic and superstitious. Tradition is handed on to satisfy a contemporary audience, not to carry hidden clues for the scholar.

After all, a new tradition can adopt a quite deliberate patina of age. The story of St Collen is a case in point. After many adventures this saint retired to a hermitage in the Somerset Levels, where he was scandalised to hear the locals talking with much respect of Gwyn ap Nudd. He shook his fists at them, and said that their friend was nothing but a demon. That evening, a sprucely dressed young man came to the lonely hermitage and asked Collen to dine at the house of his master, Gwyn. They passed unseen over the moors until they came to a castle set on 'the hill of Glastonbury' (by which is meant the Tor). Within its walls, all was music, feasting and laughter, with Gwyn himself presiding at the high seat. He greeted Collen courteously, and asked him to partake of the food, but the saint said, 'No: I do not eat the leaves of a tree.' A shudder ran through the company. Gwyn rallied and asked his guest, 'What do you think of the livery of my servants, so red and so blue?' Collen said, 'They are well for what they are. The blue is for eternal ice, and the red is for the endless burning.' Then he pulled a flask of holy water out of his robes, and sprinkled it all around him. Everything went dark, and Collen found himself alone on the dewy slopes of the Tor.

It is a memorable tale of the conflict between two worlds, and many readers have found it clear proof of Glastonbury's pre-Christian roots as a sacred place. In this they are following the lead of the original author, who wrote in the 15th or 16th century, drawing on ideas about Gwyn that had come together in medieval tradition – among them the belief that this shadowy character was something to do with Annwn, or the realm of Faerie. From the 12th century onwards, characters from Welsh tradition had been found homes at Glastonbury or elsewhere in north Somerset and Devon; originally these naturalised heroes were all saints, but as the appropriation of tradition gathered pace, it began to pick up themes from ancient or invented paganism as well. In many ways it must have prefigured the Celticism of our own era, except that in the 15th century paganism was the old effete religion overwhelmed by the new teachings of

Christianity, whereas nowadays it is supposed to be the other way round.

It is probable (though only someone as ill-mannered as St Collen would say it out loud) that Glastonbury is just a middle-Saxon monastery with a gift for inventing pedigrees and finding previously unsuspected sacred places. Certainly the Tor was never consecrated to any religion but Christianity, as far as archaeology can tell, and it was not until the 13th century that the church of St Michael was built at its highest point. But the Tor is only one among many hills which belonged to St Michael. Elsewhere in Somerset there were Burrowbridge Mump and Montacute (Fig. 10.4), both with conspicuous chapels, and a string of dedications extends westwards to St Michael's Mount itself, at the furthest reaches of Britain. It is not just a modern antiquarian fancy that links these hills together, for William Worcestre listed

Fig. 10.4 St Michael's Hill at Montacute *was a landmark for Roman roads, which after the Norman Conquest supported a castle, and then in 1760 a lookout tower.*

them in order after he had made his journey to the West in 1478. But the idea that they could form a sacred chain, running through and consecrating the landscape, had to wait until the 20th century. Wellesley Tudor Pole was a mystic and man of action who served as guardian for what may (or may not) have been the Holy Grail, and until his death in 1968 he sent this relic on many pilgrimages to awaken the sacred shrines of St Michael.[5] Catholic and Protestant could agree in paying respect to the guardian angel of Scripture, and when Christian spirituality lost its power to enchant, the new pagan synthesis took over. The St Michael Line was re-imagined, first as a primary ley, and then as a twisting pathway of dowsable energies.[6]

Like his old opponent the Devil, St Michael has taken on many different personalities through the years. The spiritual meaning of his shrines is transformed, while their monuments remain to suggest a reassuring continuity. Old stories are reinterpreted, and not just stories, for in times of transformation even the primary encounter with the sacred becomes ambiguous. Take the hill at Montacute. 'I felt compelled to climb it one very wet day,' writes the earth mysteries researcher John Billingsley, 'and on the field up to it went through an experience which I call "the veil" – sometimes I feel like I'm passing through an invisible boundary.' He came to the tower at the summit (Montacute, like Blaise Castle, is crowned by an 18th-century folly) and climbed up. 'Arriving at the top landing, I looked out of one of the windows and in the clouds – alone and/or near, I think, the location of Cadbury Castle – a clear image of a man's face appeared, bearded, with jaw-length hair and with a steady gaze looking straight at me.' Who was he? What did he appear for? That was left unsaid.[7]

This face was not the first vision in the history of Montacute. In fact the hill acquired its sacred status after the village blacksmith had a dream, back in the 11th century. A figure of divine beauty appeared to him, telling him to climb to the summit and dig for a marvellous treasure. The blacksmith shuffled the bedclothes around him and went back to sleep, but a few weeks later the dream came back, though now the shining figure wore a frown. The blacksmith was still a bit reluctant, but when the third dream came, the mysterious visitor lost his temper and pinched the workman so hard that the scratches were still visible as he tumbled out of bed. He threw some clothes on and went to the priest, showing his scars and pleading for something to be done. That morning, the villagers gathered together and marched up the hill, praying and singing, with the priest and blacksmith at their head. After long hours of digging, they came to bedrock and there, shining inside a dark cleft, they found a wonderful crucifix of bright black stone. Eventually this was lost to Somerset, for Tovi the Proud, standard-bearer to King Cnut, owned the village and he announced that the cross would need to rest at some more fitting shrine. He had it taken downhill to the churchyard, where it was loaded on to a cart drawn by 24 oxen, while a list of every sacred place in England was read aloud to them. The oxen seemed quite indifferent to this, but then a stranger in the crowd mentioned somewhere called Waltham, and they suddenly pricked up their ears and set off at a brisk pace in the direction of Essex. Waltham belonged to Earl Tovi – it was a hunting lodge of which he was particularly fond – but he yielded to the will of God and founded a monastery there instead.

The story of the miraculous cross was current at Waltham in the 1180s. By 1246 a chapel had been built on the hill, for the prior of Montacute was chartered to hold a fair there on the feast of the Translation of St Edward. Clearly the demarcation between sacred and secular did not rule out commerce, and as the fair was intended to compete with others in the neighbourhood, a hill must have been regarded as the best possible site. So it seems that hilltops were not isolated places; they were the nodes, the central points at which a scattered society could come together. Trade, like religion, has its own history of continuity, and both are often to be found within the boundaries of hillforts. The giant-built rings of Spetisbury also served as an early fair, if the finds of 10th-century pennies there count for anything.

At Woodbury, the hillfort was kept busy with buying and selling well into the 20th century. It was the Greenhill of Thomas Hardy's novels, 'the Nijni Novgorod of South Wessex; and the busiest, merriest, noisiest day of the whole statute number was the day of the sheep fair ... To each of the chief openings on opposite sides a winding road ascended, and the level green space of ten or fifteen acres enclosed by the bank was the site of the fair. A few permanent erections dotted the spot, but the majority of visitors patronised canvas alone for resting and feeding.'

The first charter for the fair was in 1232 but this may have simply authorised an established gathering. The popular story suggests as much. One day, it seems, a pedlar was carrying his pack over the hill to Bere when a sudden squall of rain came on. All his cloth and his fine things were drenched, but the storm soon blew over, and when the sun came out he sat on the old banks and spread his wares around him to let them dry. Some women from the village were passing that way, and the bright fabrics caught their eye. They climbed up to investigate, and what they found pleased them so much that after a little bargaining everything was sold. The pedlar came back the next year, and the year after that he brought his friends, and so the fair grew.[8] It all sounds very convincing, though in fact this story is a migratory tale type and Woodbury is not the only fair to lay claim to it. But it fills the same need as any other story of origins: it shows how something came out of nothing, and all by accident. Woodbury Hill Fair was an important landmark, in time as well as space. Boys wore their first breeches for Fair Day on 21 September, and domestic fires were never lit until the night after, whatever the temperature. It would be almost a letdown that this should have come about by mere human decisions, the fiat of some king or abbot: how much better to put it down to the providential workings of chance.

Towards the end, the element of funfair began to predominate at Woodbury, bringing it in line with other hilltop festivals such as Dover's Games. These had been instituted on the rising ground that overlooks Chipping Camden by Robert

Dover. They lasted until 1852, and were then revived a century later. Modern entertainments are not those of the original games, which involved horse-racing, shin-kicking, pitching the hammer and generous amounts of food.[9] Cudgelling and races were also on offer at Maiden Castle, along with grinning for tobacco and running after a pig to catch it by its tail. These sports made their appearance in 1798, under royal patronage, but following the crisis of the Napoleonic years they were not continued. Not even the attraction of cheese-rolling down the vertiginous slopes of the hillfort was enough to attract spectators for a second year. And yet in Gloucestershire, at Coopers Hill, cheese-rolling alone has formed the nucleus of a long-lasting festival, where the young men of the neighbourhood hurl themselves down a one-in-two gradient with reckless disregard for life, limb, and Public Liability Insurance.

Cheese-rolling at Coopers Hill has taken on a life of its own. Quite apart from the sport itself, it has acquired the value that comes from honouring tradition: this, people say, is something that we do, because we always have done it. That is true of many events, and it is a complete reversal of the doctrine current among Victorian folklorists – the idea that forgotten rituals linger on as popular customs. In fact it is much more common for a practice to begin as part of the ordinary range of social diversions, and then to perpetuate itself from year to year, becoming stranger and more ritualised as it loses touch with practices in the wider society. The maypoles of Sturminster Marshall and Chipping Camden have acquired an iconic status that would have surprised 17th-century villagers, for whom they were just a routine way of marking dance-floors.

With customs, as with stories, the patina of archaism might sometimes be created quite deliberately. On May Day, the young men of Newent and district climbed May Hill and fought vigorously among themselves for possession of it, parish against parish. A later account from the 19th century has more picturesque details. They were divided into two troops: one wore the livery of winter while the other was dressed as spring, covered in green branches and May blossom. The fight was rigged so that winter would lose, and then after the lads had limped back down the slopes, their fathers would get together on the same spot to apportion grazing rights.[10] This was essential for men with competing claims to a finite hectarage of pasture, and it is easy to see how the same conflict of interest could have been played out in straight violence among the youngsters, and how the familiar symbolic combat of summer and winter would have channelled the mayhem into a more acceptable form.

But the ritual combat would never have made sense without the sense of ceremony, even of mystery, which surrounded these hilltop customs. Hills had a queer reputation, and it was only during the day that they belonged to humankind. No one could remain on Maiden Castle overnight, for sooner or later they would always be forced to go down the hill. At Lamberts Castle, once the racing and wrestling of the games was over and the crowds began to drift away, 'the Countrie People will show you an Hole near the toppe of the Hill ... They will tell you more Fables than I list to write ... of the Spirits haunting that Place.' Yet there were always a brave few who would confront the hills at night, like the doctor from Broomfield who heard of an iron castle, which lay beneath Ruborough Camp, full of gold and silver. Being 'an uncommon book-learned man', he soon found out the day and hour at which the door into the hill would be revealed. He must have been something of a dowser, too, since he was able to mark the right spot with a hazel wand. Come the night of the full moon, the doctor hired a trustworthy labourer and the two men set off to work, one with a spade and the other with a bible. 'At last the servant's spade struck on the iron door; and at once horrible groans and shrieks and cries were heard underground in the castle, and spirits of all sorts began to come out at the door, ready to carry away the poor servant.' It took some nifty work with the bible to get him out, and at once the earth closed up again, leaving green turf where the trench had been.[11]

Fig. 10.5 A clump of beeches clothes Culliford Tree, *part of a Bronze Age barrow cemetery that lies along the Ridgeway on the chalk downs of central Dorset.*

Fig. 10.6 Cadbury Castle – *built in the Iron Age, stormed by the Romans, and then reoccupied and fortified in the obscure period of the 6th century.*

There is a hint of the Montacute story here, but the doctor was searching for more worldly goods, and he did not have the authority of a dream. Without the consent of the hidden guardians, a hunt for treasure is always doomed, though that has never restrained its hold on the imagination. People in Uley whispered how gates of silver opened to unknown marvels beneath Crawley Hill. In Glastonbury they knew that doomed Abbot Whiting had concealed the most precious treasures of his abbey behind a pair of golden gates. And if these are only hints and rumours, then there are the iron gates of Cadbury, whose location is known for certain. They lie 'close by the original British roadway into the fort ... Father often used to say that when a boy he had seen the upper corner of the iron durns and the corner of an iron door.' This was not the only passage underground, since the hill was honeycombed by secret tunnels. Clap down the cover on one well, and you could hear the echo reverberate inside another, even though the whole body of the hill stood between them. Naturally, being so undermined, the ground within the hillfort was beginning to collapse, and a stack of barley which could be seen over the ramparts in September would be quite invisible by March.

So Cadbury was a hollow hill, just like Glastonbury Tor, except that there the image was a poetical one and here it took a more literal form. The fairies lived in hills, or to be a little less prosaic, if you went to a hill you might be able to encounter the fairy world. It did not matter what kind of hill: a tussocky barrow was as good as the Mendips, for those who wanted to make contact. Lie down on Bincombe Bumps at mid-day, with your ears held close to the ground, and you will hear the sweetest singing. A little further down the Dorset Ridgeway, the same tale is told of Culliford Tree barrow, although this has an updated version (Fig. 10.5). A woman visited the site once or twice in the 1970s, while worrying about the purchase of her new house. 'She states firmly that on both occasions she heard the voice of an invisible speaker who warned her to desist from her plan. After the second occasion she told her agent she had changed her mind.'

Along with fairies went treasure. Cadbury was as full of gold as Ruborough, but it had lost its guardians when the fairies abandoned Somerset. They left when people started building churches everywhere, since the sound of bellringing was as unwelcome to them as the touch of holy water; but before they went, they had been on quite good terms with their neighbours in the valley. Aubrey was told, at the end of the 17th century, how they used to lend out kitchenware for festivals in the village, making no conditions except that the goods had to be returned on time. This lasted until an ungrateful human coveted their great cauldron and failed to return it, and so the commerce between two worlds came to an end.

But it is not to trace the fairies, or to dig for gold, that visitors clamber through the bluebell woods and explore the old fort (Fig. 10.6). Cadbury/Camelot has become synonymous with Arthur. 'Have you come to take the king out?', asked an anxious old man when a party of antiquarians visited in 1902, and since then there have been several attempts to bring out the king, at least in a metaphorical sense. They culminated in the excavations of 1966–70, when fundraising bodies included the Pendragon Society and the Honourable Society of Knights of the Round Table. The dig was inspired by a brief note from the Tudor antiquary, John Leland: 'the people tell nothing thar but that they have hard say that Arture much resorted to Camalat'. Other gossip from his 1542 visit included the discovery of various finds, including a horseshoe of pure silver.[12]

By 1890, local people were able to tell the visitor much more than they had in Leland's time. King Arthur is at rest within the hill, surrounded by his knights; if you are pure of life, and you climb up to wash your eyes in Arthur's Well on St John's Eve, you will see the iron gates swing open and catch a glimpse of the sleeping king. That is the night when he wakes to ride out with his men, or as others say, it happens on every night of the full moon: at all events, the riders troop down King Arthur's Hunting Causeway and water their horses at the spring by Sutton Montis church before they return to the hollow hill. Their horses are shod with silver that glints in the moonlight. There was an unbeliever in the village who used to scoff at all this, but he was silenced one morning after Midsummer Night when he found a silver horseshoe in the trackway.[13]

That story sounds like an imaginative elaboration of the comment in Leland, and if so, it can only have come from someone who knew of his book. In fact the whole Arthurian tradition at South Cadbury smells of the lamp. His night rides with his men, a source of dread to anyone who encounters them, are typical of the French *chasse Artu*. The lost leader who lies buried in some landmark, and rides around it at night on a silver-shod horse, sounds very much like the great O'Donoghue of Killarney, whose traditions had been retailed to English tourists since the 1820s. It would not have taken much in the way of a dialogue between obliging locals and eager visitors before these other stories of a sleeping king were grafted on to the gold-filled, fairy-haunted hill in Somerset.

In this way tales from local tradition find themselves being woven into the great national narratives, of which the Arthurian cycle is the chief. And at Glastonbury, even Arthur forms only part of a great web, one which seems to bring together every imaginable myth from these isles. The monks may have made the connection back in 1191, when they uncovered, or claimed to

*Fig. 10.7 **The thorn tree which can be seen today on Wirral Hill** descends from cuttings of the original Glastonbury Thorn, and retains its winter-flowering habit.*

uncover, the majestic bones which lay beneath a leaden cross marked 'Here the Famed King Arthur Lies Buried in the Isle of Avalon'. Or they may have been drawing on earlier tradition. That's the way with Glastonbury, you can never be sure. One thing is certain: as soon as a tradition gets going in this quiet market town, it will put down roots like bindweed.

The winter-flowering Glastonbury Thorn (Fig. 10.7), for instance, first appears in 1520 as a tree that 'do burge and bear green leaves at Christmas/ As fresh as other in May'. Its fame began to spread after the Reformation, when it filled an ambiguous role, somewhere between a natural curiosity and a relic. In the 1660s visitors were told how a Puritan (Elizabethan or Civil War, the sources are divided) tried to cut it down but was blinded by a chip from the trunk. By 1716, when the chances of a real Catholic revival were slim, it was safe to give the Thorn a legend and it was revealed to have been the staff of Joseph of Arimathea, planted in the ground when he rested on Wirrall Hill (now officially renamed Weary-All) and gazed down on the holiest earth of Glastonbury.

The old Thorn had died by the time its legend started to grow, but numerous shoots had been planted in the town by pub landlords and others with an interest in the tourist trade. Fortunately the winter-flowering habit is preserved by clones of the original tree, which by now had been propagated throughout the country. When calendar reform came in 1752, the Bristol newspapers reported a failure of Glastonbury Thorns to flower in Buckinghamshire, where people had gone back home and refused to attend Christmas church services until 6 January, New Style. So in the secular 18th century, the tree acquired a religious authority which it had never had in the days of the monks.[14]

At least the Thorn had attracted visitors in the medieval period, which is more than can be said for Glastonbury's holy well. In 1751 Matthew Chancelor, a long-time sufferer from asthma, dreamed that he was following the bridlepath out of Glastonbury, when he bent down to drink from some water that welled up by the track. In his dream, he thought someone told him that if he returned, and drank from these waters on seven successive Sundays, he would be cured. When he awoke, Chancelor hurried on down to Glastonbury. There was the water trickling by the road, just as he had hoped (it ran from a disused medieval conduit) and everything followed as it did in his dream. His cure was described in a broadsheet which caught the public imagination, and soon a stone-lined chamber was cleaned out at the ruins of the old well, which was visited by hopeful invalids from every village between Bristol and Street.[15]

Fig. 10.8 Traces of iron stain the waters of Chalice Well to a dry blood colour, but they were still used to supply Glastonbury monastery in the 12th century.

But a spa, even a divinely revealed one, was rather tame by Glastonbury standards. It seems to have been lost from view between the 1780s and the beginning of the last century, when the well formed a feature in the grounds of a Catholic seminary, and was rumoured to have supplied water to 12 anchorite disciples of Joseph of Arimathea. This was enough to attract the attention of Alice Buckton, a spiritual seeker who bought the site at auction in 1912. The price was high, but she was assisted by the hand of God, who arranged for a rival bidder to be stranded by train failure in a country station some distance away. In the years that followed, it became clear that Chalice Well (as it was now called) was the place where Joseph had kept the Grail, staining its chalybeate waters into an everlasting red with the holy blood (Fig. 10.8). Before Joseph it had been in the hands of the Druids, or possibly the Egyptians. By the time that Buckton died, in 1944, the well had become part of the round of sacred sites in Glastonbury.

The idea that a mysterious treasure lies buried deep within a well is not confined to Glastonbury, nor to tales of healing saints. Nothing could be more different from these tranquil waters than the home of brave Lady Bankes, the heroine who held Corfe Castle for her king against the Roundheads. Eventually, as England fell under its new rulers, she stood alone and after eight weeks of siege in the winter of 1645–6, a traitor in her garrison sold out to the enemy. But before she quit the old grey walls, knowing that her goods would be robbed for the Parliamentary cause, Lady Bankes threw all her plate and jewels down a well and lobbed in a keg of live gunpowder after them. As the smoke of the explosion cleared, she uttered a solemn curse on anyone who should search the well. Then she seized the unsuspecting traitor and had him hanged from the keep, before reluctantly grating open the castle gates.[16]

Well, Lady Bankes was real enough, and one could imagine that there might be some truth in that story about the well. But then we are told how the abbot of St Augustine's in Bristol, hearing that the suppression of religious houses was imminent, paid a midnight visit to the fishpond at Abbots Leigh and entrusted the abbey treasures to its dark waters, hoping to return when there was a change in religion. And there is the story of a golden table from Buckland Newton, which has an almost mythical ring, with its hint of underworld guardians. It lay at the bottom of a well in the earthworks of Dungeon Castle. '"They" once tried to get it up, but this caused the foundations of a house nearby to shake, and the attempt was abandoned.'

So much for legend. Are these empty tales, or is there anything to support them in archaeology? Certainly we find that real treasure has been concealed in wells: for instance, the hoard of Roman coins found next to a perpetual spring in Hanham, beside the River Avon upstream of Bristol. These offerings seem to have been part of religious practice throughout the district. When excavated, the hilltop shrine at Pagans Hill contained a Romano-British temple aligned on a deep well, which received votive offerings until the mid-4th century. Then, after years of neglect, people began to return with offerings for the well in the 7th century, only this time they were Christians.[17]

Here we have a hill, used in its last phase as a scene of Christian pilgrimage, with a venerated well into which people throw their precious things. Look southwards to Woodbury Hill, and we have the hillfort, the shrine, the annual festival … and the legend of Anchorets Well, to which people flocked on the last of the three fair days to drink healing waters, and which was rumoured to contain a golden table. People's ideas have run in parallel at the two sites, although that does not necessarily mean that the Bere Regis site must be concealing a Romano-British holy well. Legends do not exist as a memory of historical facts. Rather, both the legend and the fact are an embodiment, for two successive cultures in the same region, of the same magical image of gold shining through the water.

History and legend combine their forces in the sacred springs at Bath. Certainly there is continuity enough for anyone here; the hot waters have seen every form of human activity, from the veneration of capricious gods to draft applications for European Union funding. But though the waters remain a constant, ideas about them have not. For most of the last two millennia, the Bath springs have not even been regarded as sacred. Visions of their spiritual meaning have only revived in recent decades, so that there is now more than one version of what the springs are really about: a split which has been accommodated in truly English fashion by dedicating the Cross Bath as a cult site, the King's Bath as a heritage centre and the Hot Bath as the venue for a multi-million-pound spa development.

And just as each generation raises its own new buildings over the unfailing springs, so the legends of Bath are under continual reconstruction. Today, you will most likely hear the story of Prince Bladud, son of the mighty King Lud. He was a handsome and promising youth, so gifted that his father allowed him to go and learn wisdom in far-off Athens. On his return from Academe, tragedy struck: young Bladud was afflicted with disfiguring leprosy. Making a solemn vow never to bring disgrace upon his royal parents, he fled the haunts of men, and eked out a miserable living herding swine. Very little in his previous career had prepared him for this, and the pigs began to lose condition. Their once glossy hides were cracked and broken, and their master led them listlessly from grove to grove, hoping to improve their lot by a change of pannage. Then, one morning, as the pigs were being driven out to feed, they saw a waterhole in the valley below. A thin mist rose from the marsh and the pigs broke into a run as they jostled towards it, with Bladud in the rear trying to keep up with the herd. Soon every beast was wallowing in the glutinous mud, as their master nervously watched over his charges. They seemed different somehow … healthier. At once Bladud was a man of action again, he threw off his leprous rags and plunged into the marvellous waters: when he emerged, he found himself restored to health. Need we say more of his glorious return to court, of his subsequent reign as a wise and enlightened king or of the noble structure which he built in honour of the gods over the sanitive waters?

This tale of Bladud and the pigs first appears in the 1670s, part of the traditional lore, which Bath people liked to pass on to those who were visiting the springs. Before then, Bladud had featured as the hero of a quite different kind of story. It was he, visitors were told, who had created the hot springs by burying molten brass and brimstone – a splendidly medieval combination of magic and chemistry. This was the version still current in the learned Selden's notes to *Poly-Olbion*, in the early 17th century: no leprosy, no pigs. And it is precisely this conventional view of Bladud as the wise magician that is being guyed in the later tale, by making him into a pig-keeper. Otherwise it is simply one amongst many stories that explain how a spa was discovered when a quick-witted countryman saw an animal making use of its curative waters. Pigs at Bath, doves at Cheltenham, sheep at Nottington, a cow at Epsom: there is a whole menagerie of them.

At first Bladud's adventure was presented as a simple country tradition, helped out in some versions by appalling puns – the pigs come from Hogs Norton, they cross the river at Swineford, and so on. In 1673 the story was versified in cod-rustic dialect. And when the dissolute but polished Earl of Rochester came to town, the city fathers took down a public inscription that referred to the legend, just in case it should become the butt of his wit.[18]

But turn the clock forward, and see how different a picture can be coloured in from the same outline. Two hundred years on, the steam which reeked above the mud-bath has softened into a fine Celtic mist, and Bladud is no longer the comic swineherd but a wounded Fisher King, set to tend the magic beasts of the Other-world. 'An illness forces the hero into exile,' explains the bardic teacher Bob Stewart. 'He is led by totem beasts to a sacred site … he acquires magic powers, which he uses for the benefit of the people, and to the glory of the Goddess.'[19] Now that's more like a foundation myth.

As this suggests, a living tradition can speak in many voices, from flippancy to reverence: it is forever growing through reflection and commentary on itself. Take the cycle of stories from Cerne Abbas. Legend tells how, when the Christian faith was still young and uncertain in the hearts of Dorset folk, St Augustine came tramping over the dry downs to bring his message to the country people. They had very little time for him, and stood about jeering. But Augustine beat the ground with his staff, and at once an unquenchable spring began to flow (Fig. 10.9). This was something they understood, for water is scarce in these hills in summer. At first they only praised the saint for satisfying their thirst, but then gradually they realised that his holy words, too, could bring new strength to their parched lives.

Fig. 10.9 The monks of Cerne built a chapel over St Augustine's Well *in the late medieval period and the healing reputation of its waters survived the Dissolution.*

This is the kind of legend that is common at holy wells. St Laurence, a companion of Augustine, made a spring flow at Didmarton, as did St Keyne at Keynsham, and the Virgin Mary herself at Hempsted (Fig. 10.10). She had been on her way to visit Joseph of Arimathea at Glastonbury when her ship was swept up-river by the Severn bore. The exegetical use of these tales is obvious, and they were repeated from place to place whenever the symbolism of cleansing and thirst-quenching could ornament a medieval sermon.

Fig. 10.10 The Lady Well at Hempsted *was originally a conduit head, providing a flow of pure water to Llanthony Priory in the suburbs of Gloucester.*

When St Augustine created the well at Cerne, he looked up to Heaven and said '*Cerno Hel*', which is mixed Latin and Hebrew for 'I see God'. Hence the name of the village (*Cernel* in Domesday). And here the story becomes more complicated, because Hel, or Helith, is a name traditionally associated with the Cerne Giant. This massive chalk-cut hill-figure is not recorded until the 17th century – possibly because he did not exist until then. But today Cerne is synonymous with its giant, just as Cadbury is with Arthur, and he has to be smuggled into the stories somehow. After all, Walter of Coventry did write in the 13th century that a god called Helith used to be worshipped in Dorset; and while he may have been misunderstanding an earlier allusion to the prophet Elijah (Helias in medieval Latin), he might just have been on to something. Then again, the antiquary William Stukeley was sure that Heil had something to do with the Phoenician Hercules ... and so speculation goes on. Like Vincent and Goram, the Giant has taken over a Christian landscape and given it new meanings. But he has done this very much in the manner of our own times – not by wiping out the old legends, but by reinterpreting them in a seemingly endless web of stories about stories. St Augustine's Well is still there, but its meanings have changed. Like Bath, it is now seen as a primordial Celtic shrine. Like the Giant, it is a place for fertility ritual.

As far as folklore is concerned, it does not really matter when the Giant was made, but it does matter very much that neither his age nor his meaning can be pinned down. In 1996 he was put on trial by a team from Bournemouth University, hoping to establish his true date, but the jury is still out.[20] When we study the landscape legends of the West, we arrive at no authoritative interpretation of them, no learned proof of origin: rather, we find ourselves exploring the ten thousand meanings that myth has had for different cultures at different times. Sue Clifford of Common Ground summed up the feelings of many when she said at the trial in Cerne, 'He is a giant, he diminishes all of us. He is a giant, a figure of the imagination ... While we did not give him life, it is only through us that he lingers.'

NOTES

1   Quinn 1996.
2   Harte 1986, 75; Waring 1977, 48.
3   Worcestre 1969, 292–3.
4   Harte 2000.
5   Benham 1993, 140.
6   Miller & Broadhurst 1989.
7   Richardson 2001, 56–7.
8   Pickard-Cambridge 1885.
9   Briggs 1974, 26–7.
10   Palmer 1994, 35, 291.
11   Collins 1857.
12   Robinson 1921; Alcock & Ashe 1968, 125.
13   Bennett 1890; St George Gray 1913.
14   Vickery 1979.
15   Coleman 1897; Rahtz & Watts 2003, 134–8 and 161.
16   Beard 1933, 338.
17   Quinn 1999, 151, 169; Rahtz 1991.
18   Clark 1994.
19   Stewart 1989.
20   Darvill *et al.* 1999, 152.

11

West Country Spas

SAM HUNT

Before the widespread availability of mains supplies natural springs were an important source of fresh water. The city of Wells and towns such as Stogursey in Somerset were sited close to local springs, as were many other settlements where rivers and streams either did not exist or were too contaminated for domestic use. Springs also provided an important focus for cult worship and religious practice. They were commonly associated with the worship of Celtic deities and, as sacred sites, later became absorbed into the Christian Church as 'holy wells', for example St Decuman's Well at Watchet. Villages were often named after holy wells; Holwell near Sherborne and Holy Well Lake just west of Wellington indicate the importance once attached to local springs. The Chalice Well at Glastonbury and St Anne's Well at Clifton were important pilgrimage centres in the medieval period, as was St Augustine's Well at Cerne Abbas in Dorset (Fig. 11.1).

Healing powers were frequently ascribed to springs and holy wells – 'eye' wells, for example, were particularly common in the West of England. The sulphur springs at Edington and Queen Camel in Somerset were frequented for the treatment of skin diseases and St Anthony's Well in the Forest of Dean had the added virtue of curing mangy dogs. Near Bath the waters of St Winifred's Well on the slopes of Lansdown were reputed to cure infertility.

But it was lower down in the Avon valley, where thermal springs emerge from the valley floor, that the healing qualities of spring waters were to be exploited on a very different scale. During the Roman occupation, and from the Norman period through into the 20th century, Bath developed to become an important medical spa and fashionable resort.

The growing popularity of water-based cures in the 18th century was to lead to the emergence of other spa resorts in the West. Hotwells near Bristol, and Cheltenham, where iron-impregnated (chalybeate) springs were discovered in 1716, were to become important curative centres. Later in the 18th century the vogue for seawater bathing was to give rise to a new generation of marine spas along the north and the south coasts, the seaside resorts of Weston-Super-Mare and Weymouth becoming important holiday destinations in the Victorian period.

The growth of inland and seaside resorts was to be important in shaping the West, bringing new wealth to both market towns and fishing villages, and stimulating the growth of road and rail networks and the development of cultural institutions – theatres, festivals and an architectural legacy of crescents, piers and pavilions.

Fig. 11.1 Direction for St Adhelm's Well at Doulting, Somerset.

CURATIVE WATERS

Bath, up until the late-Georgian period, held an undisputed position as the premier resort and its social institutions provided a model for others to follow.

It was also the leading centre for curative treatment. From three spring heads more than a million litres of thermal water gush forth daily at a temperature of around 40°C, sufficient to sustain a substantial complex of hot and tepid bathing facilities. Because they were heavily mineralised with sodium and calcium sulphates the Bath waters were also promoted as a drinking cure for a range of internal ailments.

Although Bath was an important centre for water treatments in the medieval period its development as a spa town dates from the 16th century. The publication of a series of medical tracts advocating the use of the Bath waters was to have an important effect on its growth by encouraging wider interest among physicians in Britain. Among the most influential of these publications were *A Book of the Natures and Properties, as well of the Baths of England as of other Baths in Germany and Italy*, written in 1562 by Dr William Turner, Physician to Edward VI , later to become Dean of Wells, and Dr Edward Jorden's *Discourse of Natural Bathes and Mineral Waters*, which first appeared in 1631 and ran into five editions.[1] Bathing in spa water was recommended for the treatment of a range of ailments from skin complaints to arthritis, sciatica and rheumatism. Immersion in spa water was also advocated for the treatment of palsy, a condition that was caused by the adulteration of cider and port with lead acetate, which was used as an early and particularly dangerous form of artificial sweetener.[2] Spa water was pumped as a form of hydraulic massage, the jets of hot water being directed on to the affected part of the body. Pumping replaced the rather inefficient treatment of bucketing, which was performed by the tallest and strongest of the bath attendants.

As at other spas, a growing colony of physicians resided at Bath, undertaking diagnosis of visiting patients' ailments and advising on spa 'regimes'. Dr Thomas Guidott was one of the leading spa physicians practising at Bath in the latter part of the 17th century. His *The Register of Bath*, published in 1694, which lists 200 cures at the spa between 1663 and 1693, is of particular interest not only as a medical record of the ailments treated but also because it provides an interesting profile of patients visiting Bath during the Restoration period.[3] Although most came from London, the Home Counties and the West Country, there are references to patients from other parts of the country, including Scotland and Ireland. Gout, rheumatism and 'lameness' figure prominently among the cures.

Fig. 11.2 Humphrey Repton, **Taking the Waters at the Pump Room, Bath,** *1784, watercolour.*

A 70-year-old merchant from London was cured of the gout in 1676 after three seasons of bathing in the Cross Bath and 'rubbing well of the guide's hands'. Sciatica was a common complaint and pumping was the recommended treatment – 20,000 'strokes' at the pump cured Benjamin Baber, a Bath alderman, in 1665. Patients with skin complaints and ulcers also benefited from the water cure, including Emmanuel Weston who was cured of the 'scurf' after having washed his head 20 times in the Leper's Bath. Others required more prolonged treatment, such as Henry Johnson, 'a dane' with old sore and running ulcers on the legs, hands and face, who had to return for the cure over several seasons. Sporting injuries were also mentioned: Viscount Hereford, who fell from his horse while hunting, was successfully treated for an arm injury by a combination of pumping and swimming in the baths.

From the 17th century onwards drinking the spa water became increasingly popular as a cure for internal disorders, including gout brought on by the high-protein diet of the wealthy classes. Guidott's *Register* records drinking cures as being successful in the treatment of palsy, stomach pains and corpulence. To accommodate the growing numbers of patients pump rooms were built adjacent to the King's Bath and Hot Bath springs in the early 18th century (Fig. 11.2).

Further west from Bath three tepid thermal springs emerge in the Avon Gorge at Bristol, and in the 17th century Hotwells, on the edge of the River Avon, became an important spa centre. A pump house and assembly rooms were built in 1722 with a gravelled promenade commanding picturesque views of the Gorge. Drinking the waters was recommended for the treatment of diabetes, kidney complaints and skin disorders. In 1754 John Wesley was successfully treated for the disease at the spa. Clifton, on the edge of Bristol Downs, was developed to provide accommodation for patients. In later years Hotwells acquired a reputation for the treatment of consumption and in 1799 Thomas Beddoes established his Pneumatic Institute there, offering inhalation cures of nitrous oxide and cow's breath. The Institute, however, was short-lived although Beddoes' research established that water cures were ineffectual in treating the disease.

The chalybeate and saline springs at Cheltenham offered an alternative treatment to the thermal springs at Bath and Hotwells, and from the late 18th century the town developed rapidly as a spa centre following the publication of a series of medical treatises advocating the virtues of the waters (Fig. 11.3). Cheltenham was principally a drinking spa. The original spring, later to become the Royal Well, was discovered around 1716. As Cheltenham grew in popularity, however, other wells were sunk to tap new supplies of mineral water. By 1830 the Cambray, Montpellier, Imperial and Pittville wells offered a choice of spa waters ranging in mineral strength and composition. Unlike the spa at Bath, these wells were speculative ventures and because the waters were not thermal, bathing facilities were not developed on a comparable scale. The waters were, however, popular for the treatment of internal disorders, including liver complaints, loss of appetite and constipation. Cheltenham, as with Bath, sustained growing numbers of resident spa physicians who would 'carry out a diagnosis of the patients' ailments and advise a course of treatment in which control of diet and regular exercise usually formed an important part. The daily 'regime' of drinking the waters, promenading and resting was fundamental to the cure and dictated the pace of life at the spas. Coupled with a change of air and environment the regularity of the spa routine was probably as effacious as drinking and bathing in curing many ailments. Medical opinion was divided on the value of the Cheltenham waters and there is evidence that some of the springs were 'fortified' by the addition of Epsom salts.

The growing popularity of spa treatment following the Stuart Restoration brought about the emergence of several minor spas in the West Country. These were mainly chalybeate spas, and as with

Fig. 11.3 S W Fores, **Effects of the Cheltenham Waters or tis NECESSARY to quicken *your* motions after the Second Glass,** *1823, hand-coloured engraving.*

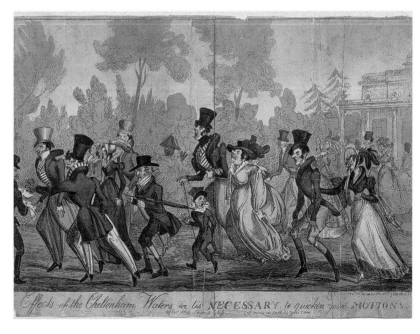

Cheltenham they were primarily developed as drinking spas, although some had cold-water and heated immersion baths as well. In the latter half of the 17th century, spas were established at Castle Cary and Box, and outside our region, in Wiltshire, at Chippenham, Holt and Seend, and in the late 18th century at Ditteredge. Most of these spa wells were short-lived speculative developments, although Holt and later Melksham, in Wiltshire, which emerged in the early years of the 19th century, proved to be more successful. The sulphur spring at Purton, also in Wiltshire, was developed as a spa in the late-Victorian period and bottled waters were sold as late as 1948. Gloucester, too, enjoyed a brief vogue as a spa centre, following the discovery of a saline chalybeate spring there in 1815. As at others of the smaller spas a pump house was built and the surrounding area was landscaped with gravelled walks for promenading. Four other spas were established in Gloucestershire Hyde Spa at Prestbury; Walton Spa near Tewkesbury; Lower Swell; and at Newent, on the edge of the Forest of Dean. In Dorset the sulphur spring at Nottington, just north of Weymouth, was to become a popular spa centre in the Georgian period and an octagonal pump house with bathing facilities was built in the late 1830s. John Crane, a Dorchester physician, described the qualities of the Nottington water in his *An Account of the Nature, Properties and Medicinal Uses of the Mineral Water at Nottington near Weymouth, Dorchester* in 1765.[4] He recommended drinking the waters as a cure for a variety of ailments, including ridding the body of worms and kidney stones, incontinence and corpulence, healing wounds and skin diseases. Many patients combined drinking the Nottington waters with seawater bathing at Weymouth.

The Chalice Well at Glastonbury has a longer history as there is evidence of Roman construction under the 12th-century well-house. The spa was revived in the 18th century when it enjoyed a brief reputation for curing blindness, ulcers, deafness and the 'King's-evil'. Bottled Glastonbury water was sold in London and from the 17th century bottled water from Bath, Cheltenham and Melksham was also widely available throughout the country, alongside imported spa water from continental spas. Bottled water from St Vincent's Spring at Bristol was popular with seamen as a prevention for scurvy and was exported to the continent, Ireland, Jamaica and the West Indies. Later, in the 19th century, J Schweppe and Co were bottling water from the Upper Hotwells Spring as part of their flourishing business manufacturing carbonated mineral waters, or 'soda' water as it later became known.

SPA VISITORS

Spa treatment required patients to undergo a daily regime of bathing and drinking over several months, sometimes longer, to be successful. For many patients visiting a spa became an annual event – some even took up permanent residence. The favoured season for taking the cure at Bath was from April to June, with a second season in autumn. The season at Cheltenham was from May to October. Hotwells likewise had a summer season. Treatment was available at most spas throughout the year, however, and as spa facilities were improved in the latter half of the 18th century seasonality was to become less important.

Royal patronage was important in securing the success of Bath and Cheltenham as places of fashionable resort. The visits of Anne of Denmark, seeking relief from gout, to Bath in 1613 and 1615 were the first of a series by Stuart monarchs. In their wake came courtiers and other members of the aristocracy. The Restoration of 1660 was to see the return from the continent of Royalist exiles, many of whom had resided at Spa in Belgium. Bath and Tonbridge Wells, in Kent, were to emerge as leading resorts over this period. By the mid-18th century Bath had eclipsed its rival, becoming the country's premier resort, a position it was to retain for the next 50 years. Writing to Lady

Suffolk in 1766, Hugh Walpole lists a number of prominent visitors at Bath including Lord Chatham, the Chancellor (Lord Camden), Lord Northington, Lady Rockingham, Lady Scarborough, Lord and Lady Powis, Lord and Lady Spencer, and Lady Vane.[5] In their wake came others. Abbé Prevost in 1734 noted the presence of card players, musicians and actors 'growing rich on the pleasure for which others pay, and sharing it with them'.[6] Bristol Hotwells also benefited from aristocratic patronage. The Duke and Duchess of Beaufort visited the spa in the 1750s and the Duke of York took the cure in 1766. The patronage of Lord Fauconberg, George III's gentleman-in-waiting and the visit of the king and his family in 1788 was to have a similar effect on the fortunes of Cheltenham.

Up until the 18th century travelling to the spas in the West of England involved a lengthy and frequently hazardous journey. Many stretches of the roads were treacherous and coaches often met with accidents or became bogged down in mud (Fig. 11.4). Maintenance of the roads was the duty of local parishes, and since resources for the regular upkeep of heavily used routes were inadequate, many parishes did little other than lay faggots and stones on the worst stretches. Added dangers were the highwaymen who frequented Hounslow Heath and Kingsdown, just outside Bath.

The growth of turnpike trusts in the West Country in the 18th century, however, resulted in the gradual emergence of an improved road system radiating outwards from the major

Fig. 11.4 **The Original Bath Mail Coach,** *1784, engraving.*

towns. The trusts evolved in a random manner, as they were dependent on local initiatives to raise the necessary capital and to secure an Act of Parliament to undertake road improvements. The London to Gloucester road required three Acts of Parliament and was not fully turnpiked until 1720. The Western Road linking Bath to London via Chippenham and Reading was developed over a longer period; the first section to be improved was undertaken by the Bath Trust in 1707, but the final section of the road, between Cherhill and Marlborough, was not completed until 1743.

By the mid-18th century the region had a well-developed infrastructure of turnpike trusts and by 1837 more than 4,800km of the road network was under the management of those trusts. The turnpike trusts were instrumental in stimulating the development of a network of stagecoach routes that was greatly to improve the speed and ease of travel in the region. By the close of the century the journey by coach from London to Bath had been reduced from three days to 38 hours, and the daily coach service linking Cheltenham to London took only 12 hours.

The numbers of visitors to the region rose rapidly as travel became cheaper and easier. Increased prosperity, particularly among the emerging professional classes in the 18th century, was to result in a changed visitor profile to the spas. Merchants, bankers, lawyers and clergymen and their families began to figure prominently among the visitors to Bath and Cheltenham. One such visitor was John Penrose, a Cornish parson from Penryn, who visited Bath with his wife and eldest daughter in 1766, seeking a cure for gout. His letters to his daughter Peggy provide a detailed chronicle of his visit, and daily life at a Georgian spa.[7]

The journey from Penryn, by chaise and stagecoach, was made in easy stages, and took a week. The Penrose family, as did most visitors, chose to stay in furnished lodgings and, not having brought their own servant, engaged a young girl to prepare their meals and keep house. Although linen was provided, most of their meals were either bought in from a pastry cook or cooked by themselves at their lodgings. Instead of engaging a local physician to advise on treatment of his gout, John Penrose secured the services of a Bath apothecary, Mr Haviland, who prescribed a drinking cure of spa water, a quarter pint (142cc) being taken twice and subsequently four times daily, the morning draught being taken in the Pump Room before breakfast.

In between drinking the waters John Penrose occupied his time with the customary diversions at Bath. During the day strolling on the Parades by the river if the weather was fine, visits to one of the many subscription libraries and artists' studios, attendance at church services and the endless rounds of private tea parties. There was also the allure of the many shops in the city. As today, both Bath and Cheltenham built up a thriving retail trade based on visitors. London retailers would visit for the season, and companies such as Wedgwood had outlets in the city. Excursions were also made. Penrose visited Prior Park to see Ralph Allen's landscape gardens and made a trip to Bristol. Indeed, the attraction of both Bath and Cheltenham was in no small part due to opportunities they presented for visiting nearby country houses such as Longleat and Bowood, as well as excursions to scenic attractions including Cheddar Gorge and Wookey Hole. Tea gardens were popular. Darke's Tea Gardens at Prestbury was a popular destination for visitors to Cheltenham as were the Lyncombe Tea Gardens outside Bath. Race meetings and country walks served to vary the routine during the afternoon. In the evening there was the theatre, subscription concerts, assemblies and balls.

Staying at a fashionable spa such as Cheltenham or Bath was not cheap and lodgings were notoriously expensive during the season. Apart from doctors' fees and payment for use of the baths, there were subscriptions to the Pump Room and public entertainments at the assembly rooms to be paid. Sedan chairs, accommodation for servants and purchase of provisions also had to be included in the budget. But it was not just the wealthy who sought relief from their ailments through the use of spa water: Bath in particular received large numbers of poor and destitute invalids. By the mid-16th century they had become a serious burden on the city and in 1572 an Act of Parliament was obtained which required those without independent means to obtain a licence signed by two Justices of the Peace with maintenance provided by their local parish. St John's Hospital, St Katherine's and Mary Magdalen in the vicinity of the Hot Bath offered free accommodation and treatment for poorer patients. Another charitable foundation, Bellot's Hospital was founded in 1617. The Mineral Water Hospital, founded in 1738, was to become an important centre for treatment of occupational diseases.

A LONG MINUET
Longa Tysonum Min

SPA SOCIETY

Social divisions in treatment and accommodation were to be accentuated as Bath entered its 'golden era' as a spa in the 18th century. Charity was the point of separation. The success of Bath and Cheltenham ultimately depended on their reputations as fashionable resorts and the ability to attract visitors who could spend freely to sustain their institutions.

Not all visitors came to recover their health. A French visitor, M Le Blanc, writing in the 1740s, noted that: 'They are much deceived who think that the waters of Bath are like those of Bourbon, where only the infirm, paralytic or valetudinarian persons are to be found. On the contrary, this is the place in all England to enjoy good health, and turn it to account.'[8] Taking the waters was to develop into an annual social event. The season favoured by physicians for the cure became part of the social calendar for high society and the rapidly expanding middle class, and from the early 18th century public entertainments – balls, concerts and theatre-going – were to become a major feature of spa life. At Bath this was developed on a scale second only to London. In the reign of George III, when the spa was at the height of its popularity, there were no fewer than three assembly rooms providing a wide choice of daily entertainment during the season, ranging from formal dress balls to informal cotillion or fancy balls that included country dancing. Public breakfasts, tea assemblies, card assemblies and concerts were also provided by the proprietors of the assembly rooms. Subscription gardens such as the Spring Gardens at Bath held a regular programme of concerts, some with illuminations and firework displays. Even the morning and afternoon rituals of drinking the waters became a social event, and the Pump Room was enlarged to accommodate the growing number of visitors and a resident band of musicians. Church-going also became part of the entertainment industry. New churches, notably the Countess of Huntington's Chapel and the Octagon Chapel in Milsom Street, were built to meet the influx of visitors, attracting leading preachers during the season. Together with actors, professional gamblers, dancing masters, dressmakers and portrait painters preachers formed a significant element of Bath's mobile population. Fortune-hunters and fraudsters, splendidly portrayed in the character of Captain Cormorant in Charles Anstey's *New Bath Guide* of 1820,[9] were also attracted to the spa, preying on gullible visitors with money to spend, as did 'the nymphs of Avon Street' in the lower part of the town.

Gambling was a major feature of spa life, particularly at Bath where it had, according to Daniel Defoe, developed 'to a scandalous degree'.[10] Play centred on card games, notably lansquenet and piquet and games of chance, such as hazard. EO (Even and Odd), a simple form of roulette, brought enormous profits to the assembly rooms and gambling houses in the city. A series of gaming acts were introduced in the 18th century and in 1755 all games of chance, except card

Fig. 11.5 Bunbury, **A Long Minuet as Danced Bath,** *1787, coloured engraving.*

play, were prohibited. Gambling continued in private sessions, however, and the assembly rooms offered daily card assemblies for whist players.

The seasonal influx of visitors posed a unique challenge for the emerging spa towns. Whether for reasons of health, or in quest of diversion, people from different parts of the country and all walks of life were thrown together. Ministers of State drank the same waters as their tailor, and might dance a minuet with a sugar-planter's daughter (Fig. 11.5). A new balance had to be struck between social regulation and social licence. Ordering of entertainment and social intercourse was essential for social harmony and a precedent lay in the ordering of court entertainment. Bath was the first spa to appoint a Master of Ceremonies. Cheltenham and Hotwells soon followed. 'Beau' Nash, who held the post at Bath from 1704 to 1761, ordered the programmes of entertainment and strictly enforced etiquette and social conduct at the spa. Dress and precedence was regulated at public balls, as was conduct in the baths. The wearing of swords was banned. Courtesy and good manners were expected from all visitors, regardless of wealth, birth and rank. Nash's rules, drawn up in 1764, were to remain in force with little change well into the Regency period and were adopted by other spa towns.

Spa society, however, was not socially inclusive. Admission to 'the company' was decided by the conventions of Georgian society in which dress and gentlemanly conduct were paramount. The Master of Ceremonies effectively controlled admission to spa society by force of personality. The subscription system for admissions to concerts, balls and circulating libraries ensured the exclusion of the socially undesirable. Tradesmen and servants were specifically banned from public assemblies. Spa society was an artificial society, constantly changing as people arrived and departed. It encouraged familiarity, and even friendship. Goldsmith, in his *Life of Beau Nash* of 1762, observed that gentlemen at the Bath coffee houses conversed 'on the news of the day, with a freedom and ease, not to be found in the metropolis'.[11] Acquaintances made at the spa, however, were limited to its confines. Some years earlier than Goldsmith, in 1753, Tobias Smollett in *The Adventures of Ferdinand Count Fathom* noted that 'a maxim universally prevails among the English people to overlook and wholly neglect, on their return to the metropolis, all the connections they have chanced to acquire during their residence at any of the medical wells'.[12]

BUILDERS AND SPECULATORS

At the beginning of the 18th century Bath was in many respects still a medieval town encompassed by defensive walls, its skyline dominated by the abbey and many of its poorer buildings still roofed in thatch. Beyond the walls lay orchards and open fields. By the close of the century the city presented a very different appearance, having increased its size fourfold, with extensive residential developments on the southern slopes of Lansdown and eastwards on the Bathwick estate on the other side of the river. Much of the old city had also been rebuilt. Parades and terraces replaced 17th-century gabled buildings, streets were widened and new spa buildings constructed by the Corporation. The transformation from medieval town to Georgian city took place in a remarkably short period of time. A similar building boom took place at Cheltenham in the Regency period. By 1821 there were 13,388 residents, compared to just over 3,000 in 1801. Clifton also witnessed a period of growth over the same period with the construction of terraces on the downs and a new assembly room (Fig. 11.6). On a smaller scale Gloucester, Glastonbury and Melksham all increased in size as developers sought to cash in on the growing demand for accommodation at the principal spas.

Much of the building development was undertaken as piecemeal ventures by individual speculators, or through joint stock companies, as at Gloucester and

Fig. 11.6 Rolina Sharples, **The Cloak-Room, Clifton Assembly Rooms,** **c.***1817–18,* oil on canvas.

Melksham. Tontine agreements provided an alternative for small-scale investors. A tontine agreement was used to finance the construction of the Upper Assembly Rooms at Bath between 1768 and 1761; the subscribers received an annuity for life, the sum increasing proportionately as investors died. Larger schemes were usually developed by breaking the land up into smaller plots, which were sub-let to craftsmen-builders who erected houses within strictly controlled architectural guidelines. The availability of credit and development of provincial banks in the latter half of the 18th century provided the capital on which the building expansion depended.

Bath and Cheltenham offered unique opportunities for such large-scale developments. Not only was the land available, but also the increasing popularity of the two spas had led to a shortage of accommodation. The first major development scheme took place at Bath where, in the 1720s, the architect-developer John Wood proposed an ambitious plan for the total redevelopment of the city on Vitruvian principles. Published in his *Essay towards a Description of Bath*, the scheme featured an Imperial Gymnasium for 'the practice of medicinal exercises', a Royal Forum and a Grand Circus for sporting events. Although sadly Wood's scheme was never executed in full, parts of it were, notably the laying-out of Queen's Square in 1727–36 as a residential development, followed by the Parades beside the River Avon, originally projected as the northern side of his Royal Forum. This was followed by the construction of the Circus and Royal Crescent by his son, John Wood the Younger, almost certainly to his father's designs (Figs 11.7 and 11.8).

Fig. 11.7 Cozens, **The Circus, 1773,** *watercolour.*

Fig. 11.8 Aerial view of Bath showing the Circus and Royal Crescent, which *formed the focus for the residential development to the north-est of the city. Planned by John Wood and John Wood the younger, this prestigious scheme was laid out in the third quarter of the 18th century. The Upper Assembly Rooms, built by John Wood the younger, can be seen to the bottom right of the photograph.*

As examples of town planning, Wood's architectural schemes were remarkably in advance of their time, imaginatively unifying individual houses behind a common palatial façade, as at Queen Square, and in planned spatial relationships in which vistas and symmetry were paramount. Wood's designs were to influence a number of other architects including Nash, the Adam brothers and the Yorkshire architect, John Carr, whose designs for the Royal Crescent at Buxton were clearly inspired by its namesake in Bath. Wood's architectural schemes were not, however, merely intended for visual effect; behind them was a social purpose. Parades, he believed, 'were designed to

encourage walking and conversation'; squares 'for people to assemble together; and the Spot whereon they meet, ought to be separated from the Common ground to Men and Beasts, and even to Mankind in General, if Decency and good Order are necessary to be observed in such Places of Assembly'.[13] Ultimately, though, the success of the venture depended on selling leases for individual properties, and this in turn depended on securing exclusivity. Upper Bath, as it came to be known, rapidly became the premier residential area. The Duke of York purchased a house in the Royal Crescent and residents of the Circus included William Pitt MP, Lord Clive, Princess Amelia and Thomas Gainsborough.

A later major residential development at Bath took place on the Bathwick estate on the other side of the Avon. Laid out in the 1780s by Thomas Baldwin and linked to the city by Robert Adam's magnificent Pulteney Bridge, the Bathwick development fell victim to the financial crisis during the Napoleonic Wars. The Bath City Bank crashed in 1793 and Baldwin together with many of the local builders became bankrupt (Fig. 11.9). Over-supply of housing stock added to the problem, as did the decline in visitors. Clifton was also affected. On the downs the Royal York Crescent was left unfinished and in a ruinous condition.

For Cheltenham, however, the Napoleonic Wars brought prosperity. The last two decades of the 18th century saw a fourfold increase in the number of lodging houses. The streets were paved, a second assembly room was opened and a new theatre and subscription library were built. As with Bath, the major new developments took place outside the town where there was ample building space and gently sloping land sheltered by the Cotswold hills. Architecturally, however, Cheltenham's major period of expansion belongs to another era: the stern Palladian classicism of Wood's Bath gave way to the lighter and more ephemeral style of the Regency, stucco and brick replaced stone and spacious tree-lined walks and rides gave the spa a very different feel to the intensively terraced environs of Bath and the oppressive air of its lower town. Unlike Bath, Cheltenham's new estates were built around the spa wells: notable among them was the Montpellier estate, which was developed by Henry Thomason, a London and Liverpool banker, in the early years of the 19th century. The Pittville estate, promoted by the wealthy attorney and MP for Cricklade, John Pitt, who was to become the largest landowner in Cheltenham, followed the Montpellier development (Fig. 11.10). As with John Wood's vision for Bath, the planned estate was only partially realised. Only the Pump Room and its park, together with 200 of the planned 600 houses, were ever built and Pitt was deeply in debt at the time of his death in 1842. Cheltenham had passed its zenith by then, and like Bath was facing competition from a new generation of resorts.

Fig. 11.9 Bath in 1800. *Extensive building development took place in Bath in the 18th century when the spa was at the height of its popularity. The confines of the Avon valley was to result in the main focus for building activity being on the northern side of the river, radiating outwards from the medieval walled city. The single largest residential development was the Bathwick estate to the east of the River Avon. Drawn up in the late 1780s, the plans were never fully realised.*
1. Pump Room and King's Bath, 2. Cross Bath,
3. Hot Bath, 4. Hetling Pump House, 5. Mineral Water Hospital.

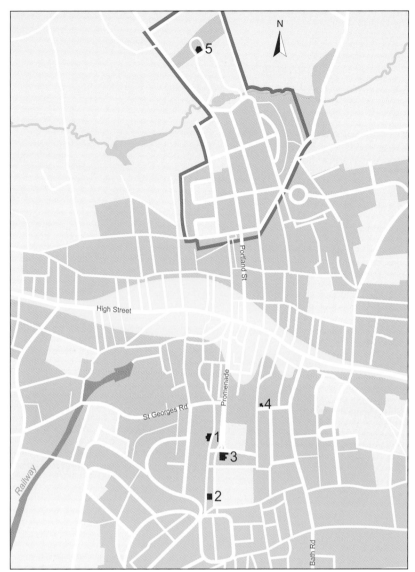

By the mid-19th century a noticeable change had taken place in the region's spa towns as they became increasingly residential in character. The availability of high-quality accommodation and the relatively low cost of living in the old spas were attractive to those seeking retirement. Cheltenham and Bath were to become popular with ex-colonial administrators, naval and army officers, clergy and others with independent means. The village of Clifton continued to grow despite the decline in popularity of Hotwells. It was to become a prestigious suburb of the expanding city of Bristol, into which it was absorbed in 1835 (Fig. 11.11).

In the 20th century the legacy of prestigious Georgian and Regency buildings continued to serve Bath and Cheltenham well, contributing in no small part to the latter's social and economic regeneration from the 1980s onwards as cosmopolitan cities in their own right and regional centres of culture.

BELOW: *Fig. 11.11 Bristol in 1815.* The *development of Clifton and Hotwells (outlined in red) was stimulated by the growing popularity of the Hotwells Spa at the foot of the Avon Gorge. The two villages became incorporated into Bristol in the late 19th century, by which time most of the area had been infilled with housing development.*

ABOVE: *Fig. 11.10 Cheltenham in 1870.* In contrast to Bath where the spring heads *clustered together within the medieval city, Cheltenham's spa wells were in open fields outside the earlier town, which grew up along the highway between Gloucester and Broadway. To the south, a tree-lined promenade linked the Montpellier and Imperial wells with the High Street and from the late 18th century onwards a series of separate estates of terraces, crescents and villas was developed in the surrounding area. Pittville to the north of the town (outlined in red) was developed as a planned estate around the Pittville Pump Room and park in the second quarter of the 19th century.* 1. The Royal Well, 2. Montpellier Spa, 3. Imperial Spa, 4. Cambray Spa, 5. Pittville Pump Room.

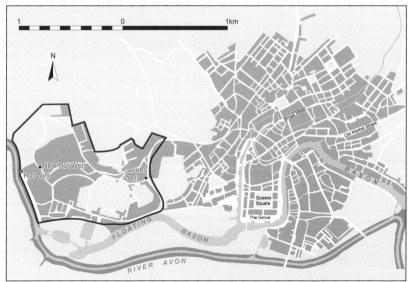

SEASIDE RESORTS

In 1752 Dr Richard Russell first published *A Dissertation Concerning the Use of Sea Water in the Diseases of the Glands*.[14] He recommended the drinking of sea water and sea-bathing as treatment for a wide range of ailments, including glandular disease, asthma, ruptures, madness, skin diseases and deafness. Although many other treatises advocating the benefits of sea water were to appear in later years, Russell's publication was undoubtedly the most influential on medical opinion. The 'air of the coast' and a mild climate in winter was also seen as beneficial for weaker patients, particularly those suffering from chest complaints, who needed an escape from the increasingly smoke-polluted towns and cities. For those afflicted by gout and rheumatism, heated seawater bathing was recommended. In 1759 Galden's Sea Baths were opened at Brighton offering hot and cold private saltwater plunges with shower facilities and vapour baths. Along with many other new seaside resorts, Brighton owed much of its success to royal patronage.

The successful Bath entrepreneur, Ralph Allen, was a regular summer visitor to Weymouth from 1750 until his death in 1764 and it was largely due to his influence that the town was to become the leading seaside resort in the region, a position it was to retain well into the Victorian period (Fig. 11.12). Allen introduced the resort to the Duke of York, and later the Duke of Gloucester was to build a summer residence overlooking the sheltered sandy bay; here, between 1789 and 1805, George III and the royal family stayed when the king visited Weymouth in order to undergo a regime of sea-bathing to recover his health (Fig. 11.13). Royal patronage resulted in the resort's rapid development over this period. Lodging houses were built around the bay and regular coach services ran from the resort to London, Exeter, Bath and Bristol. By 1800 there were more

Fig. 11.12 The seafront of Weymouth, as with many other seaside resorts, was subject to extensive building development from the close of the 18th century. John Hutchins' plan from The History and Antiquities of the County of Dorset *(Hutchins, 1774, Vol. 1)* shows the seafront prior to the construction of the esplanade, with backyards and gardens leading down to the beach and horse-drawn bathing machines.

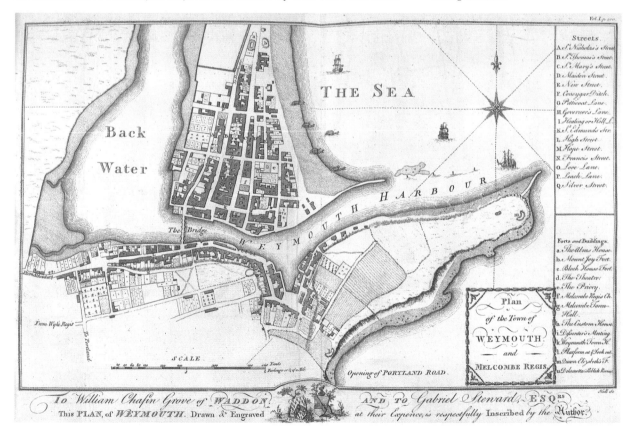

Fig. 11.13 **Royal Dipping – George III takes his first bathe at Weymouth,** *engraving.*

than 30 bathing machines in operation, together with a suite of marine baths. A new and larger assembly room was built to cater for the growing number of summer visitors, the programme of entertainments and etiquette for balls based on those at Bath and Hotwells. Indeed, the first Master of Ceremonies also presided over the Clifton rooms during the winter season.

The improvements to roads and travelling conditions in the West following the introduction of turnpike trusts during the second half of the 18th century was to stimulate the development of a number of other seaside resorts on the southern coast, and by the Regency period former fishing villages such as Sidmouth and Lyme Regis had become popular watering places. The low cost of living, compared to the inland resorts, was a major factor in their popularity. The Regency courtesan, Harriette Wilson, chose to recuperate at Charmouth. She described Lyme as

> a sort of Brighton in minature, all bustle and confusion, assembly rooms, donkey-riding, raffling, etc; etc. It was sixpence per night to attend the assemblies, and much cheaper if paid by the season. We went to a little inn and dined. From the window, I was much amused to see the smart old maids that were tripping down the streets, in turbans or artificial flowers twined round their wigs, on the light fantastic toe, to the sixpenny assembly-rooms at five in the evening! They were very pleasantly situated near the sea, and as we walked past their windows we saw them all drinking tea and playing cards. There were amongst them persons of the highest rank; but the society was chiefly composed of people of very small independent fortunes, who for economy had settled at Lyme Regis; or of such as required sea-bathing; natives, either of Exeter or any neighbouring town.[15]

It was, however, the relaxed informality of the seaside resorts which was to appeal to the rapidly changing society of the Regency. The ordered public entertainments of Bath and Cheltenham had lost their appeal; the cult of the picturesque and the open air was seen as the antithesis of an industrialised society, and from it the notion of the seaside holiday was born. Sailing and fishing trips became popular, together with excursions to Lulworth Cove, Durdle Door and Abbotsbury and other local beauty spots. The picturesque scenery of the coast at Charmouth appealed to Jane Austen in particular, who described it thus in *Persuasion*: 'its sweet retired bay, backed by dark cliffs, where fragments of low rock among the sands make it the happiest spot for watching the flow of the tide, for sitting in unwearied contemplation'.[16]

This change in attitude was to be vividly expressed in building development at the seaside resorts – individualism Georgian style. Marine villas and thatched *cottages ornés*, of which Woolbrook Cottage at Sidmouth is one of the finest surviving examples, have rural and rustic roots. The promenade, an essential feature of any spa, likewise was changed to fit the new spirit of the age – the formal gravel walks of Bath and Hotwells evolved into the esplanade, a simple carriageway, separating beach and town. At Lyme the Cobb was also popular for maritime promenading, anticipating the development of seaside piers in the Victorian period.

EXCURSIONS AND HOLIDAYS

In the early years of the 19th century marine resorts began to appear on the north Somerset coast; Clevedon and Weston-Super-Mare, both within easy reach of Bristol, developed quickly (Fig. 11.14). Despite the growing popularity of the coast the region's resorts remained fairly exclusive, most of them little more than seaside villages. But with the coming of the railways change was rapid as the coast became easily accessible and the cost of travel dramatically reduced.

Weston-Super-Mare was linked to the rapidly developing Great Western Railway (GWR) network in 1841 (Fig. 11.15). Weymouth followed in 1857,

Fig. 11.14 William Hopkins and Edmund Havell, **Weston Sands in 1864,** *oil on canvas.*

Fig. 11.15 GWR poster for Weston-super-Mare, c. 1935.

with daily train services from both Paddington and Waterloo reaching the resort in less than four hours. The GWR and Southern Region railway companies actively promoted the seaside holiday through publicity campaigns – indeed, the GWR proclaimed itself as 'The Nation's Holiday Line'. It was to have a profound effect on the development of the West Country resorts from the mid-19th century onwards. Weymouth and Weston-Super-Mare, both with ample building land, were extensively developed from the 1840s onwards to become the two leading resorts in the region. Lodging houses and hotels crowded the seafront. Piers, bandstands and theatres were built and ornamental gardens laid out. Beyond the seafront rows of terraced houses sprang up to accommodate a growing resident population as well as summer visitors. Between 1851 and 1861 Weston-Super-Mare's population rose from 4,033 to over 8,000. By 1951 it had reached 40,000.

During the second half of the 19th century the railway network was extended to include many of the smaller coastal towns. Swanage was reached in 1885, and finally in 1903 a branch line linked Lyme Regis, much to the annoyance of its wealthier residents. Although their development as seaside resorts was on a smaller scale, the advent of the railway was to profoundly affect the smaller towns. On the north coast the construction of the West Somerset Railway in 1871 acted as a major stimulus for the development of Minehead, and on the Dorset coast Bridport Harbour was rebranded as West Bay to promote the new resort.

The opening up of the coast saw the emergence of a new populist seaside culture, actively promoted by individual resorts, each competing for a share of the holiday trade. Treatment and recuperation gave way to entertainment and relaxation. Bathing machines were replaced by changing tents and beach huts, assembly rooms by pavilions and winter gardens and the post of Resort Director had taken on the role of the Master of Ceremonies. The beach was no longer the preserve of fishermen and bathers – families relaxed in the sun, built sandcastles, watched Punch and Judy shows and pierrot troupes performing their routine. Larger resorts offered a varied programme of organised entertainment. In the 1950s Weymouth offered bathing-beauty competitions, sailing regattas, carnivals and open-air dancing. Cowboy Cal McCord and his horse, Ladybird, and the Weymouth roller-skating troupe vied with touring artistes and comedians at the Pavilion.

The introduction of paid holidays for factory workers in the 1930s resulted in a surge of holidaymakers travelling to the seaside. During the summer months visitors from South Wales and the Midlands poured into Weston-Super-Mare for their annual holiday and in July 1930 over 5,000 holidaymakers descended on Weymouth from the GWR works at Swindon during 'Swindon Fortnight'. Day trips were also popular and special excursion trains were laid on at Bank Holidays. During the summer months paddle-steamers ran regular excursions from Swansea and Cardiff to Weston-Super-Mare and the north Somerset coast. Weston-Super-Mare developed a busy airport with regular flights to Cardiff and beyond. In 1937 Western Airways flew in 2,555 day-visitors during the Whitsun Bank Holiday.

REVIVING THE SPA

Although no longer centres of fashion, spa treatment continued at both Cheltenham and Bath during the Victorian period. Spa-visiting enjoyed a revival in Britain in the latter part of the 19th century, due largely to the influence of the popular continental spas such as Baden-Baden and Aix-les-Bains, which were much frequented by fashionable society up until the outbreak of the First World War. A new generation of cold-water spas emerged including Malvern and

Fig. 11.16 Schnee Bath, New Private Baths, c. 1914.

Leamington Spa, offering a range of continental hydrotherapy treatments linked to spacious and well-appointed hotels. The level of investment needed to modernise the spa facilities and accommodation was beyond many of the older spas, however; the smaller ones including Gloucester, Nottington and Radipole Spa near Weymouth, fell into disuse during the second half of the 19th century, although the Gloucester Pump House continued to function up until 1931. In 1822 the Pump House at Hotwells was demolished. An attempt was made later to revive the spa and a new pump house was built, but the venture was unsuccessful and in 1867 the building, together with Hotwells Point, was demolished to improve navigation through the Gorge.

Bath was fortunate, as the Corporation owned the thermal baths and much of the surrounding property, and from the late 1860s it embarked on an ambitious programme of modernisation and expansion. The New Royal Baths were opened adjacent to the newly built Grand Pump Room Hotel, and this was followed by the construction of an additional treatment centre adjacent to the King's Bath, and the extension of the Pump Room with a concert room to accommodate the Bath Orchestra. Despite initial opposition from the medical establishment, new treatments modelled on the 'Continental' system were introduced, including vapour baths and inhalation rooms as well as Sitz and Nauheim baths, Aix-les-Bains douches and exercise pools with chairlifts. At the same time the Royal Mineral Water Hospital was extended to meet an increase in demand for admissions and its facilities were modernised (Fig. 11.16).

ARCADES AND FESTIVALS

Bath maintained its position as a leading centre for spa therapies for another hundred years. By the mid-20th century, however, changes in ideas about medical treatment meant that practitioners no longer favoured the use of mineral water, and the facilities were closed down in the mid-1970s. Shortly afterwards public bathing was stopped when it was discovered that an amoeba contaminated the baths. The architectural and cultural legacy, however, was the salvation of both Bath and Cheltenham. Despite the ravages of post-war rebuilding programmes the two cities retained much of their historic character, attracting both tourists and well-heeled residents. The tradition of public entertainment was to find a new expression in international artistic festivals, the Bath Music Festival and Cheltenham Literature Festival becoming the focus for a new 'season'.

The last 50 years have also seen changes to the coastal resorts as the growth in cheap foreign travel has drawn off much of the summer trade. But while the popularity of the traditional resorts has declined, the south and north coasts have remained important holiday destinations. Holiday camps appeared in the post-war period, and later caravan sites and static caravan parks provided alternative low-cost holidays. Indoor leisure complexes with heated pools, amusement arcades and fast-food outlets are a more recent development as the larger resorts seek to develop year-round business. Butlin's Minehead, recently redeveloped as a holiday village around the massive Skyline Pavilion complex and attracting just under 500,000 visitors a year, is now a resort in its own right. Fortunately the most impressive areas of coast scenery have been protected while at the same time made more accessible by the opening-up of long-distance footpaths. The coastal areas of Dorset and north Somerset now form extended leisure zones, offering a variety of recreational uses to visitors.

Improvements to the road network and an accompanying increase in car and coach travel have transformed the whole region into a 'multiple' destination. The traditional spa visit and in turn the seaside summer holiday have given way to short breaks and day visits. Leisure interests increasingly influence the decision of where to visit and when. Windsurfing at Weymouth, shopping at Bath, alternative medicine at Glastonbury or the Gold Cup at Cheltenham – the region's spa towns continue to provide an important focus for tourism and the leisure industry in the region, robustly retaining their individuality and distinctiveness as they adapt to meet the needs of a changing society.

NOTES

1	Jorden 1631; Turner 1562.	8	Le Blanc 1745.
2	Rolls 1988, 77–86.	9	Anstey *c.* 1820
3	Guidott 1694.	10	Defoe 1748, 289.
4	Crane 1765.	11	Goldsmith 1762.
5	H Walpole, letter to G Montagu, Oct 18 1766, quoted in Barbeau 1904, 88.	12	Smollett 1753.
		13	Wood 1765, 345.
6	A Prevost, 1738, No38, quoted in Barbeau 1904, 80	14	Russell 1753.
		15	Marquis 1960, 233.
7	Mitchell & Penrose 1983.	16	Austen 1818.

12

Fossils and Ferns

JO DRAPER

The West is surprisingly diverse, with a solid limestone backbone running through it, contrasting with the flat peaty Somerset Levels and wide clay valleys such as the Blackmoor Vale. The plants, buildings and farming reflect this diversity, but even as late as the end of the 18th century the landscape had not been geologically mapped nor really scientifically understood. At best, topographers such as the county historians of the 18th century described the landscape, and attempted a 'Natural History', covering what in the next century would become the sciences of geology, botany and biology. John Hutchins, the county historian of Dorset, who published his two volumes in 1774, realised the deficiency and offered an apology:

> If the Reader finds himself disappointed in his expectations of a larger and more particular detail of Natural History, I beg leave ingenuously to acknowledge myself by no means master of this branch of science, in which I only profess myself an humble admirer. Several gentlemen of the county have turned their thoughts to its botanical and fossil history, and made a considerable progress in their discoveries: but as they could not be prevailed on to reduce them into one continued essay, my candid readers must allow me to decline a task I am not equal to, and content myself with pointing out a few particulars, and drawing a short sketch, in hopes it may raise and engage the future attention of some person, whose abilities and leisure health and fortune may qualify him to traverse the sea coast, islands, and quarries. As this is a subject hitherto unattempted, it will amply reward the labour of the curious enquirer, produce new and interesting discoveries of the wonders of nature and the greatness and wisdom of its Author. Certain it is, that the sea shore of this county, and isles of Brownsea, Purbeck and Portland afford an inexhaustible fund of natural curiosity.

In the generation following Hutchins several people found the 'leisure, health and fortune' to inquire into the geology of Dorset, and their labours were indeed amply rewarded.

Hutchins understood the main geological bones of the county: there were different physical areas, 'fixed and invariable. Whatever changes a county undergoes, the soil and situation are still the same: and here the down, the vale, and the heath, will be always distinct; nature has set to each its proper bounds, which it cannot pass.'

John Collinson, the Somerset county historian who published three volumes a little later (1791), had another motive too – patriotism: 'We cannot love that with which we are totally unacquainted and our attachment to our country cannot fail of being increased as the opportunities of information concerning it become more extended.' In common with Hutchins, Collinson sees information on natural history as a religious exercise:

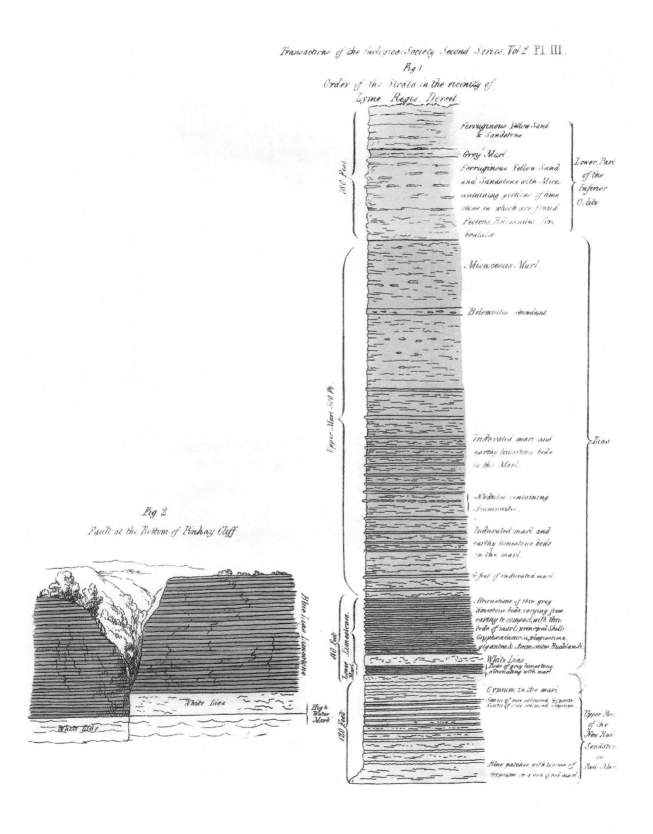

Transactions of the Geological Society Second Series, Vol 2. Pl. III.

Fig 1

Order of the Strata in the vicinity of
Lyme Regis, Dorset

Fig 2.

Fault at the Bottom of Pinhay Cliff

There is scarcely any district so defective as not to furnish some subject of entertainment and improvement; and Somersetshire *seems to have its share of the wonderful works of Providence. By an intuition of these, science is delightfully improved; the mind exults in pursuing the Deity through all his operations, and dispensing different blessings to different regions.*

The people who lived in the different regions knew them well: they had to in order to farm them and to exploit their varied resources, but there was little scientific knowledge of the countryside until the 16th century, when plants began to be formally named and studied. The flora was important to apothecaries and a detailed and accurate knowledge of the properties of plants essential to the success of their practice. The study of geology came later, in response to economic pressures. Apart from the ability to identify sources of coal and other minerals, knowledge of the local rocks brought many additional benefits. In the 1830s, for example, the geologist Sir Henry Thomas de la Beche pointed out that while huge quantities of hydraulic lime (lime that would set under water) were brought from Wales to build the Eddystone Lighthouse at Plymouth, an equally good supply was to be had much closer at hand, at Lyme Regis (Fig. 12.1). It was this region that was to feature large in the early development of geology and the new science of palaeontology.

MARY ANNING, THE LIAS AND LYME REGIS

The Blue Lias at Lyme Regis must be the region's worst building stone, used locally only because it was cheap. The walls flaked away, and failed to keep the damp out, but the lias was full of fossils. Local people were aware of them, of course, but lacked any scientific curiosity about them. Vertebrae from the backbones of reptiles were commonly noticed in the sands and stones on the shore, and were recognised for what they were. They were called 'verteberries' – but no one gave thought to why they were there (Fig. 12.2).

From the end of the 18th century locals found that they could sell fossils as curiosities to tourists who were coming in increasing numbers to the area for

OPPOSITE PAGE:
Fig. 12.1 The first section through the lias at Lyme Regis, *published in 1823 by Henry De la Beche in his article 'On the Lias of the Coast, in the vicinity of Lyme Regis, Dorset', in the* Transactions of the Geological Society.

Lyme Regis from the Charmouth Road

Fig. 12.2 Distant view of Lyme Regis about 1840, *with collapsing cliffs right foreground and along the shore. The lias is very unstable and falls reveal more fossils. Many prints were made of Lyme because of the many visitors who bought them.*

sea-bathing. The lias was always eroding and revealing more fossils (Fig. 12.3), and quarrying (mostly for cement) produced more. In 1789 one of the main curiosity dealers was based in Charmouth, close to Lyme, and from him 'those who are desirous of adding to their collection for grottos, chimney-pieces etc, may here find materials on the lowest terms'.

The science of geology was only just beginning, and the early pioneers were working on all aspects at once – basic stratigraphy and mapping of the sequences of rocks; characterising the landscapes produced by different strata; and collecting and classifying the fossils contained in them. It was a local girl, Mary Anning, who became the most influential investigator of the fossil-rich lias (Fig. 12.4). It was very unusual for a woman to become a scientist, and Mary was also a working-class girl, another disadvantage. But she was born at just the right time – when interest in collecting was beginning – and in just the right place – a land full of fossils – and with a growing number of tourists there were plenty of customers eager to buy the cheaper ones as souvenirs.

Fig. 12.3 Black Ven, Lyme Regis from the air, taken in the 1970s. *This clearly shows the continual slipping.*

Fig. 12.4 Mary Anning on the shore at Lyme Regis *looking for fossils, from a watercolour by de la Beche. Her hammer is clear, and the top hat is probably for protection from falling rocks.*

Mary and her brother discovered the first complete ichthyosaur to be scientifically described, in about 1810 (Fig. 12.5). People had called them crocodiles before that, but proper scientific examination showed that they were a totally different species, and that the species was extinct. These large specimens of strange marine reptiles from the lias were great curiosities, and the first ichthyosaur was sold to the lord of the manor for £23 (then a huge sum) and was sent to London to be displayed in Bullock's Museum of Natural History, a commercial exhibition of curiosities.

Mary Anning became a professional fossilist, regularly walking the cliffs and shore to find specimens. But in addition to their cash value as curiosities she was concerned to establish their species and get them published scientifically. She even dissected contemporary sea creatures to compare them to the fossil remains, and taught herself French so as to be able to read the works of Cuvier, the French pioneer, on comparative anatomy.

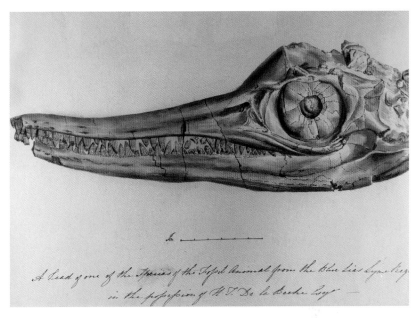

Fig. 12.5 An ichthyosaur from Lyme: *the original label says it is one of the 'species of the Fossil Animal from the Blue Lias', so it was drawn before ichtyosaurs were named in 1818.*

The preparation of the fossils was as important as the finding of them. Fossils did not appear from the rock, with all their structure exposed. They had to be prepared by removing the rock from around them, and in the early days it was only too common for people to prepare them the way they wanted them to be, rather than as they really were, and even to fake parts of the skeleton. In 1833 Mary Anning complained of one collector, Thomas Hawkins, who was working on a large ichthyosaur: 'It will be a magnificent specimen,' she wrote, 'but he is such an enthusiast that he makes things as he imagines they ought to be and not as they are really found.' Mary, herself, was acknowledged as an expert at preparation, a skill that requires great physical dexterity allied to thorough knowledge of the fossils and the rocks. The geologist de la Beche praised her work, especially 'the skill she employed in developing [preparing] the remains of the many fine skeletons of Ichthyosauri and Plesiosauri which without her care would never have been presented … in the uninjured form so desirable for their examination'.

One of the clearest examples of Mary Anning's research skills came when geologists were trying to work out what the long, often twisted, but always rounded and pebble-like fossils were. They were common finds in the lias, and Mary pointed out that they were 'most abundant in those parts of the formation in which the bones of Ichthyosauri and Plesiosauri are most numerous'. Her careful preparations showed that these pebble-like fossils could be found actually inside the ichthyosaurs. They were coprolites, fossilised excrement, and the further examination of them showed that the ichthyosaurs mostly ate fish, but occasionally each other.

This interest in excrement led to a verse popular in Oxford in the 1830s:

Approach, approach, ingenuous youth
And learn this fundamental truth
The noble science of Geology
Is bottomed firmly in Coprology

Fig. 12.6 Geological research in action: at the foot of Church Cliffs, Lyme Regis, in 1915. W D Lang (left) published detailed sections and mapping of the lias from 1903, writing over 100 papers on the local geology before his death in 1966.

Oxford was the only place teaching geology at the time, and William Buckland, the university's first professor of geology published the first paper on coprolites, using Mary Anning's work along with his own.[1]

The geology of Lyme became part of the attractions of the resort (Fig. 12.6). A visitor who wrote up his holiday as a little book entitled *A Summer Trip to Weymouth & Dorchester* in 1842 noted: 'A recent and powerful cause of attraction to visit Lyme Regis, which has been opened to the naturalist within late years, is the Blue Lias cliffs and beds in the neighbourhood. In these are now found very numerous, beautiful and highly preserved fossil remains of the Ichthyosaurus … Pleusosaurus, Pterodactylus, together with beautiful ammonites, and fishes and crustacean of many kinds, but all of extinct species.' Apart from the small matter of the spelling of Plesiosaur, the visitor, attracted by the geology to visit Lyme, was remarkably well informed in realising that the fossils were of extinct species.

Earlier attitudes at Lyme were recollected at the Scientific Congress held in Malvern in 1855, when it was recalled that two geologists visiting Lyme in 1824 '… to purchase for the Paris Museum a plesiosaurus; found that the "natives", even those who were tolerably well-informed on other matters, believed that these ancient remains [the fossils] had "recently grown in the rocks" for they were certain that no such thing had existed when they were boys and girls, and indignant they were at the bare suggestion that they might have overlooked them'. By 1855 'far different was the state of knowledge, not only amongst the trades people but even the more humble people of Lyme Regis and every other town' – a condescending piece in light of the fact that it was one of the 'humble people of Lyme Regis', Mary Anning, who had contributed so much towards the new understanding of the fossils. It does, however, illustrate the change from the 1820s to the 1850s – everyone by the 1850s was assumed to have at least a basic understanding of geology.

MUSEUMS AND COLLECTIONS

When fossils were regarded simply as oddities to be exclaimed over, it was no concern that they ended up in private cabinets of curiosities, but for scientific work to proceed permanent collections where specimens could be kept and compared were needed. Many visitors regarded Mary Anning's shop as a museum, and they could indeed see lots of fossils there, but it was not a permanent collection since she needed to sell the fossils in order to live. Generally the public, both locals and visitors, bought the cheaper, smaller fossils, and only the rich collectors or museums purchased the larger specimens.

The British Museum and the Paris Museum of Natural History bought specimens, and Adam Sedgwick acquired several for the Cambridge Museum, but it was the Bristol Institution for the Advancement of Science, Literature and the Arts that was perhaps the most important museum purchaser of her fossils. The Bristol Institution was founded in 1823, and numbered many geologists amongst its members – all men and almost all middle or upper class, as was typical of these early societies (Fig. 12.7). In 1835, the Revd William Conybeare, one of the most distinguished geologists and a member of the Bristol Institution, claimed that 'no other provincial institution was at that moment so richly furnished' with fossils and other geological material.[2] These early museums collected widely, with no restrictions on where the material came from.

Something of the excitement of these early years is given by Conybeare when he described how, in 1824, a drawing of a complete plesiosaur, a species whose existence he and other geologists had already suggested from the study of surviving fragments, arrived on the evening of a meeting of the Bristol Institution: 'to the Society I went, delighted … to pay that infant nursling of my own the compliment of making this strange monster known to the public … Such a communication could not fail to excite great interest; some of the folk ran off instantly to the printing office, whither I was obliged to follow to prevent some strange blunders.' Conybeare was trying to prevent an erroneous report in the newspapers, which in the 1820s were avidly reporting geological discoveries. The proper publication of new material was to be in scientific journals and Conybeare published the plesiosaur in the *Transactions of the Geological Society of London* the same year, with illustrations. It was important that the published type-specimens of fossils were preserved in museum collections to serve as reference material, so that they could be used for comparison and further study.

The national societies such as the Geological Society were the first to publish articles on the geology of the area, but with the rapidly growing public interest in geology, archaeology and natural history, local societies were being formed. The Bristol Institution was an early one, but by the 1840s many county-based societies had come into being, some of them publishing original research. These local societies embraced a variety of subjects, but concentrated on a limited geographical area. While many were short-lived, others have continued to perform an important function as foci for local studies.

In Dorset, for example, the Dorset County Museum (founded in 1847) has survived, but there were at least 15 other organisations in the county in the 1840s and 1850s that were fulfilling much the same purpose, several of them with

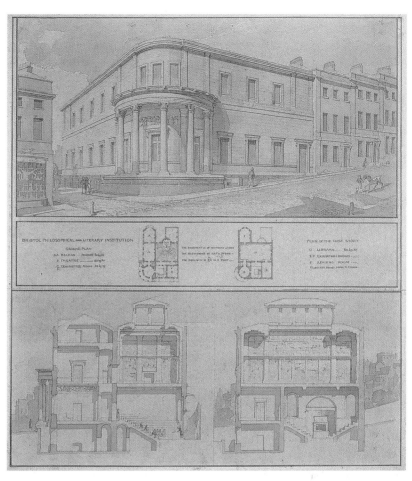

Fig. 12.7 Architectural drawings by Charles Robert Cockerell for the Bristol Institution, *an ambitious building with lecture theatre, three reading rooms, library and exhibition rooms. It cost £11,250. The exhibition rooms were a museum, but this was only open to members.*

museums of their own. Many of these were Mechanics Institutes, supposedly for the working class. Lyme Regis had one for a brief period from 1844, with a museum and reading room. It was, however, dominated by the middle classes, with a committee described as consisting of 'Gentlemen and tradesmen'. Bridport Mechanics Institute, founded in 1830, was more radical. The Literary and Scientific Institutes were more middle class, and began to be set up in Dorset from 1831. All ran lecture series and would have had far more effect on public understanding than the work of national societies such as the Geological Society. These local institutes and societies grew from a desire for education, especially in the sciences, and were motivated by a strong sense of local patriotism.

Throughout the country many of these local societies were publishing papers on history, geology and natural history, but in Dorset little was published at this early date except for the papers of an unusual group, The Purbeck Society, founded in 1855. This was an upper- and middle-class group of enthusiasts who concentrated on a small area of Dorset but managed to published two volumes of research papers on topics that ranged widely – churches, barrows, birds, folklore, geology, ancient families, wrecks off the coast and botany. 'Botany and entomology', stated the founder in 1855, 'are peculiarly ladies' pursuits.' One member recorded his recollections of the society: 'The meetings were pleasant social gatherings, made more attractive by luncheons occasionally given by some of the members and by the presence of several agreeable young ladies who usually attended them. Their presence, however, made it somewhat difficult to select subjects for discussion that were suited to bonnets as well as heads.' Presumably the bonnets of the lady members were empty, but the women nonetheless had a huge effect on the society because when 'the young ladies married and the luncheons ceased' and the main organising spirit moved away from the area, the society quietly died. The principal lasting contribution of The Purbeck Society was its creditable set of publications, which seem to bear little direct relationship to the cheerful social events described by the member.[3]

The Purbeck Society also ran a museum at Corfe, but like all these early museums in Dorset, it was open only to members, or friends of members. Even the Dorset County Museum at the time restricted entry to members and their immediate families, only council members having 'the privilege of admitting strangers to view the Museum'. But this was changing, and when the Dorset County Museum moved to large purpose-built premises in 1884 it opened its doors to everyone.

Scientific publication was vital for the development of geology and all other sciences, but the lectures and field trips organised by the various societies and even their small local museums must have been far more influential amongst the general public, many of whom were avid for instruction in the new developments.

Many societies were formed in the 1820s, and while some declared their wider interests in their very name – the late 19th-century Dorset Natural History and Antiquarian Association, for example, clearly set itself a wide remit – others were more specialised. The Poole Natural History Society, a short-lived late 19th-century group,

Fig. 12.8 Rare photograph of a 19th-century field club actually out in the field – *Poole Natural History Society visiting Dorchester and Wolfeton House in May 1899. Half are women – the Dorset societies seem to have been unusually broad-minded in allowing women members.*

suggests specialisation by the name, but in fact its members visited old buildings and archaeological sites just like their fellows in the Dorset Society (Fig. 12.8).

The Crewkerne Literary and Scientific Institution was founded in 1849, and its aims and achievements were widely reported. At the first anniversary meeting it was stated: 'The object of the Institution is to encourage learning; to lead the mind to what is good and useful; to stimulate thought and reflection; and aid the enquirer after knowledge; to promote a taste for the Arts and Sciences; and to create a kindly feeling among all classes.' This was a very wide remit, a surprising amount of which had to do with understanding the landscape: 'During the past year several talented lectures have been delivered … the mind and genius of woman – the marvels of geology – the beauties of botany – the phenomena of physical geography'. The institution had 144 members drawn from all classes, and although (like most similar groups) it published nothing except annual reports, the influence of its well-attended lectures must have been considerable.[4]

'STRATA' SMITH – SOMERSET, BIRTHPLACE OF GEOLOGY

The man who is credited with creating the science of geology is William Smith, later known as 'Strata' Smith. Before Many Anning was born, he studied the geological stratigraphy of Somerset, and became the first person to work out systematically and in detail the sequences of the strata. He, himself, described the house in which he lived at High Littleton, Somerset as 'the birthplace of geology'. And he was absolutely right.

William Smith was born in 1769, and became a land surveyor, an expanding profession in the late 18th century, a time when much of the common land was being enclosed, when surveys of big estates were becoming more frequent, and when canals were being cut across the landscape. All depended on accurate measurements and the skill of the professional surveyor.

In 1791 Smith began working in the Somerset coalfields, which had been producing coal on a small scale since medieval times. In the late 18th century production was greatly increased, with much deeper shafts being dug. No one understood the geological sequence apart from the miners themselves, who had names for each level. Smith's work took him down many of the mines, and he recorded the different strata, their positions and thicknesses, drawing up correlations between the different mines. This was a huge step forward in understanding the geological structures, but Smith took the study further by noting and comparing the fossils in each level, which gave a much more exact character to each of the strata and allowed sequences to be built up. The miners knew that the sequences were the same in all the mines, but they believed this was only true for the coalfields. Smith could not see why this should be so, and his next job offered just the opportunity he needed to extend his study.

Canals were the cheapest means of moving bulky goods to market, and the Somerset coalmine-owners were quick to embrace the new technology by deciding to build a canal from the mining area to the Kennet and Avon Canal, from where the coal could be widely distributed to Bath and beyond. Smith was appointed as surveyor to the canal company, and was to oversee a cut through more than 10km of country. By extraordinary good luck, it had been decided to cut two canals for most of the route, thus giving Smith two long samples of the geology.

Smith carefully watched and recorded the geology of the canal cuttings, and realised that, as with the coal deposits, the fossils contained in each individual stratum were vital for distinguishing the strata from one another. Having two almost parallel cuttings meant that he could check one against the other, but systematic collection of fossils from each layer, together with accurate recording, was vital to the process. From these observations Smith realised that he could predict the order of the various strata; moreover, these observations could be expanded over the whole country. In 1796 he wrote:

Fossils have long been studied as great curiosities, collected with great pains, treasured with great care and at a great expense, and showed and admired with as much pleasure as a child's rattle or a hobby-horse is shown and admired by himself and his playfellows, because it is pretty; and this has been done by thousands who have never paid the least regard to that wonderful order and regularity with which Nature has disposed of these singular productions, and assigned to each class its particular stratum.

Later he wrote about some of the difficulties he had had in these first observations:

For six years I put my notions of stratification to the test of excavation; and I generally pointed out to contractors and others, who came to undertake the work, what the various parts of the canal would be dug through. But the great similarity of the rocks of the Oolite, on and near the end of the canal towards Bath, required more than superficial observation to determine whether these hills were not composed of one, two or even three of these rocks, as by the distinctions of some parts seemed to appear. These doubts were at length removed by more particular attention to the site of the organic fossils which I had long collected. This discovery of the mode of identifying the strata by the organized fossils respectively imbedded therein led to the most important distinctions.

In 1799 Smith produced the first geological map in the world. He had been recording his observations largely in the form of sections, but this was not the clearest way to present them. Maps showing land use were already being made, coloured to show different types of soil etc, and it was on these that he modelled his geological map. The map covered a circular area of 8km around Bath, an area that was not particularly complex in geological terms. In the years to follow he was to extend his work to cover the entire country (Fig. 12.9).

Thus geological mapping, and indeed the whole principle of stratigraphy, was born in this unlikely area of early industrial Somerset.[5]

Fig. 12.9 Part of William Smith's geological map of England 1815, *showing the area covered by this book. The amount of work needed to produce this first geological map of the country was massive.*

In days of old, old William Smith,
While making a canal, Sir,
Found out how the strata dipped to the east
With a very gentle fall, Sir.
First New Red Sand and marl a-top,
With Lias on its border,
Then the Oolite and the Chalk so white
All stratified in order.[6]

LANDSCAPE: PLANTS AND COLLECTING

From the late 18th century onwards tourists came increasingly to admire
landscape, especially the more spectacular parts of the countryside: rocky hills,
mountains, lakes and cliffs. This was a new-found interest in scenery for its own
sake. Earlier it was man's control of landscape that had been the focus of
appreciation, the emphasis being on the well-farmed. Thomas Hardy made fun
of this in his novel *The Trumpet Major*: 'as Nature was hardly invented at this
early point in the century [about 1805] Bob's Matilda could not say much about
the glamour of the hill; or the shimmering of the foliage, or the wealth of glory in
the distant sea as she would doubtless have done had she lived later on'.

Even Matilda, however, would have known to exclaim over rugged rocky areas:
they had become much admired during the 18th century. One such rugged area,
Cheddar Gorge in Somerset, exactly fitted the new ideals of scenery (Fig. 12.10).

Fig. 12.10 Cheddar Gorge today:
*a dramatic landscape, contrasting with the
softer lands of the Somerset Levels beyond.*

John Collinson, the Somerset county historian, wrote of it in 1791: 'what most distinguishes the place, and occasions it to be visited by travellers, is that stupendous chasm … certainly the most striking scene of its kind in Great Britain'. Stupendous and awesome were what was required by tourists. Collinson continues:

> *In passing along this valley, the awful scenery is continually changing, but to observe all its beauties, it must be traversed backwards and forwards. In doing this, there will be found ten points of view, which are grand beyond description, and where the prospects exhibit that wild and tremendous magnificence which cannot fail impressing the mind of the spectator with awe, and astonishment at the works of that Power, whose voice even the obdurate rocks obey, and retire.*

'Awful' means 'awesome' and therefore good. The 'Power' is, of course, God. The 'ten points of view' were one of the rules governing the proper appreciation of landscape in the later 18th century. These ten places were considered to give the best, most picture-like (or picturesque) views of the subject, and were to be ticked off by visitors.

As well as the gorge itself, Collinson thought that the natural caves and springs added to the attractions of Cheddar, and the 'many curious aquatick plants … which being kept in continual motion, render the scene uncommonly beautiful'. He also noted 'many curious plants' in the cliffs 'which grow out of the fissures of the rocks right up to their very summits', but it was the Cheddar Pink (*Dianthus gratianopolitanus*) which was the main botanical attraction.

The pink must always have been known to locals, but it was not noted by botanists and named until 1724. It was admired by the many visitors to Cheddar, and this very popularity nearly brought it to extinction. Locals grubbed up roots to sell to the visitors, as reported by the *Victoria County History* in 1906, who hoped that 'it will long continue to flourish in spite of the damage to which it is exposed at the hands of those who make trade of selling the roots'. Luckily, the sensible plant grew in some completely inaccessible places and has survived. Today, it is included on the World Conservation Union's Red List of Threatened Species, which means that it is illegal 'to intentionally pick, uproot, or destroy' it, or to sell or advertise it for gain.[7]

The seashore was an early focus for mass collecting – from the mid-18th century onwards seashells and seaweeds were popular not so much for their scientific interest but for decoration. Early geologists at Lyme Regis were often taken for commercial seaweed or shell collectors, and all seaside places had curiosity dealers who made much of their stock into decorative pictures, often accompanied by badly written verses. At Lyme Regis, according to the local historian, George Roberts, writing in 1834,[8] 'Much taste was displayed in the arrangement of shells, pebbles, and sea-weed – much energy in the search after them … every sitting-room [had] some tasteful and fantastic nick-nack of the marine school … baskets made of shells, containing different kinds of sea-weed … which ladies of great taste so well know how to arrange.' Some Lyme pictures were enlivened with the following verse (which was used in many seaside resorts):

> *Oh call us not weeds, but flow'rs of the sea,*
> *For lovely, and gay, and bright-tinted are we;*
> *Our blush is as deep as the rose of the bowers,*
> *Then call us not weeds, – we are ocean's gay flow'rs.*

Many visitors collected their own seaweed or shells to arrange and take home, but it was doubtless easier to buy from the local professionals. Mary Anning's father had dealt in shells and seaweed as well as fossils.

In 1857 the beach at Lyme Regis was described as where 'an Aquarium can be furnished with most of those interesting objects required in making one of those pleasing acquisitions to the "Home of Taste". [An aquarium is] a picture of life, which has charms, that may vie with the most elaborate masterpiece of Art, increasingly attractive for its frequent changes in appearance, which unlike the productions of human artists, will never satiate by monotony.'[9]

Scientific study of seaweeds and shells went on alongside this decorative collecting. Seaside visitors collecting seaweed and shells must have had some effect on the wildlife, and indeed some rare species did become even rarer. Compared to the fern craze described below, however, the effects were slight.

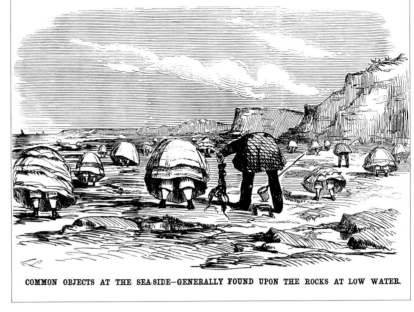

COMMON OBJECTS AT THE SEA-SIDE—GENERALLY FOUND UPON THE ROCKS AT LOW WATER.

Fig. 12.11 The peak of the craze for marine aquariums satirised by Punch in 1858 – *due to the number of collectors they were indeed the commonest creatures on the shore.*

In the 1850s the invention of the aquarium, in which sea-creatures could be kept alive, along with seaweeds, rapidly developed into a craze and led to parts of the coast being stripped of sea anemones and other creatures (Fig. 12.11). Aquariums were cheap to build, and so were widely popular. Fortunately the fashion did not last too long, and the seashores were left to recover. Most of the people with aquariums were not studying the creatures, only admiring them, but even so they were part of that more widespread interest in natural science that gave birth to the local societies described above whose members devoted themselves to the study of botany, geology and other kindred subjects.

THE FERN CRAZE

From the 1830s onwards ferns began to attract increasing interest from amateur botanists. Ferns had not hitherto been a focus for botanical study, perhaps because they lack flowers, but they have one irresistible characteristic: they produce attractive variants or sports that are completely different from the original plant. The collectors' desire to own every variant created devastation in the wild.

The craze for fern-collecting was encouraged by the invention of the closed glass case, where ferns (and indeed other plants) could thrive with only very occasional watering. Nathaniel Ward perfected his model in the 1830s, and the new gardening magazines that had sprung up wrote enthusiastically about them, spreading their fame. These Wardian cases, or Ward's Portable Greenhouses, as they became known, were easy to make and after the reduction of the heavy taxes on glass in 1845, not expensive. They not only shielded plants from the polluted air of towns, but also transformed the transport of plants from distant countries.

Amateur botany generally was already popular in the 1830s, and by the early 1840s ferns had captured the public imagination. Many books were published on them, and a class of professional collectors had arisen that was happy to supply those who did not seek the thrill of the hunt.

Charles Kingsley encouraged fern collection, or 'pteridomania' as the Victorians latinised it, writing in *Glaucus; or the Wonders of the Shore* in 1855:

Your daughters, perhaps, have been seized with the prevailing 'Pteridomania,' and are collecting and buying ferns, with Ward's cases wherein to keep them (for which you have to pay), and wrangling over unpronounceable names of species (which seem to be different in each new Fern-book that they buy), till the Pteridomania seems to you somewhat of a bore: and yet you cannot deny that they find an enjoyment in it, and are more active, more cheerful, more self-forgetful over it, than they would have been over novels and gossip, crochet and Berlin-wool.

The hobby was popular from the 1850s, with many people exploring the landscape to find the ferns, dig them up and take them home (Fig. 12.12). Local surveys of ferns were published to help the collectors, who often removed all the rare ferns over a wide area. The Devon/Dorset borders north of Lyme Regis were a particularly good hunting ground, and *Ferns of the Axe* was one of the most popular of these local guides. First published in 1862 it was in such demand that a second edition followed only four years later. The author, the Revd Z J Edwards, encouraged others to look for ferns. It was a congenial pursuit since:

There is scarcely a bog, or dripping wood, or damp shady lane, where traces of the Fern tribe are not to be found throughout this interesting neighbourhood. In many a neglected wall, or bridge, or church, or crevice of a rock, the humbler of these plants are seen creeping with their rolled-in buds, and silently demand our praise and observation. Nay, the very works of art cannot expel these dear children of nature. As certain of the feathered tribe have left their natural haunts, and thronged to the habitations of men, so certain of these Ferns have deserted their original residence among the rocks, and are scarcely ever seen except upon buildings and walls, the artificial work of man.

Fig. 12.12 Ferns in west Dorset, a wood engraving of 1971 by Reynolds Stone. *This celebrates the common Hart's Tongue, whose many variants were prized by Victorian collectors.*

He helpfully pointed out where the rarer ferns were to be found, and is particularly informative about the variants that attracted collectors:

An account has been given of very many varieties of abnormal forms of various species of our Ferns. In some of these the difference is very slight; in others so great that a person uninformed would think it impossible that they

Fig. 12.13 A large group of Victorian fern collectors depicted by the Illustrated London News *in July 1871. The couple on the left are hauling away a large selection.*

constitute the same species. It may be very properly asserted, that many are monstrosities, not varieties, and therefore not to be noticed. If, however, we cast away all monstrosities and deem them not worthy our consideration, our gardens and our shrubberies would lose much of their beauty and elegance. What is it that makes the borders and parterres of our nobility and gentry appear so lovely? For what are handsome prizes offered at our Floricultural and Horticultural Meetings? What is it that the nurseryman and gardener strive to produce by dint of the most skilful cultivation? Monstrosities. The single rose and stock is nature's production; the double rose and double stock are monstrosities, deviations from nature's ordinary course.

Edwards finished his book with encouragement to fern-seekers (Fig. 12.13), making it clear that while it was mostly a middle- and upper-class pastime, some of the lower orders were starting to collect as well:

It is hoped that these hints will serve to remove any difficulty that may arise in attempting to discover the various Ferns of the neighbourhood. Several have been drawn already to amuse themselves with this simple study as a recreation, in consequence of our observations previously thrown out in a local newspaper. The endeavour has been made to make the subject understood by every class, and it is the source of no little pleasure to find, that not only the gentry, but the humble classes and mechanics have felt interested in the wild productions of their own locality.

The man who was probably the most persistent and devoted fern-hunter in all England lived near Lyme. James Moly (1826–1910) was described in the *British Fern Gazette* after his death as 'one of the few remaining pioneers of the British Fern cult'; he had discovered 600 distinct varieties of fern, 'a considerable number of which were high-class and some absolutely unique' (Fig. 12.14). All these varieties were dug up and taken back to his huge garden: the desperate collecting instinct comes over very clearly. Moly went on collecting all his life, long after the fern cult had faded, dedicating his whole life to fern-hunting, and walking, it is said some 100,000 miles (160,000km) in Dorset and Devon seeking ferns.[10]

Fig. 12.14 James Moly of Lyme, thought to have been the greatest variety-hunter of ferns in the country. He discovered 600 distinct varieties mostly in the Lyme and Charmouth area. The photograph probably dates from the 1870s and he is dressed for fishing. A note written soon after his death described him as having been the 'handsomest man in Dorset'.

***Fig. 12.15 A detail of the Somerset
Levels,*** *with characteristic drainage by
ditches, and willows.*

THE SOMERSET LEVELS

Perhaps the strangest area of this diverse region is the Somerset Levels and moors, covering more than 518km² (Fig. 12.15). Large parts of these flatlands are covered in peat, and the development of this unusual landscape follows a similar pattern to most of the region, but at a later date because of the huge amount of drainage needed to make the land suitable for agricultural use.

Today the levels are much appreciated in their own right, but in the past the main drive was to make them useful. Collinson in 1791 approved the fact that the water 'being excluded by sluices and sea walls, the marshes have from time to time by much industry been drained and reduced to profit'. In the 18th century the area was seen as useful for wild-fowling and little more. Medieval settlement was on 'islands' of higher ground, and as the Somerset historian Robert Dunning[11] describes, in the medieval period:

> *tenants built and maintained sea-walls, embanked rivers, and gradually worked from their island and marsh-side villages, draining and reinstating the land. None of this involved much co-ordination, and winter flooding as well as much litigation was the inevitable result. Between 1770 and 1833, however, co-ordinated efforts not only attempted large-scale drainage, including the digging of the King's Sedgemoor Drain (1794), but also clay and silt was spread to alter the character of the soil. More difficult areas were and still are drained by pumping stations, the first in 1830. Greatest progress was made in the 1940s, first with the creation of the Huntspill Cut … and then the widening of the King's Sedgemoor Drain.*

The peat was used locally as a fuel from early times, but the extraction of huge quantities for horticultural purposes from the middle of the 20th century onwards has had far-reaching repercussions for conservation. The very landscape itself was being altered by peat extraction but agreements with the larger extraction companies are now ensuring that the marshes are being properly restored (Fig. 12.16).

The Somerset Levels are now the home of what was until the late 19th century a universal industry – the manufacture of willow baskets. Willows thrive on the higher parts of the levels, and the old pollarded trees are an important part of the landscape. The present-day industry, however, is based largely on intensely cultivated, closely planted very short willows, but the area still has a most distinct character – a landscape of peat, willow and flooding.

THE 20th CENTURY – DESTRUCTION AND BIODIVERSITY

It is easy to mock Victorian natural history, especially the hugely popular crazes such as the mania for aquariums or fern-collecting, which certainly damaged the

countryside, but the history of the landscape in the 20th century is even sadder. When Wordsworth wrote in 1844: 'Is then no nook of English ground/Secure from rash assault?', he was concerned about the effect of railways on wild places. From today's perspective the railways he dreaded seem of minor importance – they affected only a tiny percentage of the landscape.

The irony of the 20th into the 21st century is that an increase in research and a greatly increased public awareness of the landscape have paralleled an unprecedented destruction of the countryside. Removing all the variant ferns from a particular area is almost irrelevant in the light of the wholesale destruction of grasslands, old woods, hedgerows and heathlands, for the most part caused by modern farming methods. It has been estimated that nationally 40 per cent of hedgerows were destroyed in the 50 years following 1940, together with 95 per cent of flower-rich meadows. Hedges are still disappearing today, but at a slower rate (Fig. 12.17).

The concept of ecology – the understanding of the interdependence of different species in their habitats – was a development of the 20th century. It has led to our growing awareness of the huge importance of maintaining the biodiversity of the countryside, with its complex ecosystems and its rich mix of species embracing wide genetic variation. The preservation of the fantastic web of life alongside the need for a system of sustainable agriculture is perhaps the greatest challenge we now have to face.

Fig. 12.16 Somerset Peat-Heritage Triptych. (left) Panel 1 painted by pupils of Ashcott Primary School with artist Kate Lynch showing the Somerset peat-cutting heritage 1900–39, a lively representation of the many uses of peat from the strange and, until recent times, little known or understood landscape of the Somerset Levels; (right) Panel 3 painted by Meare Primary School with Kate Lynch showing the Somerset peat industry from 1960 to the present day, with peat extraction for horticulture, and a restored area of the marshes in the foreground.

***Fig. 12.17* The Cotswolds today,** *with arable crops in place of traditional sheep grazing, changing the whole picture of landscape as well as its biology.*

NOTES

1   Torrens 1995, 257–84.

2   Neve 1983, 179–204; Taylor & Torrens 1986, 136–48.

3   Draper 1996, 14–23; 1999, 136–8.

4   Anon. 1850, 115–18.

5   Winchester 2001.

6   A song for the Anniversary dinner by A C Ramsay in 1854.

7   Marren 1999, 76.

8   Roberts 1834, 285.

9   Brown 1857, 72–3.

10 Allen 1969; Merrill 1989, 34, includes the Kingsley quotation about the fern craze.

11 Dunning 1980, 126–7.

13

Romanticism and Recreation

TREVOR ROWLEY

POPULAR PERCEPTIONS AND ALTERNATIVE VIEWS

The 1939 *Penguin Guide to Somerset*,[1] with its maps proudly 'in three colours',
paints a landscape of small towns linked by unclassified roads, and of villages in a
maze of minor tracks. Modern social and economic reality are rarely allowed to
intrude into the picture; if they are, as at Radstock with its relics of coal mining,
they too are claimed as part of a gentle, idyllic English tapestry: 'The miners'
cottages are tidy if monotonous, and as mining villages go, Radstock is almost
picturesque.' Where the guide cannot avoid facing aspects of the 20th century,
they are treated with distaste or irony. The expanding seaside resort at Weston-
Super-Mare is condescendingly described as 'the most astonishing mushroom,
grown mainly on the fertile soil of the modern holiday habit'. Modern buildings
are dismissed as being constructed of 'cheaper and nastier building material'; the
passing of craftsmanship which this reflects is regretted as 'street after street is
rebuilt and "improved" out of recognition'. The 'second-rate vulgarity' of 'the ill-
mannered self-assertion of the newest cinema or 1930s' bungalow' is condemned
without reservation.

The landscape offered by the Somerset guide is overwhelmingly one of rural
tranquillity: 'a fragment of Old England, await[ing] the pen of the etcher', to
paraphrase one commentator. It is a landscape seen through the eyes of Miss
Marple, a land of tea rooms and picturesque village pubs. It is the landscape of
the emerging Council for the Protection of Rural England (now the Campaign to
Protect Rural England) and the National Trust, a product of new car-based
tourism mingling with unabashed nostalgia for a past rural idyll.

The very *raison d'être* for the *Penguin Guide to Somerset*, indeed, and of other
similar guides such as the popular Shell Guides, was the increased mobility
provided by train, car and motor coach, which brought the countryside and its
delights into range on a large scale for the ordinary citizen for the first time.
Places that had been known mainly only to locals became much more widely
accessible as the 20th century progressed. Mass mobility and tourism was
already well under way by the time of the outbreak of the Second World War and
was a primary factor in the democratisation of the landscape and the heritage.
The Somerset coast and Severn Estuary were convenient for the urban
population of Bristol and for the coalminers and steelworkers of South Wales,
while the Dorset seaside towns were within reach of holidaymakers from
Southampton and midland and eastern England.

Although its beguilingly attractive rural landscape was and still is one of the
region's greatest assets, the reality is that in the perceived 'Golden Age' of the
recent past there was considerable rural poverty. Many countryside people in the
region suffered particularly badly during the 19th century. The end of the
Napoleonic Wars had brought a sudden agricultural slump, as a result of which
many farmers in the region went bankrupt and the social fabric was almost torn

Fig. 13.1 The cottage in Tolpuddle where the Tolpuddle Martyrs are believed to have met.

asunder. The 'Swing Riots' of 1830, named after a fictional Captain Swing whose signature appeared on letters warning landowners and farmers of impending attacks, were fostered by low wages and long hours, especially on the larger estates. The riots were short-lived, but particularly in Berkshire, Hampshire and Wiltshire and a little later in Dorset, they triggered waves of rick-burning and machinery-breaking as revenge for the poverty and misery being suffered. Corn-producing areas were the worst affected; the saying was: 'Chalk was riotous, cheese tranquil.'

Although soon quelled, the riots led to other forms of protest. The desperation of workers in Dorset was expressed by the formation of the Friendly Society of Agricultural Labourers at Tolpuddle in 1834. Fearing revolution, the landowners acted quickly and used the old Mutiny Act of 1797 to sentence six of the Tolpuddle leaders to transportation to Botany Bay. This harsh sentence caused such a public outcry, led by Dorchester's MP, that the 'Tolpuddle Martyrs' were granted a free pardon, although in the event only one chose to return to Tolpuddle. The story is told for tourists today in the Tolpuddle Martyrs Museum, housed in memorial cottages built in 1934 by the Trades Union Congress. Tolpuddle itself is now the keystone of alternative landscapes of the region, telling a different story to that of the rural idyll (Fig. 13.1).

This alternative story is echoed by the official documents. Evidence presented a decade after the Martyrs' pardon to the Parliamentary Commission on The Employment of Women and Children in Agriculture, in 1843 provides a grim picture of rural life in Dorset. Rachel Hayward, wife of a farm labourer of Stourpaine, gave witness of the conditions in which her family lived:

> There are eleven of us in our family – myself, my husband, three daughters and six sons. We have two rooms, one down stairs and the other up stairs over it. We all sleep in the bedroom.

In 1867 yet another Parliamentary Commission (Employment of Children and Young Persons and Women in Agriculture) reported that:

> The cottages of [Dorset] are more ruinous and contain worse accommodation than those of any other county I have visited, except Shropshire; ... And such villages as Bere Regis, Fordington, Winfrith, Cranborne, or Charminster (in which there is an average of 7 persons to a house) ... are a disgrace to the owners of the land, and contain many cottages unfit for human habitation.

These conditions, particularly the absence of even the most rudimentary sanitary arrangements for many labourers' cottages, coupled with the overcrowding and poor dwellings, inevitably led to ill health on a significant scale – rheumatism, tuberculosis, bronchitis and many other diseases. A Bristol land agent of the

mid-19th century, William Sturge, who was as familiar with the slums of Bristol as with those of north Somerset villages, was in no doubt that conditions in the villages were often worse than in Bristol.

This rural deprivation continued to be a feature of the region well into the 20th century, just at the time that the rosy picture of the Penguin and Shell Guides was being disseminated. Rural poverty was accompanied by persistent migration from the land, and rural depopulation continued into the decades after the Second World War. It was only reversed towards the end of the century, when there was a move back into the villages – not by farmworkers but by a completely new type of 'country dweller', mobile, comfortably-off, retired or homeworking refugees from the cities, who modernised the 'charming' cottages that had been the wretched homes of 19th-century agricultural labourers. People and wealth returned to the countryside and the villages now shine as never before – a self-fulfilling prophecy of the 'rural idyll' (Fig. 13.2).

Fig. 13.2 The model village of Milton Abbas in Dorset. It was built in the 1780s to replace the old town which was displaced when Joseph Damers, Viscount Milton, rebuilt the country house and created a new landscaped park. In the 19th century, living conditions in these picturesque cottages were among the worst in Dorset.

LITERARY LANDSCAPES

The 20th-century view of landscape has relied heavily on literary perceptions: the land seen through the eyes of writers. Our region has more than its fair share of literary associations, although two – Thomas Hardy and the Wordsworth/Coleridge connection – stand out. Coleridge and Wordsworth came to the north Somerset coast on walking tours in the 1790s, bringing with them two new enthusiasms: romantic scenery and seabathing. William and Dorothy Wordsworth moved in 1795 to Racedown Lodge, near Bettiscombe in the Blackdown Hills, where William wrote some of his most important early poetry. In 1797 they moved on to Alfoxden Park at Holford, to be near Coleridge at

Fig. 13.3 Plaque of the poet Samuel Taylor Coleridge on the churchyard wall of Ottery St Mary, Devon, where he was born in 1772. Coleridge lived in Nether Stowey in Somerset for a few years where he was the centre of a literary circle which included Wordsworth. He wrote 'The Rime of the Ancient Mariner' and 'Kubla Khan' while living here.

Nether Stowey. Alfoxden was a fine, three-storey mansion set in a deer park high on the edge of the Quantocks, a place that Coleridge said can 'make man forget there is any necessity for treason'. Dorothy's *Alfoxden Journal* records her impressions of the area from the Quantocks to the Culbone Hills, which inspired *The Lyrical Ballads* (1798) on which Wordsworth and Coleridge collaborated: 'There is everything here; sea, woods wild as fancy ever painted, brooks clear and pebbly as in Cumberland, villages so romantic.'

While at Alfoxden, Wordsworth completed his *Lyrical Ballads*, which include 'Tintern Abbey' and 'The Nightingale'; Wordsworth felt that the latter was an appropriate memorial to his last Quantock days spent with Coleridge. Charles Lamb and William Hazlitt were among the visitors to Nether Stowey, creating a remarkable literary circle. The only drawback was the local people's suspicions. It is said that the Wordsworths' north country accents and Dorothy's dark complexion, as well as the long walks they took, often at night, with camp stools, telescopes and notebooks, led to their investigation as French revolutionary spies. A Home Office spy, nicknamed 'Spy Norya', was sent from London to investigate the 'mischievous gang of Englishmen' and reported that 'the inhabitants of Alfoxden House are a Sett of violent Democrats'; but ultimately concluded that they were 'harmless cranks'.

Samuel Taylor Coleridge and his wife took as their home the village of Nether Stowey on the eastern slopes of the Quantocks (Fig. 13.3). In the short time that the family was here, Coleridge composed many of his best-known works, including 'The Rime of the Ancient Mariner' and 'Kubla Khan'. Earlier, at Clevedon overlooking the Bristol Channel, he had completed 'The Eolian Harp' and 'Reflections on having left a Place of Retirement', two poems in which Clevedon is brought vividly to life – the evening scent of a bean field, the flash of white sails in the Bristol Channel, the 'Dim coasts, and cloud-like hills and shoreless ocean'. It was the beginning of Coleridge's love affair with the Somerset landscape, during which he was inspired by the heaths, coombs, woodlands, dells, waterfalls and hidden streams.

But it was Nether Stowey that inspired Coleridge's most famous works. Dorothy Wordsworth records that 'The Rime of the Ancient Mariner' was first conceived on a long winter walk over Quantoxhead to Watchet and Dulverton, beginning on 13 November 1797 at about 4 pm when the sun was just setting over Longstone Hill. This late start was deliberately timed so that Coleridge and Wordsworth, who accompanied him, could watch the transition from sunlight to moonlight over the sea. Wordsworth later wrote an account of their expedition, which lasted several days, with many 'droll enough recollections' of their adventures along the coast and in country inns while they composed the outline of the poem.[2]

Coleridge spent much time walking along the Somerset coast and through the countryside of the Quantocks and Exmoor with William Wordsworth and other poets. The house in which the Coleridges lived, rented from a local tanner, Tom Poole, is now owned by the National Trust and called Coleridge Cottage. In his poems of that time Coleridge draws upon the imagery of the Quantock Hills. He evokes the bare 'springy' heath of the upper hills, the damp 'ferny' dark of Holford Combe and its waterfall, and the evening sunlight on his neighbour's garden of limes, walnut trees and ancient ivy.[3] It was from the ancient port of Watchet that the Ancient Mariner's doomed crew set sail.

The Quantocks became Coleridge's poetic kingdom and for many people the landscape can only be seen in his company. He was planning a poem to be called 'The Brook' and he records that, 'My walks ... were almost daily on top of the Quantock, and among its sloping combes. With my pencil and memorandum book in hand, I was making studies, as the artists call them, and often moulding my thoughts into verse, with the objects and imagery immediately before my senses.' 'The Brook' was never written but emerged as a central theme in 'Kubla Khan':

*I sought for a subject, that should give equal room and freedom for
description, incident, and impassioned reflections on men, nature, and society,
yet supply in itself a natural connection to the parts, and unity to the whole.
Such a subject I conceived myself to have found in a stream, traced from its
source in the hills among the yellow-red moss and conical glass-shaped tufts
of bent, to the first break or fall, where its drops become audible, and it begins
to form a channel; thence to the peat and turf barn, itself built of the same
dark squares as it sheltered; to the sheepfold; to the first cultivated plot of
ground; to the lonely cottage and its bleak garden won from the heath; to the
hamlet, the villages, the market-town, the manufactories, and the seaport.*[4]

It was some time during the first fortnight of October 1797 that Coleridge went
for a long solitary walk along the coast to Lynton. He appears to have been taken
ill on his return journey and stopped off at Ash Farm above Culbone church,
where he wrote 'Kubla Khan' under the influence of opium, which he had been
given to cure his sickness. In the poem he creates a mystic land of 'milk and
honey' set 'on the coast of Granada'. But the original setting is clearly that of the
Quantock Hills, and the woods running down to the Bristol Channel at Culbone,
as he observed them that autumn at sunset, just as the moon began to rise above
the lonely farmhouse:

*The hanging woods, that touch'd by autumn seem'd
As they were blossoming hues of fire and gold,
The hanging woods, most lovely in decay,
The many clouds, the sea, the rock, the sands,
Lay in the silent moonshine; and the owl,
(Strange! very strange!) the scritch owl only wak'd
Sole voice, sole eye of all that world of beauty!*[5]

Many other places in the region are heavy with literary ghosts. At Combe Florey,
in Somerset, the essayist Sydney Smith was rector between 1829 and 1845. Here,
he said, his Georgian house (now the Old Rectory) was 'like the parsonages
described in novels'. 'My neighbours look very much like other people's
neighbours; their remarks are generally of a meteorological nature.' The novelist
Evelyn Waugh lived here too, at the manor house, between 1956 and 1966, and
wrote *Unconditional Surrender* (1961), and the last volume of his war trilogy,
Sword of Honour (1965). Waugh is buried in the churchyard;[6] Smith has a
memorial east window in the church.

Rather earlier, one of the inventors of the English novel, Henry Fielding, was
brought up at the manor house in East Stowe, a village some 6km to the west of
Shaftesbury; his most famous novel, *Tom Jones* (1749), was inspired by the
place and its characters. The ashes of the poet T S Eliot (d 1965), whose
ancestors left the village of East Coker in Somerset for America, are buried in
the church as he requested. The second section of his *Four Quartets* (1944) is
named after the village.

The old fishing port of Lyme Regis on the south-west Dorset coast offers yet
more literary associations. Jane Austen wrote of a visit here in 1804 when she
attended a ball and went bathing in the sea. Eleven years later she drew on her
memories of this and possibly other visits to the town in *Persuasion* (1818), and a
small garden on Marine Parade has been laid out that commemorates Jane
Austen's association with Lyme. The town's long curving harbour wall called the
Cobb, of medieval origin, is its most famous landmark largely because of its place
in Austen's novel. Lyme Regis was also the setting for one of cinema's most
enduring images, that of a lone woman standing on the wave-lashed Cobb, in the
film based on the novel *The French Lieutenant's Woman* by John Fowles. The
heroine (played by Meryl Streep) walks there daily with her long raven hair

blowing in the wind. Fowles himself was so taken by the resort that he retired there and for years managed the local museum. He moved to Underhill Farm in 1965 and wrote, 'The house is old, set uphill from square high-walled garden. A Fig. tree, strawberry beds, the sea beyond. I have that strange feeling that I wrote about in *The Magus* – of meeting oneself coming the other way in time. This is the place, something will be lost forever if one avoids the encounter.'[7]

In the west, Exmoor has become inextricably associated with Richard Doddridge Blackmore and his novel *Lorna Doone* (1869). Although the story was written from childhood memories of Exmoor while Blackmore was in London, many of the descriptions unmistakably correspond to specific places in the area. The Doone valley is a long enclosed sweep of green pasture and mature woodland. The now demolished medieval farm known as Hoccombe Combe is thought to have been the home of a wild and unruly Exmoor family whose real-life exploits provided the inspiration for the story. The beautiful little 15th-century church to the east, at Oare, is thought to be the setting of the heroine's dramatic, interrupted wedding. The novel is set in the 17th century at the time of the Monmouth Rebellion, yet it is quintessentially a Victorian story, evoking a nostalgic picture of rural England at a time of great technological advances. The fictional story of Lorna Doone rapidly created a real landscape and Doone Valley first appeared on Ordnance Survey maps in 1889, just 20 years after the novel was first published. Doone tourist country now covers much of Exmoor and the name is associated with a host of holiday activities, shops and restaurants, and riding and fishing holidays.

Above all, however, it is perhaps Thomas Hardy whose writing has most created our perception of the region, and has even given it a name – Wessex. Few writers can be as closely identified with an area as Hardy is with Wessex (Fig. 13.4); he placed his fictional characters and events in a thinly disguised Dorset landscape.[8] By the end of the 19th century, Dorset in particular had become an established place of pilgrimage for devotees intent upon visiting the settings of the 'Wessex Novels'.

Hardy was born, where his heart is buried, at Higher Bockhampton close to Stinsford (Mellstock). As a child he explored the surrounding countryside, getting to know his local woods, heaths, rivers and farms. He visited relatives in other Dorset villages and walked daily to his school in the expanding provincial town of Dorchester. In his teens and early twenties he travelled the county more widely as an apprentice (and later assistant) architect, inspecting houses, churches and churchyards. He later went on cycling expeditions to explore the county's historical and archaeological monuments, as a member of the Dorset Natural History and Antiquarian Field Club. In 1876–8, a period of his life he often described as 'our happiest time', Hardy and his wife Emma made their first home at Sturminster Newton, a small market town at the heart of the rich agricultural area of the Blackmoor Vale. While there he wrote *The Return of the Native*. But Hardy's later life was mostly spent in Dorchester, which he made universally famous under the alias of Casterbridge. Although he needed to spend much time in London, Hardy also required a Wessex retreat and he designed and built a house for himself to the north-east of Dorchester on the site of Mack's Tollgate, which he called Max Gate. It is now owned by the National Trust. Here he lived from 1885 until his death in 1928. Max Gate was the ideal place in which to write and the years that followed Hardy's move here saw the publication of many of his finest works, including *The Mayor of Casterbridge*, *Tess of the d'Urbervilles* and *Jude the Obscure*.

What is Hardy's landscape? How has he shaped our perception of the region? First, he championed localness, at the very beginning of the process of globalisation that so affects today's world. 'I am convinced' Hardy wrote in old age, 'that it is better for a writer to know a little bit of the world remarkably well than to know a great part of the world remarkably little.' More, he reinvented Wessex as it is popularly known today. He partly defines our region as used in

Fig. 13.4 Thomas Hardy, *author of the Wessex Novels, which have contributed to our modern concept of Wessex.*

this book. He coined the word 'Wessex' in its modern sense, or revived and adapted it, in *Far from the Madding Crowd*, as he explained in the preface:

> *It was in the chapters of* Far from the Madding Crowd, *as they appeared month by month in a popular magazine, that I first ventured to adopt the word 'Wessex' from the pages of early English history, and give it a fictitious significance as the existing name of the district once included in that extinct kingdom. The series of novels I projected being mainly of the kind called local, they seemed to require a territorial definition of some sort to lend unity to their scene. Finding that the area of a single county did not afford a canvas large enough for this purpose, and that there were objections to an invented name, I disinterred the old one.*
>
> *Since then the appellation which I had thought to reserve to the horizons and landscapes of a partly real, partly dream country, has become more and more popular as a practical provincial definition; and the dream country has, by degrees, solidified into a utilitarian region which people can go to, take a house in, and write to the papers from.*

'Dream country' can almost be a synonym for the modern use of the word 'landscape' as a perception of the world rather than as a piece of scenery.

Returning to Hardy's childhood, the two most important features in his personal landscape seem to have been the heaths and the River Frome. Even with the A35 trunk road so close, the Hardy childhood cottage at Higher Bockhampton still has the atmosphere of 'a lonely and silent spot between woodland and heathland', as Hardy descried it (Fig. 13.5). To the Dorset heaths, of which there

Fig. 13.5 Thomas Hardy's cottage at Higher Bockhampton near Dorchester.

are many, individually named, Hardy gave the collective name of Egdon Heath. This severe, unwelcoming landscape, with its harsh beauty and untameable character, became one of the grand metaphors in Hardy's imagination:

> *The outlook, lone and bare,*
> *The towering hawk and passing raven share,*
> *And all the upland round is called 'The He'th'.*[9]

It is also a symbol of Nature's indifference to human frustration and despair:

> *As evening shaped I found me on a moor*
> *Sight shunned to entertain:*
> *The black lean land, of featureless contour,*
> *Was like a tract in pain.*[10]

In the famous description of Egdon that forms the opening chapter of *The Return of the Native*, Hardy takes the grimness of the scene and emphasises the brooding darkness and sombre tones of the 'obscure, obsolete, superseded country'.

Running through Egdon Heath from west to east, however, and bisecting it, is the river that offers a strong contrast to the sombre heathland which flanks it. Hardy named this river variously the Froom, Frome or Var. He describes it and its waters in *Tess of the d'Urbervilles*, as being 'clear as the pure River of Life shown to the Evangelist, rapid as the shadow of a cloud, with pebbly shallows that prattled to the sky all day long.' The valley provides a landscape of hope and delight. It was here that Tess was courted by Angel Clare, enjoying the only sustained period of happiness in her tragic life. After she had walked across the heath from Puddletown, her first sight of the valley 'sent her spirits up wonderfully'. From its opening words – 'On a thyme-scented, bird-hatching morning in May' – this whole chapter of the book is keyed to a pitch of celebration, confronting the dourness of Egdon on either side with what Hardy calls 'the irresistible, universal, automatic tendency to find sweet pleasure somewhere, which pervades all life, from the meanest to the highest'.

Tess's first impression is in practical terms, comparing the valley with her native Blackmoor Vale and noting that:

> *The world was drawn to a larger pattern here. The enclosures numbered fifty*
> *acres instead of ten, the farmsteads were more extended, the groups of cattle*
> *formed tribes hereabout; there only families. These myriads of cows stretching*
> *under her eyes from the far east to the far west outnumbered any she had ever*
> *seen at one glance before.*

Hardy emphasises the rich fertility of the landscape and one can recognise the prosperous farming settlements that border the valley – Kingston Maurward and Stafford House, Ilsington, Woodsford and Moreton, and further downstream, Woolbridge Manor. Over the years these settlements have fluctuated between the working headquarters of a great dairy and the residences of landowning gentry. Moreton, for example, was the home of the agricultural improver, James Frampton, who is commemorated by the obelisk that since 1786 has risen among the trees on nearby Fir Hill.

When dealing with coastal areas, Hardy contrasts the insularity and stability of inland countryside with the more open aspects of the coast. He introduces a cosmopolitan sense of wider horizons, which was expressed colourfully in two seaside resorts of very different character, Weymouth and Bournemouth, or as he named them, Budmouth and Sandbourne. In his preface to *The Return of the Native*, set in the 1840s, Thomas Hardy wrote that at that time: 'Budmouth still retained sufficient afterglow from its Georgian gaiety and prestige to lend it an absorbing attractiveness to the romantic and imaginative soul of a lonely dweller inland'. He was himself such a 'soul' and wrote with the authority of personal experience:

> As a rule, the word Budmouth meant fascination on Egdon. That Royal port and watering place, if truly mirrored in the minds of the heath folk, must have combined, in a charming and indescribable manner, a Carthaginian bustle of building with Tarentine luxuriousness and Baian health and beauty.

A remarkable place indeed, which Diggory Venn described in simpler terms:

> Now Budmouth is a wonderful place – wonderful – a great salt sheening sea bending into the land like a bow – thousands of gentlepeople walking up and down – bands of music playing ...

As a young man working in an architect's office, Thomas Hardy in 1869 had lived in lodgings in Weymouth, where he rowed in the bay most summer evenings and bathed 'at seven in the morning either on the pebblebeach towards Preston, or diving off from a boat'. There were steamboats operating from Weymouth, either as pleasure trips on which 'there was dancing by moonlight, and where the couples would come suddenly down with a lurch into each other's arms', or as connections with other harbours in the vicinity. An early scene in *Desperate Remedies*, which Hardy was writing at this time, describes 'a popular local excursion by steamboat' from Weymouth to Lulworth Cove, during which harps and violins played music for dancing: Hardy himself made this excursion with his sister, Mary, in August 1868 (Fig. 13.6).[11]

Laurie Lee is another writer responsible for creating our perceptions of our region's landscape, in this case the Gloucestershire Cotswolds. Lee was born in Stroud and grew up in the small village of Slad, which lies in a narrow tributary

Fig. 13.6 A steamboat moored at Weymouth in 1908. *Trips from Weymouth were a regular feature of the summer schedule, both locally to Lulworth Cove and to the Channel Isles.*

THE HARBOUR & PAVILION. WEYMOUTH.

of the River Frome in a landscape that seems not to have changed in centuries (Fig. 13.7). 'I was set down from the carrier's cart at the age of three; and there with a sense of bewilderment and terror my life in the village began.'

So begins *Cider with Rosie*, his autobiographical story of a childhood spent in remote rural Gloucestershire around the time of the First World War. Lee tells a tale of changing rural seasons, each with a familiar sameness, of the simple pleasures of making your own entertainment, of 'knowing your place' in the grand scheme of things and never aspiring to rise above it. He described the Cotswold valley in which he spent his formative years as 'greener, and more exotically lush than is decent to the general herbaceous smugness of the English countryside'. His early life was primitive by today's standards – the Lee family cottage was lit by oil lamps and candles, and they cooked over a wood fire.

Fig. 13.7 The hamlet of Slad, Gloucestershire, which lies in a valley to the north of Stroud. The author Laurie Lee was brought up here and his autobiographical novel is set in the village where he is now buried.

Part of the attraction of Lee's writing now is that he wrote about the end of an era; after the First World War, things were never to be the same again. In short, Lee stands at the threshold of the romantic nostalgia of the Penguin and Shell Guides. Lee's evocation of summertime is a hymn to nostalgia – the long lost lazy summer days of youth:

> *When they were gone there was nothing else to look at, the village slipped back into silence. The untarred road wound away up the valley, innocent as yet of motor-cars, wound empty away to other villages, which lay empty too, the hot day long, waiting for the sight of a stranger. ... There was nothing to do. Nothing moved or happened, nothing happened at all except summer. Small heated winds blew over our faces, dandelion seeds floated by, burnt sap and roast nettles tingled our nostrils together with the dull rust smell of dry ground. The grass was June high and had come up with a rush, a massed entanglement of species, crested with flowers and spears of wild wheat, and coiled with clambering vetches, the whole of it humming with blundering bees and flickering with scarlet butterflies. Chewing grass on our backs, the grass scaffolding the sky, the summer was all we heard; cuckoos crossed distances on chains of cries, flies buzzed and choked in the ears, and the saw-toothed chatter of mowing-machines drifted on waves of air from the fields.*[12]

This world was slowly invaded and eventually taken over by the motor car, the charabanc and the motorbike. The horses died and were replaced by machines. The social, economic and even religious certainties that had bound Laurie Lee's childhood were in the process of disintegrating. The First World War and its immediate aftermath accelerated the change from a world of horses, wagons, dusty lanes, oil lamps, thatched roofs, cob walls, labour-intensive farming, locally made tools and home-made entertainments to the world of cars, lorries, motor buses, tractors, tarmacadam roads, council houses, electricity, telephones, wireless, piped water, mains drainage, standardised household articles and mass entertainment. 'Soon the village would break, dissolve, and scatter, become no more than a place for pensioners.' In the final chapter of *Cider with Rosie* – 'Last Days' – Laurie Lee recalls that, 'The last days of my childhood were also the last days of the village. I belonged to that generation which saw, by chance, the end of a thousand years' life.'

Lee's nostalgic painting of his childhood world is the world that the Guide writers were reaching for and eulogising. Our hearts may welcome this vision of rural timelessness but our brains know it to be fiction. Yet even today at a superficial level the West region seems much the same as it did almost a century ago, but tidier, cleaner, sanitised, although its inhabitants, for the most part, have no links to the countryside they inhabit apart from their appreciation of its tranquillity and fresh air.

OPENING UP

Chapter 6 has already charted the slow improvement of the road network and the building of canals and railways that opened up the region to visitors from outside as well as facilitating travel and exchange within. The historical absence of very large towns and ports, and its remoteness from London, meant that historically the region had been little visited from the outside. Except by sea, and through the Severn Estuary, communications were not easy, and accordingly much of the region remained isolated and relatively unknown until well into the 19th century. Bath was an exception with its international reputation as a spa resort from the 18th century, but even Bath was difficult to reach and its development was restricted. It was canals and the railway, in particular, that began to open up the region to outside influences. Improved communications at the same time unified the region and exposed it to outside change. The possibility of new distant markets for the region's produce eventually altered the landscape, leading for instance to the development of the dairy industry; cattle replaced sheep as the principal livestock across much of the region, and landscape therefore changed as well.

Although the canals were to be eventually eclipsed and destroyed by the railways, for a few decades their impact was enormous and they are still a significant aspect of the region's landscape character. At the peak of its activity during the 1830s and 1840s the Bridgwater and Taunton Canal was carrying annual loads of more than 70,000 tonnes, mostly of Welsh coal. Somerset coal, on the other hand, was a major component of cargoes on the Kennet and Avon Canal; the latter's rapid transport capacity encouraged a major growth in the industry and the creation of a distinctive aspect of the Somerset landscape, apparent even today despite the death of coalmining here as elsewhere in England. Canals were costly to build, and had not always given their investors adequate returns before the railways arrived and stole their traffic. Railways sometimes literally replaced canals: the Camerton to Limpley Stoke Railway took over much of the northern course of the Somerset Coal Canal and the canal tunnel at Combe Hay was drained and used for trains instead. The heyday of the canals was thus brief. They still mark our landscape with their water, bridges and locks and the settlements that were established alongside wharves, although only

Fig. 13.8 Brunel's Box tunnel near Bath opened in 1841. *It is almost 3km long.*

a few canal ports (such as Burbage, Pewsey, or Honey Street at Alton Barnes in Wiltshire) are still alive with narrowboats.

Railways on the whole have had a longer and more profound effect upon the landscape, and on the region's social and economic life. From the opening in 1841 of Brunel's broad-gauge line from London to Bristol, the network developed rapidly in the region; in view of the amount of earth moving, bridge building, tunnelling and engineering work involved, as well as the capital accumulation and legal work necessary, the rate of progress was staggering (Fig. 13.8). The fitting of the railways into the existing landscape is a fascinating study in itself. One line was known as 'Castleman's Corkscrew' or 'Castleman's Snake', because it was promoted under the leadership of an energetic Wimborne solicitor, A L Castleman, and took such a circuitous route for its short 97km length from Southampton to Dorchester. The Wiltshire, Somerset and Weymouth line, completed in 1857, passed through difficult country at Frampton and used a 640m tunnel to avoid spoiling the landscaped parkland of Frampton Court. The same line provides two other early examples of environmental concern on the outskirts of Dorchester: it tunnelled under Poundbury hillfort and adopted a tight curve, which still slows trains to this day, in order to avoid the henge at Maumbury Rings.[13]

Until the railway came in 1850, Dorchester was essentially the Casterbridge that Hardy later invented, a small county town of assizes and gentry, markets and merchants, still confined within the line of the Roman walls, and seen from afar (as Elizabeth-Jane saw it in *The Mayor of Casterbridge*) as 'an old fashioned place ... huddled all together and ... shut in by a square wall of trees, like a plot of garden ground by a box edging'. But the railways changed all that, and marked the beginning of the modern town. The names and architecture of today's streets show the stages of development clearly; history can be easily read in the townscape. Fine late-Victorian middle-class villas and smaller semi-detached lower middle-class houses are carefully segregated in places such as Prince of Wales Road and Alexandra Terrace. Elsewhere, the haphazard development of housing estates in the late 19th and early 20th centuries is clearly visible. For example, the South Court and Victoria Park estates on the south side of the town were sold for development in 1897, but plots were sold off piecemeal in the usual fashion and it was 40 years before the area was developed completely. Today, of course, Dorchester continues to expand, this time like all English towns with large sprawling estates only truly suited to movement by motor car.

The new railways also opened up northern Somerset and brought it into much closer contact with Bristol and Exeter. The following account of the summer excursion of the Somersetshire Archaeological and Natural History Society for 1898 demonstrates the convenience and flexibility of railway transport in the late 19th century:

> *The Great Western Railway Company, with their usual readiness on such occasions, issued excursion tickets for the visit, and the intention was to provide special carriages by the 10.18 a.m. express train. The party, however, turned out to be a larger one than was anticipated, numbering altogether 100. Mr Linley, the stationmaster, thereupon promptly made arrangement for a special train to convey the visitors, which left Taunton at 10.20, running in advance of the regular express. Exeter was reached without stopping after a smart run of forty minutes.[14]*

The railways allowed farmers throughout the region to obtain new equipment, new and improved breeds of cattle and sheep, artificial fertilisers, tile drains and drainage pipes, and materials such as barbed wire and corrugated-iron sheets. Most important of all, the railways opened up a large new market for liquid milk, which could now be sent to the towns. The demand from the growing population of London increased greatly after the cattle plague there in 1868 had destroyed many of the metropolitan dairies. Dairy farmers throughout the region, from the claylands of north and west Wiltshire, Marshwood Vale in Dorset, and the Somerset Levels, ceased converting the bulk of their milk into cheese and butter and began to send it to the towns by rail. The railways thus virtually killed the local small-scale production of the great variety of different West Country cheeses in favour of the liquid milk trade. The railways also had an important but adverse impact upon the fortunes of arable farmers, as they encouraged the distribution of cheap imported foodstuffs, especially wheat from North America, and thus played a crucial part in the great depression in English agriculture during the last quarter of the 19th century, during which arable and sheep farming were particularly badly hit.

On the other hand, market gardening was greatly stimulated by the coming of the railways and there was an increasing demand for flowers, fruit and vegetables to supply the markets of London and other growing towns. A notable development was strawberry-growing for the London market, which became very important in Somerset around Cheddar along the southern slopes of Mendip. An impetus was also given to various firms of seedsmen and nurserymen by the improved transport facilities. Firms such as Dunns of Gillingham, Scotts of Merriott near Crewkerne, and Kelways of Langport all found that they had a regional and even national market rather than their former purely local one. At Gillingham in north Dorset, Shadrach Dunn began his seed business in 1832, selling grass, clover, sainfoin and lucerne seed in the local markets, and establishing a reputation for his locally grown Dorset marlgrass clover seed. Thus the railways brought new prosperity and greatly increased trade to some market towns, while others that were not on a railway line rapidly declined. In Dorset, for example, the railways changed Sherborne, Gillingham, Bridport and, above all, Dorchester into thriving centres of population and enterprise, while Cerne Abbas, Beaminster, Cranborne and Bere Regis, which were not served by the railways, declined rapidly; their markets died, and they virtually ceased to be towns at all.[15]

During the 1960s, Dr Beeching's axe fell on many coastal branch lines. Modernisation of the networks and a switch from steam to diesel and electric did little to halt the decline. British Rail had a hard job of selling rail travel to a public that had tasted the freedom that the motor car could bring. Advertisements for 'Golden Rail Breaks' in the seaside guidebooks of the 1970s began to look remarkably unattractive to the motoring public. The familiar picture of empty stations and deserted tracks can be seen in many places – the line across the east Dorset heathland from Salisbury to Wimborne Minster, opened with the usual ceremonies in 1861, lasted only just over 100 years, and parts of it have already disappeared under the heathland vegetation.

Paradoxically, this has opened up a new form of nostalgic holiday attraction, and once the era of steam was well and truly over, many of the disused branch lines were transferred to enthusiastic steam-preservation societies. Some of these were at seaside towns, most notably the North Somerset line. While people no longer wanted to make their main journey by train, they were happy to relive the days of steam with a nostalgic trip along the coast. The privately owned West Somerset Railway runs southwards from Minehead on the Somerset coast to Bishop's Lydeard. At nearly 32km, it is the longest line of its kind in the country and it was formed when British Rail's 100-year-old branch line between Taunton and Minehead closed in 1971. A summer service runs between Easter and the end of October, with 10 stations along the line and the special attractions of a first-class Pullman dining car and the *Flockton Flyer*. The stations and the train make frequent appearances on television and in the cinema and play a significant role in the region's nostalgia industry.

In the second half of the 20th century, motorways and trunk roads came to change the landscape in a large number of ways, just as railways had done earlier. Perhaps the greatest symbol of the new dominance of the internal combustion engine in the region is the M5 motorway. This was designed both to move traffic from Bristol, South Wales, London and the Midlands to the West Country, and to serve Severn-mouth towns such as Portishead, Clevedon and Weston-Super-Mare, as well as Taunton. Elsewhere in the region major trunk routes such as the A303, which skirts Stonehenge on its way westwards, carry almost equally heavy volumes of traffic, swelling to breaking point during summer months. The absence of a comprehensive motorway network, however, undoubtedly helps to preserve the essentially rural image of the West and to keep it still some way beyond the limits of the insatiable hinterland of London.

SEASIDE RESORTS AND RECREATION

The resorts that began to develop during the 18th century at spas and around the southern coasts of England were at the start of a long process by which the region was to become in part a landscape of recreation. This development was, of course, closely bound up not only with the expansion and acceleration of modes of travel, but also with the region's natural resources, whether sea water, spa water or scenery, tranquillity and 'rural-ness'.

The story of the origins and growth of inland spas, and of seaside towns – of 'taking the waters' – has been told in Chapter 11. In the present chapter, Weston-Super-Mare, in Somerset, can represent this story in more detail. Other resorts, for instance Bournemouth, displayed equally dramatic explosions of population following the coming of railways along the south coast, in Bournemouth's case kick-started by a strange craze for the medicinal value of pine-scented air discovered by a London doctor, which transformed a former wilderness into what Hardy described as a 'Mediterranean lounging-place on the English Channel'. Now, of course, Bournemouth is a major regional shopping and business centre, with its own university and international airport.

The first hotel at Weston-Super-Mare was opened in 1810 and a coach service from Bristol began in 1814, but holidaymakers began to arrive in large numbers only after the coming of the railway early in 1841. The same is true of Clevedon and nearby Portishead, too, and Burnham-on-Sea. After the railway came, the growth of these resorts was extraordinarily rapid and Weston-Super-Mare in particular grew from a tiny fishing hamlet of fewer than 500 people in 1800 to being the largest town in Somerset, apart from Bath, in 1901 with a population of nearly 20,000.

Weston's first guidebook for visitors was written in 1822 and paints a vivid portrait of the village at that time. Only one hotel, two inns and a number of lodging houses catered for visitors. There was a Methodist chapel, in addition to the parish church and a post office. There was little organised entertainment – a billiard table, a reading room, two pleasure boats for hire and dances held at the Assembly Rooms. Visitors would otherwise have talked, read, sketched and walked.

Birnbeck Pier was completed in 1867, and the town continued to grow, with villas, estates and boulevards. There were drives and walks through Weston Woods, originally a private game reserve, offering views as far as Exmoor and Wales. Perhaps the most important development was the building of sea walls and a 3km promenade still in use today under the Seafront Improvement Scheme of the 1880s. Weston also finally gained a direct railway in 1884, when the present station and loop line into the town opened, making the town even more popular for thousands of visitors, many of them day trippers on Bank Holiday excursions and works outings. As the number of visitors increased so new shops opened, and private schools were set up as it became fashionable for

Fig. 13.9 The Grand Pier at Weston-super-Mare in 1907, just three years after it opened.

the wealthy to send their children to seaside boarding schools advertising themselves as the providers of the benefits of healthy sea air for delicate children.

New facilities were established to entertain visitors, including indoor swimming baths, a theatre on Knightstone, and a library and museum in The Boulevard. On the beach the bathing machines disappeared as mixed bathing became acceptable. By 1890 Birnbeck Pier offered a theatre, alpine railway, shooting gallery, park swings, merry-go-round, tea and coffee rooms, bar, bandstand, photographic studios, switchback, waterchute, flying machine, helter-skelter, maze, bioscope, cakewalk and zigzag slide, and local traders complained that many thousands of trippers arriving by steamer from Wales (15,000 on an average August Bank Holiday) never went further into the town than the pier. In 1904, therefore, a second pier – the Grand Pier – was built closer to the town centre, offering music-hall entertainment (Fig. 13.9).

In the 20th century, between the two world wars, the Marine Lake was built to provide a safe shallow beach; the Winter Gardens and Pavilion opened in 1927, followed in the 1930s by the open air pool, the first amusement arcades and an Odeon cinema. At the same time, Weston Airfield was officially opened in June 1936, bringing many South Wales miners to Weston on their days off. Over the 1937 Whitsun holiday 2,555 passengers travelled on Western Airways from Weston Airport, a world record for that time but also an omen that Weston's boom days would soon end as cheap air travel took the town's customers to more exotic destinations a few decades later.

The single most important change for holidays by the sea in the years after the Second World War, however, was the growth of car ownership. In 1951, 47 per cent of holidaymakers went by train to their destination, 27 per cent went by bus or coach and 27 per cent by private car. By 1960, nearly half of the total number of holidaymakers went by car and by the end of that decade nearly 70 per cent. By then, however, travel abroad had become easier and foreign holidays had become less expensive, and British seaside resorts faced a difficult period. Holidaymakers still came, but increasingly only for day trips; the towns became resorts for the retired and elderly on the one hand, and the boisterous and sometimes beligerent on the other. There are signs that the pendulum is beginning to swing back a little and that the bracing attractions of the English seaside resort are being rediscovered. This is due in part to increased prosperity and leisure, which allows a sizeable minority to take several holidays a year, a regime into which an English holiday experience can be accommodated, often in the form of a short break.

OPEN HOUSE – THE COUNTRY HOUSE

Fuelled partly by the Penguin and Shell Guides with which this chapter started, the region's history was soon to become just as big an attraction for visitors as its natural resources of seaside and spas. The number and accessibility of these historic attractions has increased steadily throughout the 20th century to the present time, as historic buildings and monuments have gradually been opened to a wider public, and in recent years has expanded with the inclusion of more 'manufactured' heritage centres and a plethora of 'theme museums'. A major element in this process was the transfer of stately homes to the National Trust in the years after the First World War by an aristocracy no longer able to afford their upkeep. Country houses, as Jane Austen's novels remind us, had always been available for viewing by the right sort of people, but as they fell into Trust hands (the first sizeable country house to come into its possession was Barrington Court in 1907) their audience expanded and, particularly after 1960 with mass car-ownership, the English habit of visiting grand houses at weekends became engrained. As well as houses and their estates, the Trust also acquired large tracts of countryside, such as Cheddar Gorge (1910 and 1928) and parts of Exmoor (1918 and 1943).

The generosity of the wealthy and the aristocracy in handing over these assets is a constant refrain of guidebooks throughout the 20th and into the 21st century. Although there was undoubtedly a genuinely philanthropic complexion to some of these gifts, as the 20th century progressed the economic realities of death duties and the increasing costs of running and maintaining historic buildings were the main imperative. Many country houses that were not bequeathed to the nation were converted to hospitals, schools or other uses (often after requisition during the Second World War), while others were demolished, so that gift to the Trust was a sensible long-term survival strategy for the owners.

Although country houses were primarily places of private residence, improved facilities for travel during the 19th century had already brought a steady stream of visitors to the famous houses, and formal arrangements began to be made to cater for the increased numbers. Some houses and grounds were open at set times and on an organised basis. From the mid-18th century enterprising local printers had produced guidebooks to assist the visitor. Journals and descriptions of tours made through various parts of England became an increasingly popular literary form. Owners were proud that their fine houses and carefully tended grounds should be visited by 'persons of taste and discernment'. The gardens at Stourhead were opened by Henry Hoare as soon as the landscaping, planting and building commenced during the 1740s, and the nearby inn, The Spread Eagle, provided accommodation for tourists.

As early as 1751 a guidebook to Wilton House (Wiltshire) was produced, and was sold in London, Bath and Salisbury. The task of showing visitors over a great house became a valuable perquisite of the housekeeper and other household servants. A visitor to Wilton in 1776 noted that according to the porter's book 2,324 persons had visited the house during the previous year, and by the early 19th century the tips, which ranged from 2s 6d to £1 0s 0d from each party of visitors, were collected and shared out in varying amounts between the servants.

At this stage, entrance fees were not seen as a way of supporting the house but of restricting visitor numbers. A few benevolent landowners encouraged local people to enjoy their parks and one of the most welcoming was the celebrated archaeologist General Pitt-Rivers, who during the late 19th century set up visitor facilities – a large recreation park known as the Larmer Grounds – on his estate at Tollard Royal, on the borders of Wiltshire and Dorset. The general provided shelters for picnics (for which crockery and cutlery were supplied, but alcohol prohibited), gardens, a lake, formal walks, a theatre and a bandstand. Workmen from the estate formed the band, which performed on Sunday afternoons during the summer. The Larmer Grounds became very popular and in 1893 were visited by 24,000 people.[15]

The upkeep of large-scale, elaborate houses and landscapes was increasingly difficult after the First World War, when agricultural fortunes plummeted once more. The sale of landed estates, which had already been increasing in the pre-war years, reached fever pitch between 1918 and 1922. It is estimated that as much as 25 per cent of England changed hands, a level of activity in the land market that had not been seen since the Dissolution of the monasteries, which had itself been the impetus for the creation of many country houses. The Second World War marked another watershed, as country houses and their gardens were frequently maintained by only the one or two members of the estate staff who were too old for conscription. The houses were often requisitioned by the Ministry of Defence and used for a variety of purposes, and many of their interiors were damaged and mistreated, making the decision to destroy or sell buildings that much easier after the war was over. The 'Dig for Victory' campaign changed the face of many parks and gardens, which were forced into food production. Only a handful of country houses were actually destroyed during the war, but many were commandeered for use by the army, schools or hospitals, their parks dotted by concrete roads, trenches and bunkers, and still bear traces of this phase of their story today.

Restored country houses continue to be added to the region's abundant stock. In 2003, the Trust's new acquisition of Tyntesfield, a Gothic extravaganza near Nailsea, in Somerset was opened to the public. There are in the region numerous other fine buildings and monuments in the hands of both the National Trust and English Heritage, with many more still owned privately but run as part of the same overall heritage and tourism industry. Indeed, throughout the region there is an underlying landscape of tourism, which affects not just the sites themselves and their setting, but the character of the services offered by neighbouring towns and villages by way of hotels, tea shops, tourist shops and so on. The influence extends further. The recent inscription on to the World Heritage List of the south Dorset coast is already creating radically different perceptions of the landscape, one whose first *raison d'être* is tourism rather than farming or fishing.

MUSEUMS AND OTHER DISTRACTIONS

In addition to the normal range of archaeological and historical museums, the region has an extraordinarily eclectic collection of visitor attractions. Billy Butlin's holiday camp at the east end of Minehead's esplanade has been updated and renamed Somerset World. It is the largest holiday complex in Europe with a caravan village, funfair, waterworld and shopping mall; almost all the facilities are under cover in an attempt to compete with warmer overseas resorts. Minehead has come a long way since 1890, when there was a local by-law in force that forbade anyone over the age of 10 from swimming in the sea 'except from a bathing machine, tent or other effective screen'. At Washford, some 10km south-east of Minehead, there is a Tropiquaria, a wildlife park specialising in tropical animals, snakes and spiders, while close by at Williton is the Bakelite Museum, dedicated to the 'pioneer of plastics'.

At Montacute, in addition to the Elizabethan mansion there is the TV and Radio Memorabilia Museum, which houses a large collection of vintage radios, wireless receivers and television sets. Close to Wincanton, best known for its racecourse, is the Haynes Motor Museum, which has the largest collection of veteran, vintage and classic cars and motorbikes in Britain. As Somerset's premier resort, Weston-Super-Mare has a wide range of attractions including the International Helicopter Museum, home to the world's largest collection of helicopters and autogyros, and the Time Machine Museum. At Bournemouth, there is a Teddy Bear Museum and the Casa Magni Shelley Museum, devoted to the life and works of the poet Percy Bysshe Shelley, while at Christchurch close by is a museum devoted to the history of flying boats and the Museum of Electricity. Weymouth has the Museum of Coastal Defence, housed in the Nothe Fort (the latter was built in the 1860s as part of the Portland naval base), while the 'Deep Sea Adventure', an attraction telling the story of marine exploration, occupies one of its harbour's imposing Victorian grain warehouses.

Street, to the south-west of Wells, was a small rural village up until the early 19th century, when it began to expand into an industrial town. Much of this growth was due to one family, the Clarks. In the 1820s, the Quaker brothers, Cyrus and James Clark, began to produce sheepskin slippers from the hides of local animals. Many of the town's older buildings owe their existence to the family and in particular there is the Friends' Meeting House of 1850 and the building that housed the original Millfield School. The oldest part of the Clarks factory has now been converted into a shoe museum and, although the company is one of the largest manufacturers of quality footwear in Europe, it continues to keep its headquarters in the town.[16]

In Dorset, the pride of the museums is the County Museum in Dorchester. The collection and displays are housed in a custom-built Victorian building, including a cast-iron gallery, and trace the county's history from its geological origins through to the present day. The museum also contains a collection of Hardy memorabilia and a reconstruction of his study at Max Gate: even the inventor of Wessex heritage is now heritage.

THE WEST TODAY

By the end of the 20th century the region had seen many changes and it now offers many contradictions. The downland has been put to the plough as never before, while in the valleys fish farms and watercress beds flourish again. Cattle and creameries have replaced sheep, and mushrooms are grown commercially in disused quarries. Each year the motorways and arterial roads pull the cities closer, and litter is a major problem. Each year there are more redundant churches in the region, but increased mobility and earlier retirement have saved thousands of cottages from dereliction. Oil and gas have been tapped from the southern edge of Poole Harbour, although Salisbury was still generating its electricity from the water flowing under the Town Mill when the nuclear power station on Winfrith Heath was opened in the late 1950s. Insurance and computing have become local industries, and greater leisure and affluence have meant that the 8,000 moorings for small boats between Lyme Bay and Southampton Water are no longer enough.[17] Caravans and mobile homes have created whole transient towns, much disliked by many locals along with wind farms. Amusement arcades have taken over the heart of many Edwardian seaside resorts.

Despite the changes, however, parts of the West can still communicate some sense of that beguiling illusion of timelessness and isolation that in the late 19th century rendered them so appropriate for Thomas Hardy's pastoral purposes. The lost rural way of life, whatever its drawbacks, had an integrity which still fascinates and attracts today. Its traces are still visible in the farms and churches, the lanes and trackways of a countryside that is still predominantly agricultural, and in the contours of a topography essentially unchanged.

The region still stands out as distinctively more peaceful, remote and untouched than its neighbours. Apart from Bristol at its periphery (and Bristol look as much westwards and northwards as it does towards Wessex) it does not have major cities as do all other English regions. It has the M5, but otherwise not the same extent of motorways as other regions. By and large, it is still a region to go to rather than to travel through on the way to somewhere else (the A303 excluded, perhaps). It has no very large airports. Lying immediately east of the more spectacular and popular regions of western Britain it has often been overlooked by travellers intent on reaching the perceived delights of the Celtic fringes. It is a region that for the most part has avoided the worst excesses of both the Industrial Revolution and the motor age.

The West has an historic landscape accumulated over four millennia of man's activities, and much of this landscape survives intact. There has been less hedgerow removal here than in central and eastern England, fewer new roads have been built and there has been less quarrying and less coastal development, while the towns and villages have remained relatively small and tranquil. The attractions of the quiet historic landscape have become increasingly appreciated as urban and suburban life becomes busier and noisier. Villages and hamlets that were literally poverty-stricken two centuries ago have now been restored and renovated and provide pretty, comfortable homes mainly for the affluent. Compared to many parts of contemporary Britain it is still largely rural and relatively 'unbruised'. Hardy's Wessex can still somehow be felt.

NOTES

1	Winbolt 1939.	10	Thomas Hardy, *A Meeting With Despair*.
2	Moorman 1957, 345.	11	Hawkins 1983, 1–11.
3	Holmes 1999, 154.	12	Lee 1962, 150–1.
4	Griggs 1956–71.	13	Taylor 1970.
5	Coleridge 1975, 584.	14	Bettey 1974.
6	Eagle & Carnell 1981.	15	*VCH Wiltshire* 1987, 82–3.
7	Fowles 2003.	16	Billing 2001, 310.
8	Pike 2002.	17	Welfare 1984, 90.
9	Thomas Hardy, *By The Barrows*.		

Bibliography

Alcock, L and Ashe, G 1968. 'Cadbury: is it Camelot?', *in* Ashe, G, *The Quest for Arthur's Britain*. London: Pall Mall, 123–148

Allen, D E 1969. *The Victorian Fern Craze: A History of Pteridomania*. London: Hutchinson

Allen, M J 1997. 'Landscape, land-use and farming', *in* Smith, R J C, Healy, F, Allen, M J, Morris, E L, Barnes, I and Woodward, P J, *Excavations Along the Route of the Dorchester By-pass, Dorset, 1986–8* (Wessex Archaeology Report **11)**. Salisbury: Wessex Archaeology, 277–283

Allen, M J 2000. 'Soils, pollen and lots of snails', *in* Green, M G, *A Landscape Revealed: 10,000 Years on a Chalkland Farm*. Stroud: Tempus, 36–49

Allen, M J 2002. 'The Chalkland landscape of Cranborne Chase: a prehistoric human ecology'. *Landscapes* **3**, 55–69

Anon., March 1850, 'Anniversary Meeting of the Crewkerne Literary and Scientific Institution'. *Supplement to the United Counties Miscellany*, 115–118

Anstey, C *c*.1820. *The New Bath Guide*. Bath: Meyler

Aston, M (ed.) 1988. *Aspects of the Medieval Landscape of Somerset*. Taunton: Somerset County Council

Aston M 2000. *Monasteries in the Landscape*. Stroud: Tempus

Aston, M and Iles, R (eds) 1987. *The Archaeology of Avon: A Review from the Neolithic to the Middle Ages*. Bristol: County of Avon, Public Relations and Publicity Department

Aston, M and Leech, R 1977. *Historic Towns in Somerset. Archaeology and Planning* (Comm Res Archaeol in Avon, Glos and Somerset, Survey **2**). Gloucester: Committee for Research Archaeology in Avon, Gloucestershire and Somerset

Aston, M and Lewis, C (eds) 1994. *The Medieval Landscape of Wessex* (Oxbow Monograph **46**). Oxford: Oxbow Books

Aston, M, Austin, D and Dyer, C (eds) 1989. *The Rural Settlements of Medieval England*. Oxford: Basil Blackwell

Atthill, R 1971. *Old Mendip*, 2nd edn. Newton Abbot: David and Charles

Atthill, R (ed.) 1976. *Mendip: A New Study*. Newton Abbot: David and Charles

Austen, J 1818 (1978 edn). *Persuasion*. Harmondsworth: Penguin

Barbeau, A 1904. *Life and Letters at Bath in the Eighteenth Century*. London: Heinemann

Barrett, J, Bradley, R and Green, M 1991. *Landscapes, Monuments and Society*. Cambridge: Cambridge University Press

Beard, C R 1933. *The Romance of Treasure Trove*. London: Sampson Low

Benham, P 1993. *The Avalonians*. Glastonbury: Gothic Image

Bennett, J 1985. *Sea Mills: The Roman Town of Abonae* (City of Bristol Museum and Art Gallery Monogr **3**). Bristol: City of Bristol Museum and Art Gallery

Bennett, J A 1890. 'Camelot'. *Proc Somerset Archaeol Natur Hist Soc* **36**, 1–19

Beresford, M W 1967. *New Towns of the Middle Ages*. London: Lutterworth

Bettey, J H 1974. *Dorset*. Newton Abbot: David and Charles

Bettey, J H 1986. *Wessex from AD 1000*. Harlow: Longman

Bettey, J H 1989. *Suppression of Monasteries in the West Country*. Gloucester: Alan Sutton

Bettey, J H 1993. *Estates and the English Countryside*. London: Batsford

Billing, J 2001. *Guide to Rural England: The West Country*. Aldermaston: Travel Publishing

Blair, J and Ramsay, N 1991. *English Medieval Industries*. London and Rio Grande: Hambledon

Bolton, J L 1980. *The Medieval English Economy, 1150–1500*. London: Dent

Bond, C J 1998. *Somerset Parks and Gardens: A Landscape History*. Tiverton: Somerset Books

Bond, C J 2004. *Monastic Landscapes*. Stroud: Tempus

Booker, F 1977. *The Great Western Railway: A New History*. Newton Abbot: David and Charles

Bradley, R J 1990. *The Passage of Arms*. Cambridge: Cambridge University Press

Bradley, R J 1993. *Altering the Earth: The Origins of Monuments in Britain and Continental Europe*. Edinburgh: Society of Antiquaries of Scotland

Bradley, R J 1998. *The Significance of Monuments*. London: Routledge

Braine, A 1891 (facsimile edn 1969). *The History of Kingswood Forest*. Bath: Kingsmead Bookshop

Branigan, K and Fowler, P J (eds) 1976. *The Roman West Country: Classical Culture and Celtic Society*. Newton Abbot: David and Charles

Brigden, R 1986. *Victorian Farms.* Ramsbury: The Crowood Press

Briggs, K 1974. *The Folklore of the Cotswolds.* London: Batsford

Brill, E 1987. *Life and Tradition on the Cotswolds*, 2nd edn. Gloucester: Alan Sutton

Brown, H R 1857. *The Beauties of Lyme Regis…* Lyme Regis: Daniel Dunster

Buchanan, A and Cossons, N 1969. *Industrial Archaeology of the Bristol Region.* Newton Abbot: David and Charles

Bulley, J A 1952. '"To Mendip for coal": a study of the Somerset coalfield before 1830, Part 1'. *Proc Somerset Archaeol Natur Hist Soc* **97**, 46–78

Bulley, J A 1953. '"To Mendip for coal": a study of the Somerset coalfield before 1830, Part 2'. *Proc Somerset Archaeol Natur Hist Soc* **98**, 17–54

Burnham, B C and Wacher, J 1990. *The Small Towns of Roman Britain.* Berkeley and Los Angeles: University of California Press

Cannadine, D 1984. 'The present and the past in the English Industrial Revolution 1880–1980'. *Past and Present* **103**, 149–58

Carus-Wilson, E M 1967. *Medieval Merchant Venturers*, 2nd edn. London: Metheun

Catt, J A 1978. 'The contribution of loess to soils in lowland Britain', *in* Limbrey, S and Evans, J G (eds), *The Effect of Man on the Landscape: The Lowland Zone* (Counc Brit Archaeol Res Rep **21**). London: Council for British Archaeology, 1–20

Chandler, J 1991. *The Vale of Pewsey.* Bradford-on-Avon: Ex Libris Press

Christiansen, R 1981. *Thames* and *Severn* (*A Regional History of the Railways of Great Britain*, Vol. 3). Newton Abbot: David and Charles

Clark, J 1994. 'Bladud of Bath: the archaeology of a legend'. *Folklore* **105**, 39–50

Clew, K R 1970. *The Somersetshire Coal Canal and Railways*, 2nd edn. Newton Abbot: David and Charles

Clifton-Taylor, A 1972. *The Pattern of English Building*, 3rd edn. London: Faber and Faber

Coleman, J 1897. 'Matthew Chancelor's dream'. *Somerset and Dorset Notes and Queries* **5**, 355–6

Coleridge, E H (ed.) 1975. *The Complete Poetical Works of Samuel Taylor Coleridge*, Vol. 2. Oxford: Oxford University Press

Coles, B and Coles, J 1986. *Sweet Track to Glastonbury: The Somerset Levels in Prehistory.* London: Thames and Hudson

Coles, J and Coles, B 1989. *Prehistory of the Somerset Levels.* Somerset Levels Project. Hereford: Austin & Sons Ltd

Coles, J and Minnitt, S 1995. *Industrious and Fairly Civilized: the Glastonbury Lake Village.* Taunton: Somerset Levels Project and Somerset County Council Museums Service

Collins, J W 1857. 'On Ruborough Camp, Somerset'. *J British Archaeol Ass* **13**, 294–8

Costen, M 1992. *The Origins of Somerset.* Manchester: Manchester University Press

Crane, J 1765. *An Account of the Nature, Properties and Medicinal Uses of the Mineral Water at Nottington near Weymouth, Dorchester.* Lockett

Cunliffe, B 1978. *Hengistbury Head.* London: Elek

Cunliffe, B 1986. *The City of Bath.* Gloucester: Alan Sutton

Cunliffe, B 1991. *Iron Age Communities in Britain*, 3rd edn. London: Routledge

Cunliffe, B 1993. *Wessex to AD 1000.* Harlow: Longman

Darby, H C 1977. *Domesday England.* Cambridge: Cambridge University Press

Darley, G 1978. *Villages of Vision.* London: Paladin

Darvill, T 1987. *Prehistoric Gloucestershire.* Gloucester: Alan Sutton and Gloucestershire County Library

Darvill, T, Barker, K, Bender, B and Hutton, R 1999. *The Cerne Giant: An Antiquity on Trial* (Bournemouth University School of Conservation Science Occ Paper **5**). Oxford: Oxbow

Davies, G J 1979. 'Dorset in the Newfoundland trade'. *Proc Dorset Natur Hist Archaeol Soc* **101**, 1–5

Defoe, D 1748. *A Tour Through The Whole Island of Great Britain*, Vol. 2, 2nd edn

Down, C G and Warrington, A J 1972. *The History of the Somerset Coalfield.* Newton Abbot: David and Charles

Draper, J 1996. 'The early years of the Dorset County Museum'. *Proc Dorset Natur Hist Archaeol Soc* **118**, 14–23

Draper, J 1999. 'Bridport Literary and Scientific Institute'. *Proc Dorset Natur Hist Archaeol Soc* **121**, 136–138

Dunning, R 1980. *Somerset and Avon.* Edinburgh: Bartholomew

Dunning, R 1991. *Some Somerset Country Houses: A Personal Selection.* Wimborne: Dovecote Press

Dunning, R 1995. *Somerset Castles.* Tiverton: Somerset Books

Dunning, R W 2001. *Somerset Monasteries.* Stroud: Tempus

Eagle, D and Carnell, H (eds) 1981. *The Oxford Illustrated Literary Guide to Great Britain and Ireland.* Oxford: Oxford University Press

Elkin, P W 1991. 'Aspects of the recent development of the port of Bristol', *in* Good, G L, Jones, R H and Ponsford, M W (eds) *Waterfront Archaeology. Proceedings of the Third International Conference Bristol 1988* (Counc Brit Archaeol Res Rep **74**). London: Council for British Archaeology, 27–35

Evans, J G 1975. *The Environment of Early Man in the British Isles.* London: Paul Elek

Finberg, H P R 1955. *The Making of the English Landscape: Gloucestershire.* London: Hodder and Stoughton

Finberg, H P R (ed.) 1957. *Gloucestershire Studies.* Leicester: Leicester University Press

Finberg, J 1977. *The Cotswolds* (The Regions of Britain). London: Eyre Methuen

Flower, F 1990. *Somerset Coalmining Life.* Bath: Millstream Press

Fortey, R 1994. *The Hidden Landscape: A Journey into the Geological Past.* London: Pimlico

Fowler, P J 1993. *The Farming of Prehistoric Britain.* Cambridge: Cambridge University Press

Fowles, J 1982. *A Short History of Lyme Regis*. Stainbridge: Dovecote Press

Fowles, J 2003. *The Journals*, Vol. 1. London: Jonathan Cape

French, C, Lewis, H, Allen, M J, Scaife, R G and Green, M 2003. 'Archaeological and palaeo-environmental investigations of the Upper Allen Valley, Cranborne Chase, Dorset (1998–2000): a new model of earlier Holocene landscape development'. *Proc Prehist Soc* **69**, 201–234

Gardiner, J, Allen, M J, Hamilton-Dyer, S, Laidlaw, M and Scaife, R G 2002. 'Making the most of it: late prehistoric pastoralism in the Avon Levels'. *Proc Prehist Soc* **68**, 1–40

Gelling, M and Cole, A 2000. *The Landscape of Place-Names*. Stamford: Shaun Tyas

Goldsmith, O 1762. *The Life of Nash*. London: J Newbury

Gough, J W 1967. *The Mines of Mendip*, revised edn. Newton Abbot: David and Charles

Gould, S 1999. *The Somerset Coalfield* (Somerset Industrial Archaeology Survey **11**). Taunton: Somerset Industrial Archaeology Society

Green, M G 2000. *A Landscape Revealed: 10,000 Years on a Chalkland Farm*. Stroud: Tempus

Griggs, E L 1956–71. *Collected Letters of Samuel Taylor Coleridge*. Oxford: Oxford University Press

Guidott, T 1694. *The Register of Bath*. London

Hadfield, A M 1970. *The Chartist Land Company*. Newton Abbot: David and Charles

Hadfield, C 1967. *The Canals of South West England*. Newton Abbot: David and Charles

Hadfield C and Hadfield A M (eds) 1973. *The Cotswolds: A New Study*. Newton Abbot: David and Charles

Hall, L J 1983. *The Rural Houses of North Avon and South Gloucestershire, 1400–1720* (City of Bristol Museum and Art Gallery, Monograph **6**). Bristol: City of Bristol Museum and Art Gallery

Hannah G W 1986. 'The evolution of Bridport harbour'. *Proc Dorset Natur Hist Archaeol Soc* **108**, 27–32

Harte, J 1986. *Cuckoo Pounds and Singing Barrows: The Folklore of Archaeological Sites in Dorset*. Dorchester: Dorset Natural History and Archaeology Society

Harte, J 2000. 'Legends of the fall: giants in the Anglo-Saxon imagination'. *3rd Stone* **39**, 5–11

Haslam, J (ed.) 1984. *Anglo-Saxon Towns in Southern England*. Chichester: Phillimore

Havinden, M 1981. *The Somerset Landscape*. London: Hodder and Stoughton

Hawkins, D 1983. *Hardy's Wessex*. London: Macmillan

Heighway, C 1987. *Anglo-Saxon Gloucestershire*. Gloucester: Alan Sutton and Gloucestershire County Library

Hill, D 1984. *An Atlas of Anglo-Saxon England*, 2nd edn. Oxford: Basil Blackwell

Hill, D and Rumble A R (eds) 1996. *The Defence of Wessex: The Burghal Hidage and Anglo-Saxon Fortifications*. Manchester: Manchester University Press

Holmes, R 1999. *Coleridge: Early Visions*. London: Flamingo

Horsey, I P 1992. *Excavations in Poole 1973–1983* (Dorset Natur Hist Archaeol Soc Monogr Ser **10**). Dorchester: Dorset Natural History and Archaeological Society

Housley, R 1995. 'The Environment', *in* Coles, J and Minnitt, S *Industrious and Fairly Civilized: the Glastonbury Lake Village*. Taunton: Somerset Levels Project and Somerset County Council Museums Service, 121–136 (and 188–189)

Jacobi, R J 2004. 'The Late Upper Palaeolithic lithic collection from Gough's Cave, Cheddar, Somerset and human use of the cave'. *Proc Prehist Soc* **70**, 2004

Jenkins, J G 1974. *Nets and Coracles*. Newton Abbot: David and Charles

Jones, R H 1991. 'Industry and environment in medieval Bristol', *in* Good, G L, Jones, R H and Ponsford, M W (eds) *Waterfront Archaeology. Proceedings of the Third International Conference Bristol 1988* (Counc Brit Archaeol Res Rep **74**). London: Council for British Archaeology, 19–26

Jones, R L and Keen, D H 1993. *Pleistocene Environments in the British Isles*. London: Chapman and Hall

Jope, E M 1964. 'The Saxon building stone industry in Southern and Midland England'. *Med Archaeol* **8**, 91–118

Jorden, E 1631. *A Discourse of Naturall Bathes, and Minerall Waters Especially of Our Bathes at Bathe in Sommersetshire*. London

Keen, L (ed.) 1997. *'Almost the Richest City': Bristol in the Middle Ages* (British Archaeol Assoc Conference Trans **9**). London: British Archaeological Association

Kenyon, J R 1990. *Medieval Fortifications*. Leicester and London: Leicester University Press

Kingsley, N 1989. *The Country Houses of Gloucestershire, Vol. I, 1500–1660*. Chichester: Phillimore

Kingsley, N 1992. *The Country Houses of Gloucestershire, Vol. II, 1660–1830*. Chichester: Phillimore

Kingsley, N and Hill, M 2001. *The Country Houses of Gloucestershire, Vol. III, 1830–2000*. Chichester: Phillimore

Lawrence, B 1952 (facsimile edn 1989). *Quantock Country*. Taunton: Somerset County Library

Le Blanc, A 1745. *Lettres d'un François*, Vol. 3. La Haye

Leach, P 2001. *Roman Somerset*. Wimborne: Dovecote Press

Lee, L 1962. *Cider with Rosie*. Harmondsworth: Penguin

Lobel, M D (ed.) 1975. *The Atlas of Historic Town*, Vol. 2. London: The Scolar Press for the Historic Towns Trust

Lowe, J J and Walker, M J C 1984. *Reconstructing Quaternary Environments*. London: Longman

Margary, I D 1967. *Roman Roads in Britain* (2nd edn). London: John Baker

Marquis, M 1960. *Selections from the Memoirs of Harriett Wilson*. London: Elek

Marren, P 1999. *Britain's Rarest Flowers*. London: T and A D Poyser

Massingham, H J 1937. *Cotswold Country*. London: Batsford

McNeill, T 1992. *Castles*. London: Batsford and English Heritage

McWhirr, A 1981. *Roman Gloucestershire*. Gloucester: Alan Sutton

Meirion-Jones, G I and Batt, M 1985. 'The distribution of Somerset roof tiles in Brittany: a provisional assessment'. *Vernacular Architecture* **16**, 20–4

Merrill, L L 1989. *The Romance of Victorian National History*. Oxford: Oxford University Press

Miller, H and Broadhurst, P 1989. *The Sun and the Serpent*. Launceston: Pendragon Press

Mitchell, B and Penrose, H 1983. *Letters from Bath 1766–1767 by the Rev John Penrose*. Gloucester: Alan Sutton

Moorman, M 1957. *William Wordsworth, A Biography*, Vol. I. Oxford: Oxford University Press

Mowl, T 2002. *Historic Gardens of Gloucestershire*. Stroud: Tempus

Muir, R 1986. *The Stones of Britain*. London: Michael Joseph

Neve, M 1983. 'Science in a Commercial City: Bristol 1820–60', *in* Inkster, I and Morrell, J (eds), *Metropolis and Province: Science in British Culture 1780–1850*. London: Hutchinson, 179–204

Oswald, A, Dyer, C and Barber, M (eds) 2001. *The Creation of Monuments: Neolithic Causewayed Enclosures in the British Isles*. London: English Heritage

Palmer, R 1994. *The Folklore of Gloucestershire*. Tiverton: Westcountry Books

Parsons, D (ed.) 1990. *Stone Quarrying and Building in England AD 43–1525*. Chichester: Phillimore and Royal Archaeological Institute

Penn, K J 1980. *Historic Towns in Dorset* (Dorset Natur Hist Archaeol Soc Monogr Ser **1**). Dorchester: Dorset Natural History and Archaeological Society

Pickard-Cambridge, O W 1885. 'Woodbury Hill'. *Proc Dorset Natur Hist Archaeol Soc* **7**, 93–8

Pike, R 2002. *Hardy's Geography: Wessex and the Regional Novel*. Basingstoke: Palgrave Macmillan

Platt, C 1982. *The Castle in Medieval England and Wales*. London: Secker and Warburg

Ponsford, M 1987. 'Bristol', *in* Aston, M and Iles, R (eds), *The Archaeology of Avon: A Review from the Neolithic to the Middle Ages*. Bristol: County of Avon, Public Relations and Publicity Department, Chapter 12

Ponting, K G 1971. *The Woollen Industry of South-West England*. Bath: Adams and Dart

Priestley, J B 1977 (first pubd 1934). *English Journey*. Harmondsworth: Penguin

Quinn, P 1996. 'Land and legend in suburban Bristol'. *3rd Stone* **24**, 10–13

Quinn, P 1999. *The Holy Wells of Bath and Bristol Region*. Almeley: Logaston

Rahtz, P 1991. 'Pagan and Christian by the Severn Sea', *in* Abrams, L and Carley, J P (eds) 2001, *The Archaeology and History of Glastonbury Abbey*. Woodbridge: Boydell, 3–37

Rahtz, P and Watts, L 2003. *Glastonbury: Myth and Archaeology*. Stroud: Tempus

RCHM(E) 1970. *An Inventory of the Historical Monuments in the County of Dorset, Vol. II South East, Part 2*. London: HMSO

Richardson, A 2001. *Spirits of the Stones: Visions of Sacred Britain*. London: Virgin

Rippon, S 1997. *The Severn Estuary: Landscape Evolution and Wetland Reclamation*. London: Leicester University Press

Roberts, G 1834. *History of Lyme Regis*. London: S Bagster

Robinson, J A 1921. 'King Arthur and Cadbury Castle'. *Somerset and Dorset Notes and Queries* **17**, 85–6

Rolls, R 1988. *The Hospital of the Nation. The Story of Spa Medicine and the Mineral Water Hospital at Bath*. Bath: Bird

Russell, R 1753. *A Dissertation Concerning the Use of Sea Water in Diseases of the Glands etc*. Oxford

Salzman, L F 1913. *English Industries of the Middle Ages*. London: Constable

Salzman, L F 1952. *Building in England down to 1540*. Oxford: Oxford University Press

Sampson, J 1998. *Wells Cathedral West Front*. Stroud: Sutton Publishing

Saunders, A 1997. *Channel Defences*. London: Batsford and English Heritage

Saville, A 1984 (ed.). *Archaeology in Gloucestershire: From the Earliest Hunters to the Industrial Age: Essays Dedicated to Helen O'Neil and the Late Elsie Clifford*. Cheltenham: Cheltenham Art Gallery and Museums and Bristol and Gloucestershire Archaeological Society

Smith, B S and Ralph, E 1982. A *History of Bristol and Gloucestershire*, 2nd edn. Chichester: Phillimore

Smollett, T 1753. *The Adventures of Ferdinand Count Fathom*, Vol. 2. London: Johnston

St George Gray, H 1913. 'Trial-excavations at Cadbury Castle, S. Somerset, 1913'. *Proc Somerset Archaeol Natur Hist Soc* **59**, 1–24

Stanton, W 1994. 'The case for the limestone environment', *in* Raymond, F, *Mendip Limestone Quarrying: A Conflict of Interests*. Tiverton: Somerset Books

Stewart, R J 1989. *The Waters of the Gap: Magic, Mythology and the Celtic Heritage*. Bath: Ashgrove

Storer, B 1985. *The Natural History of the Somerset Levels*, 2nd edn. Wimborne: Dovecote Press

Stroud, T 1975. *Capability Brown*, 2nd edn. London: Faber

Tann, J 1967. *Gloucestershire Woollen Mills*. Newton Abbot: David and Charles

Tatton-Brown, T (ed.) 1998. 'Building with stone in Wessex over 4000 years'. *The Hatcher Review* **5**, no. 45

Taylor, C C 1970. *The Making of the English Landscape: Dorset*. London: Hodder and Stoughton

Taylor, C C 1983. *Village and Farmstead*. London: George Philip

Taylor, M A and Torrens, H S, 1986. 'Saleswoman to a New Science: Mary Anning and the Fossil Fish *Squaloraja* from the Lias of Lyme Regis'. *Proc Dorset Natur Hist Archaeol Soc* **108**, 136–148

Torrens, H 1995, 'Mary Anning (1799–1847) of Lyme: "the greatest fossilist the world ever knew"'. *Brit J Hist Sci* **28**, 257–284

Trueman, A E 1977. *Geology and Scenery in England and Wales.* Harmondsworth: Penguin

Turner, W 1562. *A Book of the Natures and Properties as Well of the Baths in England as of Other Baths in Germany and Italy.* Cologne: Birkman

VCH Wiltshire 1987. *Victoria History of Wiltshire*, Vol. 13. Oxford: Oxford University Press

Waite, V 1969. *Portrait of the Quantocks*, 2nd edn. London: Robert Hale

Waring, E 1977. *Ghosts and Legends of the Dorset Countryside.* Tisbury: Compton

Waters, B 1987 (first pubd 1947). *Severn Tide.* Gloucester: Alan Sutton

Welfare, H, 1984. *Wessex.* London: Collins

Williams, M 1970. *The Draining of the Somerset Levels.* Cambridge: Cambridge University Press

Williams, R and Williams, R 1992. *The Somerset Levels.* Bradford-on-Avon: Ex Libris Press

Wilshire, L 1980. *Berkeley Vale and Severn Shore*, 2nd edn. London: Robert Hale

Winbolt, S E 1939. *Somerset* (The Penguin Guides). Harmondsworth: Penguin

Winchester, S 2001. *The Map that Changed the World.* London: Viking

Wood, J 1765. *Essay Towards a Description of Bath.* London

Woodward, P J 1991. *The South Dorset Ridgeway: Survey and Excavations 1977–84* (Dorset Natur Hist Archaeol Soc Monograph **8**). Dorchester: Dorset Natural History and Archaeological Society

Worcestre, W 1969. *Itineraries* (ed. J H Harvey). Oxford: Clarendon

Wymer, J 1999. *The Lower Palaeolithic Occupation of Britain.* Salisbury: Wessex Archaeology and English Heritage

Ziegler, P 1970. *The Black Death.* Harmondsworth: Penguin

Zvelebil, M 1994. 'Plant use in the Mesolithic and its role in the transition to farming'. *Proc Prehist Soc* **60**, 95–134

General reading not specifically cited in endnotes

Addison, W 1951. *English Spas.* London: Batsford

Adkins L and Adkins, R 1992. *A Field Guide to Somerset Archaeology.* Wimborne: Dovecote Press

Allen, D E 1976. *The Naturalist in Britain: A Social History.* London: Allen Lane

Bord, J and C 1985. *Sacred Waters.* London: Granada

Granville, A 1841. *Spas of England and Principal Sea-Bathing Places.* London: H Colburn

Hembry, P 1990. *The English Spa 1560–1815: A Social History.* London: Athlone

Kellaway, G 1991. *Hot Springs of Bath.* Bath: Bath City Council

Neale, R 1981. *Bath: A Social History 1680–1850.* London: Routledge

Pretty, J 1998. *The Living Land.* London: Earthscan

Robertson, C 1975. *Bath, An Architectural Guide.* London: Faber

Robertson, M 1992. *Exploring England's Heritage: Dorset to Gloucestershire.* London: HMSO

Sitwell, E 1932. *Bath.* London: Faber

Webster, C J (ed.) 2000. *Somerset Archaeology.* Taunton: Somerset County Council

Index

Picture Credits

Aerial survey acknowledgements

New English Heritage aerial photographs were taken by Damian Grady. The Aerial Reconnaissance team would like to thank the following people for their help: a special note of thanks must go to the skills and patience of the pilots Mick Webb, Marten White and Robert Bewley; the aircraft owner David Sanders; the NMR cataloguing team Rose Ogle, Katy Groves, Catherine Runciman, Cinzia Bacilieri, Philip Daniels, Geoff Hall; Jon Proudman for all the publication scanning; and Sarah Prince for laser copying thousands of aerial photographs to send to the authors.